RETHINKING MASCULINITY

New Feminist Perspectives Series
General Editor: Rosemarie Tong, Davidson College

RETHINKING MASCULINITY

Philosophical Explorations in Light of Feminism

Second Edition

edited by
Larry May, Robert Strikwerda,
and Patrick D. Hopkins

Rowman & Littlefield Publishers, Inc.
Lanham • Boulder • New York • London

ROWMAN & LITTLEFIELD PUBLISHERS, INC.

Published in the United States of America
by Rowman & Littlefield Publishers, Inc.
4720 Boston Way, Lanham, Maryland 20706

3 Henrietta Street
London WC2E 8LU, England

British Cataloging-in-Publication Information Available

Library of Congress Cataloging-in-Publication Data

Rethinking masculinity : philosophical explorations in light of
    feminism / edited by Larry May, Robert Strikwerda and Patrick
    Hopkins.—2nd ed.
        p.   cm.
    ISBN 0-8476-8256-0 (cloth : alk. paper).—ISBN 0-8476-8257-9
(pbk. : alk. paper)
        1. Men—United States.   2. Sex role—United States.
    3. Masculinity (Psychology)—United States.   4. Feminist theory.
    I. May, Larry.   II. Strikwerda, Robert A.   III. Hopkins, Patrick D.
HQ1090.3.R48   1996
305.31—dc20   96-21390
                                                                          CIP

ISBN 0–8476–8256–0 (cloth : alk. paper)
ISBN 0–8476–8257–9 (pbk. : alk. paper)

Printed in the United States of America

⊗ ™ The paper used in this publication meets the minimum requirements of
American National Standard for Information Sciences—Permanence of Paper
for Printed Library Materials, ANSI Z39.48–1984.

Contents

Acknowledgments

"Sex and Social Roles: How to Deal with the Data" by Patrick Grim originally appeared in *Femininity, Masculinity, and Androgyny*, edited by Mary Vetterling-Braggin (Lanham, Md.: Littlefield Adams, 1982). Reprinted by permission of Rowman & Littlefield.

"The Enduring Appeals of Battle" by J. Glenn Gray originally appeared in *The Warriors: Reflections on Men in Battle* (New York: Harcourt Brace, 1959). Copyright extended by Ursula A. Gray, 1987. Reprinted by permission.

"Masculinity and Violence" by Victor Seidler originally appeared in *Recreating Sexual Politics* (London: Routledge, 1991). Reprinted by permission.

"Do Black Men Have a Moral Duty to Marry Black Women?" by Charles Mills originally appeared in the *Journal of Social Philosophy*, 25 (1994): 131–53. Reprinted by permission.

"Bioethics and Fatherhood" by Daniel Callahan originally appeared in the *Utah Law Review*, 735 (1992). Reprinted by permission.

"The Facts of Fatherhood" by Thomas W. Laqueur originally appeared in *Conflicts in Feminism*, edited by Marianne Hirsch and Evelyn Fox Keller (New York: Routledge, 1990). Reprinted by permission.

"Fatherhood and Nurturance" by Larry May and Robert Strikwerda originally appeared in the *Journal of Social Philosophy*, 22, no. 2 (1991): 28–39. Reprinted by permission.

"Pornography and the Alienation of Male Sexuality" by Harry Brod originally appeared in *Social Theory and Practice*, 14, no. 3 (1988): 265–84. Reprinted by permission.

Introduction

Several years ago two of us attended a lecture by Sandra Harding in which she spoke of a need for writings by men who are committed to feminism who "speak specifically as men, of themselves, of their bodies and lives, of texts and of politics, using feminist insights to see the world. . . ." She warned that the task would be "difficult and painful" but that it was tremendously important for men to come to a self-understanding of their experiences as men in a way that women had done in the early stages of the feminist movement.[1] This anthology owes its conception to Harding's words of inspiration.

The essays in this anthology all have the following in common: they are written by men, most of whom call themselves feminists; they are philosophical essays that attempt to come to terms with some issue or question arising out of the authors' experiences; they are exploratory, often merely attempting to survey an experiential terrain in conceptual terms; they approach the variety of experiences of being a male in Western culture in an attempt to find non-oppressive alternatives for men and for our children and grandchildren. The authors come from a varied set of backgrounds, yet all but two of us are academic philosophers, which explains our emphasis on conceptual analysis. Each of the authors has tried to write in a rigorous way that is nonetheless accessible to those not schooled in philosophy, and in a way that remains rooted in his experiences.

Feminist philosophers have shown how much philosophy has attempted to speak of "human experience" or "human nature" while ignoring or distorting the experiences of women. This has come about because Western philosophy has tended to ignore gender or failed to see the influence of gender on philosophy. And while it is true that philosophers have by and large ignored the experiences of women, it is also true that the experiences of many men have also not been taken seriously. Many male philosophers have been influenced by feminism, but have not seen it as requiring real change in how they do philosophy. Feminist philosophy has been viewed as being for, and about, women. Our anthology takes a different tack. Just as historians and anthropologists have realized the importance of the category of gender, so we believe that gender is a valuable analytic category.[2] We look to the experiences of men in our culture not to uncover the "essence" of maleness, but because we believe that good social philosophy needs to take gender fully into account.

Although there have been many popular books on masculinity, as well as many books in social science and literature, there have been very few books on philosophy and masculinity. Three of our authors in this anthology have written or edited the very few books in this field. Kenneth Clatterbaugh's book *Contemporary Perspectives on Masculinity*[3] surveys in a comprehensive fashion the spectrum of views that men currently take toward the topic of masculinity. Victor Seidler's book *Rediscovering Masculinity*[4] combines conceptual analysis and political theorizing about many of the central topics of our anthology. And Harry Brod's edited collection, *The Making of Masculinities*,[5] contains many interesting essays by men trying to construct a model of men's studies and to relate this model to current controversies in feminist theory. But there are very few other books on philosophy and masculinity.

In this brief introduction we will do two things. First, we will discuss two of the more popular books on masculinity, John Stoltenberg's *Refusing to Be a Man*,[6] and Robert Bly's *Iron John*,[7] in an attempt to locate our anthology. These two books represent two extreme poles of the current reaction to changes in gender roles inspired by feminism. Unlike some authors who reject or attack feminism, both claim to take feminism seriously and to respond to it supportively. Stoltenberg responds by claiming that men should give up completely on the traditional model of masculinity, and Bly proposes a return to an even more traditional model. Second, we will situate the various essays collected in our anthology and compare them with one another. But this will be very brief, for we want this anthology to stand on the strength of the voices of our authors' own words as they try to grapple with the incredibly difficult task of explaining, criticizing, and reconceptualizing what it means to be male in contemporary Western culture.

Denying and Affirming Traditional Male Roles

In his book, *Refusing to Be a Man*, John Stoltenberg presents us with a very powerful popular call "for the end of manhood as we know it.''[8] He argues that manhood has been inextricably connected with patriarchy and injustice toward women. In one of the book's most powerful moments, Stoltenberg claims that "The male sex is socially constructed. It is a political entity that flourishes only through acts of force and sexual terrorism.''[9] Stoltenberg describes the subtle and not-so-subtle ways that men force women to submit to gender roles. He contends that "the act of prevailing upon another to admit of penetration without full and knowledgeable assent so sets the standard in the repertoire of male-defining behaviors that it is not at all inaccurate to suggest that the ethics of male sexual identity are essentially rapist.''[10]

But Stoltenberg also displays the more subtle side of male sexual identity that similarly forces women to do what men want:

> A "he," being a he, can get away with murder—figuratively, and sometimes even literally—simply by virtue of the fact that he dissembles so sincerely, or he uses up someone's life with such single-minded purpose, or he betrays someone's trust with such resolute passion, or he abandons commitments with such panache. When men are held to account for what they do in their lives to women—which happens relatively rarely—their tunnel vision, their obliviousness to consequences, their egotism, their willfulness, all tend to excuse, rather than compound, their most horrific interpersonal offenses.[11]

All of this is part of a "value system in which some acts are deemed 'good' and 'right' because they serve to make an individual's idea of maleness real, and others 'bad' or 'wrong' because they numb it.''[12]

Stoltenberg asks us to imagine that the variety of people's sex organs can be placed along a continuum, rather than falling into distinctly male or female sex organs. He also urges that men think of their penises as not significantly different from a woman's clitoris. And throughout this book he supports a view of eroticism that is polymorphic. While he does not say this explicitly, he seeks to replace the category of masculinity (as well as femininity) with that of androgyny. For, in the end, there are no differences between men and women that Stoltenberg allows to be a basis for differential sexual roles. At the end of one of the earlier chapters, he says, "I invite you to become an erotic traitor to male supremacy.''[13]

While many of Stoltenberg's proposals are laudable, he leaves us with very little to grasp hold of once we have refused to be a man. What is positive in Stoltenberg's book is the "idea" that men can choose something different from the traditional roles they seem to be thrown into. But it is as if men should start from scratch, since all of their past conceptions of masculinity are to be rejected on this account. Yet we believe that many changes in gender roles have to be much more incremental to be successful. (There are exceptions—male recourse to violence, for example, should be stopped immediately.) One must recognize the powerful forces of socialization that must be overcome; and one must set intermediate goals that open the door for more moderate change to be regarded as "success." Relying on radical feminist insights, Stoltenberg persuasively criticizes many aspects of contemporary American masculinity. But there is very little attention to the positive aspects of masculinity that could be mined once the negative aspects have been rejected. Indeed, it is no accident that the title of Stoltenberg's book calls for a refusal not to be masculine in some of its manifestations, but a refusal to be a man. We are not convinced that such a step is necessary. As the papers that follow will indicate, there are many other positions one can take, also inspired by feminism, that offer more options to those who find it difficult or impossible to reject masculinity altogether.

Robert Bly has also provided a very popular recent book on masculinity called *Iron John*. Bly is primarily concerned to overcome the historical changes in men's relationships (centering on fathers and sons, but neglecting fathers and daughters) brought about by industrialization. But the current situation for men is often cast as a reaction to feminism's critique of contemporary masculinity; namely, that men no longer feel that they have the inner strength and self-assurance necessary to assume the leadership roles in society they traditionally played. Here is how he states this view:

> The women of twenty years ago were definitely saying that they preferred the softer receptive male. . . . Young men for various reasons wanted their women harder, and women began to desire softer men. It seemed like a nice arrangement for a while, but we've lived with it long enough now to see that it isn't working out.[14]

According to Bly, men who have chosen to reject the traditional role of the strong, aggressive male are now not happy because of a "lack of energy in them." They are anguished and unsure of themselves, incapable of making decisions and incapable of taking the lead on matters they consider important.

While Bly claims that he is not opposed to feminism, he nonetheless implies that the women's movement must bear some of the blame for the current state of emasculated manhood. Indeed, most of the myths that Bly retells place a woman, normally the mother, at the center of men's difficulties. Bly claims to provide a third alternative between the machismo male and the soft male in his stories of the "Wild Man." The Wild Man "resembles a Zen priest, a shaman, or a woodsman more than a savage," he tells us.[15] But it is women who have created the situation in which "Men are suffering right now—young men especially."[16] And it is only other men, especially older men like Bly himself, who can lead the way toward salvation.

What Bly envisions is a return to a much earlier tradition than that of the machismo male, a tradition in which "the divine also was associated with mad dancers, fierce fanged men, and being entirely underwater, covered with hair."[17] Unlike Stoltenberg, Bly thinks that there are essential differences between men and women, differences that we will deny at our own peril. "Geneticists have discovered recently that the genetic difference in DNA between men and women amounts to just over three percent. That isn't much. However the difference exists in every cell of the body."[18] We must move away from the rejection of masculinity, says Bly, and eventually reclaim all that was positive in the images of men as heroes and even men as "Lord."[19]

The model of masculinity that Robert Bly sketches has gone too far in the opposite direction from the model sketched by Stoltenberg. Instead of envisioning new ways for men and women to interact, ways that resolve the problems that Bly insightfully discusses, he turns uncritically to the past. As many other commentators have noted, Bly sets the stage for another round of blaming women for the problems in men's lives. And this sets the stage for another round of male violence against women. Why should we think that the boys and men Bly describes, who work so hard at being ferocious, will rein themselves in when confronted with women who do not wish to go along with their warlike games? Bly's image of masculinity is as one-sided as that of Stoltenberg. But surely there are more diverse and moderate views of a revised understanding of masculinity in today's society. Our anthology aims at just such a variety of reappraisals of traditional roles and constructive explorations of alternatives available to men today.

Assessments of, and Alternatives to, Traditional Masculinity

Our selection of readings begins with Patrick Grim's assessment of the scientific evidence used by those who claim that there are differences between men and women that justify various social practices. Grim begins by pointing out that for sexual differences to be supported by evidence, that evidence "must be something more than merely a record of how men and women raised in our society have happened to turn out." Some of the evidence used to buttress the claim that men and women should be assigned different roles in society misconstrues the social nature of the evidence. But even where there is good evidence for thinking that men have more of one natural trait than do women—aggressiveness, for instance—it is not clear that society should require or encourage only men to pursue the role which is associated with that trait. As Grim writes, "we must consider whether differences ought to be exploited or compensated." Grim argues that given the potential for abuse, it would be best simply to end research into sex differences.

Robert Stufflebeam examines the debate over biological sex differences as well, and while agreeing that the scientific data in no way justifies assigning the sexes to different kinds of jobs or social roles, he argues against Patrick Grim and some feminist critics who claim research into sex differences ought to be abandoned altogether. For one thing, if there are real sex differences, abandoning research only ignores this phenomenon and does not eliminate it. For another, many critics wrongly assume that biology = determinism. However, just because something is biologically based does not mean it is not alterable. For example, if men are biologically more aggressive than women, psychological or hormonal therapy might be in order for some. All in all, Stufflebeam argues, it would be better to educate the public on the standards of good science and the actual implications of research data, rather than merely attempt to eliminate certain scientific research. After discussing the logic and politics of sex research, Stufflebeam ends by examining the actual state of such research. He looks at five well-established behavioral/cognitive differences between women and men—including differences in verbal ability, motor skills, spatial ability, math ability, and aggression—and discusses whether brain structures, genetics, hormones, or environment provides the best explanation for such differences.

J. Glenn Gray's essay is the oldest in our anthology and the only one not written in the light of feminism. It is included here because it is the most provocative account ever written of the contradictions that men have felt in wartime situations. Reflecting on his own experiences in World War II, Gray says: "many men both hate and love combat. They know why they hate it; it is harder to know and to be articulate about why they love it." Gray examines three "attractions of war": "the delight in seeing" that comes especially from the grand spectacle of battlefield encounters; "the delight in comradeship" that comes from the communal sense one achieves through mutual willingness to engage in self-sacrifice; and "the delight in destruction" that is as rooted in the psyche as is the delight in creation. In all three cases, it is the ecstatic dimension of experience that is the key. But the drives of destruction and self-sacrifice are very problematic for most men. As Gray puts it: "What our moral self tells us is abhorrent, our religious self and our aesthetic self yearns for as the ultimate good." But ultimately, the delights of war are passing and empty. As Gray concludes: "Our society has not begun to wrestle with this problem of how to provide fulfillment to human life, to which war is so often an illusory path."

Victor Seidler also discusses the connection between violence and masculinity, but in different contexts than that of war. Seidler explic-

lactation and birth, women are more likely to be able to think of their erogenous zones in radically different ways. Men's bodies, on the other hand do not display similar dualities of function and so for them, sexuality and sensuality are often indistinguishable. Also, while women may experience sexual arousal without any obvious physical changes in their bodies, men's erections make sexual arousal largely unambiguous and therefore more threatening. While Thomas does not resort here to a biopsychological determinism, he does argue that women are favored by nature to view sensuality in more complex ways than men. He ends by asking whether men could learn to experience a more complex and satisfying affectional sensuality between themselves, similar to that of women.

Leonard Harris examines the concept of honor and tries to explain why this social good has been so elusive for African American males. He considers the popular image of Martin Luther King, Jr., as a "feminine" role model and asks what it would mean to honor King for his "feminine" characteristics of love, care, compassion, and sacrifice. Harris is interested in how honoring King might affect the tendency to perceive honor in strictly "masculine" terms. But Harris contends that racism continues to be pervasive in American society, virtually excluding African American males from the moral community and thus from that group which is afforded honor. In spite of the honor bestowed on King, our society is reluctant to honor African American males and this has contributed to their lack of empowerment.

Kenneth Clatterbaugh wades into another aspect of the relationship between men and feminist values—the claim that men as men also experience oppression, by society, or by feminism itself. He argues that men have not been oppressed by feminism. Indeed, after a detailed analysis of what is right and wrong with various theories of oppression, he defends a theory of oppression that makes it impossible for a member of a dominant group in society to be oppressed. If oppression is understood as relative dehumanization, then men *as men* (not as Hispanic, or as gay) have not been oppressed by society at large or by feminism, but women *as women* have been oppressed. Even though only men are drafted and used as cannon fodder, given the high social status assigned to combat soldiers, men are not oppressed even by a system that sends them (and not women) to be slaughtered on the battlefield.

These essays, written from a wide variety of philosophical perspectives, are all related in wanting to provide characterizations of masculinity that are empowering, or at least enlightening, for men, without contributing to the further oppression of women. We do not view this anthology as self-sufficient, standing by itself, for there are many more perspectives and issues of importance that we have not addressed than those that we have. Rather, our hope is that this anthology will

stimulate other philosophers and social theorists to work on topics we
have not been able to include, especially those who can draw on
experiences quite different from those of our authors. And while the
jury is still out, we believe that this collection of essays will strike its
readers as providing reasonable analyses of what is wrong with the
traditional model of masculinity and with plausible suggestions for
change that will benefit both men and women today.

We are grateful to Jon Sisk, Jennifer Ruark, and Rosemary Tong for
encouraging this project. We would also like to thank Penny Weiss and
Marilyn Friedman for providing many helpful suggestions at various
stages in the process of completing this project. We thank Ron Broach
for compiling the index.

Notes

1. See Sandra Harding's essay "After the End of 'Philosophy'," delivered
at Purdue University's Matchette Conference in 1989.

2. See John Dupre's essay "Global versus Local Perspectives on Sexual
Difference," in *Theoretical Perspectives on Sexual Difference*, edited by
Deborah Rhode (New Haven: Yale University Press, 1990), pp. 47–62.

3. Kenneth Clatterbaugh, *Contemporary Perspectives on Masculinity*
(Boulder, CO: Westview Press, 1990).

4. Victor J. Seidler, *Rediscovering Masculinity* (London: Routledge, 1989).

5. Harry Brod, *The Making of Masculinities: The New Men's Studies*
(Boston: Allen and Unwin, 1987).

6. John Stoltenberg, *Refusing to Be a Man* (Portland, OR: Breitenbush
Books, 1989).

7. Robert Bly, *Iron John* (Reading, MA: Addison-Wesley, 1990).

8. Stoltenberg, op. cit., p. 4.

9. Ibid., p. 30.

10. Ibid., p. 19.

11. Ibid., p. 17.

12. Ibid., p. 24.

13. Ibid., p. 39.

14. Bly, op. cit., p. 3.

15. Ibid., p. x.

16. Ibid., p. 27.

17. Ibid., p. 26.

18. Ibid., p. 234.

19. Ibid., p. 237.

PART ONE

Sex Differences

1

Sex and Social Roles: How to Deal with the Data

Patrick Grim

Women consistently score higher on verbal aptitude tests than do men, whereas males generally do better on tests involving "visual-spatial" skills: that is, depth perception, mazes, picture completion, map

---

This chapter was first published in 1982; I am pleased that it has aged as well as it has. As Robert Stufflebeam notes in the accompanying piece, the arguments are primarily a priori, and thus continue to stand as a challenge to further research.

The core points, to my mind, remain (1) the fact that familiar arguments from data on sex differences to social recommendations are almost invariably logically bad arguments, and (2) an incomplete but suggestive sketch as to how we might properly deliberate regarding ethical action even in cases of significant ignorance. Significant ignorance is of course the human condition.

Stufflebeam and I agree on (1). Because the arguments at issue are almost invariably bad arguments, however, he thinks they "can readily be countered." I am not so sanguine; neither the arguments nor their influence, I'm afraid, has disappeared since 1982.

The fact that a body of research is still so standardly used to defend unjust social policy, with little counter-balancing positive gain, must surely count against appeals for its continued pursuit. My conclusion was perhaps never as forceful as Stufflebeam portrays it; I argue neither that ignorance is bliss nor for any suppression of scientific inquiry. Given the variety of genuinely pressing demands on our limited resources, however, and given the perennial problems in this area with inadequate data questionably interpreted and improperly applied, I cannot see that continued testing regarding sex differences merits any high social priority.

3

reading, and the like.[1] On questionnaires women rate moving, marriage, and loss of a job as more stressful than do men.[2] Women appear to be more sensitive to sound volume and higher frequencies than men, are better at fine coordination and rapid decisions,[3] and it has been proposed that women are able to "read" facial expressions more readily.[4] Men consistently test out as more aggressive.[5]

What are we to do with data of this sort? One way such data are often used is as a justification for social practices involving a division of labor on sexual lines. If women are more sensitive to stress and less aggressive than men, it is argued, we should leave those tasks calling for aggression and tolerance of stress to men. If women are "communicative" animals and men are "manipulative" animals, we should leave the "communicative" tasks of childrearing to women.[6] If men excel at mathematical tasks and women have superior verbal skills, our engineers should be male and our telephone operators should be female. Fine coordination and rapid decision making qualify women as excellent typists, whereas better spatial perception indicates that jet pilots should be male.

The form of this argument should be familiar: our data show that men and women differ in certain ways, and those differences (so the story goes) justify a differentiation of social roles along sexual lines. The argument is quite clearly public property and appears with tedious regularity in common conversation. But it also appears in one guise or another throughout much of the literature on sex differences.[7] It is this form of argument I wish to attack.

My attack is in three parts. In the first section I hope to raise briefly some embarrassing questions concerning the data themselves. The data on which arguments of this form rely may not always be as objective, nor as clearly indicative of fundamental differences, as is often made out. In the second section I hope to address a general practical problem regarding sexual differences and our own ignorance. In the final section I will argue that the inferences often drawn from data regarding sexual differences are neither as direct nor as tight as is commonly assumed. Even if we have appropriately hard data demonstrating clearly fundamental sexual differences, the data may not support the conclusions regarding social roles which they appear to support.

I. Questioning the Data

Without an authoritative appeal to scientific data regarding sexual differences, an argument of this type would not even get off the ground. The argument as a whole, in fact, might be seen as an attempt to transfer to its social conclusions the scientific respectability of the data on which it relies. In a later section we will consider whether the argument succeeds; whether the data, however good, support the social conclusions they appear to. But for now let us consider the data themselves. Are they always as tight as they appear to be?

In order for the data to supply appropriate support for the argument at issue, they must be something more than merely a record of how men and women raised in our society have happened to turn out. That alone would not tell us whether observed characteristics are fundamental characteristics, independent of social influence, and would not show that people might not turn out quite differently in some other social context. Thus it wouldn't show, as the argument is designed to show, that social roles should quite generally be distinguished along sexual lines. If the differences at issue are merely a reflection of our own social order, they are part of what can be changed, rather than invariables which dictate the form that social change can or should take. So any data relied on in arguing for general social role differentiation along sexual lines must give some indication that observed differences are more than mere social epiphenomena. Only data which in some way go beyond a simple record of differences between women and men in the context of a particular status quo can do this.

It is because of this basic requirement that our data must in several ways be free of social influence. To the extent that our data reflect a given social situation rather than indicating sexual differences independent of social influence, they will be of little help in deciding, however indirectly, how society ought to be.

There are at least two ways in which data regarding sexual differences may be a reflection of our society rather than of something more. The data may not, first of all, be appropriately *hard* data; the apparent differences such data show may in fact be the result of social influences on or inherent in the ways in which the data are collected, counted, and represented. The data of a sexist observer might not be hard in this sense; the differences observed are in fact merely in the eye of the observer. But even if our data are appropriately hard—even if the ways in which our data are accumulated are free from illegitimate social influence—the differences for which we then have evidence may themselves be the result of social influences. Given the systematically different ways in which children of different sexes are brought up in our society, it would be surprising indeed if no psychological differences showed up on our tests.[8] But this is not the data we need. Somehow we must have an indication that our data are not to be explained in social terms; that the differences objectively recorded are genuinely *fundamental* differences.[9]

Though in principle distinct, the requirement that our data be hard data and the requirement that recorded differences be genuinely

fundamental differences tend to blur in practice. The concern I want
to raise here tends toward worries regarding the hardness of some of
our data, though questions of fundamentality are clearly at issue as
well. My objections are not intended to impugn all data we have or
might collect. But they are intended as a warning by example of how
easily implicit operation of social factors may be overlooked.

Consider first the question of aggression. Is one sex more aggressive
than the other? Perhaps no other question in the history of testing for
sex differences has had so long a history involving such a variety of
test procedures. But despite the apparent simplicity of the question, a
bit of reflection shows that any attempt to put it to the test involves a
number of pitfalls. That in turn is good reason to think that much of
the testing already done has been subject to those pitfalls, and thus
good reason to be generally suspicious of the data regarding sexual
differences with regard to aggression.

One difficulty is what gets counted as aggression. In a sexist society
such as ours it would not be surprising to find that male and female
behavior is interpreted differently as aggressive. A guffawing, hand-
clamping, back-slapping female is more likely to be considered aggressive than is her male counterpart, who is merely considered outgoing
or friendly. A rumor-spreading male, on the other hand, may more
readily be considered aggressive than his female counterpart, who is
merely "catty." It may also be that whether or not an individual's
behavior is perceived as aggressive depends on the sex (and social
conditioning) of the perceiver; a female observer is more likely to see
Joe's constant sexual overtures to women as aggressive than is another
male. If "aggression" is socially loaded in these ways, it is hardly a
proper tool for collecting or representing objective data; any tests we
try to perform concerning the relative aggressiveness of the sexes will
be shot through with social prejudices from the start. Another way of
putting the point is this: "aggressive" may be a term which in subtle
ways is applied differently to men than to women. If so, it is not a
neutral characteristic which we can compare in the two cases. Asking
whether one sex is more aggressive than the other is more like asking
whether one is generally taller; neither "aggressive" nor "attractive"
is applied to each group with the objective impartiality of a yardstick.

Consider another piece of data mentioned earlier; the fact that
women generally rate moving, marriage, or loss of a job as more
stressful than men. This has been taken as an indication that women
are more sensitive to, and less tolerant of, stress.[10] But we might
draw other conclusions instead. In a job market in which women are
consistently discriminated against, the loss of a job is a greater disaster
for a woman than for a man. Women may be more stressful about
losing jobs, not because they are such delicate creatures, but because,
things being as they are, the loss of a job is in fact a more serious

themselves independent of social influences. Only in exceptional instances does some crucial experiment decide the case. Such disputes are resolved, to the extent that they are resolved at all, by a subtle accumulation of plausibility—none of it clearly decisive—on one side or the other. Often even this does not occur; the additional tests appealed to are themselves ambiguous enough to allow for either interpretation. A gray area remains and for the sake of unanimity each side may blur the dispute by speaking of what various data suggest rather than of what they show and by speaking of differential tendencies which may involve both social and fundamental factors, rather than of differential characteristics of solely one kind or the other.

To some extent we are presently ignorant of whether certain differences between men and women reveal fundamental differences or are to be attributed to social causes. To some extent, we will always be ignorant. Does this matter? If whether certain differences are fundamental or social in origin may be of moral relevance in shaping a society—an issue more fully considered in the following section—then our ignorance does matter. What we don't know may hurt us in the attempt to make our society what it ought to be.

This in effect saddles us with a quandary as to how to act in ignorance. There are differences between men and women which may be genuinely fundamental or which may be social in origin. How we ought to treat men and women may depend on which explanation is correct, but we cannot claim to *know* which explanation is correct. In that case which ought we assume; should we treat the differences at issue as fundamental until proven otherwise, or as social in origin until and unless the evidence indicates otherwise? The dilemma is both of practical importance and as unavoidable as our own ignorance.

It might be thought that in such a situation the decision we face is genuinely arbitrary; since the available evidence cannot tell us which alternative to choose, nothing can, and we might lose either way. I am not sure, however, that this is quite our predicament. Allow me to sketch in broad outlines a form of argument which would suggest that there are ethical reasons for treating men and women as if one explanation were correct even if we don't know which explanation is correct. Because of a number of fairly obvious complications the argument here is merely a sketch, and all I would claim for it at present is that it is suggestive. But it is, I think, an argument worthy of further development, and for that reason, although "merely suggestive," is not to be despised.[12]

The argument can be presented conveniently in the form of a gain-loss grid, similar to simple models of economic decision making. We might assume a fundamental explanation for differences at issue, and might be either right or wrong. We might assume a social explanation for the differences, and once again might be either right or wrong. My strategy will be to propose that the risks we run are less significant and the prospective gains greater on the assumption of a social explanation, and thus that to the extent that we are ignorant we should assume that observed sex differences are to be explained in social terms.

There is one class of prospective gains and losses which appear to balance out between our alternatives: the promise of social efficiency and the threat of social disutility. If we assume either explanation for observed differences, and if we're right, other things being equal, we can expect the social programs we introduce or the social structures we build on the basis of our theories to work more smoothly overall. If our assumed theory is wrong, we can expect to suffer on the same score.[13]

But consider also the matter of social injustice. The treatment of differences which are in fact merely social as if they were fundamental—the outcome represented by (2)—seems to be a clear instance of socially unjust treatment. Standard paradigms of racism and sexism involve precisely this feature; that differences between individuals or groups, real or imagined, are taken to be inherent and fundamental which are not. The stereotypical black is thought to be *inherently* lazy and stupid, not merely socially handicapped, and racism would be quite a different matter were this not the case. The true sexist holds not just that some particular group of women are by force of circumstance scatter-brained and fragile, but that women are so by nature. Part of the injustice of racism and sexism is simply that the stereotypes don't fit. But even if they did, sexist and racist treatment would be unjust because the characteristics involved are not the *fundamental* characteristics they are assumed to be.

On this model, I think, we must envisage social injustice of an all-too-familiar sort as one of the potential losses to be entered against the assumption of a fundamental explanation for observed differences.[14] Is there a comparable threat of injustice on the other side?

It must be admitted that the outcome envisaged in (3) includes losses

Theory True

	Fundamental	Social
Fundamental	1	2
Social	3	4

Theory Assumed

assigned tasks t_1, t_2, . . . t_n and women are assigned tasks t'_1, t'_2, . . . t'_n? It at least does not follow as night the day; allow me to catalog a number of major qualifications required in any such inference.

There are very few tasks indeed which call for one and only one simple qualification. Brain surgery demands dexterity, but not dexterity alone, and plumbing demands physical strength and a degree of limberness, but not these alone. The most dexterous of brain surgeons and the strongest and most limber of plumbers might nonetheless be a very bad brain surgeon and a very bad plumber; each might lack foresight, experience, spatial perception, and appropriate forms of mechanical imagination. The general lesson here is that qualification for most tasks is a complicated matter of balance of different abilities, some of which may be tied to fundamental characteristics and many of which may not be. Thus no single simple characteristic, and no small group of characteristics, however fundamental, can alone be expected to decide the question of who should be assigned which tasks; some other capacity or group of capacities, fundamental or social in origin, might always outweigh the significance of any inherent difference. Thus even given fundamental sexual differences, and even given that some of those differences involve characteristics which are qualifications for different sets of tasks, we cannot conclude that those tasks ought to be divided on sexual lines without considering *all* qualifications relevant to those tasks, including qualifications which are not tied to fundamental differences.

Consider also a second difficulty. There are precious few fundamental differences in the data which are not at best merely statistical differences, often very slight, which show up in testing large groups of men and women. A statistical difference of this type may not alone indicate very much. That women score higher on average in a characteristic f_1 is perfectly consistent with each of the following; that those who score most highly on f_1 are men, and that a finite number of occupational slots calling for only characteristic f_1 will best be filled entirely by men.[16] A statistical difference of this type is even consistent with the claim that your chances of selecting an individual satisfying a specific requirement for a high f_1 score are greater if you draw from a pool exclusively of men than from either a pool exclusively of women or from a randomly mixed pool.[17] A higher average score on f_1 among women does not entail that any woman scores above all men, that most women score above all men, that the highest score is a woman's or that the lowest is a man's, or that the majority of women score more highly than the majority of men.[18] Nonetheless the statistical difference in such a case is quite standardly represented by saying that "women score more highly with regard to f_1 than do men," and this latter phrase has a peculiar tendency to be misread (and misused in argument) as if it were the quite different claim that all women score more highly with regard to f_1 than all men. This subtle shift can, of course, make all the difference between truth and falsity.[19]

The importance here of this elementary error is that a *clear* justification of universally applied sex-role differentiation would require the stronger universal claim: that all women score more highly with regard to f_1 than do all men. From the mere fact that the average score for women with regard to f_1 is higher than the average score for men it simply does not follow that tasks calling for f_1 ought to be assigned to any particular group at all, unless we nominate those with high f_1 scores as such a group. Consistent with the truth of the statistical claim, and depending on the circumstances, that group might be composed exclusively of women, might be composed exclusively of men, or might be composed of any proportion of the two.

We are assuming, for the moment, that the data regarding sexual differences on which arguments of the type at issue rely are beyond reproach, i.e., genuinely hard data revealing genuinely fundamental sexual differences. But this is not the only data required if the argument is to go through. Given different characteristics f_1 and f_2, and sets of tasks $t_1, t_2, \ldots t_n$ and $t'_1, t'_2, \ldots t'_n$, we must also have firm and objective data concerning the importance of those characteristics for those tasks. Oddly enough, those who present arguments for social role differentiation on the basis of sexual differences generally neglect to supply this second batch of data, substituting instead a form of armchair speculation which they would rightly reject in other contexts. From the fact (if it is a fact) that women have greater fine coordination and are better at rapid decisions, it is too often concluded that they would make good typists.[20] But why not brain surgeons or astronauts?; these too call for the characteristics in question. The fact (if it is a fact) that men are more aggressive is similarly taken to justify a role-assignment as soldiers and businessmen. But is not aggression also a qualification for the protective role of babysitters? In order for the link from fundamental traits to social roles to be a properly logical link, free from the corrupting influence of social prejudice, we would need independent demonstration of a correlation between certain traits and certain tasks or occupations. That data would have to be as hard as the data regarding the fundamental differences themselves. At this point the argument for social role differentiation characteristically takes the form of armchair speculation as to what makes a good typist, a good businessman, and the like. But if we allow armchair speculation at this point, we might as well have allowed armchair speculation as to basic sexual differences to begin with.

Another group of major assumptions lies hidden in the argument as well. Let us assume that a particular characteristic—aggression, for example—is a salient characteristic of contemporary businesspeople and is perhaps even essential to the current structure of business itself.

Let us also assume that men are more aggressive than women, and here we might even assume that men are *universally* more aggressive. Does it follow that businesspeople ought to be male? Only if we add an additional ethical premise: that contemporary businesspeople are as businesspeople ought to be, and that the current social structure of business is as it ought to be. What this shows is that no form of the argument at issue can be a pure extrapolation from data, however good; it must always involve a premise as to how society *ought* to be as well. In actual use, I think, the hidden assumption is always that our society is at least by and large as it ought to be. So it shouldn't be too surprising that the argument is generally used as a defense of the status quo; it relies on an assumption in favor of the status quo. But with different assumptions as to how society ought to be we would get different results. If aggression in business is a social handicap rather than a social strength—if, for example, it is that aggression which generates the ills of corporate capitalism—then we ought not encourage aggression in business, and perhaps quite generally ought not encourage aggression in positions of power. If males were universally more aggressive than females, we should do all we can to deny them a role in business and to keep them from occupying positions of power.

Consider finally the question of whether certain differences ought to be exploited or compensated. The fact (if it is a fact) that men and women differ in particular ways does not alone dictate how we ought to deal with those differences. Some differences between people are differences we rely on in constructing a social order—differences as to interests, needs, and desires, for example. But some differences are ones we attempt to correct or compensate for rather than to exploit. We don't give the curably ill different jobs simply because they are ill; we try to cure them. We don't simply arrange work for amputees which is better done without certain limbs; we at least attempt to supply mechanical replacements. If there are differences which *cannot* be corrected or compensated for, of course, we learn to live with them. But nothing has been said to indicate, and as far as I know none of the data show, that any of the supposed differences between men and women are differences for which correction or compensatory treatment is impossible. The statistics on aggression do not show that males could not be trained to be less aggressive, or females to be more so. Superior verbal ability on the part of females does not mean that males could not, with proper compensatory training, reach the same level. Thus one might conclude from the data regarding sexual differences not that we ought to assign career-roles along sexual lines, but that we owe each group compensatory training as a corrective for its shortcomings, so that in the end the only determinant of social role will be individual interest and desire. The point here is simply that differences alone do not show that our society ought to be constructed so as to exploit those differences; we might equally well conclude that society ought to attempt to correct them or compensate for them.

This is, I am sure, radically incomplete as a catalog of weaknesses in the inference from data regarding sexual differences to recommendations regarding social roles. But it is sufficient to show that the argument with which we began is a simple non sequitur as it stands. We have assumed that the data at issue are suitably hard data revealing genuinely fundamental differences, an assumption challenged in the beginning. But even given that assumption the conclusions generally drawn regarding social roles do not follow. In order legitimately to conclude anything at all regarding the desirability of social role differentiation we must deal with a number of additional and complicating factors. We must consider whether differences ought to be exploited or compensated, we must make explicit and defend assumptions as to how society ought to be, and we need firm evidence rather than armchair speculation as to links between particular characteristics and effectiveness at certain tasks. We must be wary of misreading statistical generalizations as universal claims, and must avoid treating prima facie and partial qualifications for particular roles as if they were sole qualifications. Without these the argument simply falls short, no matter how tight our data regarding sexual differences.

Does this indicate that the data, even if legitimate, show nothing which might be of significance to social decisions? That would be too strong. If there *are* fundamental sexual differences, that fact may be one of moral importance in deciding how society ought to be. Together with other claims and arguments it *could* even be part of a satisfactory justification of social role differentiation along sexual lines. But no data of this type, however good, would alone dictate the shape our society ought to take.

IV. Conclusion

The discussion above has a clear central theme, even if it does not build to a conclusive agrumentative climax. Contemporary data regarding sex differences are quite often taken as a justification for social recommendations involving social role differentiation on sexual lines. I have tried to detail a number of objections against the use of such an argument and against some assumptions behind it. The data on which such arguments rest are often data of which we should be suspicious, for a variety of reasons. In cases in which we are significantly ignorant, there may be ethical reasons for preferring a social explanation rather than the fundamental difference on which the standard argument relies. And even where the data are as tight and conclusive as one might like, the conclusion generally drawn is not one which follows in any rigorous sense.

It is not unusual for discussions of sex differences to end with an appeal for further testing. I will not make such an appeal. In light of the deep difficulties of attempting any satisfactory test, in light of the social dangers of a test gone wrong, in light of the inconclusiveness of the best of data for any social purposes, and given the variety of genuinely pressing demands on our social energies, I see little reason for continuing such testing.

Notes

1. See E.E. Maccoby and C.N. Jacklin, *The Psychology of Sex Differences* (Stanford: Stanford University Press, 1974). A more recent piece on visual-spatial abilities is L.J. Harris, "Sex Differences in Spatial Ability: Possible Environmental, Genetic, and Neurological Factors," in *Asymmetrical Function of the Brain*, ed. M. Kinsbourne (Cambridge: Cambridge University Press, 1979), pp. 405–522.

2. Monte Buchsbaum cites this difference and offers a biochemical explanation in "The Sensoriat in the Brain," *Psychology Today* 11 (May 1978): 96–104.

3. See Diane McGuinness and Karl H. Pribram, "The Origins of Sensory Bias in the Development of Gender Differences in Perception and Cognition," in *Cognitive Growth and Development: Essays in Memory of Herbert G. Birch*, ed. Morton Bortner (New York: Brunner/Mazel, 1979), pp. 3–56.

4. Sandra F. Witelson, "Sex and the Single Hemisphere: Specialization of the Right Hemisphere for Spatial Processing," *Science* 193, no. 4521 (1976), pp. 425–27.

5. Aggression is probably *the* standard sex difference, with more studies to its credit than any other. See E.E. Maccoby, *The Development of Sex Differences* (Stanford: Stanford University Press, 1966) and E.E. Maccoby and C.N. Jacklin, *The Psychology of Sex Differences*, op. cit.

6. The terms "manipulative" and "communicative," and various echoes of the argument, appear in Diane McGuinness and Karl H. Pribram, "The Origins of Sensory Bias," op. cit.

7. Some examples include Witelson, "Sex and the Single Hemisphere," McGuinness and Pribram, "The Origins of Sensory Bias," Monte Buchsbaum, "The Sensoriat in the Brain," and informal quotations from Jerre Levy in Daniel Goleman, "Special Abilities of the Sexes: Do They Begin in the Brain?," *Psychology Today* 11 (November 1978): 48–59, 120. A history of this and related arguments appears in Stephanie A. Shields, "Functionalism, Darwinism, and the Psychology of Women: A Study in Social Myth," *American Psychologist* 30, no. 7 (1975): 739–54.

8. Were our data to show no sex differences at all then it might be proposed that we would have a very strong case for there being fundamental differences somehow "compensated" by differential social treatment.

A distinction is sometimes drawn between biological and psychological sex differences; between height in inches, for example, and tendencies toward aggression. In what follows I concentrate for the most part on questions of psychological differences, simply because these seem the most interesting. But in most respects the argument would apply equally well to either type of trait, and I am wary of attempting a sharp demarcation between them.

9. One might also distinguish between psychological and behavioral traits on the grounds that the same psychological traits might have different behavioral manifestations in different settings or within different socially enforced roles. Though I have not relied on this distinction, and though it seems to me to be one very difficult to distinguish in practice, the discussion below of aggression and stress seems to emphasize this importance.

10. From Monte Buchsbaum, "The Sensoriat in the Brain," op. cit.

11. It might be suggested that in such cases the data can be of no help to us at all; that the data cannot decide between competing theories because it is that data that each of the theories is to explain. But this would overlook the dual role of scientific data vis-à-vis scientific theories. That which a theory explains (or seems to explain) is at the same time evidence for the truth of the theory.

The issue, of course, is which of the competing theories *better* explain the data, a matter involving the complexities and subtleties of breadth, ties with other bodies of theory and simplicity.

12. The argument has the general form of Pascal's wager, and like Pascal's wager shows strictly not that a particular alternative is true but that a particular alternative ought to be believed, or that one ought to act as if it is true. In "The Subjection of Women," J.S. Mill comes at least close to this form of argument in maintaining that given natural sex differences, there would be no need to enforce socially distinct roles. Since what women "can do, but not so well as the men who are their competitors, competition suffices to exclude them from . . ." we have nothing to lose in acting as if there are no fundamental differences. But the argument presented here differs from Mill's in a number of major respects. A convenient abridgment of Mill's essay is included in *The Feminist Papers*, ed. Alice R. Rossi (New York: Bantam Books, 1974), pp. 196–238.

13. Whether the loss of efficiency we risk in each case is the same is, perhaps, a more complicated question. Depending on how we (wrongly) treat certain differences and on what effects our incorrect treatment in fact has, these might not balance out. I am obliged to David Pomerantz for bringing this complication to my attention.

14. It should be noted, however, that all possible forms of treatment of social differences as if they were fundamental may not involve equal degrees of injustice. Exploitation of merely social differences as if they were fundamental, for example, may be a more extreme case than attempted correction of social differences as if they were fundamental.

15. Were these prospective losses *only* characteristic of (3), we might still argue that they fail to balance out the radical injustice of (2). But that would call for a more complex argument concerning the assignment of various weights to various social goals, which I have not attempted to provide here.

16. Consider, for example, a hypothetical sample such as the following, using W_1 through W_5 to represent five women and M_1 through M_5 to represent five men:

W_1	.75	M_1	1.0
W_2	.75	M_2	1.0
W_3	.75	M_3	.5
W_4	.75	M_4	.5
W_5	.75	M_5	.5
Average:	.75	Average:	.70

The average score for women is .75, and for men is a mere .70. But those two individuals who score highest are male, and if we have two openings best filled by highest scorers, with no other considerations at issue, they will best be filled by these two men.

17. Consider, for instance, the following sample:

W_1	.85	M_1	.85
W_2	.75	M_2	.85
W_3	.75	M_3	.85
W_4	.75	M_4	.85
W_5	.65	M_5	.10
Average:	.75	Average:	.70

Let us suppose that we have an opening which demands a high score, and that we have set .80 as a specific requirement. Our chances of drawing a satisfactory candidate from the pool on the left are 1/5, from a randomly mixed pool are 5/10, and from the pool on the right are 4/5, despite the fact that the average score for the right-hand column is lower than the average for that on the left.

18. The sample in footnote 16 is one in which the highest score is not a woman's. A sample in which the lowest score is not a man's, though the average male score is lower, can easily be constructed:

W_1	1.0	M_1	.70
W_2	.5	M_2	.70
Average:	.75	Average:	.70

The following sample is one in which the score of the majority of men is higher than the score of the majority of women:

W_1	.75	M_1	.80
W_2	.75	M_2	.80
W_3	.75	M_3	.80
W_4	.75	M_4	.55
W_5	.75	M_5	.55
Average:	.75	Average:	.70

For a somewhat simpler discussion of statistical frequencies and sex differences, see Joyce Trebilcot, "Sex Roles: The Argument From Nature," in *Feminity, Masculinity and Androgyny,* ed., Mary Vetterling-Braggin (Lanham, Md.: Littlefield, Adams, 1982) pp. 40–48. The general spirit of Trebilcot's discussion and mine are, I think, very similar.

19. Interestingly enough, "branching quantifiers" appear quite frequently in trying to represent the data. Some of the difficulties and ambiguities of grammatical and logical forms are made clear in Jon Barwise, "On Branching Quantifiers in English," *Journal of Philosophical Logic* 8 (1979): 47–80.

20. An example taken from Diane McGuinness and Karl H. Pribram, "The Origins of Sensory Bias." In "Sex Differences in Mental and Behavioral Traits," *Genetic Psychological Monographs* (1968), J.E. Garai and A. Schienfeld classify those abilities which favor females as "clerical skills" (pp. 169–299).

21. I am grateful to Mary Vetterling-Braggin, David Pomerantz, and Kriste Taylor for their help with revisions of an earlier draft.

2

Behavior, Biology, and the Brain: Addressing Feminist Worries about Research into Sex Differences

Robert Stufflebeam

Like it or not, men and women are different. If for no other reason, the sexes are different because each fulfills a different reproductive function: women bear children; men beget them. What isn't so certain, however, is the *extent* to which the sexes differ and what *causes* sex-related differences in behavior and ability. To resolve these issues requires biological and cognitive research into sex differences, the very enterprise (some) feminists (including Patrick Grim [1982, 1996]) want to see abandoned. Here's why: Men are better at performing certain tasks than are women, and vice versa. So, if researchers discover that sex-related differences in ability arise because of sex-specific differences in biology (e.g., brain oganization, sex hormomes, etc.), then the data will be used to justify a division of labor along sexual lines. Not only do many feminists contend that sex differences are best seen as the result of society, not biology, nearly all contend that the consequences of such research will be injurious to women. Indeed, in the definitive feminist critique of research into sex differences, *Myths of Gender* (1992), Ann Fausto-Sterling argues that sex-related discrimination is among the "inevitable consequences" of such research. Thus, society would be better off being "ignorant" of any sex differences, and doubly so if they arose from biological causes. Therefore, it is claimed, such research ought to be abandoned. I disagree.

My purpose for this chapter is to defend cognitive and biological research into sex differences. Doing so requires that I do three things. First, I need to address the main feminist worry about such research; viz., that the data will inevitably be used to justify discrimination against women. I don't think this worry is well-founded. Indeed, I don't think this worry is well-founded for precisely the *same reasons* feminists argue that research into sex differences ought to be abandoned. So, second, defending research into sex differences requires that I address the main feminist claims about such research; viz., (1) that sex differences are best seen as the result of social not biological causes; (2) that society would be better off being ignorant of any sex differences; and (3) that research into sex differences ought to be abandoned. Against these claims I argue that one *cannot* predict how any one male or female will perform any given task simply because men, on average, are better than women at performing certain tasks, and vice versa. As such (and for other reasons), the statistical nature of sex difference generalizations cannot "justify" discrimination or a division of labor along sex lines. All things being equal, educating the public regarding the limitations of the data is a far better solution to combating any potential abuse (of the data) than is either ignorance or abandoning such research altogether. Moreover, if cognitive models of information processing ought to be constrained by how brains actually work (a widely held assumption in both philosophy of mind and cognitive science), then to inform and constrain the model-building endeavor, biological research into cognitive sex differences needs to continue. Finally, defending research into sex differences requires that I be clear about not only what the differences in question are, but which among the following causes most reasonably explains them: structurally dimorphic brains, differences in brain organization, hormones, genes, or the environment.

Since this chapter appears in an anthology dedicated toward a reexamination of masculinity in light of feminism, I shall be defending research into sex differences against two well-established feminist critics of such research: Grim (1996), whose arguments are mostly of an a priori nature, and Fausto-Sterling (1992), whose criticisms are mostly of an empirical nature. But while Fausto-Sterling is explicit about being a feminist, Grim is not.[1] Nevertheless, their concerns and conclusions are very much the same, even if how they view themselves is not. So, out of convenience, I shall label their criticisms as "feminist." But bear this in mind: the worries feminists have about the consequences of research into sex differences aren't *just* feminist worries, and they should not be read as such.

What Makes the Sexes Different? Preliminaries

No one seriously questions the fact that males are different from females. But even limiting our discussion to humans, ignoring the ambiguities of "different," and assuming that "male" and "female" are mutually exclusive and exhaustive kinds, it isn't obvious what *makes* the sexes different. For example, how should the blanks be filled in the following expressions?

(1) It is in virtue of _____ that males are males; [or] X is a male just in case X is/has _____.

(2) It is in virtue of _____ that females are females; [or] X is a female just in case X is/has _____.

Since such type identity questions arise in the context of *being* a thing of a certain sort, they are metaphysical questions. Metaphysically speaking, to use a hackneyed example, it is in virtue of (a) being a male, (b) being unmarried, (c) being of marriageable age, and (d) not being a priest that one either is or is not a member of the class of things called "bachelors." The problem here, however, is that metaphysical questions regarding *sex identity* are often confused with metaphysical questions regarding *gender identity*.

For example, is it in virtue of one's appearance that one is either a male or a female? By an individual's appearance alone, most of us, most of the time, would find it easy to ascribe his or her correct sex. After all, males and females just look different. But clothing styles, hairstyles, the use of makeup, whether one shaves (and if so, what), and so on, are social conventions. They vary not only across cultures, but they also vary within any one culture over time. Still, all things being equal, few people would find it difficult to identify a man as such even if he were in drag, or to identify a woman as such even if she were dressed in combat boots and utilities.[2] Clearly, therefore, it isn't in virtue of how one dresses that one *is* female (or male). Pardon the cliché, but clothes really don't make a man or a woman. Yet social conventions *do* figure in the individuation of gender. Gender, it is widely held, reduces to those "social, cultural, and psychological aspects linked to males and females through particular social contexts" (Lindsey 1994, 3). Thus, contrary to the extreme claims of biological reductionists, metaphysical questions regarding *gender* identity reduce to sociology (broadly construed). But whether one *is* a male or a female—i.e., one's sex—requires something else.

Consider another example. Suppose that while traveling along a deserted country road on your way to a very important engagement, your car stalls, and you find yourself stranded. Since you don't have a cellular phone and you haven't seen a fellow driver for hours, you realize that without assistance soon, you will miss your pressing engagement. Out of the corner of your eye, you notice a sign posted in front of some tall bushes near a gate across the road. It reads "SUNNY DAYS NUDIST COLONY." Because you assume there will be a phone in the colony, you enter through the gate. Off in the distance you see a dozen people playing volleyball. As you approach them, you realize that aside from everyone being completely unadorned, they are all hairless. Would you nevertheless be able to ascribe the correct sex to these naked, hairless individuals? Chances are, yes you would: you would simply note the presence or absence of penises.

The following question suggests itself: Is having the right sort of genitalia sufficient to make one male or female? Again the answer is no. Although ascriptions based on such features may be justified, even correct, it isn't in virtue of having the correct "sex organs" that one is a male or a female. A postoperative "female" transsexual may appear to be a female, but most of us, if we were apprised of the facts, would say that the "female" is not *really* a female, but "a man who has undergone surgical and hormonal therapy to make him look and feel like a woman" (Posner 1992, 26–27). We do so because the individuation of sex identity ultimately depends on a conjunction of biological features (but not merely having the right sex organs); viz., "chromosomal, anatomical, reproductive, hormonal, and other physiological characteristics" (Lindsey 1994, 3). So contrary to the extreme claims of social reductionists, metaphysical questions regarding *sex* differentiation reduce to biology (broadly construed).

Thus, questions of *gender identity* reduce to the environment, whereas questions of *sex identity* ultimately reduce to biology. Neither of these claims is terribly problematic.[3] The topic of concern here is whether *sex differences*—certain sex-related differences in behavior and ability—arise because of differences in gender or differences in biology. It is the latter possibility that both bridles and worries so many feminists. And for good reason. Before saying why, let me first be specific about some of the differences in question.

Five Behavior-Related Sex Differences

MacCoby and Jacklin (1974), whose study remains the standard, identified four significant behavioral differences that are sex-related. I've added another (the second) for this difference is also well-established.

1. *Females have greater verbal fluency than males.* At about age eleven, test scores involving language production and comprehension begin to diverge. Female superiority in verbal fluency tasks—such as naming or listing words that begin with a target letter—increases through high school and beyond (Kimura 1992). "Overall, the magnitude of female superiority at verbal skills is small, in the range of one-quarter of a standard deviation" (Kolb

& Whishaw 1990, 391). Though the difference is slight, there *is* a difference.

2. *Females are better than males at precision motor tasks.* Females are better than males on tasks requiring fine motor coordination; e.g., placing pegs in holes on a board (Kimura 1992, 80).

3. *Males are better than females in visual-spatial ability.* Males perform better than females "on tests of recall and detection of shapes, mental rotation of two- or three-dimensional figures, geometry, maze learning, map reading, aiming at and tracking objects, and geographical knowledge" (Kolb & Whishaw 1990, 391–93). "Like the verbal advantage of females, the spatial advantage of males is not absolute, the difference being only about 0.4 of a standard deviation" (Kolb & Whishaw 1990, 393). Here too, though the difference is slight, there *is* a difference.

4. *Males perform better at math than females.* At about twelve, the mathematical skills of boys increases faster than that of girls (Kolb & Whishaw 1990, 393). Although girls achieve higher scores in the classroom, boys achieve higher scores on standardized tests (such as the SAT) (Fausto-Sterling 1992, 58–59). Although "women do better than men on mathematical calculation tests, . . . men do better than women on tests of mathematical reasoning" (Kimura 1992, 80–81).

5. *Males are more aggressive than females.* "A sex difference is present as early as social play begins, at age 2 to 3 years, and remains through the college years" (Kolb & Whishaw 1990, 393).

Feminist Worries about Biological Research into Sex Differences

Critics of research into sex differences claim: (1) that the data have been used to justify a division of labor along sexual lines; (2) that society would be better off if we abandoned such research altogether; and (3) for a variety of reasons, some (or most) of the data is untrustworthy. These claims engender some obvious worries about research into sex differences. My aim here is to evaluate both the claims and their attendant worries. However, since so much hinges upon the reliability of the data itself, I have reserved most of my analysis of the third claim for the next section.

Do Sex Differences Justify Discrimination against Women?

Without question, data identifying sex differences have been used to defend the relegation of women to specific social roles and to only certain (usually menial) jobs. A generation ago, the scenario Grim depicts below was appallingly common.

Women consistently score higher on verbal aptitude tests than do men.
. . . What are we to do with data of this sort? One way it is often used is
as a justification for social practices involving a division of labor on
sexual lines. . . . If women are more "communicative" animals . . . , we
should leave the "communicative" tasks of childrearing to women. . . .
[If] women have superior verbal skills, our . . . telephone operators
should be female. (Grim 1996, 4)

Even today, the data may *potentially* be misused. For example, there
really isn't anything to prevent someone from making the following
related inferences: If women are more communicative, they should be
operators and drive-through window tellers, whereas men, given their
superior visual-spatial skills, should be jet pilots and architects. Indeed, the potential for misuse of data from research into sex differences is one reason why such research "is regarded with suspicion by
those who fear it may be used against women, as past patterns
suggest" (Lindsey 1994, 46).

But people reason fallaciously all the time. If someone is bent on
making claims unsupported by the evidence, there is precious little
anyone can do to stop him (or her). Here's the rub: the *potential* for
misuse of the data does not entail that abuse is "inevitable" (Fausto-
Sterling 1992, 5). Moreover, the emphasis should not be on what
someone *wants* the data to entail; rather, the emphasis should be on
what the data *do* entail, which isn't very much. Here's why.

First, if it's true that women, on average, have greater verbal ability
than men, does it follow that women should be relegated to only such
menial positions as operators, tellers, and the like? Of course not. The
secretary of state, psychologists, college professors, and a host of
white-collar jobs *also* require superior verbal ability. So, if it follows
(as some have indeed claimed) that women and only women should
occupy jobs that will take advantage of their superior verbal ability,
then women should be given preference to *all* such jobs, not just the
menial ones.

Second, qualifications for jobs rarely (if ever) hinge upon any of the
above sex differences alone. As Grim (1996) notes, "[t]here are very
few tasks indeed which call for one and only one simple qualification"
(13). For example, high-status jobs such as engineers *do* require
superior math skills, but not *just* superior math skills; other
abilities—e.g., facility with computers, teamwork, etc.—are also required. Hence, even granting that the sexes differ in certain abilities,
it isn't obvious why any of the above sex differences *alone* should be
a difference that makes a difference in hiring practices or social roles.

Third, what can we tell about the abilities of any one male or female
because males, on average, perform certain tasks better than women,
and women, on average, perform certain tasks better than men?

Does it follow from the fact that men, on average, have superior mathematical reasoning skills, that any one man has superior mathematical reasoning skills? Again, of course not: it never follows from a statistical generalization of the form "Group *X,* on average, has feature *F*" that each each and every member of *X* has *F.* For example, men, on average, are larger and taller than women. While this is true, it should be obvious that not every man is larger and taller than every woman. Similarly, it never follows that "*X* is an *F*" simply because an empirical generalization of the form "Most members of *X* are *F*" is true. To reason thus is to reason fallaciously. Period. So, even if men on average have superior mathematical reasoning ability, any one woman could have mathematical reasoning skills superior to any man. And given that the differences themselves are very slight, not only does Fausto-Sterling (1992) rightfully question how much emphasis should be placed on such data, she asks: "If all you knew about a person was his or her score on a test for verbal ability, how accurately could you guess at his/her sex?" (Fausto-Sterling 1992, 29). Citing Plomin and Foch (1981), she rightfully concludes, "not very." Neither can we predict a person's test score on the basis of her or his sex (384).

But if sex differences are slight, and the differences themselves don't tell us how any particular individual will behave, and if the sex differences themselves aren't a sufficient qualification for any social role or job, then why be worried about how such data can be abused? Far from "justifying" a division of labor along sex lines, inferences to particular individuals based on the above generalities are almost always mistaken and illogical. As such, any abuse of the data from studies into sex differences can readily be countered. And abuse needs to be countered: for while people may be easily persuaded by rhetoric about sex differences, it doesn't follow that they ought to be. About this much at least, I agree with feminists. But whereas feminists aim to curb abuse of the data by eliminating research into sex differences, I opt for another solution: education.

Should Research into Sex Differences Be Abandoned?

The history of research into sex differences is replete with claims that by current standards would be unwarranted, absurd, or even dangerous. Not even luminaries in the history of neuroscience have been immune from such nonsense. For example, Paul Broca (for whom we name both a type of aphasia and the area of neocortex associated with language production) attempted to show that brain size correlated with intelligence:

> In general, the brain is larger in men than in women, in eminent men than in men of mediocre talent, in superior races than in inferior races.

Other things being equal, there is a remarkable relationship between the development of intelligence and the volume of the brain. (quoted in Gould 1980, 150)

If one draws an analogy between strength and intelligence, then since strength is directly proportional to muscle mass, it is reasonable to hypothesize that there *is* a correlation between brain size and intelligence. After all, men's brains, on average, *are* larger than women's brains. This doesn't have anything to do with intelligence however. Rather, larger bodies have larger brains, and men, on average, are larger than women. Broca and his colleagues should have seen this. Their error was in forcing the data to conform to their prejudices, rather than allowing the data to falsify their hypothesis. Thankfully, as Gould (1980) notes, "such overt [sexism] and racism is no longer common among scientists" (151).

Yet if sex differences are the result of differences in biology, then since brains mediate all our behavior, it stands to reason that differences in brain anatomy may be the differences that make a difference. Only someone caught in the grip of an aprioristic dogma would claim otherwise. And the fact that researchers haven't found many significant differences between the brains of men and women does not entail that further differences don't exist. The only way to resolve the issue is to do more science. But doing further research is precisely what many feminists do not want: "further research into sex differences in cognition or brain laterality," says Fausto-Sterling, "seems to me uncalled for" (1992, 221).[4]

Grim (1996) proposes that our continued "ignorance" of the biological role in causing sex differences is acceptable, given the untoward social and psychological consequences of learning the truth—the biological facts of the matter. According to Grim, there are "ethical reasons" for valuing social explanations over biological ones. Above all, the social risks "are less significant and the prospective gains greater on the assumption of the social explanation" (10). Here's why:

To the extent that observed differences are social in origin rather than fundamental [biological], they can in principle be socially avoided; society might be constructed such that those differences did not appear at all. . . . One of our standard social ideals is that of a truly egalitarian society, a society of equals. When that ideal is criticized, it is generally criticized as utopian or unrealistic. But it is not criticized . . . as ethically undesirable. This is important because to the extent that differences at issue are merely social, an approximation of the ideal of egalitarianism is a real possibility. To the extent that differences are fundamental, we will always fall short of that goal. Thus [assuming sex differences are the result of social causes] allows a prospect of egalitarianism . . . a closer approximation of a deeply seated ethical ideal. (Grim 1996, 11–12)

So not only should we remain in ignorance of any biological causes of sex differences, it would be better for society, he feels, if we simply assumed that sex differences arise from the environment alone.

I disagree.

First, "a truly egalitarian society," as Grim notes, would be "a society of equals" (1996, 11). But whether egalitarianism should be lauded as a social ideal depends on how one fleshes out "equality." Grim gives few specifics. I shall therefore assume that what he has in mind is a society where—regardless of sex, sexual orientation, race, ethnicity, and so on—everyone is given an equal education and everyone has an equal opportunity to compete for available employment. In such a society, no member from any one group would be privileged; the playing field, as it were, would be level. I find it problematic whether such a society is consistent with most strains of feminism. My principal concern, however, is that *equal opportunity does not entail equal ability*. Even in an egalitarian society, some people will be better at performing certain tasks than will others. How then will the choice jobs be doled out? It can't be by ability, for that would: (1) discriminate against those of lesser ability; (2) tacitly admit that people just aren't equal; and (3) violate the "equal treatment" that is necessary for "distributive justice" (Grim 1996, 11). What about by lottery? I hope not, for who would want to go under the knife of any surgeon selected by such a process? Thus, if the moral highroad requires both abandoning research into sex differences and valuing social causes over biological ones, then because equal treatment doesn't entail equal ability, far from solving the problem of how to deal with sex differences, taking the moral highroad only ignores it: wishing the problem away doesn't eliminate the problem.

Second, even in sex-related behavioral differences are caused by biological factors alone, it does not follow that they are incorrigible: remedial training or some other sort of corrective could compensate for biologically caused limitations. For instance, some gene or other predisposes certain people to be myopic, but corrective lenses can compensate for their inferior eyesight. Similarly, if male aggressiveness is due to biological causes, say genes or hormones, it doesn't follow that society ought to sanction male aggressiveness. Such aggressiveness could be tempered by some sort of therapy—hormonal, psychological, or otherwise. And assuming that males are inherently inferior to females at precision motor tasks, given that there is only a slight difference between female and male performance averages, it stands to reason that male performance as a whole could be improved by some sort of compensatory training. The same holds for the other sex differences, *mutatis mutandis*. Indeed, Grim (1996, 15) makes this very point: "none of the data shows that any of the supposed differences between men and women are differences for which correction or compensatory treatment is impossible." So, even if sex differences arise from biological causes, it does not follow that training or some other therapy couldn't compensate for "inherent" limitations. Simply put, acceptance of a biological base for sex-related differences in ability is *not* an endorsement of determinism. But if research into the biological causes of sex differences is abandoned, then we shall never know how best to compensate for inherent limitations (assuming there are inherent limitations), so individual performance would never be maximized. Thus, abandoning research into the causes of sex differences is inconsistent with egalitarian ideals.

Third, ignorance of the real causes of sex differences is an unacceptable solution to potential abuse of the data or psychological discomfort, particularly given the meager nature of differences themselves. Others agree, even where differences *do* make a difference. For example, consider the following remarks by Simon LeVay, a prominent researcher into biological causes of sexual orientation:

> "If scientists find a gay gene, and I think they will, it opens the possibility—even a probability—of misuse." The dangers he foresees include discriminatory employment tests and fetal tests followed by abortions of potentially gay children. That doesn't mean the search to understand sexual orientation should be given up, argues LeVay. "You avoid misuse by helping along the process of society accepting gay people. I would be very unhappy if mothers aborted fetuses more likely to be gay, but you don't prevent that by inhibiting research, or by prohibiting testing or abortion. You do it by education, by helping people understand that it's okay to have gay kids." (LeVay 1994/March, 70)

Similarly, the way to mitigate the potential misuse of the data is *not* to eliminate scientific inquiry. Rather, the solution is to educate the public on what the data do and do not entail, to educate the public in the standards of good science, and to demand that scientists conduct themselves accordingly. "Good science," Fausto-Sterling notes, "can prevail only when the social and political atmosphere offers it space to grow and develop" (Fausto-Sterling 1992, 213). Agreed. But surely such an atmosphere won't obtain either in the absence of education or the abandonment of unpopular research whose data may *potentially* be misused.

Last, truth isn't what we can defend against all comers. Neither is it what we can maintain in the face of all criticism. Truth is truth, indifferent to its popularity. All things being equal, if naturalistic explanations are to be driven by any ideal, that ideal ought to be truth. Hallowed be its name. The price, however, is that sometimes our most cherished beliefs turn out to be false. The belief that sex differences arise from *biological* causes may be one of them. But the belief that sex differences arise from only *social* causes may be false as well. No one said determining the facts of the matter would be easy. Let the ideological chips fall where they may.

Explaining Sex Differences

There are five sorts theories that are often advanced to explain sex-linked cognitive differences: sex-specific differences in *brain morphology,* sex-related differences in *brain organization, hormones, genes,* and finally, the *environment.* I shall evaluate each in turn. Two points will quickly become obvious. First, not every theory will account for each of the above sex differences. Second, we simply don't know what the true causal mechanisms are—or at least the complete story.

Are the Brains of Males and Females Structurally Dimorphic?

The raison d'être of neuroscience is to explain and model how brains work. Because all human cognitive behavior is mediated by brains, given that there *are* cognitive sex differences, it is reasonable to suppose that what explains these differences is that male and female brains are built differently—that the brains of males and females are structurally dimorphic. At this point, there's no need to determine whether sex-related variations in anatomical organization correlate to any of the above cognitive sex differences. Rather, we need to focus on whether there *are* any sex-related differences in brain structure. Given the immeasurable complexity and variation in brain morphology from individual to individual, determining the facts of the matter has proven to be difficult.

A sufficiently mature neuroscience would be such that, if the brains of males and females (or heterosexuals and homosexuals) were in fact structurally dimorphic, a neuroanatomist, when given a brain, would definitively be able to individuate both the sex and sexual orientation of the individual to whom it once belonged. At present, such is not the case. Part of the problem lies in the sheer complexity of neural organization. There are about 180 billion cells in the brain, approximately 50 billion of which are directly involved in information processing. But each of these 50 billion or so neurons receives up to 15,000 connections from other neurons. As someone once said, there are more possible patterns of synaptic activation in a normal adult brain than there are elementary particles in the entire universe!

As if that weren't enough, bear in mind that no two brains are exactly alike. The brains of healthy adults not only differ in size—from between 1100g to 2000g—but also in "gyral patterns, distribution of gray and white matter, cytoarchitectonics, vascular patterns, [and] neurochemistry'' (Kolb & Whishaw 1990, 383; also see 3–4). For Fausto-Sterling (1992), these differences among brains

> bear witness to the extensive yet futile attempts to derive biological explanations for alleged sex differences in cognition. . . . [E]ach person's brain may have more physical individuality than do the person's finger-prints. . . . [This] implies that attempts to lump people together according to broad categories such as race or sex are doomed to failure. (60; also see 49)

If this line of reasoning is right, then neuroscience, cognitive science, psychology, and a host of methodologically similar disciplines—disciplines based on empirical generalities—would go by the boards.

There is no reason to throw out the baby with the bathwater just yet; for while no two brains are *exactly* alike, it doesn't follow that there aren't *any* regularities. There are. (If there weren't, neurosurgery would be even harder than it is.) Consider the following:

1. Because males have larger bodies, male brains are larger than female brains. But because any one female can be larger than any one male, not all female brains are smaller than every male brain. The converse is also true.
2. Normal brains are bilaterally organized into two hemispheres connected by a fiber tract of approximately 200 million neurons (which is about 0.4 percent of all the processing neurons) called the *corpus callosum*.
3. Although the two hemispheres are functionally and anatomically asymmetrical,[5] the laterality of the hemispheres is not absolute: both hemispheres play a role in nearly every human behavior. Nevertheless, in right-handed people, the *left* hemisphere is the primary seat of language processing, whereas the *right* is the primary seat of visual-spatial processing.
4. Each hemisphere is composed of four lobes. Each lobe contains an area for a specific type of information processing: (a) FRONTAL LOBE—motor processing; (b) PARIETAL LOBE—somatosensory processing; (c) TEMPORAL LOBE—auditory processing; (d) OCCIPITAL LOBE—visual processing.

Aside from the already discussed difference in brain size, do any of the above anatomical regularities relate to sex? The answer appears to be yes. Based on a study of fourteen whole normal brains taken at autopsy (nine males, five females), de LaCose-Utamsing and Holloway (1982) report that the *splenium*—the posterior part of the corpus callosum—is significantly larger in females than in males (see Figure 1). They also reported a qualitative difference: ''The female splenium

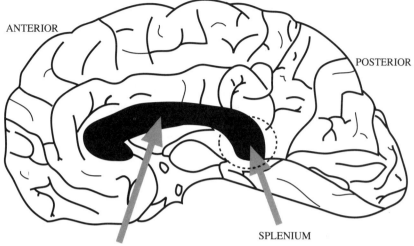

ANTERIOR

POSTERIOR

SPLENIUM

CORPUS CALLOSUM

Figure 1. Medial view of the right hemisphere. The corpus callosum is the primary fiber tract that conveys information between the two hemispheres. In callosal studies, the subdivisions that are typically measured are the entire length, and anterior and posterior halves, and the splenium.

is bulbous and widens markedly with respect to the body of the callosum; the male counterpart is approximately cylindrical and is relatively continuous with the body of the corpus callosum'' (Kolb & Whishaw 1990, 386). Given that men are larger than women, and hence male brains are larger than female ones, it *should* be the case that the male callosum is proportionally larger than the female callosum. It's not.

Attempts to duplicate the de Lacose-Utamsing and Holloway (1982) findings have met with mixed success: only about 50 percent of subsequent studies have fully or partially corroborated their findings (Kolb & Whishaw 1990, 386). One recent study by Allen et al. (1991), with a sample size of 122 adults and 24 children (there were an even number of males and females, who also corresponded by age) using magnetic resonance imaging (MRI), corroborated de Lacose-Utamsing and Holloway's identification of sex-based shape differences of the splenium.

Several problems continue to plague research into sex- and sexuality-related differences in the brain. The most glaring problem concerns the nature of some of the samples themselves. As in the LeVay (1994/ May, 1994/March) study of structural dimorphism between the brains of homosexuals and heterosexuals, test samples may have been tainted by neurological disease (or in the case of the brains studied by LeVay,

AIDS). While one must be wary of generalizing from the atypical, "it is difficult to be certain that observed differences truly reflect differences in . . . the population [as a whole]" (Kolb & Whishaw 1990, 395). Other problems include inconsistencies, procedural differences, small samples, and great variability in results, to name a few.

In addition, even if there are the structural sex and sexuality differences suggested by the callosal and hypothalamic data (see LeVay, 1994/May, 1994/March), we don't know whether such differences were congenital or arose from experience (Fausto-Sterling 1992, 240). The point here, however, is that there *are* such differences. And like the other biological characteristics that figure in sex identity— chromosomes, sex organs, hormone levels, and so on—differences that are in themselves of no moral or political significance, anatomical differences between the brains of women and men are so as well, regardless of their origin. Because as a society we are supposed to value diversity, why should splenium size be treated any differently than such unproblematic biological indicators of diversity as skin color? It shouldn't.

Although finding sex-related structural differences in brains has been difficult, it has nevertheless been done. The tasks now include determining how these differences arose and whether they play some causal role in engendering any of the behavior-related sex differences. Yet if we follow Grim and Fausto-Sterling's advice to altogether abandon sex difference research, then we shall never be able to answer these questions.

Are Sex Differences Due to Differences in Brain Organization?

Thanks in part to studies by McGlone (1977, 1980), one of the first researchers to study sex differences in neurological patients, there is good evidence that lesions affect the sexes differently. In McGlone's population, for example, the likelihood of *aphasia* (a language disorder of either production or comprehension, or both) was three times greater in males than in females (Kolb & Whishaw 1990, 396). This result suggests that the female brain is more symmetrically organized for language than the male brain. In other words, male language processing occurs more or less exclusively in the left hemisphere (and hence the male brain ought to be more asymmetrical than the female brain), while female language processing occurs less-exclusively in the left. Thus, lesions in the left hemisphere of males should (and in fact do) make them more susceptible to language disorders. Conversely, if a lesion occurs in the female left hemisphere, because of the increased language processing in the right, the right hemisphere could compensate, so females would be less susceptible to aphasia. The symmetry underlying female language processing could account for their greater verbal competence. Similarly, male right hemisphere dominance in visual-spatial processing could account for the higher male performance averages in visual-spatial tests.

Until recently, McGlone's conclusion (that the female brain is more symmetrical than the male brain) was viewed as "too simple to account for the data" (Kolb & Whishaw 1990, 396–97). For while there is "good evidence that lesions affect males and females differently, . . . it has not been proved that this is due to differences in brain organization" (Kolb & Whishaw 1990, 398). In fact, several positron emission tomography (PET) studies of language processing failed to show any differences in cerebral organization between males and females (see Petersen et al. 1988; Petersen & Fiez 1993; Petersen et al. 1993).[6] So given the immunological superiority of the additional X chromosome, females may be less susceptible to language disorders; as such, the difference in aphasia rates (between males and females) could be due to genetics.[7]

However, McGlone's conclusions have recently been corroborated by Shaywitz et al. (1995). She and her colleagues used functional magnetic resonance imaging (fMRI) to study female and male subjects performing a phonological matching task. Their data clearly provide "direct evidence" for the notion that language processing is lateralized in the left hemisphere in men, but is processed bilaterally in women (Rugg 1995, 561): an area of inferior frontal cortex in *both hemispheres was active when women performed the task, but only the inferior frontal cortex of the left* was active when men performed the task. Still, since only a total of thirty-eight subjects were studied—nineteen men and nineteen women—it doesn't follow that women *in general* process language bilaterally; nor does it follow that the brains of women *in general* are functionally more symmetrical than men. To justify these general claims, the pool of tested subjects must substantially increase. Nevertheless, some progress has clearly been made.

But positing sex-specific differences in brain organization isn't the only way to explain the cognitive sex differences. For example, the differences in verbal and visual-spatial tasks could be due to either maturational constraints on cerebral organization, or to sex-specific strategies in performing the tasks. Regarding the latter, even if there are sex-linked cognitive problem-solving strategies, we don't know whether the factors that influence such predispositions are genetic, maturational, or environmental. Regarding the former, it is unproblematic that girls physically mature earlier than do boys. It is therefore reasonable to suppose that the brains of girls mature faster as well. Since the left hemisphere is functionally organized *before* the right hemisphere, girls may thus have a maturational edge on verbal ability. And the corresponding slower development of boys may enhance visual and spatial ability (Kolb & Whishaw 1990, 400). Bear in mind,

however, that although *minor* anatomical differences in cerebral structure have been identified, *significant* structural dimorphism has not.
And with regard to the minor sex-related anatomical differences, we
simply don't know whether they cause any of the sex-linked differences in behavior.

Hormonal Effects

It is the influence of gonadal hormones on the brain that leads to sex
differentiation. This isn't really problematic. To refresh the reader's
memory as to how this occurs, I offer the following summary:

> Hormones are internal secretions produced by the endocrine glands that
> are carried by the blood throughout the body, which affect target cells in
> other organs. Both sexes possess the same hormones, but they differ in
> the amounts secreted. . . . [S]ex hormones have two key functions. . . .
> (1) They shape the development of the brain and sex organs and (2) [they]
> then determine how these organs will be activated. . . . During fetal
> development when certain tissues are highly sensitive to hormones, the
> secretion of testosterone both masculinizes and defeminizes key cellular
> structures throughout the brain and reproductive organs. (Lindsey 1994,
> 22)

In effect, as Christen (1991, 29) reports, "the male can be regarded as
a female transformed by testosterone" (also see Kimura 1992; Fausto-
Sterling 1992, fig. 3.8).

Because "studies with nonhuman primates . . . show that the
increased aggression in males is probably the result of the male
hormone androgen both pre- and postnatally" (Kolb & Whishaw 1990,
393; also see 387), it is reasonable to suppose that sex hormones—
testosterone in particular—play some role in male aggressiveness.
However, a positive correlation between testosterone and aggression
does not entail that testosterone *causes* aggression. In fact, elevated
levels of testosterone in aggressive male subjects may be *the result,*
not *the cause* of aggressive behavior (Fausto-Sterling 1992, 127).
Moreover, "the apparent biological predisposition in males toward
aggression is mediated by social influences" (Lindsey 1994, 25).[8] Thus,
we cannot conclude that testosterone or any other hormone is the
critical variable in explaining male aggressiveness.

Genetic Sex-Linkage

Fausto-Sterling (1992) spends a disproportionate amount of time
attempting to debunk research into "genetically caused behavior"
(12). To put the issue thus, however, is a straw man, for only the most
committed genetic reductionist would make such a claim. Strictly

speaking, genes code protein sequences that develop into structures, not programs, not behaviors. It is these structures (and circuits of structures), which when presented with an appropriate stimulus, engender a specific response. Genes can predispose one toward a particular behavior, say, language learning, but unless certain environmental conditions obtain, neither will the behavior (see Fausto-Sterling 1992, 71, 89). Thus, if genes are among the factors that *cause* any of the sex-related differences in behavior, they do so only indirectly, and never in isolation from environmental influences.

The paradigm examples of genes contributing to behavior are studies of (male) homosexual preference among identical twins, where one twin is homosexual. Concordance rates as high as 88 percent have been reported: in fifty of the fifty-seven pairs of identical twins in one study, where one twin was a homosexual, both were homosexuals. In studies involving fraternal twins where one twin was a homosexual, both twins were homosexual in approximately 50 percent of the cases. In studies involving biologically related (and/or adopted brothers), the concordance rate was about 10 percent. Because identical twins have 100 percent of their genes in common, the high correlation suggests a genetic role in (homo)sexual orientation (Posner 1992, 101).

However, as Fausto-Sterling (1992) notes, the similar sexual orientation of the identical twins "could as easily be due to environment as genetics," given that identical twins have more experiences in common than do either fraternal twins or non-twin brothers; e.g., they dress alike, are mistaken for one another, etc. (257–58). Although the gist of her criticism is correct, the criticism itself is overstated: it implies an *either* genetics *or* environment framework that even she denies. But there is a way to resolve the issue: conduct a similar study on identical twins who were reared in separate environments. Until such a study is done, disentangling the genetic causes of sexual orientation from the environmental ones remains problematic.

Environment or Experience

Environment-based explanations have been offered not only for each of the above sex-linked differences in behavior and ability, they have been offered to explain gender, sexual preference, and even sex identity. One could give such an explanation for the difference in visual-spatial ability, for example, (as we have already seen) by appealing to sex-related childrearing and play practices. A similar explanation for both male aggression and mathematical ability could also be made, but the math explanation is more complicated, for it must include an appeal such as the following: "Girls are discouraged from math-dependent occupations like engineering." Although boys take more math classes than girls (which would certainly contribute to the higher scores of boys), the girls who *do* take the classes not only receive the same instruction, they also get better grades. The following question suggests itself: How can the girls get better grades yet score poorer on standardized math tests? Fausto-Sterling (1992) not only denies that girls receive the same instruction, she attributes the lower standardized test performance to male bias. Aside from the conspiratorial flavor of such "explanations," she is right about one thing: Until we can eliminate math-related social biases against girls (assuming they still exist), we won't be able to identify any further biological basis for the math difference beyond the right hemisphere's role in visual-spatial tasks (which includes mathematics).

But to admit *any* biological factor when explaining sex-linked behavioral differences is to deny social reductionism. This leads us full circle back to the issue of whether sex identity and sexual orientation are social constructs. I have already established that the former is primarily biological. The findings from twin and hypothalamic studies clearly support the notion that the latter minimally has a biological component, though sexual orientation need not—as is the case with one's sex—reduce to biology.

For example, consider the following case study involving the sex reassignment of a 17-month-old genetic male, one of a pair of identical twins.

> During a circumcision procedure at seven months, the electrical current used to remove the foreskin was set too high, which resulted in the loss of the entire penis. . . . Reconstructive surgery with the creation of a vagina began the process which would be followed by hormonal and estrogen therapy at puberty. . . . By age five, the twins were demonstrating almost stereotypical gender roles. . . . A follow-up of the girl at age thirteen . . . suggested she demonstrated significant psychological problems relative to her role as a female. . . . The choice was made to reconstruct a penis. As an adult, he prefers females as sexual partners. (Lindsey 1994, 23–24)

This case was heralded as the paradigmatic instance of sexual malleability—at least until 1992, when the facts regarding the reconstruction and re-assignment came to light. What is now clear, however, is that even after construction of the vagina, hormone therapy, and female socialization, "the effects of [his] first biological sex could not be completely altered" (Lindsey 1994, 24). Despite the great sexual plasticity humans exhibit, environmental determinism, like its biological counterpart, is an oversimplification. Fausto-Sterling agrees (1992, 75): "Beware (especially feminists) of replacing a biologically reductive theory with a socially reductive one" (Fausto-Sterling 1992, 108).

Although environmental explanations for sex-related differences in ability and behavior are both common and appealing, "there is no evidence that the observed sex differences . . . can be accounted for solely on the basis of environmental or social factors" (Kolb & Whishaw 1990, 400).

Conclusion

As yet, the following question has remained unanswered: What is the most reasonable theory that explains sex differences, particularly sex-liked differences in ability and behavior? The consensus among scientists is that because human development is a "mosaic of biological inheritance and social experience" (Lindsey 1994, 26), both biology *and* experience underlie all human behavior. As such, the most explanatory theory won't reduce completely to either biology or experience. Herein lies the dilemma: Fausto-Sterling (1992) is correct to note that questions regarding what part (of behavior and ability) is biology and what part is experience are questions that "remain unanswered" (14). Grim (1996) too is correct in noting that in *some* respects, we shall always be ignorant. My point, however, is that unless cognitive and biological research into sex differences continues, our ignorance will be pervasive; worse still, it will be permanent.

Notes

1. Indeed, not even once does Grim (1996) use the word 'feminist'. However, in note 18, he is quite explicit about *some* of his criticisms being in the same "general spirit" as those of one well established feminist, Joyce Trebilcot (1982).
2. The term 'utilities' is the Marine Corps name for the camouflaged uniform. Incidentally, the upper-body portion of this uniform is called a 'blouse', regardless of the Marine's sex.
3. That isn't to say that each claim doesn't have its gainsayers. For example, 'evolutionary psychologists' and 'sociobiologists' would clearly deny the former (see Horgan, 1995/Oct.). But given that sociobiological explanations aren't falsifiable, they run counter to the goal of naturalistic explanations of cognitive processing. As such, I won't have much to say about sociobiological explanations for sex and/or gender differences. For criticisms, see Gould (1980) and Fausto-Sterling (1992).
4. She makes this claim, in part, because each brain is unique. Lest I get ahead of myself, I won't here say anything about differences in brain anatomy, sex-related or otherwise. I shall explore the issue at length in the following section.
5. The following are among the major asymmetries between the hemispheres: (1) the right hemisphere is larger, but the left has more gray matter; (2) the structure of each temporal lobe is different; (3) the slope of the *Sylvian fissure* (the cleft that separates the temporal and parietal lobes) is less acute in

the left hemisphere; (4) the *frontal operculum* (also called *Broca's area*, the region of frontal cortex associated with speech production) has a more complex organization in the left (Kolb & Whishaw 1990, 348–349).

6. One reason why the PET studies have failed to corroborate the Shaywitz et al. (1995) findings is that few woman took part in any of the above studies.

7. "It is the lack or presence of the Y chromosome which determines if the baby will be a male or female. . . . The extra X chromosome is associated with a superior immune system and lower female mortality at all stages of the life cycle" (Lindsey 1994, 22–23, 34).

8. "MacCoby and Jacklin make no connection between their conclusion in one chapter that boys are more aggressive and another in the following chapter that parents mete out more physical punishment to boys, stimulate gross motor behavior in male infants more often than in females, and are more concerned with the development of appropriate sex typing (play attitudes and general behavior) in boys and in girls" (Fausto-Sterling 1992, 151).

References

Allen, L. Richey, M., Chai, Y. & Gorski, R. (1991). Sex differences in the corpus callosum of the living human being. *Journal of Neuroscience* 11:933–942.

Christen, Y. (1991). *Sex differences: Modern biology and the unisex fallacy.* N. Davidson (Trans.). New Brunswick, NJ: Transaction.

Fausto-Sterling, A. (1992). *Myths of gender: Biological theories about women and men.* (Rev. ed.). New York: Basic Books.

Gould, S. (1980). Wide hats and narrow minds. *The panda's thumb: More reflections in natural history* (pp. 145–151). New York: W. W. Norton & Company.

Grim, P. (1996). Sex and social roles: How to deal with the data. In L. May and R. Strikwerda (Eds.) *Rethinking masculinity: Philosophical explorations in light of feminism,* 2nd ed. (pp. 3–20, in this volume). Lanham, MD: Rowman & Littlefield.

Horgan, J. (1995/Oct.). The new social Darwinists. *Scientific American 273:* 174–181.

Kimura, D. (1992). Sex differences in the brain. In *Mind and brain: Readings from Scientific American magazine* (pp. 79–89). New York: W. H. Freeman and Company, 1993.

Kolb, B., & Whishaw, I. (1990). *Fundamentals of human neuropsychology.* (3rd ed.). New York: W. H. Freeman and Company.

de Lacoste-Utamsing, C., and Holloway, R. (1982). Sexual dimorphism in the human corpus callosum. *Science 216:* 1431–1432.

LeVay, S. (1994/March). Sex and the brain. *Discover 15:* 64–71.

LeVay, S. & Hamer, D. (1994/May). Evidence for a biological influence in male homosexuality. *Scientific American 270:* 44–49.

Lindsey, L. (1994). *Gender roles: A sociological perspective.* (2nd ed.). Englewood Cliffs, NJ: Prentice Hall.

MacCoby, E. & Jacklin, C. (1974). *The psychology of sex differences.* Stanford, CA: Stanford University Press.

McGlone, J. (1977). Sex differences in the cerebral organization of verbal function to patients with unilateral brain lesions. *Brain 100*: 775–793.

McGlone, J. (1980). Sex differences in human brain asymmetry: A critical survey. *Behavioral and Brain Sciences 3:* 215–263.

Petersen, S. & Fiez, J. (1993). The processing of single words studied with positron emission tomography. *Annual Review of Neuroscience 16:* 509–530.

Petersen, S., Fox, P., Posner, M., Mintun, M. & Raichle, M. (1988). Positron emission tomographic studies of the cortical anatomy of single-word processing. *Nature 331:* 585–589.

Petersen, S., Fox, P., Snyder, A. & Raichle, M. (1990). Activation of extrastriate and frontal cortical areas by visual words and word-like stimuli. *Science 249:* 1041–1044.

Plomin, R. & Foch, T. (1981). Sex differences and individual difference. *Child Development 52:* 383–385.

Posner, R. (1992). *Sex and reason.* Cambridge, MA: Harvard University Press.

Rugg, M. (1995). La différence vive. *Nature 373:* 561–562.

Shaywitz, B., Shaywitz, S., Pugh, K., Constable, R., Skudlarski, P., Fulbright, R., Bronen, R., Fletcher, J. Shankweiler, D., Katz, L., & Gore, J. (1995). Sex differences in the functional organization of the brain for language. *Nature 373:* 607–609.

Trebilcot, J. (1982). Sex roles: The argument from nature. In M. Vetterling-Braggin (Ed.), *Femininity, masculinity and androgyny* (pp. 40–48). Lanham, MD: Rowman & Littlefield.

PART TWO

Aggression and Violence

3

The Enduring Appeals of Battle

J. Glenn Gray

I feel cheerful and am well-pleased. . . . What is ahead may be grim and dreadful but I shall be spiritually more at rest in the heart of the carnage than somewhere in the rear. Since I have lent myself to the war, I want to pay the price and know it at its worst. (War journal, January 31, 1944)

My friend wrote once late in the war that he often thought of me as *the soldier*. To him I had come to stand for the qualities that he associated with universal man at war. The idea, I recall, both flattered and insulted me a little at first but ended by impressing me with its truth, though I should never have conceived it on my own. I wrote in my journal: "Perhaps the worst that can be said is that I am *becoming* a soldier. To be a soldier! That is at best to be something less than a man. To say nothing of being a philosopher." Since then I have frequently wondered what it meant to be a "soldier" and why I regarded myself then, insofar as I was a soldier, as less than a man.

At the time I wrote these lines I faced the grim realization of how narrowed all our desires had become. The night before, one of the women in the town where we were staying had declared: *"Das Essen ist die Hauptsache."* Food is the main thing. And the words had burned into my brain with the force of a proverb. The majority of my fellows seemed content with the satisfaction of their natural urges— eating, drinking, and lusting for women. Interests and refinements that transcended these primitive needs, and that I had built up over the years, were rapidly falling away, and I felt that I was becoming simply one of the others.

In a German newspaper, taken from a prisoner, I read a letter from a soldier long years on the Russian front, who lamented that the war had robbed him of any sense of self-identity and that he no longer possessed an ego and a personal fate. I realize now, much better than I did then, that there was another force much more determining than simple need and desire. It was the emotional environment of warfare, more specifically, the atmosphere of violence. The threat to life and safety that the presence of the opponent, "the enemy," represented created this climate of feeling. Near the front it was impossible to ignore, consciously or unconsciously, the stark fact that out there were men who would gladly kill you, if and when they got the chance. As a consequence, an individual was dependent on others, on people who could not formerly have entered the periphery of his consciousness. For them in turn, he was of interest only as a center of force, a wielder of weapons, a means of security and survival. This confraternity of danger and exposure is unequaled in forging links among people of unlike desire and temperament, links that are utilitarian and narrow but no less passionate because of their accidental and general character.

In such a climate men may hold fast in memory to their civilian existence of yesterday and stubbornly resist, as I tried to do, the encroachments of the violent and the irrational. They may write home to their parents and sweethearts that they are unchanged, and they may even be convinced of it. But the soldier who has yielded himself to the fortunes of war, has sought to kill and to escape being killed, or who has even lived long enough in the disordered landscape of battle, is no longer what he was. He becomes in some sense a fighter, whether he wills it or not—at least most men do. His moods and disposition are affected by the presence of others and the encompassing environment of threat and fear. He must surrender in a measure to the will of others and to superior force. In a real sense he becomes a fighting man, a *Homo furens*.

This is surely part of what it means to be a soldier, and what it has always meant. *Homo furens* is, so to speak, a subspecies of the genus Homo sapiens. Obviously, man is more than a fighter and other than a fighter, in our age and formerly. In some generations—alas! too few as yet—organized war has been little more than an episode. Even those generations who have had to spend much time in combat considered themselves farmers, teachers, factory workers, and so on, as well as fighters. Man as warrior is only partly a man, yet, fatefully enough, this aspect of him is capable of transforming the whole. When given free play, it is able to subordinate other aspects of the personality, repress civilian habits of mind, and make the soldier as fighter a different kind of creature from the former worker, farmer, or clerk.

Millions of men in our day—like millions before us—have learned to live in war's strange element and have discovered in it a powerful fascination. The emotional environment of warfare has always been compelling; it has drawn most men under its spell. Reflection and calm reasoning are alien to it. I wrote in my war journal that I was obsessed with "the tyranny of the present"; the past and the future did not concern me. It was hard for me to think, to be alone. When the signs of peace were visible, I wrote, in some regret: "The purgative force of danger which makes men coarser but perhaps more human will soon be lost and the first months of peace will make some of us yearn for the old days of conflict."

Beyond doubt there are many who simply endure war, hating every moment. Though they may enjoy garrison life or military maneuvers, they experience nothing but distaste and horror for combat itself. Still, those who complain the most may not be immune from war's appeals. Soldiers complain as an inherited right and traditional duty, and few wish to admit to a taste for war. Yet many men both hate and love combat. They know why they hate it; it is harder to know and to be articulate about why they love it. The novice may be eager at times to describe his emotions in combat, but it is the battle-hardened veterans to whom battle has offered the deeper appeals. For some of them the war years are what Dixon Wecter has well called "the one great lyric passage in their lives."

What are these secret attractions of war, the ones that have persisted in the West despite revolutionary changes in the methods of warfare? I believe that they are: the delight in seeing, the delight in comradeship, the delight in destruction. Some fighters know one appeal and not the others, some experience all three, and some may, of course, feel other appeals that I do not know. These three had reality for me, and I have found them also throughout the literature of war.

War as a spectacle, as something to see, ought never to be underestimated. There is in all of us what the Bible calls "the lust of the eye," a phrase at once precise and of the widest connotation. It is precise because human beings possess as a primitive urge this love of watching. We fear we will miss something worth seeing. This passion to see surely precedes in most of us the urge to participate in or to aid. Anyone who has watched people crowding around the scene of an accident on the highway realizes that the lust of the eye is real. Anyone who has watched the faces of people at a fire knows it is real. Seeing sometimes absorbs us utterly; it is as though the human being became one great eye. The eye is lustful because it requires the novel, the unusual, the spectacular. It cannot satiate itself on the familiar, the routine, the everyday.

This lust may stoop to mindless curiosity, a primordial impulse. Its typical response is an open-minded gaping at a parade or at the explosion of a hydrogen bomb. How many men in each generation have been drawn into the twilight of confused and murderous battle

"to see what it is like"? This appeal of war is usually described as
the desire to escape the monotony of civilian life and the cramping
restrictions of an unadventurous existence. People are often bored
with a day that does not offer variety, distraction, threat, and insecurity. They crave the satisfaction of the astonishing. Although war
notoriously offers monotony and boredom enough, it also offers the
outlandish, the exotic, and the strange. It offers the opportunity of
gaping at other lands and other peoples, at curious implements of war,
at groups of others like themselves marching in order, and at the
captured enemy in a cage.

However, sensuous curiosity is only one level of seeing. The word
"see," with its many derivatives, like "insight" and "vision," has an
imaginative and intellectual connotation which is far more expansive
than the physical. Frequently we are unable to separate these levels of
seeing, to distinguish the outer from the inner eye. This is probably no
accident. The human being is, after all, a unity, and the sensuous,
imaginative, and intellectual elements of his nature can fuse when he
is absorbed. Mindless curiosity is not separated as much as we like to
believe from what art lovers call the disinterested contemplation of
beauty. The delight in battle as a mere spectacle may progress almost
insensibly to an aesthetic contemplation or to a more dominantly
intellectual contemplation of its awfulness. From the simplest soldier
who gazes openmouthed at the panorama of battle in his portion of the
field to the trained artist observing the scene, there is, I believe, only
a difference of degree. The "seeing" both are engaged in is for them
an end in itself before it becomes a spur to action. The dominant
motive in both cases appears to be neither the desire for knowledge,
though there is much that is instructive in the scene, nor the need to
act, though that, too, will become imperative. Their "seeing" is for
the sake of seeing, the lust of the eye, where the eye stands for the
whole human being, for man the observer.

There is a popular conviction that war and battle are the sphere of
ugliness, and, since aesthetic delight is associated with the beautiful, it
may be concluded that war is the natural enemy of the aesthetic. I fear
that this is in large part an illusion. It is, first of all, wrong to believe
that only beauty can give us aesthetic delight; the ugly can please us
too, as every artist knows. And furthermore, beauty in various guises
is hardly foreign to scenes of battle. While it is undeniable that the
disorder and distortion and the violation of nature that conflict brings
are ugly beyond compare, there are also color and movement, variety,
panoramic sweep, and sometimes even momentary proportion and
harmony. If we think of beauty and ugliness without their usual moral
overtones, there is often a weird but genuine beauty in the sight of
massed men and weapons in combat. Reputedly, it was the sight of
advancing columns of men under fire that impelled General Robert E.

Lee to remark to one of his staff: "It is well that war is so terrible—we would grow too fond of it."

As I reflect further, it becomes clear, however, that the term "beauty," used in any ordinary sense, is not the major appeal in such spectacles. Instead, it is the fascination that manifestations of power and magnitude hold for the human spirit. Some scenes of battle, much like storms over the ocean or sunsets on the desert or the night sky seen through a telescope, are able to overawe the single individual and hold him in a spell. He is lost in their majesty. His ego temporarily deserts him, and he is absorbed into what he sees. An awareness of power that far surpasses his limited imagination transports him into a state of mind unknown in his everyday experiences. Fleeting as these rapt moments may be, they are, for the majority of men, an escape from themselves that is very different from the escapes induced by sexual love or alcohol. This raptness is a joining and not a losing, a deprivation of self in exchange for a union with objects that were hitherto foreign. Yes, the chief aesthetic appeal of war surely lies in this feeling of the sublime, to which we, children of nature, are directed whether we desire it or not. Astonishment and wonder and awe appear to be part of our deepest being, and war offers them an exercise field par excellence. As I wrote:

> Yesterday morning we left Rome and took up the pursuit of the rapidly fleeing Germans. And again the march was past ruined, blackened villages, destroyed vehicles, dead and mangled corpses of German soldiers, dead and stinking horses, blown bridges, and clouds of dust that blackened our faces and filled our clothes. . . . Later I watched a full moon sail through a cloudy sky . . . saw German bombers fly past and our antiaircraft bursts around them. . . . I felt again the aching beauty of this incomparable land. I remembered everything that I had ever been and was. It was painful and glorious.

What takes place in us when we are under the spell of this powerful mood? It is often said that its deepest satisfaction lies in the sense of personal exemption from the fate of others. We watch them exposed to powers that overwhelm them, and we enjoy the feelings of superiority of the secure. When human beings are not involved, and feelings of the sublime steal over us at the majestic in nature, this can be traced to a heightened sense of the ego in one way or another. As spectators we are superior to that which we survey. In my journal are these words:

> This evening we watched a beautiful sunset over the Tyrrhenian Sea. From our window we looked out on the wall-enclosed gardens of Carano, where flowers blossomed and peach trees made the air sweet with their white blossoms. Beyond them stretched fields and, farther, the

mountains, Formia, Gaeta, the sea. As the sun sank behind the mountains, it illumined a cloud that was hanging low. As we watched the
wonderful pageantry of nature, the sound of cannon was carried in on the
evening air. We were forced to realize that a few miles away, in this area
we were gazing at, men lurked with death in their hearts. We were looking
over no man's land. As it grew dark, huge signs of fire appeared on the
mountain. It was mysterious, but we had no doubt that it had to do with
death and destruction.

The feeling of momentary depression, as Kant puts it, which we
initially succumb to when looking through a telescope at the vastness
of the heavens and the insignificance of ourselves in comparison is
soon supplanted by the consciousness that we are the astronomers. It
is we who know that the heavens are empty and vast, and the heavens
presumably know nothing of us. The human spirit triumphs over these
blind forces and lifeless powers of nature. Such scenes as I described
above could be explained, by this view, as the exultation of the
spectators that they were not actors or sufferers, for the sublime mood
derives from a separation of the spectator from the spectacle, and its
pleasantness consists in the superiority the ego feels.

But such a view is wrong, or, at the very least, one-sided. It is the
viewpoint of an egoistic, atomistic psychology rather than the product
of close observation. The awe that steals over us at such times is not
essentially a feeling of triumph, but, on the contrary, a recognition of
power and grandeur to which we are subject. There is not so much a
separation of the self from the world as a subordination of the self to
it. We are able to disregard personal danger at such moments by
transcending the self, by forgetting our separateness.

Last evening I sat on a rock outside the town and watched a modern
battle, an artillery duel . . . the panorama was so farreaching that I could
see both the explosion of the guns and where their speedy messengers
struck. . . . Several shells of replying batteries landed fairly close and
made my perch not the safest of vantage points. But it was an interesting,
stirring sight. After a while the firing died down and evening shadows
came over the valley. A townsman carrying a pail of swill for his hogs
came by, fell into conversation, and then asked me to await his return,
when he would take me to his home for a glass of wine.

Perhaps the majority of men cannot become so absorbed in a
spectacle that they overcome fear of pain and death. Still, it is a
common-enough phenomenon on the battlefield that men expose themselves quite recklessly for the sake of seeing. If ever the world is blown
to bits by some superbomb, there will be those who will watch the
spectacle to the last minute, without fear, disinterestedly and with
detachment. I do not mean that there is lack of interest in this

disinterestedness or lack of emotion in this detachment. Quite the contrary. But the self is no longer important to the observer; it is absorbed into the objects with which it is concerned.

I think the distinctive thing about the feeling of the sublime is its ecstatic character, ecstatic in the original meaning of the term, namely, a state of being outside the self. Even in the common experience of mindless curiosity there is a momentary suppression of the ego, a slight breaking down of the barriers of the self, though insignificant in comparison with the rarer moods when we are filled with awe. This ecstasy satisfies because we are conscious of a power outside us with which we can merge in the relation of parts to whole. Feelings neither of triumph nor of depression predominate. The pervasive sense of wonder satisfies us because we are assured that we are part of this circling world, not divorced from it, or shut up within the walls of the self and delivered over to the insufficiency of the ego. Certain psychologists would call this just another escape from the unpleasant facts of the self's situation. If so, it is an escape of a very different sort from the usual. We feel rescued from the emptiness within us. In losing ourselves we gain a relationship to something greater than the self, and the foreign character of the surrounding world is drastically reduced.

Another appeal of war, the communal experience we call comradeship, is thought, on the other hand, to be especially moral and the one genuine advantage of battle that peace can seldom offer. Whether this is true or not deserves to be investigated. The term "comradeship" covers a large number of relationships, from the most personal to the anonymous and general, and here I will consider only some essentials of military comradeship. What calls it into being in battle, what strengthens or weakens it, what is its essential attraction?

The feeling of belonging together that men in battle often find a cementing force needs first to be awakened by an external reason for fighting, but the feeling is by no means dependent on this reason. The cause that calls comradeship into being may be the defense of one's country, the propagation of the one true religious faith, or a passionate political ideology; it may be the maintenance of honor or the recovery of a Helen of Troy. So long as there is a cause, the hoped-for objective may be relatively unimportant in itself. When, through military reverses or the fatiguing and often horrible experiences of combat, the original purpose becomes obscured, the fighter is often sustained solely by the determination not to let down his comrades.

Numberless soldiers have died, more or less willingly, not for country or honor or religious faith or for any other abstract good, but because they realized that by fleeing their post and rescuing themselves, they would expose their companions to greater danger. Such loyalty to the group is the essence of fighting morale. The commander who can preserve and strengthen it knows that all other psychological or physical factors are little in comparison. The feeling of loyalty, it is clear, is the result, and not the cause, of comradeship. Comrades are loyal to each other spontaneously and without any need for reasons. Men may learn to be loyal out of fear or from rational conviction, loyal even to those they dislike. But such loyalty is rarely reliable with great masses of men unless it has some cement in spontaneous liking and the feeling of belonging.

Though comradeship is dependent on being together physically in time and space, it is not a herding animal instinct. Little can be learned, I am convinced, from attempting to compare animal and human forms of association. In extreme danger and need, there is undeniably a minimal satisfaction in having others of your own species in your vicinity. The proverb that "misery loves company" is not without basis, particularly in situations where defense and aggression are involved. But it is equally true that men can live in the same room and share the same suffering without any sense of belonging together. They can live past each other and be irresponsible toward each other, even when their welfare is clearly dependent on co-operation.

German soldiers who endured Russian prisoner-of-war camps in the decade after World War II have described convincingly how the Communist system succeeded in destroying any sense of comradeship among prisoners simply by making the results of individual labor the basis of food allotments. Under a system like this, men can not only eat their fill but also enjoy superfluity without any concern for a mate who may slowly be starving to death. This lamentable fact about human nature has too often been observed to require much further confirmation. The physical proximity of men can do no more than create the minimal conditions of comradeship. It no more explains the communal appeal of war than it explains why people love cities.

What then are the important components of comradeship, if physical presence is only a minimal condition? The one that occurs immediately is organization for a common goal. Even a very loose type of organization can induce many people to moderate their self-assertiveness and accommodate themselves to the direction of a superpersonal will. Everyone is aware of the vast difference between a number of men as a chance collection of individuals and the same number as an organized group or community. A community has purpose and plan, and there is in us an almost instinctive recognition of the connection between unity and strength.

Those who stand in disorganized masses against smaller groups of the organized are always aware of the tremendous odds against them. The sight of huge crowds of prisoners of war being herded toward collection centers by a few guards with rifles slung over their backs is one filled with pathos. It is not the absence of weapons that makes these prisoners helpless before their guards. It is the absence of a common will, the failing assurance that others will act in concert with you against the conquerors.

But organization is of many kinds, and the military kind is special in aiming at common and concrete goals. The organization of a civilian community, a city, for example, is not without goals, but they are rarely concrete, and many members are hardly aware of their existence. If a civilian community has goals with more reality and power to endure than military goals, as I believe it does, its goals are, nevertheless, unable to generate the degree of loyalty that a military organization can.

In war it is a commonplace of command that the goals of the fighting forces need to be clear and to be known. Naturally, the overall goal is to win the war and then go home. But in any given action, the goal is to overcome the attacking enemy or, if you are the attacker, to win the stated objective. Any fighting unit must have a limited and specific objective, and the more defined and bounded it is, the greater the willingness, as a rule, on the part of soldiers to abandon their natural desire for self-preservation. Officers soon learn to dread hazy and ill-defined orders from above. If the goal is physical, a piece of earth to take or defend, a machine-gun nest to destroy, a strong point to annihilate, officers are much more likely to evoke the sense of comradeship. They realize that comradeship at first develops through the consciousness of an obstacle to be overcome through common effort. A fighting unit with morale is one in which many are of like mind and determination, unconsciously agreed on the suppression of individual desires in the interest of a shared purpose.

Organization for a common and concrete goal in peacetime organizations does not evoke anything like the degree of comradeship commonly known in war. Evidently, the presence of danger is distinctive and important. Men then are organized for a goal whose realization involves the real possibility of death or injury. How does danger break down the barriers of the self and give man an experience of community? The answer to this question is the key to one of the oldest and most enduring incitements to battle.

Danger provides a certain spice to experience; this is common knowledge. It quickens the pulse and makes us more aware of being alive by calling attention to our physical selves. The thrill of the chase in hunting, of riding a horse very fast, or of driving an automobile recklessly is of this sort. But the excitement created in us by such activities has little communal significance. Its origin appears to be sexual, if we understand sex in the wide sense given to it by Freud. The increased vitality we feel where danger is incidental is due to awareness of mastery over the environment. It is an individualist, not a communal, drive.

The excitement and thrill of battle, on the other hand, are of a different sort, for there danger is central and not incidental. There is little of the play element about combat, however much there may have been in training for it. Instead, for most soldiers there is the hovering inescapable sense of irreversibility. "This is for keeps," as soldier slang is likely to put it. This profound earnestness is by no means devoid of lightheartedness, as seen in teasing and horseplay, but men are conscious that they are on a one-way street, so to speak, and what they do or fail to do can be of great consequence. Those who enter into battle, as distinguished from those who only hover on its fringes, do not fight as duelists fight. Almost automatically, they fight as a unit, a group. Training can help a great deal in bringing this about more quickly and easily in an early stage. But training can only help to make actual what is inherent. As any commander knows, an hour or two of combat can do more to weld a unit together than can months of intensive training.

Many veterans who are honest with themselves will admit, I believe, that the experience of communal effort in battle, even under the altered conditions of modern war, has been a high point in their lives. Despite the horror, the weariness, the grime, and the hatred, participation with others in the chances of battle had its unforgettable side, which they would not want to have missed. For anyone who has not experienced it himself, the feeling is hard to comprehend, and, for the participant, hard to explain to anyone else. Probably the feeling of liberation is nearly basic. It is this feeling that explains the curious combination of earnestness and lightheartedness so often noted in men in battle.

Many of us can experience freedom as a thrilling reality, something both serious and joyous, only when we are acting in unison with others for a concrete goal that costs something absolute for its attainment. Individual freedom to do what we will with our lives and our talents, the freedom of self-determination, appears to us most of the time as frivolous or burdensome. Such freedom leaves us empty and alone, feeling undirected and insignificant. Only comparatively few of us know how to make this individual freedom productive and joyous. But communal freedom can pervade nearly everyone and carry everything before it. This elemental fact about freedom the opponents of democracy have learned well, and it constitutes for them a large initial advantage.

The lightheartedness that communal participation brings has little of the sensuous or merely pleasant about it, just as the earnestness has little of the calculating or rational. Both derive instead from a consciousness of power that is supra-individual. We feel earnest and gay at such moments because we are liberated from our individual impotence and are drunk with the power that union with our fellows brings. In moments like these many have a vague awareness of how isolated and separate their lives have hitherto been and how much they have missed by living in the narrow circle of family or a few friends. With the boundaries of the self expanded, they sense a kinship never known before. Their "I" passes insensibly into a "we," "my" becomes "our," and individual fate loses its central importance.

At its height, this sense of comradeship is an ecstasy not unlike the aesthetic ecstasy previously described, though occasioned by different forces. In most of us there is a genuine longing for community with our human species, and at the same time an awkwardness and helplessness about finding the way to achieve it. Some extreme experience—mortal danger or the threat of destruction—is necessary to bring us fully together with our comrades or with nature. This is a great pity, for there are surely alternative ways more creative and less dreadful, if men would only seek them out. Until now, war has appealed because we discover some of the mysteries of communal joy in its forbidden depths. Comradeship reaches its peak in battle.

The secret of comradeship has not been exhausted, however, in the feeling of freedom and power instilled in us by communal effort in combat. There is something more and equally important. The sense of power and liberation that comes over men at such moments stems from a source beyond the union of men. I believe it is nothing less than the assurance of immortality that makes self-sacrifice at these moments so relatively easy. Men are true comrades only when each is ready to give up his life for the other, without reflection and without thought of personal loss. Who can doubt that every war, the two world wars no less than former ones, has produced true comradeship like this?

Such sacrifice seems hard and heroic to those who have never felt communal ecstasy. In fact, it is not nearly so difficult as many less absolute acts in peacetime and in civilian life, for death becomes in a measure unreal and unbelievable to one who is sharing his life with his companions. Immortality is not something remote and otherworldly, possibly or probably true and real; on the contrary, it becomes a present and self-evident fact.

Nothing is further from the truth than the insistence of certain existentialist philosophers that each person must die his own death and experience it unsharably. If that were so, how many lives would have been spared on the battlefield! But in fact, death for men united with each other can be shared as few other of life's great moments can be. To be sure, it is not death as we know it usually in civilian life. In the German language men never die in battle. They *fall*. The term is exact for the expression of self-sacrifice when it is motivated by the feeling of comradeship. I may fall, but I do not die, for that which is real in me goes forward and lives on in the comrades for whom I gave up my physical life.

Let me not be misunderstood. It is unquestionably true that thousands of soldiers die in battle, miserable, alone, and embittered, without any conviction of self-sacrifice and without any other satisfactions. I suspect the percentage of such soldiers has increased markedly in recent wars. But for those who in every battle are seized by the passion for self-sacrifice, dying has lost its terrors because its reality has vanished.

There must be a similarity between this willingness of soldier-comrades for self-sacrifice and the willingness of saints and martyrs to die for their religious faith. It is probably no accident that the religions of the West have not cast away their military terminology or even their militant character—"Onward, Christian soldiers! Marching as to war . . ." nor that our wars are defended in terms of devotion and salvation. The true believer must be ready to give up his life for the faith. And if he is a genuine saint he will regard this sacrifice as no loss, for the self has become indestructible in being united with a supreme reality. There are, of course, important differences. The reality for which the martyr sacrifices himself is not visible and intimate like the soldier's. The martyr usually dies alone, scorned by the multitude. In this sense his lot is infinitely harder. It is hardly surprising that few men are capable of dying joyfully as martyrs whereas thousands are capable of self-sacrifice in wartime. Nevertheless, a basic point of resemblance remains, namely, that death has lost not only its sting but its reality, too, for the self that dies is little in comparison with that which survives and triumphs.

It is true that we in the West are frequently infatuated with the idea of sacrifice, particularly self-sacrifice. Why are some people so strongly repelled and others again and again attracted by the impulse to self-sacrifice? Or why do both attraction and repulsion have place in the same breast at different moments? As moralists, we are repelled, I suspect, because the impulse to sacrifice is not subject to rational judgment and control. It takes hold of us and forces us against our will, later claiming justification from some higher authority than the human. As often as not, it puts itself at the service of an evil cause, perhaps more frequently than in the service of the good. The mysterious power that such leaders as Napoleon, Hitler, and Stalin had in their being that enabled them to create a love for self-sacrifice perplexes us endlessly. We cannot condemn it with full conviction, since it seems likely that both leaders and led were in large degree powerless to prevent the impulses that dominated them.

Yet such power is appalling beyond measure and from a rational viewpoint deserving of the deepest condemnation. The limits of free will and morality are transgressed, and man is forced to seek religious and metaphysical justification for self-sacrifice, even when committed in an evil cause. As in the aesthetic appeal of war, when we reach the impulse of the sublime, so in the communal appeal of comradeship, when we reach the impulse to self-sacrifice, we are confronted with contradictions that are deeply embedded in our culture, if not in human nature itself. What our moral self tells us is abhorrent, our religious self and our aesthetic self yearn for as the ultimate good. This is part of the riddle of war.

If we are truly wise, perhaps we should not want to alter these capacities of our human nature, even though we suffer from them immeasurably and may yet succumb to their threat. For the willingness to sacrifice self, like the attraction of the sublime, is what makes possible the higher reaches of the spirit into the realms of poetry, philosophy, and genuine religion. They prevent our best men from losing interest in and hope for our species. They stand in the way of discouragement and cynicism. As moralists, we can condemn Saint Paul and Saint Augustine for their mystical conviction that without sacrifice no purgation from sin is possible. But we should be cautious in so doing, for they were convinced that without the supra-moral act, we human beings are not able to lead even a normally moral existence. Though they were not disposed to believe that God was without moral qualities, they were quite certain that there was more in His universe than the determinations of good and evil. For them the "I am" preceded logically and in time the "I ought." And vast numbers of people have agreed with them that the religious order is superior to the moral, though they continue to be confused about how the two are related.

Are we not right in honoring the fighter's impulse to sacrifice himself for a comrade, even though it be done, as it so frequently is, in an evil cause? I think so. It is some kind of world historical pathos that the striving for union and for immortality must again and again be consummated while men are in the service of destruction. I do not doubt for a moment that wars are made many times more deadly because of this striving and this impulse. Yet I would not want to be without the assurance their existence gives me that our species has a different destiny than is granted to other animals. Though we often sink below them, we can at moments rise above them, too.

If the lust of the eye and the yearning for communication with our fellows were the only appeals of combat, we might be confident that they would be ultimately capable of satisfaction in other ways. But my own observation and the history of warfare both convince me that there is a third impulse to battle much more sinister than these. Anyone who has watched men on the battlefield at work with artillery, or looked into the eyes of veteran killers fresh from slaughter, or studied the descriptions of bombardiers' feelings while smashing their targets, finds hard to escape the conclusion that there is a delight in destruction. A walk across any battlefield shortly after the guns have fallen silent is convincing enough. A sensitive person is sure to be oppressed by a spirit of evil there, a radical evil which suddenly makes the medieval images of hell and the thousand devils of that imagination believable. This evil appears to surpass mere human malice and to demand explanation in cosmological and religious terms.

Men who have lived in the zone of combat long enough to be veterans are sometimes possessed by a fury that makes them capable of anything. Blinded by the rage to destroy and supremely careless of consequences, they storm against the enemy until they are either victorious, dead, or utterly exhausted. It is as if they are seized by a demon and are no longer in control of themselves. From the Homeric account of the sacking of Troy to the conquest of Dienbienphu, Western literature is filled with descriptions of soldiers as berserkers and mad destroyers.

Perhaps the following account from the diary of Ernst Juenger in World War I may stand for many because it is so concise and exactly drawn. It describes the beginning of the last German offensive in the West.

> The great moment had come. The curtain of fire lifted from the front trenches. We stood up.
>
> With a mixture of feelings, evoked by bloodthirstiness, rage, and intoxication, we moved in step, ponderously but irresistibly toward the enemy lines. I was well ahead of the company, followed by Vinke and a one-year veteran named Haake. My right hand embraced the shaft of my pistol, my left a riding stick of bamboo cane. I was boiling with a mad rage, which had taken hold of me and all the others in an incomprehensible fashion. The overwhelming wish to kill gave wings to my feet. Rage pressed bitter tears from my eyes.
>
> The monstrous desire for annihilation, which hovered over the battlefield, thickened the brains of the men and submerged them in a red fog. We called to each other in sobs and stammered disconnected sentences. A neutral observer might have perhaps believed that we were seized by an excess of happiness.

Happiness is doubtless the wrong word for the satisfaction that men experience when they are possessed by the lust to destroy and to kill their kind. Most men would never admit that they enjoy killing, and there are a great many who do not. On the other hand, thousands of youths who never suspected the presence of such an impulse in themselves have learned in military life the mad excitement of destroying. The appetite is one that requires cultivation in the environment of disorder and deprivation common to life at the front. It usually marks the great difference between green troops and veterans. Generals often name it "the will to close with the enemy." This innocent-sounding phrase conceals the very substance of the delight in destruction slumbering in most of us. When soldiers step over the line that separates self-defense from fighting for its own sake, as it is so easy for them to do, they experience something that stirs deep chords in their being. The soldier-killer is learning to serve a different deity, and his concern is with death and not life, destruction and not construction.

Of the many writers who are preoccupied today with man's urge toward destruction, Ernest Hemingway stands out as one who has succeeded in incorporating the spirit of violence in his men and women. In his *For Whom the Bell Tolls*, he has his hero say at one point: "Stop making dubious literature about the Berbers and the old Iberians and admit that you have liked to kill as all who are soldiers by choice have enjoyed it at some time whether they lie about it or not." And his old colonel in the more recent book *Across the River and into the Trees* is as profound a portrait of the soldier-killer as we have seen in recent literature. The colonel is so far aware of this impulse to destruction in himself that he tries to counterbalance it by the contrary appeal, namely, Eros, in the form of the young and beautiful countess. This latter book has been harshly criticized from an artistic point of view, and not many have seen, I believe, how well Hemingway grasps the two primordial forces that are in conflict within the colonel, as within many a professional warrior, conflicts that can be resolved in a fashion only by death.

Sigmund Freud has labeled these forces in human nature the Eros drive or instinct, the impulse within us that strives for closer union with others and seeks to preserve and conserve, and the Thanatos (death) drive or instinct, the impulse that works for the dissolution of everything living or united. Freud felt that these two are in eternal conflict within man, and he became, consequently, pessimistic about ever eradicating war as an institution. Men are in one part of their being in love with death, and periods of war in human society represent the dominance of this impulsion.

Of course, this idea of an independent destructive force in life is age-old. The early Greek philosopher Empedocles gave imaginative form to a cosmology in which two universal principles explain the universe. Empedocles taught that the universe is in ceaseless change, in generation and decay, because Love and Strife are ever at work in the animate and the inanimate. Love unites all forms of life, for a period holding the upper hand, and Strife tears them apart and breaks down what previously belonged together. The original components are not annihilated, but simply dispersed in various forms by Strife. They are able to form new unions once more, and the endless process of composition and decomposition continues. Empedocles conceived both forces as of equal strength, both eternal, and both mixed equally in all things. In this imaginative vision of the world process, he sees, also, a necessary relationship between these cosmological powers, an insight that is sounder and more fruitful than most modern conceptions.

We are tempted under the influence of Darwinian thought to explain away man's delight in destruction as a regressive impulse, a return to primitivism and to animal nature. We picture, sometimes with the help of Freudians, all our cultural institutions as a kind of mask covering up the animalistic instincts that lie beneath the surface of all behavior. Such a view tends to explain all phenomena of human destructiveness, from the boyish pleasure in the tinkle of broken glass to the sadistic orgies of concentration camps, as a reassertion of man's animal nature under the veneer of culture. Man when he destroys is an animal; when he conserves he is distinctively human.

I cannot escape the conviction that this is an illusion, and a dangerous one. When man is at his destructive work, he is on a different plane from the animal altogether. And destructive urges are as capable of being found in highly cultivated natures as in the simpler ones, if not more so. The satisfaction in destroying seems to me peculiarly human, or, more exactly put, devilish in a way animals can never be. We sense in it always the Mephistophelean cry that all created things deserve to be destroyed. Sometimes there is no more concrete motive for destroying than this one, just as there is no expressible motive for creating. I described this kind of wanton behavior in my journal one night.

> It was an unforgivable spectacle. They shamed us as Americans, as colleagues and junior officers, they shamed us before our hired people. Our President lay on his bier in Washington, boys from our Division lay wounded and dying on the battlefields round about, and these lordly colonels drank themselves senseless and wantonly destroyed property with their pistols. It was a commentary on the war, on the uselessness of fighting for ideals, on the depravity of the military life.

Indeed, there are many important similarities, I feel, between the creative and destructive urges in most of us. Surely the immediate sense of release that is the satisfaction in accomplishment and mastery is not very different in the two impulses. One may become a master in one field as in the other, and there are perhaps as many levels of accomplishment. Few men ever reach superlatives in the realm of destruction; most of us remain, as in the domain of creation, moderately capable.

But artistry in destruction is qualitatively different in its effects upon the individual, in a way that minimizes similarities. It loosens one by one our ties with others and leaves us in the end isolated and alone. Destruction is an artistry directed not toward perfection and fulfillment, but toward chaos and moral anarchy. Its delights may be deep and within the reach of more men than are the joys of creation, but their capacity to reproduce and to endure is very limited. Just as creation raises us above the level of the animal, destruction forces us below it by eliminating communication. As creativity can unite us with our natural and human environment, destruction isolates us from both. That is why destruction in retrospect usually appears so repellent in its inmost nature.

If we ask what the points of similarity are between the appeal of destruction and the two appeals of war I have already examined, I think it is not difficult to recognize that the delight in destroying has, like the others, an ecstatic character. But in one sense only. Men feel overpowered by it, seized from without, and relatively helpless to change or control it. Nevertheless, it is an ecstasy without a union, for comradeship among killers is terribly difficult, and the kinship with nature that aesthetic vision often affords is closed to them. Nor is the breaking down of the barriers of self a quality of the appeal of destroying. On the contrary, I think that destruction is ultimately an individual matter, a function of the person and not the group. This is not to deny, of course, that men go berserk in groups and kill more easily together than when alone. Yet the satisfaction it brings appears to lie, not in losing themselves and their egos, but precisely in greater consciousness of themselves. If they hold together as partners in destruction, it is not so much from a feeling of belonging as from fear of retaliation when alone.

The willingness to sacrifice self for comrades is no longer character-istic of soldiers who have become killers for pleasure. War henceforth becomes for them increasingly what the philosopher Hobbes thought to be the primal condition of all human life, a war of every man against every man. That soldier-killers seldom reach this stage must be attributed to the presence of other impulses in their nature and to the episodical character of battle and combat. I can hardly doubt that the delight in destruction leads in this direction.

This is not the only melancholy consequence of this impulse, for its very nature is to be totalitarian and exclusive. Unlike other delights, it becomes, relatively soon in most men, a consuming lust which swal-lows up other pleasures. It tends to turn men inward upon themselves and make them inaccessible to more normal satisfactions. Because they rarely can feel remorse, they experience no purgation and cannot grow. The utter absence of love in this inverted kind of creation makes the delight essentially sterile. Though there may be a fierce pride in the numbers destroyed and in their reputation for proficiency, soldier-killers usually experience an ineffable sameness and boredom in their lives. The restlessness of such men in rest areas behind the front is notorious.

How deeply is this impulse to destroy rooted and persistent in human nature? Are the imaginative visions of Empedocles and Freud true in conceiving that the destructive element in man and nature is as strong and recurrent as the conserving, erotic element? Or can our delight in destruction be channeled into other activities than the traditional one of warfare? We are not far advanced on the way to these answers. We do not know whether a peaceful society can be made attractive enough to wean men away from the appeals of battle. Today we are seeking to make war so horrible that men will be frightened away from it. But this is hardly likely to be more fruitful in the future than it has been in the past. More productive will certainly be our efforts to eliminate the social, economic, and political injustices that are always the immediate occasion of hostilities. Even then, we shall be confronted with the spiritual emptiness and inner hunger that impel many men toward combat. Our society has not begun to wrestle with this problem of how to provide fulfillment of human life, to which war is so often an illusory path.

The weather has been unspeakably bad also, and what with the dawning realization that the war may continue through the winter, it has been sufficient to lower my previous high spirits. Perhaps "high spirits" is not the proper term for the nervous excitement and tension of this war front. I experience so much as in a dream or as on a stage, and at times I can step aside, as one does in a dream, and say: Is this really I? "Sad and laughable and strange" is the best combination of adjectives to describe these twilight days of our old world—the words that Plato used to describe his great myth at the end of *The Republic*. I would say, first strange, then sad, then laughable—but the laugh is not the same as the laugh of one in love when his beloved has delighted him with some idiosyncrasy of love. It is the laugh of the fallen angels who have renounced heaven but find hell hard to endure. (War journal, October 2, 1944)

4

Masculinity and Violence

Victor Seidler

As men, we often grow up to be strangers to ourselves. We experience little connection with our emotions and feelings. This is not the way we are born, nor is it a feature of our biological nature as men. As Anne-Marie Fearon has expressed it,

> I believe that all human beings, even male ones, are born (or are at any rate conceived) sensitive, loving, intelligent, open and real. We all know that they don't stay that way for very long and that males in particular tend to grow up arrogant, insensitive, alienated and, above all, violent.[1]

This is part of the price we have been forced to pay for being effective and competent in the world. This can make consciousness-raising a particularly threatening and difficult experience for men. It is often easier for us to talk about our experience in an intellectualised way than actually to express how we are feeling. This can be yet another way in which we retain a certain distance from ourselves. We can envy the access that women seem to have to their histories and experience, and, particularly with the development of the women's movement, the relationships they have with each other. This can make us more aware of lacks in our own lives.

Contact with feminist ideas can drive many men into a deeper silence about ourselves, guilty about our position within the relationships of power and subordination. The idea that "all men are violent" or that "all men are potential rapists" can deeply challenge our sense of our masculinity.[2] It can produce a sense of despair, guilt and a paralysing self-hatred. It leaves no room for us as men to change. In a strange way, it can leave many men untouched as they accept this judgement of themselves intellectually. We can find ourselves giving tokenistic or uncritical support to the women's movement. In this way, men can credit themselves with supporting the women's movement while not really having to challenge themselves.

I do not think we should underestimate the difficulties of changing ourselves. We each have our own histories. We need to be aware of the deeper pattern in our experience and relationships. Sometimes the men's movement has tended to concentrate on a change of manner in which we have wanted to identify with the softer qualities of warmth, emotionality, caring and kindness, but we need to be aware of the depth of the legacy of our socialisation and the ways this continues to influence our experiences and relationships. We cannot simply wish away our angry and violent impulses or our tendencies to control and dominate. It is important, however, for any men's movement which would seek to take the challenge of feminism seriously to engage critically and attend to the nature of these impulses. They have formed the ground on which certain powerful radical feminist claims have been built, to the effect that men's will to power is ultimately and finally irreconcilable with a sexual politics which aspires to freedom and fulfillment.

It is partly because of the ways in which we are made strangers to ourselves that our violence can erupt in such frightening ways. It can take us by surprise. Often for men, anger can be used to dispel feelings of vulnerability and need which are taken to be signs of weakness. I remember the constant anxiety of having to prove my masculinity. Because I was not tall or strong, I felt vulnerable at school to being called a "weed," "soft," or "puny." These were different ways of not being a "proper man." This creates constant anxiety and tension. We get so used to living with it that it comes to feel "normal."

Masculinity is never something you can feel at ease with. It is always something that you have to be ready to defend and prove. You have to prove that you are as much a man as everyone else. Often this means putting others down, especially girls. It is because feelings of softness, vulnerability and need are so peculiarly threatening to our very sense of ourselves as men, that we fight them off so strongly, but this can also give us an ambiguous relation to our anger, especially if we do not feel the confidence of being able to defend ourselves physically. I was scared of getting involved in physical fights. This meant that I could not feel confident in my anger.

Anger, Fear and Violence

I did not really want to know that I was angry because this was threatening. I learnt to suppress angry feelings, but I was constantly aware of the threat of physical violence. At school there was the constant fear of being "bashed up." This was an aspect of the relationships between children as much as it was an aspect of the authority and power of teachers. Competition was always combined with the threat of physical violence. Adorno is right to remind us that

> In fact, competition itself never was the law according to which middle class society operated. The true bond of bourgeois society had always been the threat of bodily violence . . . In the age of the concentration camp, castration is more characteristic of social reality than competitiveness . . .
>
> (quoted from 'Social Sciences and Sociological Tendencies in Psychoanalysis,' *New Left Review*)[3]

As boys, we have to be constantly on the alert. We always have to be ready to defend ourselves, constantly on our guard. I think I felt this acutely because I could not be confident in defending myself physically.

This builds enormous tension and anxiety into the very organisation of our bodies. It makes it difficult to let go or relax, and fits with the ways in which we are encouraged to treat our bodies as efficient machines that we use. This deeply marks our sexuality. Often we have very little relationship with our bodies. We do not see them as a source of joy or satisfaction. We are estranged from our bodies. This makes it easier for us to use them in an unfeeling way. Sexuality becomes an issue of conquest. It becomes a question of how many women you can get off with and how many times you can screw them. In this sense, sexuality is closely identified with power. For men, it can become almost second nature. Often it becomes connected to violence. This is partly because this form of sexuality can leave us frustrated and unfulfilled, and it can be easier to take that out on others than to look at ourselves. The roots go very deep.

Anne-Marie Fearon shares how her son came home from nursery school one day with the information: "Girls are soppies." She points out that "This did not emanate from the school which is consciously opposed to sexism; but the active members of the male 'club' seem to say these things with such conviction that it only takes one or two of them to affect the whole class." As a boy, you have to be ready to defend yourself. You cannot admit your fear. If someone challenges you, you cannot afford to be a "scaredy-cat." You have to learn to fight, or at least pretend to be ready to fight. You cannot afford to let others think of you as "wet" or a "drip." This partly explains the symbolic importance of boxing within masculine culture. At school we were expected to do it, even if we hated it. Luckily we did not have to do it often. This becomes the training ground for masculinity. As Anne-Marie Fearon says:

> You teach him to deny his fear and hurt. This is very hard and puts him under constant tension; so you give him a gun and a monster mask, and now whenever he feels that tension he can channel it into aggression and project his fears onto someone else . . . But it doesn't do to feel it and discharge it by crying and trembling; and this is forbidden. So he is stuck with it; fear, tension and aggression become a way of life, and the only consolation is that the Club tells him: it's natural, that's what boys are meant to be like—now you're one of us!
>
> (Fearon 1978)

I want to explore this theme through looking at certain scenes in Martin Scorsese's film, *Raging Bull,* and the discussion which this generated. I want to use this film to bring out issues in the relationship between masculinity and violence, rather than simply to offer a review of it as a film.[4]

Many people refused to see the film. There are moments when it seems to me all too close to a glorification of violence. The camera almost seems transfixed with certain brutal scenes in the boxing ring. The use of slow motion serves to romanticise. I do not want to defend any of this.

I want to use the film to illuminate different conceptions of the ways in which we can change as men. I do not want the contrast to be too crude. I want to suggest the importance of particular forms of therapy for men, ways in which we can explore our anger, resentments, fear, hurt and violence. This involves developing more contact and experience of ourselves, rather than simply denying these feelings as "unacceptable." If we repress these feelings, we will often act them out unknowingly in our relationships with others, often without realising how controlling we are being because we deny these very feelings in ourselves.

The film is about the life of Jack La Motta, the 1949 middleweight boxing champion. It is about life in the Italian community in the Bronx, New York, in the 1940s. It is about a world that is very different from the suburban Jewish middle class in which I grew up. But the film is about masculinity, male violence, frustration and pride. It hits home. In parts the violence is unbearable and out of control. But it did not estrange me. It was painful but understandable for most of the time.

I want to argue that our violence and anger cannot be denied. We have to learn to distinguish the different aspects of these feelings, rather than simply deny them. Therapy is important within this process, especially if it helps us grasp the ways in which our violence is a sign not just of our strength but of our impotence and frustration. Scorsese's *Raging Bull* helps us understand how male violence works, even if it leaves us with little sense of how men change. He shows how masculinity can be used up. Jake is used up by the crowd. He is often incapable of expressing himself. He fights his way out of situations. In the end nobody wants to know him. He is imprisoned by his own masculinity.

Raging Bull can help us connect to an aspect of our masculinity that we too easily deny. It can put us back in touch with our own "raging bull"—the desire to hit out and hit back. Scorsese himself is no tough guy. In an interview which Don Macpherson and Judith Wiliamson did with him for *Time Out,* he admits that "I don't punch people in the face. I'm too short, and I can't run—and I've got asthma" (p. 20, 6 Feb 1981). The film can also help us face our rage and anger, rather than think that they will disappear if we feel uneasy and ashamed about them. Rather than keep these feelings to ourselves, it feels better to socialise them, to bring them into the open where they can be explored, possibly in a safe environment men create with each other.

This is to suggest a different conception of the ways in which people can change. Often if we deny our feelings, they simply reorganise themselves at a deeper level, expressing themselves in more spiteful and hidden ways. It can be through exploring our anger and rage that we come to be more familiar with these feelings, clearer about the different feelings of need and vulnerability which they sometimes cover and hide. This can give us more control of our emotional life. This will not be a control based on repression, but rather on an experience of connection. At the moment we often take out these fears and frustrations on those we are closest to, often the women and men we are sexually involved with. Sometimes this is the only situation in which we can feel safe enough to share them. Often our negative feelings and our resentments have a very different source, existing at a level of which we have little awareness. We can find ourselves hitting out blindly.

There is an early scene with Jake at home in his Bronx apartment. He is sitting at the table as his wife is standing cooking him a steak. He is impatient. He does not want to wait. He gets annoyed at his wife because the steak is not ready. He blames her. It is her fault. He wants it to be ready when *he* wants to eat it. She cannot take it any more. She gets angry and lets him have it as it is. She locks herself in their bedroom. She stands up to him. He hits her. He takes out his frustration on her. She will not take it. The relationship breaks up.

The film shows Jake developing a second relationship and eventually marrying Vikki, a young woman from the neighborhood. He is infatuated with her, though he hardly knows her. He is introduced to her by his brother, who also likes her. His brother is brighter and more intelligent, but Jake is going to be the champion. There is a scene when Jake gets his brother to hit him as hard as he can in the face. His brother thinks that this is stupid but Jake forces him to do it. Jake wants to prove that he can take anything that is given to him. In the final moments of his boxing career when he is eventually beaten for the championship, he stands there almost letting himself take whatever punishment is given to him. When he has finally lost, he goes up to Sugar Ray Robinson who has beaten him and, with blood pouring from his face, he says with stupid pride, "I could take it. You never got me down." Robinson just laughed. Jake seems to have proved something to himself. He has proved that he can take whatever the world has to throw at him. It is a difficult moment. I did not understand it completely.

This connects to another incident which takes place when Jake has won the championship. He has moved into a new house with Vikki. He has never been able to satisfy her in their sexual relationship and is suspicious that she is having relationships with other men. He is madly jealous. You witness some tenderness in their early sexual relationship, but even here he is always telling her what to do. He gives her a series of instructions. He will not allow her spontaneity. He is forced to withdraw to reassert his control of the situation. He always needs to have control; he cannot surrender to his desire.

In this later scene, Jack is watching TV in his living room with his brother. His wife Vikki is upstairs. As he messes with the faulty set, Jake's huge, powerful body is useless, and his pent-up frustration builds at this thing he cannot make work by hitting—like his home life. Confronted with something too complex to be bent to his will in the only way that he knows, Jake goes berserk on a quite different tack. His suspicions rise to an accusation of his brother: "You fucked my wife? You fucked my wife?" "You ask me that, your own brother? You expect me to answer that?" Both are outraged with a sentimental pride that is peculiarly masculine. Jake goes upstairs to his wife. His insane jealousy takes the form of both physical obsession with what he imagines to have happened—"You sucked his cock?"—and of physical revenge. In the culmination of the episode, he beats up both his wife and his brother.

The success of *Raging Bull* lies in *not* just showing more male violence, but in the fact that the TV set build-up is inseparable from the whole sequence, and creates, not the sense of Jake's strength, but of his impotence. This is also made clear when in another scene, Vikki observes idly that a young contender has a pretty face. Jake cannot rest until he has knocked the boy's nose halfway to his ear, in one of the film's most brutal boxing scenes: "He ain't pretty no more"; but again, instead of power, we feel the inadequacy of using the ring to work out a paranoid personal obsession.

Jake takes out his anger and frustration on this young contender. In this way, he thinks that he is getting even with Vikki, or even proving something to her. But this is not even something that she knows about, or could guess about. This is a kind of acting-out of emotions and feelings that is less familiar within a middle-class masculine experience. Jake's emotions and feelings are much nearer to the surface. He has less control over them. We gain little sense of his ongoing relationship with Vikki. We simply learn of the restrictions that he places upon her freedom and the intensity of his jealousy whenever she makes contact with other men. We have little sense of his need in the relationship, of his vulnerability. It is this sense of "self-sufficiency" that is deeply related to masculinity. This is often what makes our relationships difficult. We are brought up to feel that needing things from others is a sign of weakness. We grow fearful of acknowledging and getting to know these needs, lest they have grown to such proportions that they threaten to overwhelm us.

Control, Frustration and Violence

Within a middle-class setting, our bull is less likely to rage. It is too firmly controlled. We are more likely to be cynical and spiteful. We are brought up to use language to control and moderate our emotions. We are likely to be greater strangers to our violence. This does not make it any the less threatening for being veiled. It does not necessarily mean that we are more capable of asking for what we need in our relationships, but it becomes easier to feel self-sufficient, to feel that we do not really need things for ourselves. We can pride ourselves on our reliability and our dependability.

This does not mean that we do not expect women to cook and clean for us and that we do not get irritated when things do not go our way. It is our invulnerability that can block us from deepening the relationships we have, since it is hard for us to recognise the kinds of needs we bring into a relationship. Rather, we often expect women to be able to interpret our needs for us. It is tempting to feel that we do not want to have to ask for what we need, but want people who love us to have some kind of intuitive grasp of what we need. Often this is an avoidance. It means that we do not have to take the risk of asking. It means that we do not have to accept the pain of rejection. I remember the difficulty of asking girls to dance at the local youth club when I was fourteen. I would find a way of asking without really asking. In this way I would never have to feel rejected.

If Scorsese is right that "You have to claw your way through . . . the 'negative' aspects'' because you come to a point in your life when you cannot any longer deny them, we have to be sensitive to the differences in our class and racial backgrounds. This means coming to terms with our individual histories, with the experiences that have shaped our masculinity. This has been part of the importance of consciousness-raising for men, but it has also shown the needs for different kinds of therapy since, especially for middle-class men, talking can be a way of avoiding facing difficulties in our experience. We need to find ways of coming to know and explore the broader extent and depths of our feelings and emotions, not judging them too early and too easily.

This involves acknowledging the full range and force of our emotions and feelings, often resentful, painful and spiteful feelings that we would prefer not to acknowledge. Therapy understands the importance of expressing these feelings, not simply talking about them, and thereby promises to give us a fuller contact with ourselves. Sometimes we will learn how our feelings and experiences are shared by others. This itself can be a form of liberation as we are often brought up to assume that our fears and inhibitions are completely private and individual. We learn the significance of class and ethnic differences, but also what we have been brought up to share in our experience of masculinity.

Some of this became clearer to me in our *Achilles' Heel* collective discussions.[5] It showed that Scorsese had expressed something of more general significance. When Tony asked a friend whether she saw him as violent, she first said "no," and then she said, "Well, yeah. I think in some ways you are. My experience of your violence is always in relation to things going wrong, and frustration with machinery and with inanimate things which frustrate you." This helped Tony understand that it is when arrangements go wrong which seem important to him at the time, when, for example, the car does not work, that his anger and frustration are brought out. He also realised that

> the thing is that the only person who kind of sees that very much is actually S, and it often happens when I'm with her. It's got a lot to do with our relationship. And that's partly to do with a feeling of licence that I can let things out. That she knows me that well that I can let things out.

At a more complex level, Tony explained,

> it's also something else as well. I can let things out but at the same time I feel that somehow exposing myself to her means I have less power or something. It means I feel vulnerable. And that makes it worse. It means I feel more frustrated and more angry about it and end up being increasingly uptight. I don't feel that angry when things go wrong with other people. It's something about taking it out on her in a kind of oblique way.

I know how I can avoid feelings of vulnerability in a similar way. It is not easy even to know when we are doing this. Often we need the help and support of others to recognise these patterns, which sometimes have deeper sources in our earlier relationships. This is something therapy can help us with. It is also something that consciousness-raising can help us to develop different patterns about.

Sharing this experience reminds Andy of a similar pattern:

> I haven't cleaned up and the place is a mess and I feel depressed with that. She comes and says the place is in a mess, and that reminds me I feel depressed and I'm immediately hostile and angry with myself because she's kind of exposed me to myself, I suppose. And I feel frustrated with myself that I haven't got things together for myself . . . I feel frustrated that it takes her to remind me that the place is in a mess. I don't want to be reminded and . . . oh . . . it's really painful. And so I get all gritty faced.

Often we do not thank people for putting us more in touch with ourselves, even when it is women or men we are particularly close to. It is easy to feel exposed, found out. Sometimes we can feel that we are doing reasonably well and it only takes the presence of someone else to make us realise we are feeling bad. It can be difficult to accept this in a straightforward way, often easier to hit out. This can connect to an impulsive feeling to reject the support and help others are ready to offer us, even when this is exactly what we need. Again it can be difficult to acknowledge this need and vulnerability because at some level we continue to feel this as a form of weakness and defeat, even if we have consciously rejected these notions of self-sufficient masculinity.

Often these patterns have deep sources. As men, we are often brought up to get our way. We can find it hard to accept changes, even if we want them intellectually. Sometimes we can retain control in our relationships through the very unspoken sanction of our tempers. This can create fear and uncertainty in others. It can give us power within the relationship as others find it difficult to challenge us directly. This can only change slowly. It involves a different process of transformation for men and women, which has to happen at different levels.[6]

Sometimes, for men, it is through coming to acknowledge and accept our vulnerability, pain, longing, and fear, that we can escape from the need to respond so immediately with anger and violence. This can help us to a different kind of control of ourselves as we do this emotional work for ourselves, rather than relying upon the women and men in our close relationships. This involves taking a different kind of responsibility for ourselves as we learn to gain more support and understanding from other men. It is partly through coming to more understanding and experience of our own "raging bulls" that we can begin to re-evaluate what matters to us in our lives and what kind of relationships we want to have with others. This will mean learning to ask more directly for what we need but also accepting we will not always get it.

Men, Responsibility and Violence

At another level, this remains a totally inadequate response to male violence, especially when it is taken out on women and gay people. Nothing can justify this violence. Individual men have to be held responsible for their verbal and physical violence. It is up to all of us to say that this behaviour is unacceptable, whether it is going on within a relationship or not. Often we collude in silence. We are brought up within liberal society to think that it is a "private concern" that we should not interfere with. Often we remain silent rather than challenge friends who are involved in violent relationships, or people we see harassing women in the street.

Until we experience this sort of behaviour not simply as a violation of others, but also as a violation of our own humanity, we are likely to collude. Often it is difficult when a man responds to us saying, "I'm only having a bit of fun—why are you taking it so seriously?" We can easily feel that we open ourselves for ridicule if we intervene. These are situations we need to confront openly and directly. We are surrounded by them most of the time. It is easy to collude in denying the significance of the pain and violation that are taking place.

Andrea Medea and Kathleen Thompson, in an article "Little Rapes," talk about the gradual effects on women of having to endure walking down a city street at night, or even during the day:

> If you are subjected to this kind of violation every day, a gradual erosion begins—an erosion of your self-respect and privacy. You lose a little when you are shaken out of your day-dreams by the whistles and comments of the construction workers you have to pass. You lose a little when a junior executive looks down your blouse or gives you a familiar pat at work . . . In themselves these incidents are disgusting, repellant—in fact, intolerable. Acceptance of them as normal is dangerous . . . Learning to avoid being hassled in the street is as much a part of living in the city as learning to cope with public transport. To see a black person subjected to this kind of abuse would make one sick. It would be painful to watch them lower their head and try to get past a group of whites unmolested. Today black people are no longer expected to 'know their place', although deliberate humiliation and discrimination against them still exists. But women face this kind of badgering and taunting and accept it. They have come to think of it as an unavoidable part of life.

(Peace News, 22 April 1977)

At the same time as it is important for us to be able to identify with other men in the ways they behave towards women, understanding the frustration out of which they sometimes respond, it is important to know that this behaviour is completely unacceptable. This very much has to do with the relationships of men with each other. Too often the Left has limited understanding of the women's movement to a support of demands and campaigns which have then been left to women to organise. This has been a comfortable tactic since it has meant that the Left has not had to challenge the sexist practices which are often deeply endemic, for example, within the trade union movement.[7] If we are not to fall into a moralistic position, we need much deeper discussion of the experience of masculinity. This has been slow and uneven in development.

Partly because as men we often do not have a language in which to identify and express our experience, we may feel uneasy and nervous in personal discussions and often have little sense that there is much to be gained from this kind of exploration. We feel confident enough in the public language we have been brought up to use. At some level, we often feel guilty for the ways we treat others and do not want to be reminded of this. We have been brought up to expect that women will do our cooking, cleaning and emotional servicing for us and it can be difficult for men to accept that this has to change.

We often hurt those we feel closest to as we take out our tensions and frustrations on them. As men, we often have little confidence that things could change if we were ready to talk our feelings through. Often we lock them tightly within ourselves until they explode or we tend to disappear into ourselves. Somehow we need to connect the frustrations that are generated through the indignities and subordination people have to endure at work with the strains and tensions in our closer relationships. This involves developing a socialist theory and practice that does not divide work from other areas of our lives. This has been one of the significant contributions of feminism.

With the strains of a more intensive work life and the frustrations of unemployment that have dominated the 1980s and look set to dominate the 1990s, we are often finding the family a locus of violence, tension and abuse.[8] Often people are left in isolation to work things out, though there is increasing recognition that issues of physical and sexual violence and abuse cannot be exclusively considered as issues of communication within the family unless they are also connected to issues of masculinity. This is a difficult insight for practitioners of family therapy to integrate because issues of gender are often left implicit. Through sharing our different experiences of masculinity, isolation can be challenged and new ways of working with men developed.[9]

But this involves the development of different forms of socialist politics which refuse to marginalise these issues as "personal," recognising how they emerge out of central tensions within culture and society. It has been an enduring influence of radical feminist work to place issues of male violence at the centre of an understanding of social relations, although often this has been done in a way that forecloses the possibilities of men to change. In this context, it is crucial not to treat masculinity as a unified and homogeneous category, fixed within particular relations of power, but to explore the emergence and experience of different masculinities. This has to be done in a way that can recognise the centrality of masculinity within an Enlightenment vision of modernity that has largely been cast in its image.

Notes

1. Anne-Marie Fearon, 'Come in, Tarzan, your time is up' in *Shrew*, issue on 'Feminism and non-violence', spring 1978.

2. These universalised images of men and male violence are explored in Susan Brownmiller's *Against Our Will: Men, Women and Rape*. Susan Griffin has also argued that rape and male violence play a central role in establishing and perpetuating male power, and they are a recurring theme in Andrea Dworkin's *Pornography: Men Possessing Women*. Lynne Segal in *Slow Motion: Changing Masculinities, Changing Men*, argues against Brownmiller's universalism, using some of Roy Porter's work—'Rape—does it have a historical meaning?'' in *Rape*, S. Tomaselli and R. Porter (eds)—to show that rape has not always been used as the principal agent to subordinate women. At the same time she recognises the significance of the ideas that not all men are potential rapists and that some women face greater risk of male violence than others—'both these statements, however, are not just controversial but explosive in feminist discourse. They need the most careful study.' (p. 240).

3. Adorno questions our accepted understandings of bourgeois society which tend to marginalise issues of bodily threat and violence, in *Minima moralia*. It is a recurring insight in his writings. A useful introduction to his writings is provided by Susan Bucks-Morss in *The Origin of Negative Dialectics: Theodor W. Adorno, Walter Benjamin and the Frankfurt Institute*. See also *The Melancholy Science: An Introduction to the Thought of Theodor W. Adorno* by Gillian Rose.

4. Scorsese seems well aware of some of the issues of masculinity and violence, which are in many ways the central themes of *Raging Bull*. These issues of displacement, violence and control are never far from the surface of the film. But hopefully the argument that I am making does not depend on a familiarity with the film, though obviously this helps.

5. This refers to the collective discussion within the *Achilles' Heel* collective as we were preparing the issue on violence. A number of the articles in the issue reflect the discussions we were having. See also the article by Tony Eardley on 'Violence and Sexuality' in *The Sexuality of Men*, ed. M. Humphries and A. Metcalf.

6. See the article on 'Masculinity and Violence' by David Morgan in *Women, Violence and Social Control*, ed. J. Hanmer and M. Maynard. It is also illuminating to connect these issues with the different views expressed in

Susan Griffin's *Pornography and Silence* and Lynne Segals' *Is the Future Female?—Troubled Thoughts on Contemporary Feminism*.

7. Issues about men and masculinity as they emerge within the trade union movement are usefully discussed in a roundtable discussion, 'Mending the broken heart of socialism' in *Male Order: Unwrapping Masculinity*, edited by Rowena Chapman and Jonathan Rutherford. See also the discussion in Lynne Segal's *Slow Motion: Changing Masculinities, Changing Men*, ch. 10, where in her attempt to make a relatively uncontentious point that we need to think in terms of 'masculinities' rather than any single masculinity, she tends to misconstrue the *Achilles' Heel* project. We affirmed men's engagement in trade union struggles and in political struggles against patriarchy but said that in our experience, men's support for feminism will tend to remain 'abstract' if it does not allow for the importance of consciousness-raising. Nor did we see masculinity simply as 'a personality issue' rather than as constructed around assumptions of social power. She offers another version of the false idea that sexual politics in the 1970s, at least as it influenced men, was only concerned with the personal and the psychological and not with the political. This allows her to argue that 'like some feminists' we were supposedly travelling on a road 'which would finally reduce politics in its entirety to the individual struggles in personal life' (p. 283).

8. An interesting set of discussions around issues of abuse are presented in Lina Gordon's *Heroes of Their Own Lives: The Politics and History of Family Violence,* in Jan Pahl's *Private Violence and Public Policy,* and in Patricia Mrazek and C. Henry Kempe, *Sexually Abused Children and Their Families.* See also the work that was done by such groups as 'Emerge' in the United States, who were working with men who abused in Boston, in 'Emerge: a men's counselling service on domestic violence: organising and implementing services for men who batter', copyright 1981, Emerge Inc.; and the work Ray Wyre has being doing amongst others in England reported in *Men, Women and Rape.*

9. Developments in working with men are presented and explored in the newsletter 'Working with men' ed Trefor Lloyd. This shows how the 1980s saw an enormous spread and diversity of men's involvement with anti-sexist activities.

PART THREE

Intimacy and Sexual Identity

5

Male Friendship and Intimacy

Robert A. Strikwerda and Larry May

> Life is so very different when you have a good friend. I've seen people without special friends, close friends. Other men, especially. For some reason men don't often make and keep friends. This is a real tragedy, I think, because in a way, without a tight male friend, you never really are able to see yourself. That is because part of shaping ourselves is done by others; and a lot of our shaping comes from that one close friend who is something like us.
>
> —Mr. Hal[1]

The "tradition" in the West has made comradeship between men the paradigm of friendship. Friendships in their purest form have been thought to exist more often among men than among women. Vera Brittain summarizes:

> From the days of Homer the friendships of men have enjoyed glory and acclamation, but the friendships of women, despite Ruth and Naomi, have usually been not merely unsung, but mocked, belittled. . . .[2]

For the most part the characteristics of loyalty, fellow feeling, and concern for the other's interests have been stressed much more heavily than intimacy in male friendships. Moreover, the presence of these characteristics has been thought to make male friendship superior to female friendship.

In contrast, recent studies of Americans indicate that men tend not to have same-sex friendships that are as satisfying to them as same-sex friendships are to women.[3] And men are beginning to wonder why this is so. Daniel Levinson writes that in "our interviews, friendship was largely noticeable by its absence. As a tentative generalization, we would say that close friendship with a man or a woman is rarely experienced by American men."[4] In 1985, after a ten-year study of 5,000 American men and women, Michael McGill stated:

> To say that men have no intimate friends seems on the surface too harsh. . . . But the data indicate that it is not far from the truth. . . . Their relationships with other men are superficial, even shallow.[5]

This recognition of a connection between the absence of intimacy in friendships among men and dissatisfaction with these friendships is our starting point. What we provide here is an exploration of the *concept* of intimacy, especially in adult male relationships. We begin with an examination of comradeship, one form of male friendship, and use this to help develop, in the second section, an account of the nature and value of intimacy in friendship. We follow this with an account of obstacles to intimacy. In our fourth section, we suggest how our view parallels certain Aristotelian themes. In the final section, we focus on the process of developing intimacy among men, discussing some moments in that process and resources that men can employ in the attainment of intimacy, even if in a fashion different from that typical of women.

In developing our account of intimacy, we draw heavily on our own experiences, supplementing them with conceptual analysis, the accounts of others, and sociological and psychological research. This is not a survey of the literature. Our primary intent is the philosophic one of building a more adequate account of what intimacy can be in the context of male friendships. Our own experiences, from which this paper originated, are admittedly limited. Both of us are male, heterosexual, white, North American, and middle class. And both of us consider ourselves feminists, and we have tried to reassess male experience from a feminist perspective. Our experiences may not be typical, although our conversations and research lead us to think that our experiences are far from unique.

We believe that our topic deserves attention by feminist philosophers, whether male or female. Much feminist writing has focused on a reassessment of female experience in order to counter oppression against women. The social practice of men failing to develop and express their feelings does have the consequence that men in general are more able to oppress than would be true otherwise.[6] Phenomenologically, however, men simply do not see themselves as oppressors in this way. It does not seem to us that most men *intentionally* oppress women by failing to disclose their feelings; rather, many men are not even aware that they could be acting otherwise. Nonetheless, they do increasingly see themselves as lacking in intimate relationships. Thus we try to provide a positive sense of what male friendship could be like in a less oppressive society.[7] It is our hope that if men do become more intimate and caring with each other, they will also become so with the women and children in their lives, thus making it less likely that oppression will continue at its present level.

I. Comradeship and Male Bonding

Male friendships often resemble the relationships between very young children who engage in "parallel play." These children want to be close to each other in the sandbox, for example, but they just move the sand around without sharing or helping and *usually* without hurting each other. They don't really interact *with* each other; they merely play side-by-side—hence the term parallel play.

Here is a rather common adult example of parallel play. Two men sit in a bar, each sipping his third beer. Every few minutes one speaks, more by way of a speech (about last night's baseball game or the new beer on tap); the other nods in agreement but waits a while before speaking himself, and then often on a different topic altogether. The men are not concerned by the lack of conversation; indeed, they might tell you that they know each other so well that they don't need to have lengthy conversations, adding that it is the peace and quiet of one another's company that they each prize most highly. When they depart for home, they clasp hands or perhaps merely salute one another.[8]

Such companionship is enjoyable; at least, we have enjoyed it. Our point is not to criticize such relationships. Not every friendship needs to be intimate. However, it seems to us that if *all* of one's friendships display such a lack of intimacy, then one's life will be impoverished and unsatisfying. Such friendships are not in themselves impoverished, but a steady diet of them may lead one either to nutritional deficiency or to hunger for something more. Similarly, if men are open to intimacy only with female friends or partners, they cut themselves off from deeply rewarding relationships with other men, as well as help perpetuate a debilitating gender pattern in which women do the emotional work for men.

Some traditional male experiences have led to a form of friendship that may pass for intimacy—what we call comradeship. The sharing of certain kinds of experiences—such as those of teenage boys in a summer resort community, of soldiers in the trenches, or of sailors on long sea voyages—provides the occasion for mutual self-disclosure among males. In these situations, one is in a period of some stress, whether puberty or physical danger, with plenty of time and not enough activity to fill it. In war, men are forced to be with one another, and they report that in this situation they often reflect on aspects of their lives they normally would block. Soldiers not only fight shoulder to shoulder, but they sit for long hours in cramped quarters wondering if their lives will end in the next barrage of gunfire. Such occasions can bring men to talk about deeply personal matters in their lives and hence to form bonds with one another that may last long after the common experiences have ended.[9]

Loyalty clearly plays a significant role in comradeship. In *The Warriors*, J. Glenn Gray provides a phenomenological account of the experiences of comradeship that develop in combat settings.

> Near the front it was impossible to ignore, consciously or unconsciously, the stark fact that out there were men who would gladly kill you, if and when they got the chance. As a consequence, an individual was dependent on others . . . [and] in turn he was of interest only as a center of force, a wielder of weapons, a means of security and survival. This confraternity of danger and exposure is unequaled in forging links among people of unlike desire and temperament. . . .[10]

In combat situations, some men recognize that they are exposed and vulnerable in ways men normally do not acknowledge. From the position of mutual vulnerability, they come to seek out others on whom they can depend, rather than withdraw into their own self-contained egos.

Interestingly, in wartime situations comrades come to see each other in abstract rather than highly personal terms. As Gray points out, "comrades are loyal to each other spontaneously, and without any need for reasons."[11] But, as Gray also notes, this loyalty is fragile since it is not necessarily connected to "spontaneous liking and the feeling of belonging."[12] Indeed, the bonding that epitomizes comradeship is strictly non-particularistic. "Men are true comrades only when each is ready to give up his life for the other, without reflection and without thought of personal loss."[13]

This lack of reflection in comradeship has had terrible, destructive consequences, both in wartime and in so-called peacetime. The high rate of involvement of fraternities in college rapes is a case in point. Mary Daly explores this idea in *Gyn/Ecology*, building in part on Gray's phenomenological account. Accepting his distinction between comradeship and male friendship, she contrasts these with sisterhood and female friendship. Whereas for women sisterhood has a potential to become friendship, she sees comradeship as not leading to true friendship for men.[14] Our contention is that it is possible to expand the forms of friendship that occur, such that it will no longer be true, as Daly claims, that "male bonding/comradeship *requires* the stunting of individuality."[15]

Comrades are not necessarily intimate friends, for they are often bound to one another as generalized others, not in terms of who each one is as a unique member of the human race. Somewhat paradoxically, comrades are loyal to each other not out of concern for the particularity of the individual other, but out of an almost impartial respect for people of a certain type or in a certain situation: fellow soldiers, compatriots, coworkers, etc. Thus there can be a wide diversity of backgrounds and personality types among comrades in combat, without the reciprocal willingness to sacrifice one's life for the other varying as a result. Comradeship is a deontological regard for a generalized other and, in this sense, is quite different from intimate friendships, which are based on a regard for a particularized other and where consequences and contexts matter quite a bit.

In intimate friendship, the psychic boundary that normally encloses the male self, allowing for the characteristically self-confident, competent, single-minded pursuit of one's public roles, is temporarily opened to allow a new focus to develop, one that includes the man and another person. It is not the formation of a new boundary as typical in comradeship, but an expansion of one's concentration of attention from self to include the other. This new concentration may look similar to our stereotyped notion of male bonding. What often passes for intimate male bonding is really the deep loyalty of comradeship, which is based on so little information about the person to whom one is loyal that it is quite fragile and likely to change as new people come to instantiate the type to whom the comrade is loyal. In contrast, because intimate bonding is based on particular characteristics of the other, it will not generally break apart unless the people themselves change significantly.

Perhaps the following analogy is apropos. Just as some anthropologists describe the typical American marriage pattern as "serial monogamy" (just one spouse at a time), so for many men having friends is "serial best-friendship." As Stanley Bing puts it, a bit facetiously, "I don't miss my formerly essential friends, because I have been able to re-create over and over again the same satisfying infantile relationship with any number of adult males within lunching distance. Every one of these guys is precious, and every one can be replaced."[16] Similarly, we have friends who are "workfriends" or "next-door friends" or "racketball partners," involving more or less constricted friendships, limited in time, place, or social situation. Thus these friendships are likely to change when the situation does. As in marriages, "divorces" and "remarriages" occur in friendships, but perhaps it is time to reconsider what intimacy in a relationship is when one is marrying for the fifth time or, as Bing would put it, "re-creating one's fifth set of essential friends."

II. The Nature and Value of Intimacy

Intimacy paradigmatically occurs in a reciprocal relationship between two or more people. Knowing oneself intimately seems to us a derivative notion, though we will suggest self-knowledge does have an essential role to play in enabling reciprocal intimacy. Although there is a substantial knowledge element involved in intimacy, there is also a degree of what one might call understanding. It is not simply knowledge of facts about the person, or an ability to predict behavior, but also an understanding of why something is the way it is, of priorities and relations. As one might expect from its etymological roots (as the superlative form of *interior*—"innermost"), intimacy typically involves a sense of a deep or profound relationship. Finally, intimacy includes an element of warmth in two dimensions, that of caring receptivity and that of being comfortable, as in "an intimate club."

Intimacy in a friendship involves a mutual relation; one cannot really be an intimate friend without a reciprocity of intimacy from another. Indeed, the reciprocal enrichment and enjoyment that typically flow from intimate relationships may constitute the chief value of such relationships. Consider the friendships that might start with one coworker asking another, "Wanna get some lunch?" Having once learned something about the other person and liking him, one typically acts to further the relationship, not just with a directly work-related suggestion, but with something that is optional. If one finds another person interesting but that person is not willing to make time for lunch or a beer, the relationship is unlikely to get off the ground. He has not given a sign of the mutuality of interest and respect that grounds intimate friendship. Nor is there a place for the simple enjoyment of each other's company or conversation.

Genuine intimacy involves a deep or intense mutual knowledge that allows the participants to grow in both self-understanding and understanding of others. That knowledge includes understanding the defining personal characteristics of an individual, conjoined with enjoyment of and loyalty to that person. Whereas one can speak of certain kinds of friends—for example, sports buddies—that one doesn't know very well, one wouldn't say this about an intimate friend. One might say, after some unexpected event, "I guess I didn't know my friend very well, but he's still my friend," but it would be quite odd to say, "I don't know him very well, but we're still intimate friends."

Even if mutual knowledge is linked to strongly positive emotional feelings for one another, these are not enough to constitute intimate friendship. It is possible for two people to know a great deal about each other and feel positively toward each other without that counting as intimate friendship. The relationship of counselor and counselee, especially when they both like each other, may involve knowledge and positive feelings without being an intimate friendship. The constrained nature and the distinctly different roles of the two people make it something other than an intimate friendship, at least until some other dimensions are added to their relationship.

Perhaps the most significant step in friendship is the achievement of a mutual trust based on some form of shared experience. To attain this trust, people usually need time in each other's company. Over time, that common experience leads to self-disclosure as a sign of trust. This trust engenders a corresponding loyalty and a further relaxation to heighten each other's enjoyment of shared activities.

As we saw in the examination of comradeship, to be intimate with another person one cannot be loyal to that person as a mere abstract other. Intimacy is not mere "fellow feeling" or mutual respect, although intimacy shares much in common with each of these concepts. Intimacy involves the kind of self-revelatory disclosures that go beyond what is necessary to generate sympathy or respect. Indeed, self-disclosure by itself often makes sympathy and respect more difficult. That is why one wants a sign of trustworthiness before one becomes intimate friends with another. When these elements of knowledge, positive feelings, trust, and reciprocity coalesce, then self-disclosure is a form of mutual enclosure in which two selves create a new, inclusive focus of attention, what Aristotle terms a complete friendship.

III. Obstacles to Intimacy in Male Friendships

As we have noted, many male friendships lack the dimension of mutual self-disclosure. The women we know report forming friendships through self-revealing discussion, whereas the men we know report that they typically form friendships based on common activities, such as work or participation in some sport, with self-revelation being at best tangential to the activity. On one level, it is certainly easier to engage in self-disclosure through discussion than by other, less-straightforward means, since one is able to disclose one's feelings with the least ambiguity by simply saying how one feels. But that presupposes capacities that many men currently lack. It is not a logical necessity that self-disclosure occur by means of discussion. Insofar as what we are is created by what we do as much as the reverse, action can be as vital a form of disclosure as speech.[17]

However, if one cannot accompany another person in the various aspects of the other's life, full disclosure through action is virtually impossible, and thus disclosure via speech becomes a practical necessity. Actions cannot easily disclose the past or project into the future without words to set the context. When one shares a past with another and shares a variety of activities—working at the same place, shopping at the same stores, attending the same church or synagogue—one can expect to disclose oneself gradually through action. The increasing diversity and mobility of North American life means that the route to intimacy through a shared past linked with shared present activities is not open to many of us. Thus, self-disclosure through speech is the only realistic possibility we have found.

The difficulties are not simply social or logistical. In order to be able to engage in self-disclosure, persons must be able to gain access to the feelings they are trying to disclose to their friends. And in order to gain this access, they must in some sense be aware of having certain feelings and be able to conceptualize them. Yet males in contemporary Western culture are encouraged not to show their feelings; indeed, from the dispassionate reasoner model of the philosopher to the Clint Eastwood image of manhood, males are encouraged not to let their feelings interfere at all with the conduct of their lives.[18] The culturally ingrained habit of hiding, rejecting, and denying legitimacy to one's feelings makes it much harder for these males, for us, to gain access to feelings and impedes the disclosure of these feelings to intimate friends.[19] We need others to help understand ourselves, as G. H. Mead has stressed, yet without some degree of self-awareness or self-intimacy we can only with great difficulty communicate what is most important about ourselves.

Larry had a revealing experience several years ago. Right before setting out for his grandfather's funeral, several friends remarked that he was keeping remarkably cool in the face of what must have been very emotionally difficult times. In reflecting on this on the way to the funeral, he discovered, much to his own amazement, that he simply had no feelings about the death of his grandfather. It was not that he and his grandfather had been distant or enemies; indeed, they had once been fairly close. But over the years, he had let the thought of his grandfather become less and less important until there simply were no positive or negative feelings attached to him. While there were no feelings here, except indifference, to disclose to his friends, the very lack of emotions could have been, but was not at that time, a basis for self-disclosure and self-realization.

It is our experience that most males we know have fewer and/or less complex emotional responses to situations than do most females. It is also true that men have been socialized to display callousness in those situations where their feelings might otherwise manifest themselves. Callousness is a lack of emotional response, or a diminished emotional responsiveness, to certain stimuli. Culturally ingrained callousness may lead to a lack of feeling, just as the metaphor suggests: the finger that has a callus will not feel as much pain as the finger without one. Callousness in men is produced by, among other ways, habitual association of a negative emotional response with images of people who are not considered (good or real) men. Negative psychological association stifles emotional feeling, just as the encrusting of nerve endings deadens sensory feeling. Over time, callousness may lead to the elimination of a certain kind of emotional response.[20] In our culture, men may disclose fewer feelings than do women simply because they have been socialized to be less aware of the few feelings they do have. They may thus be content with comradeship as we have described it as their paradigm of friendship. This socialization helps many men avoid dealing with the emotional consequences for others of their acts, at least for the short term.

At the very least, many men, ourselves included, report that they have been bewildered by the task of understanding their own feelings. For men, feelings simply seem inchoate in ways that generally do not seem to be true for women. A number of years ago Bob was almost entirely stymied when he tried to role-play the part of a woman friend in a variation of a common male-female interaction. He could recall how she had acted in the past but could not place himself in her position. He tried and failed, whereas she could play the male much better. He could not imaginatively experience how she might have felt and acted. This seems to be a much more typically male incapacity.[21] And this limits reciprocity and may also help explain why males report fewer intimate relationships than women do.

In order to have strongly positive emotional feelings for another person, as well as sustained mutual self-disclosure, it is important to be able both to have such feelings and to express them. To express such feelings, one must be able to trust another person. Yet sociological studies indicate that the dominant model is one of competition rather than trust between men.[22] Competition creates bonds between teammates but it also makes men reluctant to reveal things about themselves that would make them vulnerable, and hence cause them to risk being taken advantage of. Completing this paper took longer than anticipated because Bob's inability to admit that he simply works more slowly than Larry made it difficult to maintain their work schedule. Instead of working cooperatively, albeit differently, Bob slipped into seeing Larry more as a competitor and less as a partner. And this took some time to acknowledge. To have the openness to allow the mutual expressions of positive feelings toward one another, the people involved cannot be worrying about becoming more vulnerable than the other.

Men in American culture are clearly stymied in pursuing intimacy with other males because of fears involving their sexuality, especially culturally inbred homophobia. As teenagers, we learned not to display feelings toward other boys on pain of being ridiculed as "queers"; Bob and his brother were called "homos" for putting their arms around each other. The taboo against males touching, except in the firm public handshake, continues these teenage prohibitions. Such restrictions and taboos dampen the expression of deep feelings among males in much of American culture. And yet, in sports contexts for instance, there are clearly accepted exceptions to these taboos, such as the pat on the backside of a teammate. Perhaps here manliness is somehow assured. Homophobia is not an insurmountable obstacle to male intimacy, but it certainly does contribute to the difficulties that men have in expressing their deeply held feelings.

We see a complex of interacting factors—including homophobia, competitiveness, callousness, taboos against the expression of feelings, and social and cultural patterns—that culminate in many men in our society not being as well suited for intimacy as women are. The lack of socialization either to seek out the personal, defining characteristics of another person or to seek this information about oneself is significant. We don't ask! Rather, males best relate with one another on the basis of shared experiences, such as sports or work, rather than shared details of one another's personal life.

IV. Aristotle Revisited

At first, we thought we were sketching a relatively novel philosophical account of friendship. Indeed, compared to much that has been written on friendship, that is probably true. But a reading of Aristotle reveals a number of places where our account parallels his. He describes three species of friendship: friendship based on utility, friendship based on pleasure, and what he calls a complete friendship. In the first two cases, friendship is based not on a love of the friend's character but on the usefulness or pleasure provided by the friend. Aristotle says that "the beloved is loved not in so far as he is who he is, but in so far as he provides some good or pleasure" (1156a15).[23]

As we have suggested, much of male friendship is based *not* on a thoroughgoing knowledge of the other but on the surface characteristics and social activities that friends share. Male friends are those one can "do things" with, whose temperament and responses coincide with one's own in such a way that one can participate in various activities with them without having to explain or to negotiate troubling compromises. Two male friends both have the same attitude toward playing tennis, for example; both take it seriously, but not too seriously. Or a friend at work enjoys your cynical sniping at the higher administration, and you willingly go on your friend's excursions to various new restaurants for lunch. But such friendships can be fragile. If this friend gets promoted into an administrative position or your financial situation changes so that restaurant lunches are too much of a drain on monetary resources, the friendship is likely to wither away. This scenario exemplifies an Aristotelian friendship based on pleasure, not an intimate friendship.

Aristotle describes friendship among the young as typically based on pleasure: "They pursue above all what is pleasant for themselves and what is near at hand. But as they grow up what they find pleasant changes too. Hence they are quick to become friends, and quick to stop; for their friendship shifts with what they find pleasant, and the change in such pleasure is quick" (1156ab). As men grow older their pleasures may stop changing, and thus friendships last longer; the quality of the friendships, however, does not necessarily deepen. Our notion of American male friendship as serial best-friendship seems apt here. But this was not Aristotle's vision of complete adult male friendship in Athenian Greece, and it need not be our view of the future of contemporary adult male friendship either.[24]

Aristotle emphasizes that complete friendship takes time to develop, but he means more than simply time spent together. A genuine knowledge of the other is required, and this both comes from and helps sustain shared activities, or "living together":

> . . . as the proverb says, they cannot know each other before they have shared the traditional [peck of] salt, and they cannot accept each other or be friends until each appears lovable to the other and gains the other's confidence. (1156b)

Cooper claims that in the *Magna Moralia* Aristotle argues that "self-knowledge depends upon knowledge of others."[25] In that book Aristotle writes, reminding one of G. H. Mead: ". . . as when we wish to see our own face, we do so by looking into the mirror, in the same way when we wish to know ourselves we can obtain that knowledge by looking at our friend. For the friend is . . . a second self."[26]

There is a noteworthy difference in translations of another Greek proverb mentioned by Aristotle in the *Nicomachean Ethics*. W. D. Ross translates it as "Out of sight, out of mind,"[27] whereas Terence Irwin translates it as "Lack of conversation has dissolved many a friendship" (1156b8). The latter translation seems to us to capture more fully Aristotle's accompanying discussion: that physical distance does not necessarily "dissolve the friendship unconditionally" but merely requires a suspension of friendship until it can become active again. We might say, analogously, that the current failure of contemporary American males to have self-disclosing conversations has not destroyed the *potential* for intimacy. It is likely true, however, that just as a *long* absence due to distance can dissolve a friendship, so a *sustained* lack of self-disclosure can allow those necessary capacities to become so atrophied that intimate friendship may become impossible.

We differ from Aristotle in explicitly focusing on men. We place a greater emphasis on the psychological aspects of friendship. And we recognize that few friends today can emulate Aristotle's aristocratic Athenian friends, with their substantial leisure time—"Some friends drink together, others play dice, . . . or do philosophy. They spend their days together on whichever pursuit in life they like most" (1172a). We share with Aristotle the recognition that complete friendship is not just shared activities, parallel play; it also involves the "sharing of conversation and thought, not [just] sharing the same pasture, as in the case of grazing animals" (1170b).

V. Resources for Greater Male Intimacy

Supposing we want greater intimacy in our friendships, how can we move toward it? What are the obstacles one might face, and what resources might one draw on in this process? Here we are interested in the situation of the man who recognizes the inadequacy of typical contemporary American models for men, who does not aspire to be, for example, a hypermasculine warrior or laconic cowboy, but who also recognizes that intimacy does not come easily for him. This question has no simple answer for us; at the same time, we do not agree with Montaigne that "so many circumstances are needed to build [male friendship] up that it is something if fate achieves it once in three centuries."[28]

We do not think there is any good reason to hold that men are by nature less caring than women. Indeed, at most, the biological, sociological, and psychological evidence suggests that being female correlates more frequently with being caring, and that this is best explained in terms of socialized rather than natural differences between men and women.[29] While there are many reasons why men are in fact less likely to have intimate same-sex friendships than women are, there are also good reasons to think that it is both feasible and desirable for many men to change their attitudes so that being male and expressing intimacy correlate more frequently in the future.

Certainly, male friendships will continue to be constrained by the varieties of socially oppressive practices—sexism, heterosexism, racism, classism, and more. Nonetheless we believe that intimacy for men does not require their prior elimination, only their recognition and a serious effort to reduce their efficacy. For example, efforts to restructure work relations to make them less hierarchical and competitive could free some space for friendships to grow more easily. Given the male proclivity to emphasize shared activity over sharing disclosures, men can begin by doing things together. For us, friendship began with helping each other move into new homes, going with our families on political marches, talking about our children on jaunts with them to the library on Saturday mornings, and especially discussing philosophy and academic politics over lunch.[30]

For many men it is difficult to pursue the personal information about one another that would allow for intimate bonding. Yet they may openly describe their employment or financial problems to one another and may attempt to gain such information about those associates who seem to be in financial trouble—at least, as long as these can be presented as problems in the public realm. And this information is just as likely to display vulnerability as is more deeply personal information. Indeed, since males are generally socialized to view the public world as much more important than the private, one would think that it would be easier for men to reveal information about their private selves, since less is risked.

Unfortunately it is not easy to transfer these public skills into the realm of the personal. What is more consistent with the complexity of the phenomena we have been examining is to emphasize that intimate bonds can be as strong and as enjoyable as comradeship bonds and certainly can lead to greater personal support and growth. In wartime situations, those comrades who spend the time to find out who their comrades really are will often find that they are more rather than less motivated to sacrifice their lives for their fellow soldiers. It is almost impossible to care deeply for a person who is merely a generalized other. Gray recognized this in his account of wartime comrades, observing that "loyalty is rarely reliable with great masses of men unless it has some cement" in the feelings of liking or love.[31] And this can occur only out of sentiment for who the person is as a particular individual.

The fact that some men have developed intimacy in relationships that began as comradeships lends hope. Only if men were somehow blocked from realizing the value of intimacy would there be cause for despair. There are emotional resources that males have available to them that could, but normally do not, lead them to form intimate friendships. Among these are the ability to find common ground with those one meets for the first time, the ability to be constructively critical without adversely affecting the future of a relationship, and the ability to form longlasting bonds of loyalty with other males. Indeed, there are several types of feeling that men are generally socialized to express more readily than do women. Just as men already feel entitled to express anger, rage, and hostility, there is no reason to think that other feelings will be permanently blocked. Surely, though, what is most in need of change here is the current lack of attention on the part of most males in Western culture toward an understanding of their own feelings.

How can men learn to become intimate with each other? Not

quickly, but most likely through a process of learning while doing things together and talking about themselves. Indeed, achieving intimacy is a process, as opposed to an event to make happen or a goal to be achieved. The situation seems similar to the hedonistic paradox that those who directly seek happiness are often least likely to achieve that goal, since happiness often comes in the seeking of other things. Recently, Bob drew back from a new friend because that friend's personal disclosures made Bob quite uncomfortable; fortunately, because they continued to work together a greater *mutual* openness developed. We have not participated in the workshops or "gatherings" of the so-called Men's Movement, and so we hesitate to comment on it. If these do allow many men moments of intimacy with selves and others, they are still very different from the building of an intimate friendship.

In our own interactions, it seems that we have gotten to know each other best—achieved greater intimacy—in those conversations where we relaxed our boundaries and simply talked. We felt the tug of hesitations, inhibitions each of us has to confront one by one. Should I mention this, should I criticize or let it pass, should I ask about that, can I admit to this? Opportunities are lost, disclosure prevented. And men—we—need to develop a greater ability and inclination to reflect, both as individuals and as friends. This requires us to approach our relationships as more than "undigested interactions,"[32] as things upon which we are already reflecting, and make that more explicit. Instead of just swapping stories about our childhoods, we grew by asking ourselves questions such as, "Why did Bob react to his father in one way when disciplined and Larry to his father in a different fashion?" and, "Why did we not mention our mothers in this respect?" Here the beginnings of intimacy can enable more intimacy.

This process will not teach us to become caring, but how to develop and express our caring. We do not want to be interpreted as claiming that many men do not care about one another. Men do care, often very deeply, but at the same time in a stunted and inchoate fashion. The narrowness of our relations hinders the realization and expression of care. A friend's brother dies unexpectedly and we realize that we have little idea of what sort of relationship the two had. We don't know what to say. Perhaps they were intense rivals, drifting apart as one gained more success than the other. Perhaps not. We don't know.

Men can, however, come to know each other. We can learn to form together the intimate friendships that many women have. And just like women's friendships, eventually intimate male friendships can benefit us all.[33]

Notes

1. Alice Walker, *The Temple of My Familiar* (New York: Harcourt, Brace, Jovanovich, 1989), p. 114.

2. Vera Brittain, *Testament of Friendship: The Story of Winifred Holtby* (London: Macmillan, 1947). This passage is quoted by Blanche Cook in "Female Support Networks and Political Activism: Lillian Wald, Crystal Eastman, and Emma Goldman," *Chrysalis*, vol. 3 (1977), p. 44, who also perceptively discusses the scholarly disregard of female friendships.

3. See the summary of this research in Chapter 13 of Letty Cottin Pogrebin's *Among Friends* (New York: McGraw-Hill, 1987). See also Drury Sherrod, "The Influence of Gender on Same-Sex Friendships," in *Close Relationships*, edited by Clyde Hendrick (Newbury Park, CA: Sage Publishing Co., 1989); and Barry McCarthy, "Adult Friendships," in *Person to Person*, edited by George Graham and Hugh LaFollette (Philadelphia: Temple University Press, 1989).

4. Cited in Pogrebin, ibid., p. 253.

5. Ibid.

6. Jack W. Sattel, "The Inexpressive Male: Tragedy or Sexual Politics?" *Social Problems*, vol. 23/4 (1976), pp. 469–77.

7. See Sandra Harding's paper "After the End of 'Philosophy'," delivered at the 1989 Matchette conference at Purdue University. An earlier version of this paper is called "Who Knows? Identities and Feminist Epistemologies," in *Critical Issues in Feminist Inquiry*, edited by Ellen Messer Davidow and Joan Hartman, forthcoming.

8. Gerry Philipsen, in "Speaking 'like a man' in Teamsterville: Cultural Patterns of Role Enactment in an Urban Neighborhood," *Quarterly Journal of Speech*, vol. 61 (1975), pp. 13–22, insightfully examines how situational expectations govern male speech in one American community.

9. For a cautionary note on the durability of these relationships, see Roger Little, "Friendships in the Military Community," in *Friendship*, volume 2 of *Research in the Interweave of Social Roles*, edited by Helena Znaniecka Lopata and David Maines (Greenwich, CT: JAI Press, 1981).

10. J. Glenn Gray, *The Warriors* (New York: Harper Torchbooks, 1959), pp. 26–27 (p. 46 of this volume).

11. Ibid., p. 40 (p. 52 of this volume).

12. Ibid. (p. 52 of this volume).

13. Ibid., p. 46 (p. 55 of this volume).

14. Mary Daly, *Gyn/Ecology* (Boston: Beacon Press, 1978), p. 269.

15. Ibid., p. 279, emphasis added.

16. Stanley Bing, "No Man is an Isthmus," *Esquire*, August 1989, p. 53.

17. See Sherrod, op. cit., for a discussion of this question.

18. Judith Mayne explores some of the often overlooked complexities of Clint Eastwood movies in her essay "Walking the Tightrope of Feminism and Male Desire," in *Men and Feminism*, edited by Alice Jardine and Paul Smith (New York: Methuen, 1987).

19. See Susan Pollack and Carol Gilligan, "Images of Violence in Thematic Apperception Test Stories," *Journal of Personality and Social Psychology*, vol. 42 (1982), pp. 159–67.

20. See Larry May's essay "Insensitivity and Moral Responsibility," *Journal of Value Inquiry*, vol. 26 (1992), pp. 7–22.

21. Lillian B. Rubin, *Intimate Strangers: Men and Women Together* (New York: Harper and Row, 1983), pp. 69–70.

22. See, for example, *Beyond Patriarchy*, edited by Michael Kaufman (Toronto: Oxford University Press, 1987).

23. This and other quotations from Aristotle, unless otherwise cited, are taken from *Nicomachean Ethics*, translated by Terence Irwin (Indianapolis: Hackett Publishing Co., 1985).

24. See Pat Easterling, "Friendship and the Greeks," in *The Dialectics of Friendship*, edited by Roy Porter and Sylvana Tomaselli (London: Routledge, 1989).

25. See John M. Cooper, "Friendship and the Good in Aristotle," *Philosophical Review*, vol. 86/3 (1977), pp. 290–315.

26. Aristotle, *Magna Moralia* 1213a translated by George Stock in vol. 9 of *The Works of Aristotle* (Oxford: Oxford University Press, 1925).

27. Aristotle, *Nicomachean Ethics*, translated by W. D. Ross in *The Basic Works of Aristotle*, edited by Richard McKeon (New York: Random House, 1941).

28. Michel de Montaigne, "On Friendship," *Essays*, translated by J. M. Cohen (Baltimore: Penguin Books, 1958), p. 92.

29. For supporting arguments for this point see, for example, Richard Lee and Richard Daly, "Man's Domination and Woman's Oppression: The Question of Origins," and Carmen Schifellite, "Beyond Tarzan and Jane Genes: Toward a Critique of Biological Determinism," in *Beyond Patriarchy*, op. cit.; and John Dupre, "Global versus Local Perspectives on Sexual Difference," in *Theoretical Perspectives on Sexual Difference*, edited by Deborah Rhode (New Haven, CT: Yale University Press, 1990).

30. For one result see Larry May and Robert Strikwerda, "Fatherhood and Nurturance," *Journal of Social Philosophy*, vol. 22/2 (1991), pp. 28–39.

31. Gray, op. cit., p. 40 (p. 52 of this volume).

32. This phrase was borrowed from Steve Duck and Kris Pond, "Friends, Romans, Countrymen: Rhetoric and Reality in Personal Relationships," in *Close Relationships*, op. cit.

33. We have benefited from the comments of Marilyn Friedman, Penny Weiss, Clark Rountree, and those who attended our presentation of an earlier version of this paper in the Purdue University Women's Studies Program Spring 1990 "Brown Bag Lecture Series." We also thank the referees and editor at *Hypatia* for valuable comments on the penultimate version of this paper.

6

Gender Treachery: Homophobia, Masculinity, and Threatened Identities[1]

Patrick D. Hopkins

One of my first critical insights into the pervasive structure of sex and gender categories occurred to me during my senior year of high school. The seating arrangement in my American Government class was typical—the "brains" up front and at the edge, the "jocks" at the back and in the center. Every day before and after class, the male jocks bandied insults back and forth. Typically, this "good-natured" fun included name-calling. Name-calling, like most pop-cultural phenomena, circulates in fads, with various names waxing and waning in popularity. During the time I was taking this class, the most popular insult/name was used over and over again, *ad nauseam*. What was the insult?

It was simply, "girl."

Suggestively, "girl" was the insult of choice among the male jocks. If a male student was annoying, they called him "girl." If he made a mistake during some athletic event, he was called "girl." Sometimes "girl" was used to challenge boys to do their masculine best ("don't let us down, girl"). Eventually, after its explicitly derogatory use, "girl" came to be used among the male jocks as merely a term of greeting ("hey, girl").

But the blatantly sexist use of the word "girl" as an insult was not the only thing that struck me as interesting in this case. There was something different about this school, which in retrospect leads to my insight. My high school was a conservative Christian institution; no profanity (of a defined type) was allowed. Using "bad" words was considered sinful, was against the rules, and was formally punished. There was, therefore, a regulated lack of access to the more commonly used insults available in secular schools. "Faggot," "queer," "homo," or "cocksucker" were not available for use unless one was willing to risk being overheard by school staff, and thus risk being punished. However, it is important to note that, for the most part, these words were not restricted because of any sense of hurtfulness to a particular group or because they expressed prejudice. They were restricted merely because they were "dirty" words, "filthy" words, gutter-language words, like "shit" or "asshole." "Girl" was not a dirty word, and so presented no risk. It was used flagrantly in the presence of staff members, and even used by staff members themselves.[2]

In a curious twist, the very restriction of discursive access to these more common profanities (in the name of morality and decency) reveals a deeper structure of all these significations. "Girl," as an allowable, non-profane substitute for "faggot," "homo," and "cocksucker," mirrors and thus reveals a common essence of these insults. It signifies "not-male," and as related to the male speaker, "not-me."

"Girl," like these other terms, signifies a failure of masculinity, a failure of living up to a gendered standard of behavior, and a gendered standard of identity. Whether it was the case that a "failure of masculinity" actually occurred (as in fumbling the football) or whether it was only the "good-natured" intimation that it would occur (challenging future masculine functioning), the use of such terms demonstrates that to levy a successful insult, it was enough for these young men to claim that their target was insufficiently male; he was inadequately masculine, inadequately gendered.[3]

This story can, of course, be subjected to countless analyses, countless interpretations. For my purposes here, however, I want to present this story as an illustration of how important gender is to the concept of one's self. For these young males, being a man was not merely another contingent feature of their personhood. They did not conceive of themselves as people who were also male. They were, or wanted to be, *Men*. "Person" could only be a less descriptive, more generic way of talking about humans in the abstract. But there are no abstract humans; there are no "persons," rigorously speaking. There are only men and women. Or so we believe.

In what follows, I use this insight into gendered identity to make a preliminary exploration of the relationships between masculinity and homophobia. I find that one way to read homophobia and heterosexism in men is in terms of homosexuality's threat to masculinity, which in light of the connection between gender and personal identity translates into a threat to what constitutes a man's sense of self. To form a genuine challenge to homophobia, therefore, will not result from or result in merely increased social tolerance, but will be situated in a fundamental challenge to traditional concepts of masculinity itself.

What It Means To Be (A) Gendered Me

Categories of gender, in different ways, produce a multiplicity of other categories in a society. They affect—if not determine—labor, reproduction-associated responsibilities, childrearing roles, distributions of political power, economic status, sexual practices, uses of language, application of certain cognitive skills, possession of personality traits, spirituality and religious beliefs, and more. In fact, all members of a given society have their material and psychological statuses heavily determined by their identification as a particular gender. However, not only individuals' physical, economic, and sexual situations are determined by gender categories, but also their own sense of personal identity—their personhood. I use "personhood" here as a metaphor for describing individuals' beliefs about how they fit into a society, how they fit into a world, who and what they think they *are*.[4] Personhood is critically linked (or perhaps worse, uncritically linked) to the influence of the gender categories under which an individual develops.

Individuals' sense of personhood, their sense-of-self, is largely a result of their construction as members of particular social groups within society-at-large: religions, ethnicities, regional affinities, cultural heritages, classes, races, political parties, family lineages, etc. Some of the most pervasive, powerful, and hidden of these identity-constructing "groups" are the genders; pervasive because no individual escapes being gendered, powerful because so much else depends on gender, and hidden because gender is uncritically presented as a natural, biological given, about which much can be discovered but little can (or should) be altered. In most cultures, though not all, sex/gender identity, and thus much of personal identity, is regulated by a binary system—man and woman.[5] The socially meaningful categories of "men" and "women" are immediately extrapolated and constructed from the material of newborn human bodies—a culturally varied process that legitimates itself as purely "natural," even in all its variation.[6] To a very large extent, what it means to be a member of society, and thus what it means to be a person, *is* what it means to be a girl or boy, a man or woman. There is no such thing as a sexually or gender undifferentiated person.[7]

Identity is fundamentally relational. What it means to have a particular identity depends on what it means not to have some other identity, and by the kinds of relationships one has to other possible and actual identities. To have personhood, sense-of-self, regulated by a binary sex/gender system means that the one identity must be different from the other identity; a situation requiring that there be identifiable, performative, behavioral, and psychological characteristics that allow for clear differentiation. Binary identities demand criteria for differentiation.

For a "man" to qualify as a man, he must possess a certain (or worse, uncertain) number of demonstrable characteristics that make it clear that he is not a woman, and a woman must possess characteristics demonstrating she is not a man. These characteristics are, of course, culturally relative, and even intraculturally dynamic, but in late twentieth-century U.S. culture the cluster of behaviors and qualities that situate men in relation to women include the by now well-known litany: (hetero)sexual prowess, sexual conquest of women, heading a nuclear family, siring children, physical and material competition with other men, independence, behavioral autonomy, rationality, strict emotional control, aggressiveness, obsession with success and status, a certain way of walking, a certain way of talking, having buddies rather than intimate friends, etc.[8]

Because personal identity (and all its concomitant social, political, religious, psychological, biological, and economic relations) is so heavily gendered, any threat to sex/gender categories is derivatively (though primarily non-consciously) interpreted as a threat to personal identity—a threat to what it means to be and especially what it means to be me. A threat to manhood (masculinity) is a threat to personhood (personal identity). Not surprisingly then, a threat to established gender categories, like most other serious threats, is often met with grave resistance, for challenging the regulatory operations of a gender system means to destabilize fundamental social, political, and personal categories (a profoundly anxiety-producing state), and society is always prejudiced toward the protection of established categories. Inertia is a force in culture as well as in physics.

There are many different threats to gendered identity, but I think they can all be generally grouped together under the rubric of "gender treachery."[9] A gender traitor can be thought of as anyone who violates the "rules" of gender identity/gender performance, i.e., someone who rejects or appears to reject the criteria by which the genders are differentiated.[10] At its most obvious, gender treachery occurs as homosexuality, bisexuality, cross-dressing, and feminist activism. Any of these traitorous activities may result in a serious reaction from those individuals and groups whose concept of personal and political identity is most deeply and thoroughly sexed by traditional binary categories.[11] However, homosexuality is particularly effective in producing the extreme (though not uncommon) reaction of homophobia—a response that is often manifested in acts of physical, economic, and verbal assault against perceived gender traitors, queers.[12] Homosexuals, intentionally or not, directly challenge assumptions concerning the relational aspects of the binary categories of sex/gender, and as such threaten individual identities. Since the homophobic reaction can be lethal and so theoretically suggestive, it deserves serious attention.

Homophobia/Heterosexism

Theorists debate the value of using the term "homophobia." For some, the "phobia" suffix codes anti-gay and anti-lesbian activity as appertaining to psychiatric discourse—the realm of irrationality, uncontrollable fear, a realm where moral responsibility or political critique seems inapplicable due to the clinical nature of the phobia.[13] We do not punish people for being claustrophobic; we do not accuse agoraphobics of ignorance or intolerance; why should we treat homophobics any differently?

Other terms have been used to describe the aggregation of prejudices against gays and lesbians, including homoerotophobia, homosexism, homonegativism, anti-homosexualism, anti-homosexuality, and homohatred.[14] "Heterosexism" has become the terminology of choice for some theorists, emphasizing similarities to racism and sexism. "Heterosexism" characterizes a political situation in which heterosexuality is presented and perceived as natural, moral, practical, and superior to any non-heterosexual option. As such, heterosexuals are *justly* accorded the privileges granted them—political power, sexual freedom, religious sanction, moral status, cultural validation, psychiatric and juridical non-interference, occupational and tax privilege, freedom to have or adopt children and raise families, civil rights protection, recourse against unfair hiring practices, public representation in media and entertainment industries, etc.

For many of us, however, "heterosexism," though accurate and useful, does not possess the rhetorical and emotional impact that "homophobia" does. "Heterosexism" is appropriate for describing why all television couples are straight, why marriage and joint tax returns are reserved for heterosexuals, why openly lesbian or gay candidates face inordinate difficulty in being elected to office, or why only heterosexuals can adopt children or be foster parents. But "heterosexism," though perhaps still technically accurate, does not seem strong enough to describe the scene of ten Texas teenage boys beating a gay man with nail-studded boards and stabbing him to death.[15] The blood pooling up on the ground beneath that dying body is evidence for something more than the protection of heterosexual privilege. It is evidence for a radical kind of evil.

It is neither my goal nor my desire here to set out specific definitions of homophobia. Though I will use the term primarily with reference to physical violence and strong verbal, economic, and juridical abuse against gays, I do not claim to establish a clear boundary between homophobia and heterosexism. No stable boundary could be set, nor would it be particularly useful to try to do so—they are not discrete. "Homophobia" and "heterosexism" are political words, political tools; they are ours to use as specific situations present specific needs.

However, for my purposes here, heterosexism—loosely characterized as valorizing and privileging heterosexuality (morally, economically, religiously, politically)—can be seen as the necessary precursor to homophobia. Heterosexism is the backdrop of the binary division into heterosexual and homosexual (parasitic on the man/woman binary), with, as usual, the first term of the binary good and second term bad. Heterosexism constructs the field of concepts and behaviors so that some heterosexists' hierarchical view of this binary will be reactionary, for a variety of reasons, thus becoming homophobic (read: violent/abusive/coercive). In the same way that a person doesn't have to be a member of a white supremacist organization to be racist, a person doesn't have to be homophobic to be heterosexist. This is not to say that heterosexism is not as bad as homophobia, but rather that though heterosexism presents less of an obvious, direct, personal physical threat to gays, it nonetheless situates the political arena such that homophobia can and is bound to exist. Heterosexism is culpable for the production of homophobia. Heterosexists are politically culpable for the production of homophobics.

But even when we choose to use the term "homophobia" for cases of brutality, fanatic claims, petitions for fascistic laws, or arbitrarily firing gay employees, this does not mean that we must always characterize homophobia as an irrational, psychiatric/clinical response. Such a characterization would be grossly inadequate. "Homophobia" has evolved as primarily a political term, not as a psychiatric one, and does not parallel claustrophobia or agoraphobia, for the political field is not the same.

Religious and political rhetorics of moral turpitude and moral danger do not attach to closed-in spaces or wide-open spaces in the way they attach to same-sex eroticism. In other words, the fear and abhorrence of homosexuals is often taught as a moral and practical virtue and political oppression is massed against gays and lesbians. As a result, oppositional strategies to homophobia must be located in political discourse, not just psychiatric or pop-psychiatric discourse. Homophobia is supported and subsidized by cultural and governmental institutions in ways that demand the need for a variety of analyses. Though homophobia may often seem irrational or semi-psychotic in appearance, it must not be dismissed as simply an obsessive individual psychological aberration. Homophobia is a product of institutional heterosexism and gendered identity.

How do people explain homophobia? And especially, though not exclusively, how do people in queer communities explain homophobia? Being the victims of it, what do they see in it? Why is it that some men react so strongly and so virulently to the mere presence of gay men?

The Repression Hypothesis

One of the most common explanations of homophobia among gay men is that of repressed homosexuality. Men who constantly make anti-gay slurs, tell anti-gay jokes, use anti-gay language, obsess about the dire political and moral impact of homosexuality on the family and country, or even who are known to attack gays physically are often thought to be repressing their own sexual attraction toward men. As a result of their terror in coming to grips with their own sexuality, they overcompensate, metastasizing into toxic, hypermasculine, ultra-butch homophobes who seem to spend far more time worrying about homosexuality than openly gay men do.

This kind of repressed-homosexual explanation was aptly demonstrated by one of my straight undergraduate ethics professors. While teaching a section on sexual ethics, my professor and the entire class read a series in the college newspaper by our Young Republican student editor about how "the homosexuals" were taking over the country and converting all the children. Finally, after yet another repetition of the "but they can't have babies and they're unnatural" columns, my exasperated professor wrote a response to the paper, and after a lengthy list of counterarguments, ended by saying simply, "Methinks thou doth protest too much."

His intimation was clear. He believed that the Young Republican's arguments were more for his benefit than for his readers'. As the typical response goes among gays who hear men constantly ranting about the perils of homosexuality and the virtues of heterosexuality— "He's not trying to convince us. He's trying to convince himself."

I think for many men this theory of repression is accurate. It is not unusual for openly gay men to talk about their days in the closet and report that they were assertively heterosexist/homophobic—and that yes, they were desperately trying to convince themselves that they were really heterosexual. Sadly enough, many of these repressed homosexuals manage to maintain their repression at great cost to themselves and often at great cost to others. Some marry and live a lie, unfulfilled emotionally and sexually, deceiving their wives and children, sometimes having furtive, sexual affairs with other men. They manage psychologically to compartmentalize their erotic orientation and same-sex sexual experiences so radically that they live two separate, torturous lives. Some repressives become anti-gay activists and spend their lives trying to force gays and lesbians back into the closet, working against gay civil rights and protections.[16] Horrifyingly, some others undergo an even worse schism in their personalities, resulting in a bizarre, malignant, and persistent internalized war between homophobia and homophilia. This war can culminate in what John Money calls the exorcist syndrome, in which the repressive picks up, seduces, or even rapes a gay man, and then beats him or kills him in order to exorcise the repressive's "homosexual guilt."[17]

But while the repressive hypothesis is certainly accurate for some men, it is not accurate for all. I have no doubt that there are indubitably heterosexual men who hate and assault gays. To some extent, the explanation of repressed homosexuality may be wish fulfillment on the part of some gays. Forced by necessity of survival to be secretive and cryptic themselves, many gay men find it eminently reasonable to suspect any man of potential homosexual desire, and in fact, want such to be the case. It is reasonable, if optimistic, to hope that there are really more of you than there seem to be. And in light of the fact that many openly gay men report that they used to be homophobic themselves, the repression theory seems to be both empirically sound as well as emotionally attractive. There is also a certain sense of self-empowerment resulting from the repression hypothesis—out gays may see themselves as morally, cognitively, and emotionally superior to the men who continue to repress their sexuality. But homophobia is not so simple. What about those homophobes who clearly are not repressing their own homosexuality? What explanation fits them?

The Irrationality/Ignorance Hypothesis

Another explanation, one in perfect keeping with the roots of the word, is that homophobia is an irrational fear, based in ignorance and resulting from social training.[18] This explanation is also popular among liberal heterosexuals as well as liberal lesbians and gays. The stereotype of this kind of cultural/developmental homophobia is that of a little boy who grows up in a poorly educated, very conservative family, often in a rural area, who hears his parents and other relatives talk about the fags on TV or the homo child molester they caught in the next county and how he ought to be "strung up and shot." As the little boy grows, he models his parents' behavior, identifying with their emotions and desiring to emulate them. Although the boy has no idea of what a "fag" or "homo" is, he nevertheless learns the appropriate cues for application of those terms to situations and individuals, and the emotions associated with that application. He begins to use them himself, often as a general-use insult (like young children calling each other "nigger" even when they do not know what it means). He learns that certain kinds of behaviors elicit being called a fag and that he can achieve a degree of peer approval when he uses those terms. So he stands on the playground at recess and calls the boy who takes piano lessons a homo; his friends laugh. He asks the girls who are jumping rope with another boy why they are playing with a faggot; his friends laugh. Simultaneously, of course, the boy is learning all the other dictums of traditional heteromasculinity—girls are weak, boys are strong, girls play stupid games, boys play real games, girls that want to play football are weird, boys that do not want to play football are faggots. Eventually the boy learns the more complete definition of "faggot," "homo," "queer." Homos aren't just sissies who act like girls; they aren't just weak. They like to "do things" with other boys. Sick things. Perverted things.

A little knowledge is a very dangerous thing and the boy becomes a full-fledged homophobe who thinks boys who play the piano and do not like football want to touch him "down there." He learns that grown-up homos like to grab young boys and "do bad things to them." He learns that just as one can become a tougher, stronger, more masculine man by killing deer and by "slaughtering" the guys on the opposing football team, one can become more masculine, or prove one's masculinity, by verbally abusing or beating up queers.

Though this scenario may seem hyperbolic, it certainly does occur. I have seen it happen myself. The lesson that gets learned is that of the recurring conflict of essence and performance.

Essence: You (the little boy) have a natural, core, normal, good, essential identity; you are a *boy*, a *young man*, male, not-a-girl. This is just what you are. You were born this way. Little girls will like you. You have buddies. You're lucky. You are our *son*. It's natural and obvious that you will grow up and get married and be a *daddy*.

Performance: But even though you just *are* a little *boy*, even though it's perfectly natural, you must make sure you do not act (how? why?) like a girl. You must always make sure that you exhibit the right behavior for a boy (but isn't it natural?). Don't ever act like not-a-boy! Don't betray that which you are naturally, comfortably, normally. Don't not-be what you are. Perform like a man.

The stage is set. The child knows that he is a he and that being a he is a good, normal, natural thing. Being a he requires no effort. You just are a boy. But at the same time, there is lingering on the horizon the possibility, amorphous and not always spoken, that you might do something which violates what you are. It might be quiet—"Now put those down, son. Boys don't play with dolls." It might be loud— "What the hell are you doing playing with dolls like some sissy??!!" The little boy internalizes the expectations of masculinity.

This kind of explanation of homophobia, though useful and accurate for many purposes, tends to characterize homophobia as learned but completely irrational, unfounded, arbitrary, ignorant, counterproductive, and dysfunctional. However, such a simple analysis excludes much of the experience of the homophobe. It is not actually the case that the poor mindless homophobe simply veers through life distorting reality and obsessing over nothing, frothing at the mouth and seeing faggots behind every corner and homosexual conspiracies in every liberal platform, ruining his own life as well as others. In fact, homophobia is not dysfunctional in the way that agoraphobia is. Homophobia has functional characteristics.[19]

For example, in the story given above, the boy does not simply "catch" the obsessive, dysfunctional view of the world that his parents have. He learns that certain kinds of behaviors elicit rewarding emotions not only from his parents directly, but also from within himself when away from his parents. When the little boy plays with toy soldiers and pretends to slaughter communists or Indians, his parents smile, encourage him, and even play with him sometimes. If he plays house with his little sister, he is always the daddy and she is always the mommy and he pretends to get home from work and she pretends to have supper fixed for him—a game in which roles are correctly modeled and are thus emotionally rewarding—"I'm just like my daddy."

However, the emotional (and sometimes corporal) punishments function the same way. If the boy is caught playing with dolls, or pretending to be the mommy, he may be told that he is doing something wrong, or be punished, or may simply detect a sense of worry, disapproval, or distaste from his parents. Homophobic tendencies will be carried along with all the other traits of conservative masculinity. He will be "just like his daddy" when he calls some effeminate boy a sissy—an emotionally rewarding experience. He will receive approval from his peers when he pushes the class homo around—he will be tough and formidable in their eyes. And perhaps most importantly, he will be clearly and unambiguously performing the masculine role he perceives (correctly in context) to be so valued—an advantage in power, safety, admiration, and self-esteem. It is also in no small sense that homophobia can be functional in keeping other heterosexuals in line. The potential to accuse another boy of being a faggot, to threaten ostracism or physical assault, is a significant power.[20]

Thus, it is not the case that homophobia is somehow obviously dysfunctional on an individual or group level.[21] Homophobic activity carries with it certain rewards and a certain power to influence. In the case of the repressed homosexual, it externalizes the intra-psychic conflict and reaffirms a man's appearance of heterosexuality and thus his sense of stability, safety, and self. In the case of childhood modeling, homophobic activity wins approval from peers and authority figures, protects one from becoming the target of other homophobes, and reaffirms one's place in a larger context of gender appropriate behavior—protecting one's personal identity.

The Political Response Hypothesis

The recognition that there are rational, functional aspects of homophobia (in a heteropatriarchal context) leads to a third explanation of homophobia that reverses the second. This theory says that queers are a genuine political threat to heterosexuals and really do intend to eliminate heterosexual privilege. Homophobia, therefore, is a rational political response.[22] Radical feminist lesbians and certain radical gay men directly challenge the hetero-male-dominated structure of society, rejecting patriarchal rule, conventional morality, and patriarchal modes of power distribution. All of the primary institutional sites of power that have maintained patriarchal domination—the state, the church, the family, the medical profession, the corporation—are being challenged from without by queers who do not want merely to be accepted, or tolerated, or left alone, but who want to dismantle heteropatriarchal society and build something different in its place. In response to liberal heterosexuals who promote the irrationalist theory of homophobia, supporters of this theory might say that many of the so-called "ignorant" and "false" stereotypes of queers are in fact correct, but they are not bad stereotypes; they are good and should be praised, should be revered, should replace heterosexual values. Yes, lesbians do hate men. Yes, fags do want to destroy the nuclear family. Yes, dykes do want to convert children. Yes, homos are promiscuous.

The impetus for this theory of homophobia comes from lesbians and gays who view their sexuality as primarily a political identity, having chosen to reject heterosexuality and become lesbian or gay as a political act of resistance. They have chosen this identification because they want to fight, destroy, or separate from hetero-male-dominated society. According to this theory, homophobia is a perfectly rational, reasonable reaction to the presence of queers, because queers pose a genuine threat to the status of heterosexual privilege. It is only logical that heterosexuals would fight back, because if they do not fight back, their privilege, their power, and their dominance will be stripped away all the sooner.

There are people who seem, at least partially, to confirm this theory. It has been interesting to see that over the past ten years or so, it has become common for neo-conservative activist organizations to use the word "family" in their names. Among many gay, lesbian, and feminists activists, any organization with "Family" as part of its name is automatically suspected to be anti-gay, anti-lesbian, anti-feminist.[23] The frequency of the word "family" as an identification tag is seen as signifying a belief in the moral superiority of the traditional, heterosexual, nuclear family. This suggests that some "pro-family" activists trace and justify their anti-homosexual activism to the belief that lesbians and gays are threatening to destroy The Family and thus to destroy heterosexual morality.

It is also true that over the past twenty years or so, lesbian and gay thought has become radicalized in a variety of ways. Lesbians and gays have moved away from merely the hope of demedicalization and decriminalization to the hope of building cultures, ethics, practices, and politics of their own, hopes that include the destruction of heterosexist, or even heterosexual, society. There are some radical, separatist lesbians and separatist gays who view most human behavior in terms of rational, political aims, and for them homophobia is a predictable political response to their own oppositional politics. Nineteen ninety-two Republican presidential candidate Pat Buchanan was not simply being hyperbolic when he gravely predicted that the 1990s would be the decade of the radical homosexual. One of his campaign ads, featuring a film clip of near-nude, dancing, gay leathermen, formed the background for an attack on the grant policies of the National Endowment for the Arts. Such ads demonstrate that his homophobia is partially directed against queer-specific political and sexual challenges to his conservative Christian morality.

However, the political response hypothesis, like the others, accounts only for some homophobes, and I think, relatively few. This hypothesis suffers from too great a dose of modernist political rationalism. Like many traditional models of political activity, it overrationalizes the subjects involved. It assumes that members of the oppressor class interpret the world in political terms similar to that of members of an oppositional movement. Thus, the characterization of a homophobe is that of a rational individual with immoral goals who recognizes that the particular oppositional group of gays and lesbians is a genuine political threat to his or her power and privilege, and as such must take an active stand against that insurgent group. One of the best tactics for resisting the insurgents is terror—on individual levels with violence, on institutional levels with oppressive laws, and on sociocultural levels with boogeyfag propaganda.[24]

While this model has merit and may be partially accurate in accounting for some homophobia, it endows homophobes (and homosexuals) with a hyperrationality that does not seem to be in evidence. Most homophobes, even those who openly admit their involvement in physical and verbal attacks on gays and lesbians, do not consider their activity to be political. Most of them, in fact, do not perceive any obvious threat from the people they attack. Gary Comstock claims that perpetrators of anti-queer violence typically list the "recreational, adventuresome aspect of pursuing, preying upon, and scaring lesbians and gay men" as the first and foremost reason for their behavior. Only secondarily and less often do they list things like the "wrongness of homosexuality" as a reason for their activity. But even this "wrongness" is not listed as an explanation or political justification for their behavior as much as a background assumption that functions as cultural permission.[25]

A recent television news program interviewed a perpetrator of anti-gay violence and, like Comstock's interviewee, he had little or no explanation for why he was doing what he was doing except that it was fun. When asked how he could have fun hurting people, he said that he had never really thought of queers as real people. I think this suggests that interpreting all, or even most, homophobic violence as conscious political activity ignores that much of the "reasoning" behind homophobia, when there is any active reasoning at all, relies on a very abstract and loosely integrated background of heterosexist assumptions. Many homophobes view gays and lesbians as politically, morally, and economically insignificant. For those who have never had any personal interaction (positive or negative) with openly gay or lesbian folk, lesbian/gay people may be such an abstract other that they do not enter into one's political and moral consideration any more than people who kick dogs for fun consider the political and moral significance of dogs, except perhaps in terms of legal consequences.

Performing Gender and Gender Treachery

All three explanations of homophobia have one thing in common. They reside on a field of unequal, binary, sexual and gender differentiation. Behind all homophobia, regardless of its development, expression, or motivation, is the background of heterosexism. Behind all heterosexism is the background of gendered identities.

The gender category of men constructs its members around at least two conflicting characterizations of the essence of manhood. First, your masculinity (being-a-man) is natural and healthy and innate. But second, you must stay masculine—do not ever let your masculinity falter. So, although being a man is seen as a natural and automatic state of affairs for a certain anatomical makeup, masculinity is so valued, so valorized, so prized, and its loss such a terrible thing, that one must always guard against losing it. Paradoxically, then, the "naturalness" of being a man, of being masculine, is constantly guarding against the danger of losing itself. Unaware, the "naturalness," the "rightness," of masculinity exposes its own uncertainties in its incessant self-monitoring—a self-monitoring often accomplished by monitoring others. In fact, although the stable performance of masculinity is presented as an *outcome* of being a man, what arises in looking at heterosexism/homophobia is that being a man, or continuing to be a man, is the *outcome* of performing masculinity. But of course, not just anybody can make the performance. Anatomy is seen as prior even as the performance is required to validate the anatomy. Thus the performance produces the man, but the performance is also limited to and compulsory for a "man."[26]

The insults of the male high school jocks are telling. Even though one is recognized as a man (or boy) prior to evidenced masculinity, evidence must also be forthcoming in order to merit that continued "unproblematic" status. Whether performative evidence is provided with ease or with difficulty, it is nonetheless a compulsory perform-ance, as compulsory as the initial anatomically based gender assign-ment. But because (proof of) masculinity has to be maintained not merely by anatomical differentiation but by performance, the possibil-ity of failure in the performance is always there. It is enough to insult, to challenge, to question personal identity, by implying that one is not being masculine enough.

The logic of masculinity is demanding—protect and maintain what you are intrinsically, or you could lose it, mutate, become something else. The insults of my student peers suggest that the "something else" is being a girl—a serious enough demotion in a patriarchal culture. But of course, this is metaphor. One does not actually become a girl; the power of prior anatomy is too spellbinding, even when the performance fails. The "something else" is a male without masculin-ity, a monster, a body without its essential spirit, a mutation with no specifiable identity.[27]

So one mutation, which is so offensive it becomes the template of all mutations, occurs when a man finds that his erotic orientation is toward other men.[28] If he acts on that erotic orientation, he violates a tenet of masculinity, he fails at masculinity, and most importantly, appears to reject standards by which real men are defined as selves, as subjects. In a binary gender system, however, to be unmasculine means to be feminine; that is the only other possibility. But even as a cultural transformation into the feminine is attempted, it appears to be seriously problematic; it is not without resistance that the unmasculine male is shunted off to the realm of the feminine, for though femininity is devalued as the repository of the unmasculine, its presence as a discernible nonmasculine essence/performance is required to maintain the boundary of masculinity, and "feminine essences" do not easily coincide with "male" bodies.

The male body, which is supposed to house masculine essence from the first time it is identified as male, is out of place in the realm of unmasculine. That body is a manifestation of confusion, a reminder of rejection, an arrogant affront to all that is good and true about men, real men, normal men, natural men. How could this "man" give up his natural power, his natural strength, his real self? Why is he rejecting what he should be, what I am?

If the male is neither masculine, nor feminine enough, what is he? He becomes a homosexual, a member of that relatively new species of creature, originally delineated by psychiatry, which does not simply engage in unmasculine behavior, but which has an essential, unmasculine essence; no positive essence of his own, mind you, but rather a negative essence, an absence of legitimate essence, and thus the absence of legitimate personhood.[29] But what is the response to a creature with an illegitimate essence, to a creature with the husk of a man but with the extremely present absence of masculinity? That depends entirely on the situatedness of the responder in the distribution of gender identities and personal identities.

The repressive sees and fears becoming *that,* and must distance himself from *that* by any means necessary, often overcompensating, revealing his repression through his obsession, sometimes through active malignancy—assaulting or killing or merely registering disgust at that which he hates embodied in that which he desires.[30]

The ignorant will dismiss *those* as not really human, creatures so unidentified that they do not merit the response given to genuine identities (whether positive or negative—even enemies have genuine, if hated, identities). *It* can be killed, can be beaten, can be played with, can be dismissed.

The heterosupremacist reactionary will raise the warning—*They* are dangerous! *They* are getting out of hand! *They* are here! *They* are threatening your homes, your churches, your families, your children! And in some sense the threat may be real; *they* really do reject many of the beliefs upon which the heterosupremacists' political and personal identities are maintained.

Fortunately, the logic of masculinity, like any other logic, is neither universal nor irresistibly stable. Not every individual classified as a male in this culture will be adequately represented in my sketchy characterization of masculine personhood. My characterization is not to be interpreted so much as an empirically accurate description of all men in this society as it is a description of the mythology of masculinity that informs all constructions of men, the masculine, the "self" in Western culture, and that which could threaten them. I do not claim that all heterosexual males are homophobic (although I do think that the vast majority of heterosexual males are heterosexist). While I describe three homophobic reactions to the identity threat represented by gay men (repression, abusive ignorant bigotry, political reactionism), these in no way exhaust the variety of male reactions.

Some men, though they hate and are sickened by gays, lack the bravado to do anything more about their hate than make private slurs. Others, particularly liberals, are tolerantly heterosexist; they have no "real" problem with gays provided they are discreet and replicate the model of conventional heterosexual morality and family. And then there is the rare, genuinely subversive heterosexual man, a kind of gender traitor himself, whose identity is not coextensive with his assignment as a man. Although comfortable with himself, he wouldn't mind being gay, or mind being a woman—those are not the categories by which he defines, or wants to define, his personhood.

Do not, however, take this as a disclaimer to the effect that homophobia is the exception, the out-of-nowhere, the unusual case. Heterosexism may be the father of homophobia, modeling in public what is done more blatantly in hiding, but hidden does not mean rare. Do not think that homophobes, even violent ones, are few and far between— occasional atavistics "suffering" from paleolithic conceptions of sex roles. Even though many instances of anti-gay/anti-lesbian crime go unreported due to fear of outing, lack of proof, fear of retaliation, or police hostility, evidence is accumulating that such crime is widespread and that violent attack is higher among gays and lesbians than for the population at large. In a recent Philadelphia study, 24 percent of gay men and 10 percent of lesbians *responding* said that they had been physically attacked—a victimization rate twice as high for lesbians and four times as high for gay men than for women and men in the urban population at large.[31] Economic threat and verbal assault are, of course, even more common.

The gender demographics of physical homophobic attack suggest something about the correlation between masculinity and homophobia. Consider the findings in a recent study on violence against lesbians and gays by Gary Comstock: 1) 94 percent of all attackers were male; 2) 99 percent of perpetrators who attacked gay men were male, while 83 percent of those who attacked lesbians were male; 3) while 15 percent of attacks on lesbians were made by women, only 1 percent of attacks on gay men were made by women.[32]

Homophobic violence seems to be predominantly a male activity. What is the relationship between homophobia and masculinity? Is the man who attacks gay men affirming or reaffirming, consciously or subconsciously, his own masculinity/heterosexuality and thus his own sense of self? How is masculinity implicated in homophobia?

I have suggested in this essay that one reading of homophobia is that queers pose a threat to (compulsory) masculinity and as such, pose a threat to men whose personhood is coextensive with their identity as men. Certainly, homophobia could not exist without the background assumptions of (heterosexist) masculine identity. There could be no fear or hatred of gays and lesbians if there were no concept of a proper gender identity and a proper sexual orientation. Masculinity assumes, essentializes, naturalizes, and privileges heterosexuality. A violation of heterosexuality can be seen as treachery against masculinity, which can register as an affront or threat to a man's core sense of self, a threat to his (male) identity. In this sense, homophobia requires masculinity (and femininity); it is necessarily parasitic on traditional categories of sex/gender identity. Homophobia is the malignant "correction" to a destabilizing deviation. Without gendered standards of identity, there could be nothing from which to deviate, and thus nothing to "correct."

If this reading is accurate, homophobia is not just a social prejudice (on the xenophobic/minoritarian model) that can be eliminated by education or tolerance training.[33] It will not be eliminated just by persuading people to be "more accepting." While these approaches may be helpful, they do not get at the basis of homophobia—binary gender systems and heterosexism. The only way to ensure that heterosexism and its virulent manifestation homophobia are genuinely eliminated is to eliminate the binary itself—challenge the assumption that one must be sexed or gendered to be a person. Eliminate the binary and it would be impossible to have heterosexism or homophobia, because hetero and homo would have no meaning. This does not mean humans would have to be "fused" into some androgynous entity ("androgyny" has no meaning without the binary). It means simply that identities would no longer be distributed according to anatomically based "sexes."

While this hope may seem utopian and may have theoretical problems of its own, it nonetheless suggests an approach to studies of masculinity that may be incommensurable with other approaches. When using the model of masculinity (and femininity) as a social construct that has no intrinsic interpretation, there seems to be little use in trying to reconstruct masculinity into more "positive" forms, at least as long as masculinity is somehow viewed as an intrinsically appropriate feature of certain bodies. To make masculinity "positive" could easily devolve into retracing the boundaries of appropriate behavior without challenging the compulsory nature of that behavior. Delving into mythology and folklore (along the lines of some of the men's movement models) to "rediscover" some archetypal masculine image upon which to base new male identities is not so much wrong or sexist as it is arbitrary. Discovering what it means, or should mean, to be a "real man" is an exercise in uselessness. A "real man" is nothing. A "real man" could be anything. This is not to say that searching through mythohistory for useful metaphors for living today is not useful. I believe that it is.[34] But such a search will never get anyone closer to being a "real man" or even to being just a "man." There is no such thing. Nor should there be.

For some of us who have been embattled our entire lives because our desires/performances/identities were "immorally" or "illegally" or "illegitimately" cross-coded with our anatomies, we fear the flight into "rediscovering" masculinity will be a repetition of what has gone before. Gendered epistemologies will only reproduce gendered identities. I personally do not want to be a "real man," or even an "unreal man." I want to be unmanned altogether. I want to evaluate courses of behavior and desire open to me on their pragmatic consequences, not on their appropriateness to my "sex." I want to delve into the wisdom of mythology, but without the prior restrictions of anatomy.

I want to betray gender.

Notes

1. I want to thank Larry May for his encouragement and editing suggestions throughout the writing of this paper. I also want to make it clear that although I think some of this essay is applicable to hatred and violence directed against lesbians (sometimes called lesbophobia), for the purposes of a volume specifically on masculinity I have deliberately (though not exclusively) focused on males and hatred and violence directed against gay males. Even with this focus, however, I am indebted to work on homophobia by lesbian researchers and theorists. In a future, more comprehensive project I will explore the oppression and marginalization of a wider variety of gender traitors.

2. Although the scope of this essay prevents a lengthy discussion, it should be pointed out that many male teachers and coaches call their students and team members "girls": to be playful, to be insulting, or to shame them into playing more roughly.

3. It should also be pointed out that gay men often use the word "girl" to refer to each other. In these cases, however, signifying a lack of masculinity is not registering insult. Often, it is expressing a sentiment of community—a community formed by the shared rejection of compulsory heterosexuality and compulsory forms of masculinity.

4. I deliberately sidestep the philosophical debate over the existence of a "self" in this discussion. While I am quite skeptical of the existence of any stable, core self, I do not think the argument in this paper turns on the answer to that problem. "Self" could simply be interpreted as a metaphor for social situatedness. In any case, I do not mean to suggest that subverting gender is a way to purify an essential human "self."

5. For work on Native American societies that do not operate with a simple gender binary, see Walter L. Williams, *The Spirit and the Flesh: Sexual Diversity in American Indian Culture* (Boston: Beacon Press, 1986) and Will Roscoe (ed.), *Living The Spirit: A Gay American Indian Anthology* (New York: St. Martin's Press, 1988).

6. For works on the social construction of gender and sexuality see: Judith Butler, *Gender Trouble: Feminism and the Subversion of Identity* (New York: Routledge, 1990); Michel Foucault, *Herculine Barbin: Being the Recently Discovered Memoirs of a Nineteenth Century French Hermaphrodite* (New York: Pantheon, 1980); Michel Foucault, *The History of Sexuality: Volume I, An Introduction* (New York: Vintage Books, 1980); Montique Wittig, *The*

Straight Mind and Other Essays (Boston: Beacon Press, 1992). I do wish to point out that the notion of being "socially constructed" is often simplistically treated—even by its proponents—as merely a radical form of socialization which denies any constitutive influence of biology. Social constructivism does not have to imply irrealism or metaphysical idealism, however. It is possible consistently to hold that characteristics of bodies, including behaviors and cognitive abilities, are biologically produced and constrained while still holding that the *meaning* of these biologically-based differences are socially interpreted. For example, while skin color and physiognomy are largely biologically generated features of bodies, *race* is a social interpretation of these biological variations. Similarly, to say that sex and gender are socially constructed is not to say that there are not biologically determined differences among bodies with regard to reproductive capacities, cognition, size, strength, and appearance. It is to say that these differences mean nothing in and of themselves, but only achieve meaning after being socially interpreted. I am currently working on a paper that navigates a have-it-all position between social constructivism and biological realism.

7. In the United States and many other countries, if a baby is born with anatomical genital features that do not easily lend themselves to a classification within the gender/sex system in place, they are surgically and hormonally altered to fit into the categories of male or female, girl or boy.

8. I am grateful to Bob Strikwerda for pointing out that none of these characteristics taken by itself is absolutely necessary to be perceived as masculine in contemporary U.S. culture (except perhaps heterosexuality). In fact, a man who possessed every characteristic would be seen as a parody.

9. I borrow the insightful term "gender treachery" from Margaret Atwood. In her brilliant dystopian novel, *The Handmaids' Tale* (Boston: Houghton Mifflin, 1986), set in a post-fundamentalist Christian takeover America, criminals are executed and hanged on a public wall with the name of their crime around their necks for citizens to see. Homosexuals bear the placard "gender traitor."

10. It doesn't matter if this rejection is "deliberate" or not in the sense of direct refusal. Any deviant behavior can be seen as treacherous unless perhaps the individual admits "guilt" and seeks a "cure" or "forgiveness."

11. Someone might ask: But why those people most *thoroughly* sexed rather than those most insecure in their sexuality? My point here is a broad one about the categories of gender. Even those people who are insecure in their sexuality will be laboring under the compulsory ideal of traditional binary gender identities.

12. "Queers"—the name itself bespeaks curiosity, treachery, radical unidentifiability, the uncategorized, perverse entities, infectious otherness.

13. See Gregory M. Herek, "On Heterosexual Masculinity: Some Psychical Consequences of the Social Construction of Gender and Sexuality," *American Behavioral Scientist*, vol. 29, no. 5, May/June 1986, 563–77.

14. For all these terms except "homohatred," see Gregory M. Herek, "Stigma, Prejudice, and Violence Against Lesbians and Gay Men," pp. 60–80, in J. C. Gonsiorek and J. D. Weinrich (eds.), *Homosexuality: Research Implications for Public Policy* (London: Sage Publications, Inc., 1991). For "homohatred," see Marshall Kirk and Hunter Madsen, *After the Ball: How*

America Will Conquer its Fear & Hatred of Gays in the 90's (New York: Penguin Books, 1989).

15. See Jacob Smith Yang's article in *Gay Community News*, August 18–24, vol. 19, no. 6, 1991, p. 1. The brutal July 4 murder of Paul Broussard sparked an uproar in Houston's queer community over anti-gay violence and police indifference. To "quell the recent uproar," Houston police undertook an undercover operation in which officers posed as gay men in a well-known gay district. Although police were skeptical of gays' claims of the frequency of violence, within one hour of posing as gay men, undercover officers were sprayed with mace and attacked by punks wielding baseball bats.

16. See Kirk and Madsen, p. 127. They mention the case of Rose Mary Denman, a United Methodist minister who was a vocal opponent of the ordinations of gays and lesbians until she eventually acknowledged her own lesbianism. Upon announcing this, however, she was defrocked. Kirk and Madsen quote a *New York Times* article that states: "In retrospect, she attributed her previous vehement stand against ordaining homosexuals to the effects of denying her unacknowledged lesbian feelings."

17. See John Money, *Gay, Straight and In-Between: The Sexology of Erotic Orientation* (Oxford: Oxford University Press, 1988), pp. 109–110.

18. See Suzanne Pharr, *Homophobia: A Weapon of Sexism* (Little Rock, AR: Chardon Press, 1988) and also Kirk and Madsen, *After The Ball*. The stereotypical story is one I have elaborated on from Kirk and Madsen's book, chapter 2.

19. See Herek, "On Heterosexual Masculinity . . .", especially pp. 572–573.

20. One can think of the typical scene where one boy challenges another boy to do something dangerous or cruel by claiming that if he does not do so, he is afraid—a sissy. Similarly, boys who are friends/peers of homophobes may be expected to engage in cruel physical or verbal behavior in order to appear strong, reliable, and most importantly of all, not faggots themselves. They know what happens to faggots.

21. See Herek, "On Heterosexual Masculinity . . ." p. 573.

22. See Celia Kitzinger, *The Social Construction of Lesbianism* (London: Sage Publications, Inc., 1987).

23. For example, in my own area of the country we have Rev. Don Wildmon's American Family Association, headquartered in Tupelo, Mississippi—an ultraconservative media watchdog group dedicated to the elimination of any media image not in keeping with right-wing Christian morality. Also, in Memphis, Tennessee, there is FLARE (Family Life America for Responsible Education Under God, Inc.), a group lobbying for Christian prayer in public schools, the elimination of sex education programs, and the installation of a "Family Life Curriculum" in public schools that would stress sexual abstinence and teach that the only form of morally acceptable sexual activity is married, heterosexual sex.

24. I borrow the term "boogeyfag" from David G. Powell's excellent unpublished manuscript, *Deviations of a Queen: Episodic Gay Theory*. Powell deconstructs California Congressman Robert Dornan's claim that "The biggest mass murderers in history are gay."

25. Gary David Comstock, *Violence Against Lesbians and Gay Men* (New York: Columbia University Press, 1991), p. 172.

26. For this analysis of masculinity and performance, I owe much to insights garnered from Judith Butler's article "Imitation and Gender Insubordiation," in Diana Fuss, *Inside/Out: Lesbian Theories, Gay Theories* (New York: Routledge, 1991).

27. I use the term "monster" here in a way similar to that of Donna Haraway in her essay "A Cyborg Manifesto: Science, Technology, and Socialist-Feminism in the Late Twentieth Century," reprinted in her book *Simians, Cyborgs, and Women: The Reinvention of Nature* (New York: Routledge, 1991). Haraway says: "Monsters have always defined the limits of community in Western imaginations. The Centaurs and Amazons of ancient Greece established the limits of the centred polis of the Greek male human by their disruption of marriage and boundary pollutions of the warrior with animality and woman" (p. 180). I loosely use "monster" in referring to homosexuality in the sense that the homosexual disrupts gender boundaries and must therefore be categorized into its own species so as to prevent destabilizing those boundaries.

28. Aquinas, for example, viewed the "vice of sodomy" as the second worst "unnatural vice," worse even than rape—a view echoed in contemporary legal decisions such as *Bowers v. Hardwick* (106 S. Ct. 2841, 1986), which upheld the criminal status of homosexuality. See Arthur N. Gilbert, "Conceptions of Homosexuality and Sodomy in Western History," in Salvatore J. Licata and Robert P. Peterson (eds.), *The Gay Past: A Collection of Historical Essays* (New York: Harrington Park Press, 1985), pp. 57–68.

29. On the creation of homosexuality as a category, see Foucault, *The History of Sexuality*.

30. In this sense: The repressive hates the species "homosexual," but nonetheless desires the body "man." It is only an historically contingent construction that desiring a certain kind of body "makes" you a certain kind of person, "makes" you have a certain kind of "lifestyle." Unfortunately, it is also true that being a certain "kind" of person can carry with it serious dangers, as is the case for homosexuals.

31. See Comstock, p. 55.

32. See Comstock, p. 59.

33. This is not to say that gays and lesbians are not often treated as a minority; good arguments have been made that they are. See Richard D. Mohr, "Gay Studies as Moral Vision," *Educational Theory*, vol. 39, no. 2, 1989.

34. In fact, I very much enjoy studies in applied mythology, particularly the work of Joseph Campbell. However, I am extremely skeptical about any application of mythology that characterizes itself as returning us to some primal experience of masculinity that contemporary culture has somehow marred or diminished. There is always the specter of essentialism in such moves.

PART FOUR

Romance and Marriage

7

Real Men

Hugh LaFollette

"Ah, for the good old days, when men were men and women were women." Men who express such sentiments long for the world where homosexuals were ensconced in their closets and women were sexy, demure, and subservient. That is a world well lost—though not as lost as I would like. More than a few men still practice misogyny and homophobia. The defects of such attitudes are obvious. My concern here is not to document these defects but to ask how real men, men who reject stereotypical male-female roles—men who are sensitive to the insights of feminism—should relate with women. In particular, how should men and women relate in intimate, sexually oriented, i.e., "romantic," relationships.

The Problem of Relationships

Intimate (close personal) relationships are relationships in which each person relates to the other as a unique individual whose interests she wishes to promote. Such relationships are exemplified by care, trust, sensitivity, and mutual support. In the best of circumstances, intimacy is difficult to establish and arduous to maintain. Even when we have the noblest of intentions, we often despoil our closest relationships. We know that from experience. The task of the philosopher is to explain why this is so, hoping thereby that we can learn how to overcome these difficulties.

Relationships falter for any number of reasons. For instance, intimate relationships can be neither established nor maintained unless the partners know and trust one another. Unless they know each other, they cannot promote each other's needs. Unless they trust each other, their fear of being hurt will circumscribe communication. Moreover, their interests—although they need not be identical—must be sufficiently overlapping so neither continuous conflict nor absolute acquiescense is inevitable.

Even when two people know, love, and trust one another and have reasonably similar interests, external conditions can undermine intimacy. Job pressures, family illness, or difficulties with children make regular and sustained conversations between partners difficult. Without intimate communication to nourish them, they will grow apart. Small troubles evolve into big problems. Big problems become insurmountable hurdles. Relationships are dashed on the rocks of miscommunication and misunderstanding.

Other relationships suffer because the partners are so desirous of intimacy that they squelch their own interests. For instance, Joan may strive to make Betty happy, even if she (Joan) is thereby unhappy. In and of itself there is nothing wrong with Joan's behavior. Altruism of some form must infuse every successful relationship. But it is far too easy for well-intentioned altruism to run amuck, particularly between partners who are not honest with one another. Each may accommodate to the other so often that she becomes angry. Each may accommodate so often that she does not know what she really wants.

These are substantial hurdles for anyone wishing to establish or preserve an intimate relationship. But these are especially problematic for a man and a woman—and perhaps even more so for a man and a woman engaged in a romantic relationship. We are products of a pervasively sexist culture. The sexism in which we were all acculturated is especially difficult to escape. It permeates our society. It pervades our attitudes. It haunts and—if allowed to run wild—devours our heterosexual relationships.

If the sexist culture had merely erected legal obstacles to equality, the battle against sexism would be relatively easy. Legal obstacles, being visible, can be attacked. The women's movement has made considerable effort to remove the most onerous legal barriers to equality. It has had considerable success.[1]

The primary engines of sexism, however, are veiled, subconscious forces. The dominant culture promulgates sexist stereotypes that pervade television, movies, books, and music. These embody well-defined gender roles that infuse the relationships children see at home, at school, and when visiting their friends. They establish expectations to which all of us are subject, images to which all of us respond—to some degree or another. They shape our desires, interests, and perspectives, thereby making informed, unbiased choice difficult if not impossible.

For instance, as men we are encouraged to be determined, strong, and perhaps even aggressive. We are taught to be interested in math and science, to crave success, to be competitive. We are discouraged from developing interests or personality traits that are deemed "feminine," e.g., an interest in children or a tendency to cry. Conversely, women are taught to fear math, to enjoy literature and art. They are encouraged to be giving, supportive, soft, maternal, and if need be, subservient.

Of course not every man or woman was shaped in precisely these ways or to this extent. But even children reared in relatively liberated, non-sexist homes are shaped, at least in part, by these dominant cultural stereotypes. The effects of such shaping cannot be obliterated. Those of us reared in a pervasively sexist culture will never be entirely free from those early influences. Even those of us sensitive to the insights of feminism will still hear sexist voices from the past. They inevitably modulate our interpersonal interactions, even as we seek to free ourselves from their influence.

Consider. Trust is important in intimate relationships. Trust involves, among other things, trusting that your partner will not intentionally harm you or your interests. Such trust requires vulnerability: I cannot trust you unless I am willing to be vulnerable with you— unless I am willing to put myself in a position where you can harm my interests.

The influences of our sexist culture make trust difficult for most men. We can "trust" our bankers and we can "trust" our colleagues: we are good at institutionalized, impersonal trust. However, our fear of being really vulnerable, of personally trusting another, has often made close relationships difficult. The cardinal sin for men is to be weak, vulnerable. We are supposed to be made of iron, spartans all. We were told we must know what to do, or, short of that, to act as if we did, since we must be "kings in our castles." We may occasionally be weak with our spouses; that is acceptable. But such weakness must be contained; most assuredly it must not be public. In short, men dominated by these standard images of masculinity cannot establish relationships as close as can those who are willing to be vulnerable.

Even those of us who are relatively free of these images, those of us who are willing to be emotional, to cry, to be vulnerable, are not free for our sexist upbringing. We often find—at the most inopportune times—that our fathers' urgings "to be strong" dominate the more informed voices that tell us to be vulnerable, to be a human being. Sexism harms men as well as women. It makes genuine, intimate, and fulfilling heterosexual relationships exceedingly difficult—as if they were not difficult enough on their own.

Or suppose you and I have a long-term relationship. At some point in our lives, I become dissatisfied with my job; I want to seek employment elsewhere. You, on the other hand, are pleased with your employer and are convinced you will have difficulty finding similarly rewarding employment in the town to which I wish to move.

Obviously there are any number of considerations we might think relevant. If we are especially concerned about financial security, perhaps we will consider the options that have the highest combined salary. Or we might concern ourselves with issues of "fairness"—you have had a job you liked for ten years, now it is my turn to have a job I like. Perhaps we might look at other amenities of the respective communities; the type of neighborhood in which we can raise our children, the climate, the nature of the public schools, or the proximity to ailing parents.

Regardless of what considerations we bring to bear, our final decision will be shaped by our desires, interests, and attitudes, and these were formed by the sexist culture in which we grew up and currently live—a culture not of our choosing. Consciously or unconsciously I may expect you to be willing, if not eager, to move. I may be uncomfortable baldly asserting that my male interests are superior. I may be uncomfortable even entertaining such thoughts—after all, I am supposedly liberated. So perhaps I find, instead, some way to rationalize my choice. You, on the other hand, may want to remain with your current employer, but the image of a dutiful spouse standing by her man may lead you to suppress your interests and to acquiesce. Perhaps neither of us will succumb to these urges, but they are likely operative, even if in attenuated form. And, although they do not dictate the outcome of our deliberations, they will likely affect it.

These urgings—what I like to think of as an internal gender police— will likewise influence our decisions about child care. Suppose we decide (perhaps on good medical grounds) to breastfeed our infant. You will inevitably be required to take additional responsibility for child care, at least for the first six months. It may then be all too easy for us to use this as an excuse for letting you continue to be the primary caregiver once the child has been weaned—after all, our upbringing has likely "convinced" us, albeit subconsciously, that this is the way it should be since, after all, you are better with children.

Escaping the Sexist Culture

If both of us wish to minimize the detrimental effects of social conditioning, we must be especially attuned to the influence our upbringing exerts over us. Then we must contain those influences. That is easier said than done. For *ex hypothesi* the sexist culture shaped not only our first-order desires—for example, the desire to be a successful professional or to play football—but also our second-order desires and abilities: our values and our ability to reason. These second-order desires govern how we evaluate and subsequently modify our first-order desires. They thereby influence the contours of the people we become.

If we wish to free ourselves from these culturally induced desires, we must first identify them. That is difficult since they are amorphous, indefinite. To the extent that we can identify them, we can do so only after careful and sustained self-examination. Consequently, we cannot easily excise them nor restrain their undesirable effects.

The difficulty of identifying and controlling these impulses has led some women to separate themselves from the sexist culture.[2] Separatists think that only by starting a new culture—constituted by new ideas, new beliefs, and new ways of relating—can they escape the mental bonds with which the sexist culture has shackled us. It is easy to see why separatists might reach this conclusion.

I am inclined to believe, however, that we cannot escape the power of the culture by separating ourselves from it. The same forces that control those of us who remain will operate on those who leave. Since the culture perpetuates itself by shaping desires, values, and attitudes, removing ourselves from the culture after these have been formed will not free us from their sway. Being physically removed from the dominant culture may even make it more difficult to identify and control these forces. Consider, for instance, an individual reared in a pervasively racist culture. Merely moving to an area of the country devoid of overt racists will not purge her of racist sentiments, although it may remove her from circumstances that elicit them. The best way to eradicate racism and sexism is to transform the dominant culture that formed and sustains them.

Perhaps, though, the separatists are correct. Perhaps we can change the dominant culture only by disengaging from it. But I would like to think them mistaken. Some of us men deeply want intimate relationships with women and would suffer a substantial loss were such relationships impossible. Some of us think women have a perspective and emotional maturity from which we can learn a great deal. Some of us sexually prefer women. It is not that we think homosexuality or bisexuality wrong, immoral, or inferior. Rather we are sexually attracted to women and think it would be more effort than it is worth to try to change our orientation. Needless to say, I cannot discuss separatism in any detail here. Consequently, I will assume for the remainder of the paper that separatism is not the only way to cope with the influences of our sexist culture. I will further assume that non-sexist male-female romantic relationships are possible, albeit difficult.

We return to the original question: how do we establish intimate heterosexual relationships within a sexist culture without succumbing to that culture's detrimental influences? We cannot immediately destroy the culture's power, nor can we eradicate its influence. We can, however, contain that influence and control its most detrimental effects.[3] However, deciding that we should rid ourselves of our sexist baggage is just the first step. We must also find a strategy for doing so. There is no algorithm for freeing ourselves from sexist stereotypes, no potion we can take to make us immune to this devastating mental virus. Yet we must find ways to control its symptoms if we wish to establish genuinely intimate relationships.

Equity

Women who choose to remain in the dominant culture, yet wish to free themselves of its sexist influence, may resort to the powerful moral tools of rights, obligations, and equality. It is easy to see why. For millennia women were systematically deprived of rights and legal standing. They could not vote, hold personal property, earn a fair wage, hold public office, or serve on a jury. The women's movement has fought to gain legal recognition for women by asserting that women had *rights* to social and political goods. That is exactly what women's advocates should have done. Rights are the appropriate medium of exchange within the impersonal political arena.

Given the power of rights to battle injustice and mistreatment within the political arena, women are naturally inclined to appeal to rights and equity to battle mistreatment in personal relationships. All too often women do the bulk of the work around the house, care for the children, etc. Even when some male partners do an equal portion of the work, that is sufficiently unusual to be worthy of comment. Such men are said to be "helping" their mates—which assumes, of course, that housework and child care are women's responsibility, work in which these great-hearted men share. Despite some positive changes in the treatment of women, this still captures standard practice within most households in the United States.

If I were a woman, I would be ticked off. Men *should* carry their share of housework. Something is fundamentally wrong if they don't. The question is: How should men understand and describe our responsibilities? Do we have an obligation to do an equal portion of the work? Do our partners have rights that we violate if we don't? It is tempting to say that we each have a right not to have to carry more than our "fair share" of the load. However, that, I think, is a grave mistake. Although talk of rights and equity is appropriate within the political domain, it is anathema to personal relationships.

Traditional wisdom says otherwise; it holds that successful personal relationships must be equitable. However, a growing minority of psychologists disagree. In a series of studies Margaret Clark found that although people expect equity in impersonal (exchange or trade) relationships, they do not expect it in personal (what she calls "communal") relationships.[4] Within exchange relationships, she claims, we are expected to benefit those who have benefited us. Such relationships continue only as long as each reciprocally benefits the other. For instance, an employer and employee exchange money for labor. As long as each receives what she or he considers fair, the relationship will likely continue.

Within close personal relationships, however, people are expected to respond to each other's needs—not to reciprocate benefits. More strongly, they are expected *not* to reciprocate benefits. For instance, if I try to return a benefit from someone with whom I have a communal relationship, I may thereby destroy the relationship—even though I would be acting exactly as expected had I been in an exchange relationship.

Moreover, we must remember that the studies which suggest that equity is important for interpersonal relationships are correlative: people claim to be satisfied in relationships they deem equitable; dissatisfied in those that aren't. That may well be true. However, that does not show that people are satisfied *because* the relationship is equitable. It may well be that they deem it equitable because they are satisfied. Perhaps many people in close relationships never consciously consider if theirs is equitable, although, if asked, they surmise that it must be since they are satisfied. Conversely, if one partner is dissatisfied, she will likely seek the cause of the dissatisfaction. In the current ideological environment, being exploited seems a plausible candidate.

Even if this does not account for all of the correlation—even if we grant that perceived inequity will lead to relationship dissatisfaction—there are two divergent explanations of why this is so. According to the first, an individual enters personal relationships *in order to obtain* specified benefits from the other but is also willing to give in return: that is, she wants an equitable exchange. When or if the exchange is no longer equitable—when the relationship ceases to be a good bargain—she is dissatisfied.

According to the second interpretation—which I endorse—people enter close personal relationships not in search of a good bargain but a good friend. Both partners expect to promote their intimate's interests, to respond to her needs. Nonetheless, given each person's belief that intimates respond to the needs of people for whom they care, it is not surprising if each expects something approximating equity.

Let me explain. We are in a relationship. You have settled views about how intimates should treat each other, namely, that neither person will take advantage of her intimate; moreover, you expect each will spontaneously satisfy one other's needs. Finally, you plausibly assume that any two people will have *roughly* equivalent needs and *roughly* equivalent abilities to satisfy another's needs.

Given these beliefs, you would reasonably expect that you and your partner will benefit and give *roughly* the same. Now suppose the relationship is notably inequitable; that is, that you have contributed much and received little. You will understandably infer that I do not really love you. Equity is the likely result of a close relationship. It is not the relationship's goal.

Still others have argued not that successful relationships *are* equitable, but that they should be. On this view, inequitable relationships are not merely unsatisfying (though usually they are); rather, they are unjust. People who take advantage of their intimates have acted unjustly or immorally, they have wronged or violated the rights of their intimates.[5] At one level this claim seems eminently reasonable, even indisputable. If Jeff lets Patty carry a full-time job, do all of the housework, and completely care for the children, while he spends his evenings watching television and his weekends golfing, then Jeff has wronged Patty. What more can be said? As it turns out, a great deal.

Doubtless one partner's behavior in a "personal" relationship may be so exploitative that we can only conclude that she has acted unjustly. On this point most people will agree. That does not show, however, that close relationships are best evaluated by standards of justice or by an appeal to rights. Rather, we should conclude that such relationships are properly evaluated by criteria of justice precisely because they are no longer close or personal. If one person regularly ignores the interests of the other, the relationship is not, properly speaking, intimate. It may have trappings of close relationships: the people may spend time together or even live together. They may have fond things to say about each other. However, these trappings in an abusive relationship are not the hallmarks of intimacy but of mere familiarity.

Let's look at the flip side of the issue. Even if rights managed to protect us from gross abuse from our intimates, they would still fail to provide what we want and expect from intimates. Rights are both too stringent and too lenient. Rights are too stringent because our friends have a license to treat us in ways we would not tolerate from strangers. Close friends may borrow from us without asking; in fact, we expect them to do so. A close friend, for instance, may enter my office in the evening to borrow a book; I would feel free to do likewise. Or, a friend may plausibly expect me to help her cope with personal trauma, even though the cost to me might be substantial; I would expect her to do the same. Or a depressed friend might become angry at me in ways I would not tolerate from a stranger. I assume I could do likewise. That is just what we expect from our good friends.[6] In these cases talk of rights is simply out of place. It does not capture the nature of the relationship. A friend who borrows a book without asking has not violated my property rights; nor have I waived my rights. A friend who interrupts me to talk about her problems has not invaded my privacy; she has done what I would have expected.[7]

On the other hand, we have higher expectations of our intimates than of strangers. We expect our intimates to care. That is something rights cannot provide. If I have a right, it is merely a claim that others accord me some minimal level of decent treatment. I do not have a right that others care for me or trust me or love me.

Additionally we also expect our intimates to have "better" motives than strangers. We expect strangers to respect our rights and to fulfill their obligations to us. We expect them, for example, not to steal our property (or to steal anyone else's, for that matter) or hit us over the head or kill us. But we will not settle for abstract respect from our friends; we want personal affirmation and affection.

Imagine how repugnant it would be to have a spouse or friend who *merely* respected us. Consider, "Don't worry, honey, I will fulfill my conjugal duties to you even though I do not want to." Or, "Sure, we will talk this evening; I realize I am obliged to do so." Such behavior makes a mockery of the relationship. We do not want our friends motivated by a sense of justice, but by the desire to be with us, to talk with us, to care for us, and to promote our interests.[8]

Of course sometimes the fact that you love someone and desire to satisfy their interests may lead you to do something you do not, for other reasons, particularly want to do at that moment. Patty may not want to listen to Jeff's problems right *now*. But she may do so because she loves him. That is rather different, however, from listening to him because she is obliged to do so. Of course intimates may occasionally be motivated by a sense of duty; perhaps that is unavoidable. But duty should not become a relationship's staple. If it does, our relationship is transformed from a close relationship into an exchange relationship. And an exchange relationship, no matter how good, can never satisfy our longing for love and personal affirmation that an intimate relationship provides.

Nonetheless, someone might say, considerations of justice must be operative in the background of personal relationships, even if they are not invoked or explicitly considered. That is true in one sense, namely, that people might appeal to considerations of justice when the relationship is seriously inequitable. But that does not show that those considerations are operative in well-functioning relationships; still less does it show that they should be.

In fact, I think that appealing to or even conceiving of our personal relationships in terms of rights is to misconstrue them and will likely subvert them. If we begin to construe our personal relationships in terms of justice or rights we will see our partner's interests as limitations on us (as we would in impersonal relationships) rather than as interests we wish to promote (as we should in personal relationships).

Rights talk is intended to govern interactions between strangers, between people who do not care for each other and who may even be in overt conflict. Thus Patty's right to property limits Jeff's ability to use that property, even if he wants or needs it. Jeff's right to life limits Patty's options; Patty cannot swing her new bat in an area occupied by Jeff's head. Rights tell us what we cannot do to each other. They thereby emphasize—or create—distance between us. Consequently, if in our personal relationships we begin to think in terms of rights, we begin to think about the other as placing limitations on us. We begin to ask: "What *must* I do for my intimate?" rather than "What *can* I do for them?" Thoughts of justice or rights constrain personal relationships.

None of this should be taken to suggest that people in personal relationships never, in fact, think it terms of rights, justice, or equality. Certainly we do. Given Western civilization's preoccupation with rights it would be surprising were it otherwise. What I am suggesting is that we would be better off if we didn't; if, instead, intimates conceptualized and dealt with their differences as two people who care about one another rather than as two people who must treat each other justly.

Consider a situation where we have an apparent clash of interests. We are trying to decide, for example, which car to purchase, where to take our vacation, or where to live. If we judge our relationship by standards of justice or rights, each of us will likely become preoccupied with our rights and our responsibilities. If there is no obvious solution to our "conflict," we will likely compromise. Compromises over important issues, however, rarely satisfy either person. Each of us will feel we sacrificed to the relationship.

Suppose, instead, that we focus on our mutual care, on the fact that I take an interest in you and you in me. I want to promote your interests as well as my own; you want to promote mine as well as yours. If we can conceive of our differences in these ways, there is no straightforward way to identify a conflict of interest between us.

Of course this does not eradicate our differences. The shift in perspective does not make disagreements vanish the way some dime store novels might suggest. It does, however, change the way we view those differences, the parameters within which we make a decision. Thus, I may recognize that my interest in you is more important than my interest in buying a new Prelude. Or you may decide that your interest in me is greater than your interest in visiting Orlando.

Even if this maneuver does not result in a quick solution, it will encourage us to consider alternative solutions that might satisfy us both, rather than settling for a compromise that satisfies neither. If we are intimates we will benefit from the resulting decision. We will each understand that our interests in ourselves and one another will be advanced. So considerations of justice, though they may in some sense lie in the background of personal relationships, are best ignored by parties within them.

Finally, if we emphasize love and care rather than rights and equity, we will be better able to cope with some of the effects of our sexist culture. At least that is what I argue in the next section.

Constraining the Sexist Influences

How, then, can we establish intimate relationships that limit sexist influences without relying on equality or rights? If we are sensitive to the insights of feminism we likely need not worry about controlling overtly sexist sentiments—presumably we do not openly advocate keeping women "barefoot and pregnant." (One who openly advocates *that* view will have no interest in limiting the effects of sexism.) For us the principal obstacles to non-sexist relationships arise from subconscious attitudes and from institutionalized practices that sustain them. Long-established practices make it all too easy for us to fall into sexist patterns of relating. Liberated partners must be cognizant of these patterns and must take steps to ensure they do not mindlessly fall into them.

Consider, for example, a common occurrence: a couple meets early in college and marries (or establishes a long-term relationship). The woman quits school and finds a job to support her man, all the while assuming she will return to school herself after he finds permanent employment.

He graduates and finds a job; she returns to college to finish her degree—unless, of course, they have had a child in the meantime, which will further delay her return to school. When she finishes, he has a two or more year "jump" on her in the job market. Thus, he likely makes more money than she does. If an opportunity later arises to relocate for a better position, they will likely move to advance his career, since he is already better established economically. Having moved, she now seeks new employment, putting her still further behind him in the competition for jobs. Their future is writ: he has become the breadwinner; she has become the little woman dependent on him.

Sensitive couples must be alert to these possibilities and must work to constrain them. However, talk of rights will not serve them well in this situation. It would be difficult to say where, in the above-cited scenario, that the woman's rights were violated; each decision seems reasonable. If, however, the partners emphasize their mutual care, they should act to ensure they do not get locked into this pattern, no matter how "reasonable" it seems. They must ensure that her opportunities are not limited. For instance, both might go to school part-time. Or perhaps he could guarantee that she will finish school and find suitable employment before he furthers his career. A man should act in these ways because he cares for his partner. That is how she should expect him to act—not because she has a right that he do so, but because she knows he cares. People who care for one another do not act in ways that close off options for the other. In short, in situations where both parties recognize the tendency for sexist institutions to direct them down pre-established gender paths, they must find ways to route themselves in more productive directions.

What happens, though, if one of the parties thinks the other is subject to sexist stereotypes in ways she does not recognize? Consider this most troubling form of the case. A woman, reared in a very traditional home, maintains the conviction that her husband should "rule the home." What should she—and her spouse—do? Should they merely let her maintain this conviction unchallenged? I think not. The woman *should* try to alter these beliefs, even if she is comfortable with them and even if she thinks it would be difficult to change them. For, if she blindly accedes to her husband's judgments, she is effectively abandoning her autonomy. This is a remnant of the sexist culture she should not tolerate.

A caring spouse should likewise urge her to change, even if she does not want to. Moreover, he should act in ways that will help her change. Doing so inevitably involves elements of paternalism—and paternalism within intimate relationships is always risky. On a rights' view, paternalism is not merely risky; it is absolutely prohibited. Yet I think that to exclude paternalism in such cases, especially since the goal is to free the woman from undue sexist influences, is to damage her and the relationship. If she always accedes to his interests and preferences, then they are not on sufficiently level footing to have a genuine relationship. Thus, the man should not permit his partner to be dependent on his judgment. That, I think, is not only unobjectionable, it is the only loving option.

This should not be taken as an across-the-board endorsement of paternalism. For as I noted, unconstrained paternalism of men toward their female partners is a sexist rut we must avoid. The only circumstances where it is permissible are in dramatic situations like those just described. In other, seemingly parallel, circumstances, paternalism is clearly out of order. For instance, I think relatively liberated people may legitimately leave remnants of our sexist upbringing in place. After all, we cannot plausibly eliminate all of them in one generation. Moreover, other effects might be alterable, but only by making efforts that "cost" more than they are worth.

Consider Ralph, a twenty-year-old man who is preparing for a career in mathematics. His father was a mathematician who imbued him with a love for math. Perhaps it is a shame the father influenced Ralph in this direction. Perhaps, with different parents, Ralph would have considered being a nurse, an accountant, an elementary school teacher, or a lawyer. But the fact is, he loves math. For him to try to alter his desires because he recognizes that, had other parents reared him he might have chosen differently, would be ludicrous. Of course if the parents had wanted him to become a criminal he should try to change (although I suspect he would have trouble doing so). But as long as it is a worthwhile and personally satisfying line of work, there is nothing wrong should he pursue math as a career. Likewise, there would be nothing wrong if Ralph decided he wanted to be a nurse. It is up to Ralph.

The problem becomes stickier, though, if we imagine a similar situation that many women face. Imagine a twenty-year-old woman completing her training to be an elementary school teacher. Although there is absolutely nothing wrong with her chosen career—it is a noble profession indeed—she likely developed her interest in teaching young children because of the gender roles into which she was inculcated. Perhaps she would have selected the same career had she been reared in a non-sexist culture; perhaps not. We will never know. Although she might have had different interests and desires, she is now the person whose first-order interests were shaped by her sexist upbringing. Under such circumstances she may decide that it would be counterproductive to try to develop different career interests. She might determine that she could not alter those interests. Or perhaps she might reason that she could alter her interests only by changing "who she is." She could diminish her desire to teach elementary school only by diminishing her interests in young children. That is something she does not want to do.

The woman does nothing wrong if she continues her preparation for teaching elementary school. Even though she (and Ralph) realize they might have pursued different careers had their upbringing been different, each decides that the cost of trying to alter their interests is either impossible, unnecessary, or imprudent.

If we are partners with a woman facing such a dilemma, it would be foolish *and* paternalistic to try to change her desires, even though these desires were largely formed by her sexist upbringing. (Of course if *she* wishes to change them, then her partner should support her in whatever way possible.) For, although the culture shaped her first-order desire to be a teacher, her second-order judgment is that her first-order desire need not be changed. If, under the circumstances, her male partner were to force her to change her career plans, it would be unacceptably paternalistic.[9] Notice, though, this case is relevantly different from the previous case in which I endorsed paternalism. There what was at issue was not some first-order desire, but rather, an all-pervasive second-order desire, which, if allowed to persist, would diminish if not eliminate her ability to make informed decisions.

Experiments in Relating

Abandoning talk of rights, equity, and egalitarianism may be especially frightening for men and women who want to relate in non-sexist ways. We all know how people encased in rights are supposed to relate—our entire culture is based on such ways of relating. We have brilliant models of people claiming their rights, demanding that they be treated justly or equitably. But, if we abandon sexist role models and refuse to build a relationship on rights, then we must establish new ways of relating. What are those new ways? We may be tempted to assume there is a preferred way of relating, a way we only need find. There is, however, nothing to find. There is no predetermined way of relating waiting to be discovered. There are no models we can emulate. We must *create* successful ways of relating through experiments in relating. We must try various arrangements, styles, and patterns, and we must critically evaluate our efforts. We must revise our efforts in light of that evaluation. There is no other way to have successful heterosexual intimate relationships. There is no well-trodden path for us to follow.

Conclusion

Having a close heterosexual relationship is difficult for those who seek to escape the constraints of sexist stereotypes. If such relationships are possible, it is only through the concerted efforts of both partners to identify and excise the sexist remnants. But the attempts to free ourselves from sexist bonds is a path rutted and full of brambles, ready to trip or ensnare us. For although we must regularly scrutinize our heterosexual relationships to ensure they are (relatively) free of sexist influence, we should not constantly scrutinize them. Constant analysis of ourselves and our relationships will make our actions stiff, ingenuine. Love involves spontaneously responding to the needs of our intimates. That is something we cannot do if we are constantly assessing our actions, motives, and relationships. We may expend so much energy ensuring that we have a non-sexist relationship that we do not have a relationship at all: we do not talk about things that are important; we cannot enjoy each other's company.

Self-reflection certainly plays an important role for humans; it is crucial for healthy personal relationships. It allows us to critically evaluate and subsequently modify our actions so they are more meaningful and productive. But its value can be fully achieved only if we are already active, if we already have a life worth evaluating. To put a twist on the well-known Socratic slogan: "the unlived life is not worth examining." Meaningful self-reflection is important. But it can all too easily become the purpose of the relationship, especially when people are on a holy crusade to excise the demons of sexism.[10]

Notes

1. I am well aware, however, that women have not made the legal and economic strides some politicians would have us believe. See Susan Faludi's *Backlash: The Undeclared War Against American Women* (New York: Crown Publishers, 1991).

2. For a philosophically sophisticated defense of separatism, and an account of a separatist ethic, see Sarah Lucia Hoagland's *Lesbian Ethics* (Palo Alto, CA: Institute of Lesbian Studies, 1988).

3. Perhaps eventually we can destroy all remnants of sexism. But doing so will take generations. For those of us who wish to have heterosexual relationships *now*, what can or will happen in a century is of little help. We must deal with the fact that we live in a sexist culture and that each of us at least partly embodies that culture.

4. "Perceptions of exploitation in communal and exchange relationships," *Journal of Social and Personal Relationships* 2, 403–18 (1985); "Record-keeping in two types of relationships," *Journal of Personality and Social Psychology* 47, 549–57 (1984); "Interpersonal attraction in exchange and communal relationships" *Journal of Personality and Social Psychology* 37, 12–24 (1979).

5. Marilyn Friedman, "Justice Among Friends," American Philosophical Association, Eastern division (1986). See Chapter 5 of her book, *What are Friends For? Feminism, Personal Relationships, and Moral Theory* (New York: Cornell University Press, 1993).

6. Perhaps the reader is not comfortable with the particular illustrations provided. Perhaps, you do not want *anyone* taking your books without permission. Or perhaps you do not want *anyone* to get angry with you—even if he or she is a friend. These examples, though, are just that: examples. My point is merely that there are some things that intimates can do without explicit permission—actions that, if performed by a stranger, would constitute a violation of your rights.

7. If I discovered that a good friend did not call when she desperately needed my help because she did not want to violate my privacy . . . I would be upset. Among other things, I would doubt whether our friendship was as important to her as it was to me.

8. In this section I draw heavily from John Hardwig's "Should Women Think in Terms of Rights," *Ethics* (1984).

9. This may be one more casualty of our sexist culture. In a completely non-sexist culture, intimates might well be justified in acting paternalistically toward their partners—at least in some cases. After all, we assume our

intimates *really do* wish to promote our best interests; likely, too, they know what those interests are. But, given the tendency of males to dominate, paternalism should be avoided in all but the most extreme cases.

10. I would like to thank the editors for their encouragement and criticism of an early draft of this paper.

8

Do Black Men Have a Moral Duty to Marry Black Women?

Charles W. Mills

It is a measure of the continuing social distance between the races that the average white liberal, I am sure, would automatically assume that only a racist could think that the answer to this question is anything but an obvious "No!" The answer may, of course, still be "No," but it might not be quite so obvious. At any rate, I want to suggest that this issue—a major point of contention in the black community for decades, particularly among black women—is worthy of philosophical investigation. What arguments could there be for such a duty? On what axiological foundation would it be based? How strong would it be?

I

Let me begin with some brief remarks about the framing of the question itself. It is not just a particularistic variant of the general "Do all people have a duty to marry within their race?" because I think that the answer to *this* question is obviously "No." In other words, as will become clearer below, I am claiming that the differential social status of subordinated and dominant races, especially blacks and whites, generated *moral* asymmetries, so that whereas the claim, e.g., that "whites should only marry whites" *will* in general be based on philosophically uninteresting racist reasons, the case for black endogamy is (at least in some versions) more respectable.

135

Some other points. (i) Because of the ideological symbolism of marriage as an institution, and the material property considerations involved, this will be the special target of critics of interracial relationships. But many of the arguments against such unions would also be made (and hold as well or as badly) for common-law cohabitation, or just long-term relationships in general (or, for the most militant opponents, even short-term relationships and one-night stands). (ii) I focus on black men/white women relationships rather than also including black women/white men relationships because of another set of asymmetries: that in a sexist society, it is the economically privileged male who usually gets to choose; that most interracial marriages *are* of the black male/white female variety; and that it is this kind which has historically stirred most controversy in the black community. (Since white men have historically had sexual access to black women, the motivations involved are usually significantly different in such cases.) (iii) Finally, it should be noted that though I have put the question in the strong, and positive, form, it is sometimes the case that what opponents really have in mind is the weaker (in the sense of ruling out less), but more pointed, *negative* injunction that black men should (above all) not marry *white* women. Other "women of color" may sometimes be deemed acceptable, or at least less unacceptable.

II

That there could be such antipathies in the black community will come as a revelation to many whites, who will, of course, be used to thinking of the prohibitions going the other way. The famous line challenging would-be integrationists, after all, was always "But would you let one marry your daughter?" Indeed in the biracial coalitions of the civil rights movements, both communist and liberal, of the 1930s–1960s, acceptance of such relationships was often seen as a kind of ultimate test of good faith, a sign of whether or not whites had genuinely overcome their racist socialization.

This final intimacy (as the Klan warned: let 'em in the classroom and they'll end up in the bedroom) has assumed such significance because of the deep connection between racism and sex. Various theories have been put forward to explain white racism: that it is just "primordial" ethnocentrism writ large and backed by the differential technological and economic power of the European conquest (so *all* human groups would have been equally racist had they gotten the chance); the "culturalist" explanations that tie it, more specifically, to militant Christianity's *jihad* against non-European infidels and heathens, and the Manichaean white/good black/evil color symbolism in many European languages, particularly English; Marxist economic explanations that see it basically as an ideological rationalization of expansionist colonial capitalism (so that a naive ethnocentrism, and admitted cultural predispositions, would easily have been *overcome* had it not been for the need to justify conquest, expropriation, and enslavement); and psycho-sexual explanations focusing on the anal and genital regions, with their powerful associations of desire and shame, and their perceived link with dirt, blackness, and the dark body. But all theories have had to come to grips—some more, some less, successfully—with the peculiar horror that black male/white female couplings have aroused in the European imagination, the fear, as in *Othello,* that "Even now . . . an old black ram/Is tupping your white ewe."[1]

In the United States in particular, there were widespread laws against what used to be (and sometimes still) called "miscegenation." And for many of the thousands of black men lynched in the post-Civil War decades, the pretext was the accusation of raping a white woman, with prolonged torture and castration often preceding the final killing (the fortunate then being hung or shot, the unfortunate being roasted alive). The fact that a black man with a white wife could gain conservative support for a seat on the Supreme Court (including backing from such well-known historical champions of the black civil-rights struggle as Senator Strom Thurmond of South Carolina) is an indicator that times have somewhat changed in the intervening century.[2] But it is by no means the case that such unions are now routine, raising only the occasional eyebrow. As late as the 1960s, in deference to white sensibilities, media representations shied away from depictions of interracial sex.[3] Even the "trail-blazing" 1967 integrationist drama *Guess Who's Coming to Dinner* did not dare to show "Super-Negro" Sidney Poitier exchanging anything more than a chaste kiss (and in the safely diminished frame of a cab's rearview mirror) with white fiancée Katharine Houghton,[4] and, as William Shatner recently revealed in his autobiography, *Star Trek's* boast that it had the "first interracial kiss" on television was actually false, real lip contact between Captain Kirk (boldly going where no white man had gone before—on television, that is) and Uhura (Nichelle Nichols) being avoided so as not to offend white viewers.[5] Many pornography catalogs have a speciality section of black-on-white videos where "big black studs meet blonde sluts," (How do I know this?, you casually inquire; a friend of a friend, I quickly reply), a testimony to the familiar Freudian point that revulsion and attraction often co-exist, or even merge. So for many this is truly, as some have called it, "the last taboo," and in a world where we're trying to eliminate racism, it would seem that interracial unions should be welcomed as a sign of progress.

Yet many blacks, particularly women, are hostile to such relationships. Perhaps the single most celebrated scene from Spike Lee's recent *Jungle Fever* (1991), an exploration of an interracial affair between a black man and a white woman, was the "war council" where the bereaved wife is consoled by her black women friends, and black men's alleged desire for "white pussy" is excoriated. (Anybody reading this article who has so far been completely bewildered by what I'm talking about could do worse than beginning by renting this video.[6]) Similarly, in a class on African American Philosophy I taught this year, this question came up in discussions, and, when I decided to pose it as an essay question, was far and away the most popular topic, the majority of students arguing for "Yes." If this notion seems strange and bizarre to most liberal white philosophers, then, this simply reflects the fact that, while the black male voice is still under-represented in the academy, the black female voice has until recently been silenced altogether. (In discussions of racism, the black man is the paradigm subject, so that, as one book title aptly puts it, *All the Women Are White, All the Blacks Are Men*, going on defiantly to assert, however, *But Some of Us Are Brave.*[7]) This chapter is, in part, an attempt to reconstruct—doubtless somewhat presumptuously— some of the possible arguments from this usually neglected perspective. So this is one for the sisters. I will go through what I take to be the most popular arguments, dealing with the weaker ones first and leaving the most interesting and challenging ones to the end.[8]

III

1. The Racial Purification, or "Let's Get the Cream Out of the Coffee," Argument

This argument is basically consequentialist in form, and obviously wouldn't apply to couples who are not planning to have children, or to short-term relationships in general. In its classic version, the Racial Purification Argument is straightforwardly biologistic, with culture, where it is invoked, being envisaged as tied to race by hereditarian links. (Where the connection is somewhat more attenuated, this shades over into what I will distinguish as a separate argument, the Racial Solidarity Argument.) The claim here is that (i) there is such a thing as a "pure" race, (ii) racial "purity" is good, either in itself and/or as a means to other ends, such as cultural preservation and future racial achievement, and (iii) members of the race should therefore regard themselves as having a duty to foster purity, or—when it has already been vitiated—to girding up their loins to restore it.

The structure of the argument is embarrassingly familiar from its better-known white supremacist version, Klan or Nazi. This version will include corollary racist eugenic notions of degraded "mongrel" types produced by racial interbreeding. However, since blacks are the subordinated rather than dominant race, the boundaries here are perforce drawn so as to *include* rather than exclude those of "mixed" race (the "one-drop" rule—some "black" blood makes you black, whereas some "white" blood *doesn't* make you white). For white racists, then, the emphasis would originally have been on *maintaining* purity against black and/or Jewish "pollution" (seen—in the times when black/Jewish relations were somewhat happier than they are now—as collaborating on this joint contaminatory project: bring on those white Christian virgins!). For blacks, on the other hand, because of the myriad rapes and economically-coerced sexual transactions of slavery and post-slavery, the emphasis is usually on *restoring* a lost purity, getting rid of the "pollution" of *white* blood. Those of mixed race are counted, sometimes reluctantly, as black, but the idea is that they should try to darken their progeny. (So for light-skinned black men, the injunction is sometimes put in the stronger terms of marrying *dark* black women.)

This argument is, of course, multiply vulnerable. To be convincing, it would really have to presuppose polygenesis, the heretical hypothesis that popped up repeatedly in racist thought in the eighteenth and nineteenth centuries (and was endorsed by such Enlightenment luminaries as Hume and Voltaire) that, *contra* Christian orthodoxy, there were really separate creations for the races, so that blacks and whites were different species.[9] The theology of the black version will necessarily be different (for example, the original Black Muslim claim that whites were created by the evil scientist Yacub[10]), but the logic, with the terms inverted, is the same. In a post-Darwinian framework that assumes a common humanity, it is harder to defend (which has not, of course, stopped twentieth-century racists), though one can, and people still do, talk about "higher" and "lower," "more" and "less" evolved, races. However, most biologists and anthropologists would today agree that there are no such things as races in the first place, so that, *a fortiori,* there cannot be "pure" races (this is, to use old-fashioned Rylean language, a kind of "category mistake"). Instead what exists are "clines," gradients of continuously-varying (i.e., *not* discretely-differentiated) phenotypical traits linked with clumpings of genetic patterns.[11] Humans share most of their genes, and, as ironists have pointed out, if you go back far enough, it turns out that we're all originally African anyway, so that even those blond-haired, blue-eyed Nordic types just happen to be grandchildren who left the continent earlier.

Moreover, even if there were natural ontological divisions between different branches of humanity, an auxillary argument would still obviously be needed to establish why maintaining these particular configurations of genes *would* be a good thing, and such a good thing that the duty to realize it overrides other claims. Culture is not tied to genotype—the familiar point that children of different "races" would, if switched at birth, take on the cultural traits of their new home. So the argument can only really plausibly get off the ground on the assumption, clearly racist whether in its white or black version, that moral character and/or propensity for intellectual achievement and/or aesthetic worth is genetically racially encoded, *and* of such a degree of difference that promoting it outweighs other considerations such as freedom of choice, staying with the person that you love, and so forth. (The character claim, less often made these days even by white racists [though some sociobiologists *are* now arguing for a hereditarian explanation of black crime rates], is somewhat more defensible as a basis for endogamy, since it has a moral dimension built into it. The black version will, of course, presuppose the innate evil of *whites*. The claim of differential intellectual ability, on the other hand, [more often made by whites than blacks, since the black version of the Racial Purification Argument usually credits whites with a real, if devious, intelligence] runs into the following set of objections. Suppose it were even true, which it isn't, that races are biologically discrete entities, and that members of race R2 are on average less intelligent than members of race R1. In the first place, *intra*-racial differences would still be greater than interracial differences; we would have overlapping normal distribution curves, slightly displaced from each other on the horizontal axis, with some members of R2 being *more* intelligent than some members of R1.[12] In the second place, do people, in searching for a marital partner, always require that their spouse be just as intelligent as they are? Obviously not; there can be all kinds of facets to a person that make him/her sexually attractive, with intelligence just being one of them. On the whole, human intelligence is a good thing, but why should promoting it be such an imperative as to generate overriding moral duties, especially when our inherited educational and cultural legacy, "social" intelligence, is what is really crucial in distinguishing us from our ancestors?[13])

Finally, as a fallback position, there is the obstinate assertion—what Anthony Appiah calls "intrinsic racism"[14]—that one race is better than another in complete *independence* of these contestable claims about ability and character, so that it is just good *in itself* that there be more pure whites (or more pure blacks). And here one would simply point out that this is not so much an argument, as a concession that there *is* no argument.

2. The Racial Caution, or "Don't Get the White Folks Mad," Argument

Another kind of consequentialist argument involves quite different kinds of considerations, not questionable claims about racial purity but pragmatic points about strategy. This rests on the uncontroversial factual claim that, as mentioned, many, indeed the majority, of whites are disturbed and angered by such unions,[15] so that entering into them will increase white hostility and opposition to integration. (As surveys during the period of civil rights activism showed, many whites were convinced that integration of the bedroom was in fact the *main thing* on the minds of blacks who were pressing for "civil rights," so that this would just confirm their worst fears.) The principle would not, of course, be that one should avoid white anger at all costs (since the advance of the black liberation struggle will *necessarily* anger some whites, and this would certainly not be a moral reason for abandoning it). Rather, the idea would be that black-on-white relationships *unnecessarily* infuriate whites. So since such unions stir up great passion, and are not a necessary component of the struggle, they should be eschewed. (Some versions might then leave it open for them to be permissible in the future non-racist society, or at least when racism has considerably diminished.)

This argument is obviously somewhat more respectable. It does, however, rest on the assumption that either no point of moral principle is involved, or that breach of the principle is justified by the overwhelmingly negative consequences for achieving black liberation of stirring such passions. The reply to the first might take the anti-utilitarian, let-the-heavens-fall line that individual rights to choice trump such considerations, and that if two people love one another, they should not forsake their relationship for the sake of expediting a cause. (Or, less nobly, it might just take the in-your-face form of the joys of *épater*-ing Whitey.) It could also be argued that such an approach panders to racism, and as such is immoral in its failure to confront it, since asserting full black personhood means exercising all the rights white persons have. Alternatively, on the second point (that any such principle is in this case overridden by likely negative repercussions), it might be conceded that a greater good sometimes requires restraint, discretion, and so forth, but denied that at this particular time, the consequences are likely to be so horrendous (so the viability of the argument may be in part conjunctural, depending on the situation, e.g., 1920s Mississippi vs. 1990s New York). Or it might be claimed that those who will be infuriated by "miscegenation" will be infuriated by the civil rights struggle *anyway,* so that it is not clear that there is a discrete differential increment of outrage which can be placed in the consequentialist balance pan, or maybe it's not clear how big it will be. (And it could be argued that the allegations of interracial sex will be made whether it's taking place or not.) Nevertheless, I think it is clear that this argument, unlike the first, does have something to be said for it, though there could be debate over how much. Note that here, of course, it will be the negative prohibition ("stay away from white women!") rather than the positive duty that is involved.

3. The Racial Solidarity, or "No Sleeping with the Enemy," Argument

This argument usually accompanies, or is actually conflated with, the Racial Purification Argument, but it's obviously conceptually distinct, if for no other reason that that it can be addressed to couples who don't plan to have children, or to those in short-term relationships. Both consequentialist and deontological versions are possible, cast in terms of the imperative to promote black liberation (and the putatively inhibitory effect of such unions on this project) or one's general duty to the race (to be elaborated on later). Note that because of the *defensibility* of this consequentialist goal, the black version of the Racial Solidarity Argument is not as immediately and clearly flawed as the corresponding white version, with the goal of preserving white *supremacy*, would be.

Let me run through the important variants, moving, as before, from less to more plausible. To begin with, there are those resting on straightforwardly racist innatist theses, whether in theological guise (whites as "blue-eyed devils"—the reactive black counterpart to the traditional claim that blacks are descendants of Ham's accursed son Canaan) or pseudo-scientific guise (whites as biologically evil "ice people" damned by melanin deficiency—the reactive black counterpart[16] to the post-Darwinian "scientific racism" of the late nineteenth-early twentieth centuries). So the idea is that all whites are intrinsically evil, not to be associated with except out of necessity (e.g., in the workplace), and certainly not to be sought out as sexual partners. They are collectively, racially responsible for the enslavement of blacks (the thesis of innate evil implies that though *these* whites are not literally responsible, they would have acted just the same had they been around at the time), so that willingly sleeping with them is like Jews voluntarily sleeping with Nazis. Both for the consequences and for the preservation of one's moral character, then, one has a duty not to enter interracial relationships.

Since moral character and responsibility are *not* generally encoded in this way (even the claims of sociobiologists wouldn't stretch to this kind of reasoning), this variant is easily dismissable. The more interesting version need not make any such fantastic assumptions. The argument here readily, or maybe grudgingly, admits that whites are just humans like all of us, born as fairly plastic entities who will both be shaped by, and in turn shape, a particular socio-cultural environment. But it will be pointed out that their socialization in a white-supremacist society makes them ineluctably beneficiaries and perpetrators of the system of oppression responsible for keeping blacks down, so that they are all, or mostly (claims of differing strength can be made), the enemy, whether through active policy or passive complicity. Even if they seem to show good faith, the entering of a social "whiteness" into their personal identity means that they will never, or only very rarely (again, claims of differing strength can be made), be able to overcome their conditioning: sooner or later, their "true colors" are going to come out. If nothing else, because of the numerous affective and cognitive ties—family, friendship, cultural attachment—that link them to this white world, and help to constitute their being, they will naturally be less sensitive to its racist character, and more reluctant to confront the radical changes that have to be made to bring about a truly just society.

In the absence of hypotheses about innate evil, the deontological version gets less of a foothold (though argument #6 below can be seen as partially falling under this category), and the consequentialist version is the one which would have to be run. The idea would be that, given these empirical claims, blacks in such unions are likely to find their efforts to attack white supremacy subtly (maybe even unconsciously) resisted and diverted, so that the long-term consequences will be to compromise black struggles. Since it is often the more successful black men (prominent black businessmen, sports stars, lawyers, entertainers, intellectuals) who marry white women, such unions usually lead to a departure from the black world of the elite who (at least on some theories) are precisely the most potentially threatening to the status quo, and their entry into an immensely seductive white world of wealth, comfort and glamour where black problems, e.g., the misery of the inner cities, will gradually seem more and more remote. (This inflection of the argument makes the class dimension of black oppression particularly salient. It has traditionally been claimed that blacks have a general duty to "uplift the race," and it is sometimes pointed out in addition that by marrying a white woman, the economic and status resources of the successful black male [material and cultural/symbolic capital] are likely to be removed from the black community.) Without even realizing it, and through familiar processes of self-deception and motivated inattention, one will gradually "sell out" to the white establishment.

Unlike the innatist version, with its dubious biology, or biotheology, this version has the merits of being more in touch with social reality, and indeed of telling a not-implausible psychological tale. One response is the blunt *denial* that blacks should regard themselves as having any particular duty to combat white supremacy, the individualist every-man-for-himself solution, though this will, of course, rarely be said out loud (as against secretly practiced). A more defensible approach might be to accept the existence of this duty while simultaneously arguing, as some contemporary ethicists have done, for a *restricted* role for consequentialist moral demands.[17] So the idea would be that of course you do have *some* free-floating obligation to resist racism, but this can't be a full-time job invading every aspect of one's life, and unless one's white wife is actually a Klan member or a Nazi (obviously somewhat unlikely), one's personal life is one's own business. (Often this is accompanied by the universalist/humanist claim that in the end, color doesn't matter, we're all just human beings, and so forth.)

Another tack would be to challenge the crucial empirical premise that whites cannot *ever* purge themselves of a whiteness commited to racial supremacy (or the weaker version that their doing so is rare enough that the injunction is warranted on Bayesian grounds). It would be pointed out that people can resist and overcome their socialization, proving by their deeds that they are committed to eradicating racism. For those white women who are naive about the pervasiveness of racism, even among their own family and friends, embarking on an interracial relationship may actually have a salutary cognitive effect, the latter's hostile response awakening her to realities to which she would otherwise have been blind. An abstract opposition to racism might then assume a more visceral force, so that the net result would be a gain for the forces of anti-racism. Once the innatist framework has been abandoned, the biological link between race and character severed, and the Racial Solidarity Argument put on the consequentialist foundation of ending white supremacy, there is the danger (for its proponents) of the argument being turned on its head. Since not all *black* women will automatically be activist foes of racism (they may have succumbed to racist socialization, or, like the vast majority of human beings, just be trying to get along without heavy-duty political commitments), the question of which spouse will be of more assistance in fighting racism might then come down to simple empirical questions, rather than *a priori* assumptions. If other kinds of arguments are excluded, the foe of interracial marriages would then have to show why, in each case, the overall outcome is likely to be a debit for the anti-racism struggle. (For short-term relationships and one-night stands, neither side will be able to make much of a case for long-term consequentialist repercussions, so—if the premises are not innatist ones—the argument will usually shift to more symbolic issues, as discussed in #6, below.)

4. The Racial Demographics, or "Where Are All the Black Men?" Argument

The Racial Demographics Argument is interesting because, of those we have looked at so far, it is least tied to the explicit political project of fighting white racism, with its accompanying ideological assumptions. This argument simply points to the relatively uncontroversial statistical fact that, because of the disproportionate numbers of black men in jail, unemployed, or dead at an early age (which may or may not be attributed to white racism), there is a significant imbalance of females to "marriageable" black males.[18] ("Marriageable" may itself, of course, seem to have classist overtones, and it is true that this complaint comes most often from middle-class, or upwardly-mobile, black women,[19] but the problem is more general.) William Julius Wilson is famous for his claim that this putative shortage is in part responsible for the perpetuation of the underclass, since single black women of poorer backgrounds will then fall into poverty if they have children.[20] (Some left critics have accused Wilson of sexism on this point, arguing that the real political demand should be for women to get what is now reserved as a "male" wage.) The traditional race/gender status hierarchy in the United States is structured basically as: white men, white women, black men, black women. Because of their low prestige in a racist society, black women have not generally been sought out as *respectable* partners (as against concubines, mistresses, prostitutes) by white men and men of other races. So if eligible black men differentially seek non-black, particularly white, women, then things will be made even worse for black women, who will then have been rejected both by their own men and the men of other races.[21]

If black men therefore have a duty arising out of this fact, what would its foundation be? Since we are considering arguments in isolation from one another, we need to differentiate this conceptually from the Racial Solidarity Argument as such, though it can obviously be seen in terms of racial solidarity. The argument would not be the *general* one, corollary of #3, to "sleep with the friend," but the claim that in *these* contingent circumstances black men have such a duty. This could be defended in deontological or utilitarian terms, i.e., as a remediable unhappiness which imposes some sort of obligation on us to relieve it. (So this, unlike the previous two arguments, does require more than just *not* marrying white women.)

How plausible is this? Note, to begin with that, as mentioned, no questionable racist claims about whites' innate characters are being made, so it is not vulnerable on that score. But one obviously unhappy feature it has is that, as a putative duty, it seems to be naturally assimilable to duties of *charity,* i.e., the standing obligations most moral theorists think we have (and invested with greater or lesser degrees of stringency) to relieve distress, e.g., through giving to the homeless, to Third World famine relief, and so forth. Isn't it insulting to the person to think that sexual relationships, or marriages, should be generally entered into on these grounds? How would one react to the declaration, or inadvertent discovery, that one had been sought out as a *charitable* obligation? (The argument for endogamous marriage on the grounds of black self-respect is different, and will be discussed later.) Black women are as beautiful and desirable as sexual partners as any other women, and it feels strange to approach the issue in such a framework. So this seems a bit problematic from the start. There is also the question of how strong this putative obligation is supposed to be. For Kant and most other deontologists, charity is an "imperfect" duty, compliance with which leaves considerable latitude for choice (timing, beneficiary, extent of commitment, and so forth). In the case of something so central to one's life-plans as a choice of partner, rights of individual autonomy and personal freedom would easily override an alleged charitable claim of this sort. Utilitarianism is in general, of course, more demanding, with—depending on the variety—less or no room for what are sometimes called agent-relative "options," if welfare can be maximized through the policy in question. In this case, then, strategies of response would have to defend (non-black) common-sense morality against utilitarianism's demands, or make a case that such a policy, if taken seriously, would be more likely to promote net *un*happiness (through the constraints on the freedoms of black men, and the demeaning knowledge or uncertainty in the minds of black women as to why they had really been chosen). Nevertheless, it is clearly possible that some opponents of interracial marriage would be prepared to bite the bullet and insist on such a duty, arguing perhaps that the situation of black women is now so dire as to easily *outweigh* black male unhappiness at restriction of choice, and that as an entry in the welfare calculus, this unhappiness is not to be taken too seriously anyway, since it is likely, or necessarily, the result of a brainwashed preference for white women, and could be removed with a Brandtian "cognitive psychotherapy."[22] So this argument could be reinforced with considerations we shall look at later.

5. The Tragic Mulattos-to-Be, or "Burden on the Children," Argument

Another possible consequentialist argument is that the mixed racial and presumably (though not necessarily) cultural legacy of such unions will impose a differential burden on children of such households, who will be caught between two worlds and fully accepted by neither. This argument is often put forward hypocritically, with the actually-motivating considerations being along the lines of #1–4. Nevertheless, it should obviously still be examined.

To begin with, of course, it only gets off the ground if the couple *do* plan to have children. It could also be argued that it presupposes the continuation of racist attitudes, and that in a non-racist world such children would be completely accepted by both sides of the family.

However, since there does not seem to be much likelihood of such a world coming into existence in the near future, this objection could not plausibly carry much weight.

(I have encountered an interesting inversion of this argument, put forward perhaps only semi-seriously, that could be termed the Racial Elimination, or "Browning of the World," Argument. The thesis is that if the bottom line is indeed fighting white racism, and/or racism in general, then interracial unions are not merely morally *permissible,* but *desirable,* to be positively encouraged as a long-term strategy for eliminating racism by making everybody some shade of brown. Unfortunately, I think this underestimates human ingenuity in finding differences upon which to erect comparative aesthetic, moral, and intellectural claims. For many decades after the nineteenth-century abolition of slavery in the Americas, there were elaborate color hierarchies in the black communities in the United States, the Caribbean, and South America, structured according to one's shade and presumed degree of "white" blood, e.g., octoroon, quadroon, mulatto, Negro, and these persist today in a continuing preference in the West for light-skinned blacks.[23] Even if [which seems genetically impossible, given the normal human variation even in the children of *one* set of parents] all of us were to become a uniform brown, there would still be differences in hair texture and facial features which could be traced back to differential racial ancestry, and which could be used as grounds for discriminatory sorting. In general, I would suggest that the notion that mere somatic difference is the sufficient, or major, cause of racism is historically and anthropologically naive. I am sympathetic to the general left position that if politico-economic differences require "racial" differentiation, then the categorization will be generated accordingly even if people are much closer somatically than they currently are. It's worth remembering that in nineteenth-century Europe, the white working class was sometimes thought of as a separate "race." Where there's a political will, it could be said, there's a conceptual way.)

But back to the burden on the children. One obvious reply would be that some parents-to-be will be able to speak with authority about the non-racist character of their side of the family. But what about those who can't? And even those who do sincerely give such assurances about others' feelings may, of course, be self-deceived, or even deceived by their relatives (whether through disingenuousness, and the fact that racism is no longer respectable, or by normal human self-opacity, and the genuine non-awareness of one's actual gut responses when faced with a flesh-and-blood "mixed" grandson or niece). The way to argue around this might be to insist that extra-loving parental care can make up for any family hostility. However, there is also the set of problems the child will face in the larger society, e.g., growing up in a school and neighborhood environment where racial polarization may lead to partial ostracism by other children of both races. So I think that this does raise genuine concerns, and even if they are outweighed by other factors, they should be given their due. (A magazine called *Interrace* addresses these and other problems of interracial couples.)

6. The Questionable Motivations, or "Maybe You Can Fool That Stupid White Bitch, Nigger, and Maybe You Can Fool Yourself, But You're Not Fooling Anybody Else," Argument

I have left to the last what I consider to be the most interesting argument, or set of arguments. This is the claim that black men who enter such unions, always, or usually (the claim can be made with differing strengths), are motivated by questionable considerations. The argument tends to be deontological in form, the presumption being that some set of normative criteria can be imposed to assess the appropriate motivations for entering a marriage—these days, basically revolving around romantic love—and that, absent these motives, and/ or present some other set, the decision to marry is wrong. Since motivation is unlikely ever to be pure, and we are not completely, or at all, self-transparent anyway, one might have to talk about the *preponderance,* and the *likelihood,* of certain kinds of motivations. In addition, there is the separate moral issue of the woman's awareness or non-awareness of the nature of the motivation. Thus one would have to distinguish cases of ignorance and deception, where the white woman doesn't know what is really driving her male spouse-to-be, from cases where both parties know what's going on. (In other kinds of non-romantic marriages, for example marriages of convenience for immigration reasons, or the standard pragmatic tradings of financial security for youthful beauty, both parties often know the score, so that if these unions are wrong, it is not because of *deception.*)

Now obviously interracial marriages have no monopoly on questionable motivations, but the claim of opponents would be that they are *more* likely to be present (or, more strongly, *always* present) in such unions. What is the basis of this claim? The argument is that because of the central historic structuring of the American policy by white racism,[24] the psychology of both whites and blacks has been negatively affected, and that this has ramifications for human sexuality. (Or, as initially mentioned, there is the more radically foundational claim that sex is in fact at the root of racism in the *first* place, so the whole thing *starts* there.) In a patriarchal society, sexuality is distorted by sexism as well as racism, so that male sexuality characteristically involves the notion of conquest, sexual competition, and a proving of one's manhood by securing the woman, or the series of women, more highly ranked in the established hierarchy of desirability. But *white women* will in general represent the female somatic ideal in our society: they are preeminently the beauty queens, fashion models, movie goddesses, magazine centerfolds, porn stars, whose images are displayed from a billion magazine covers, billboards, television screens, videos, and movie theaters.[25] Black males will inevitably be influenced by this, so that a wide range of potentially questionable motivations is generated:

(i)   sexual exoticism and forbidden fruit-picking,
(ii) racial revenge,
(iii) racially-differentiated aesthetic attraction, and
(iv) racial status-seeking and personhood by proxy.

(i) Sexual exoticism *per se*—the lure of the different—obviously has no intrinsic connection to black and white relations, and indeed need not involve *racial* difference at all, being felt across cultural, ethnic, and class lines. Moreover, on its own it would not really seem to raise any moral problems; people are sexually attracted to each other for all kinds of reasons, and if the strangeness of the Other is what is turning them on, there seems no harm in this—whatever gets you through the night, and so forth. The real concern here would be the prudential one that this is unlikely to prove a reliable foundation for a long-term relationship or marriage, exoticism rapidly being demystified in the quotidian domestic irritations of house-cleaning manias and toilet seats left up. It is really the coincidence of the exotic with the black-white racial taboo, the fact that this strange fruit is *forbidden,* that gives rise to what Spike Lee calls "jungle fever." But again, assuming a liberal view of sexuality, which would deny the legitimacy of such taboos, and taking for granted that both parties know what's going on, no moral, as against prudential, questions would really seem to be raised. I think when people advance this as a moral argument they are either unconsciously conflating it with one or more of the *other* possibilities ([ii] to [iv]), which we'll examine separately, or assuming that one party, e.g., the white woman, doesn't realize the real source of her appeal. So insofar as this is a successful moral argument, it would really just be subsumable under the general proscription against deceit in interpersonal relationships, perhaps with the added *a priori* reminder that, given people's capacity for self-deception, black men are not likely to be willing to face the fact that this *is* really what's driving them (a point we'll encounter again). For (i), then, if there is a duty, it is derivable, given certain empirical assumptions, from the conventional set of duties to the other person, which can be founded either on welfare or Kantian grounds.

(ii) By contrast, racial revenge as a motivation is clearly and uncontroversially immoral. The idea here (though this will not usually be said out loud, or at least within earshot of whites) is that marriage to, or sometimes just sex with, a white woman (or, better, *many* white women), is an appropriate form of revenge, conscious or unconscious, upon white men. This is linked, obviously, to acceptance of a sexist framework in which male combat, here interracial, takes place in part across the terrain of the female body, so that masculinity and honor are fused with ability to appropriate the woman. Sex with the enemy's woman then becomes a symbolic retribution both specific—for the thousands of rapes and other sexual abuses visited upon black women over the hundreds of years of slavery and its aftermath, which black men were in general powerless to stop—and general—for the systematic humiliations of the denial to black men of their manhood in a society created by white men. Obviously black men who enter unions with white women for such purposes are just using them.

(iii), (iv) I will discuss these together since, though the details are different, the root issue is arguably the same. Thus far the duty, insofar as it exists, has been easily derivable from standard prohibitions against deceiving and using others. These final two subsets of allegedly questionable motives are to my mind the most interesting because they raise the possibility of duties to oneself and/or duties to the race.

First, the aesthetic question. As pointed out, in this country, the white woman has traditionally represented the somatic norm of beauty.[26] It's true this has recently begun to expand somewhat, with black Miss Americas (including one chosen in 1993), and some preference in the fashion industry for "ethnic" models. But the first black Miss America, 1983 queen (though later deposed) Vanessa Williams, was so fair-skinned that the Congress of Racial Equality refused to recognize her as black, and the black models used in MTV videos will usually be light-skinned, Caucasoid blacks. White or light skin, long non-kinky hair, "fine" noses and narrow non-everted lips remain the norm, and as such are difficult or impossible to achieve without artificial assistance for black women of non-mixed heritage: hence the long-established cosmetic industry in the black community of skin bleaches, hair straighteners, wigs and hair extensions, and more recently (for those who can afford it) chemical peels, dermabrasion and plastic surgery. The argument is, then, that in choosing to marry white women, black men are admitting by this deed their acceptance of a white racist stereotype of beauty, and rejecting their own race. (Obviously there is a feminist, and indeed even more general humanist, argument that stereotypical physical attractiveness should not be the major criterion for marriageability *anyway,* but I am not endorsing these norms but merely outlining their logic. This is in fact what motivates most men, and pending the advent of a utopia where physical appearance becomes unimportant, to be systematically disadvantaged by race seems unfair. In other words, I am assuming, though I will not try to show this, that this racial dimension inflicts *additional* unfairness on top of the normal genetic lottery by which, within a race, "plain" or "ugly" people are socially disadvantaged through not meeting *intra-racial* standards of attractiveness.)

The other set of motives is conceptually distinct, though in practice it will usually go with the aesthetic set, and the ultimate source of both is arguably the same.[27] This is the project of achieving social status through one's white wife. White women are then a kind of prize who can both affirm one's self-esteem, and help to provide an entree (at least in liberal circles) to the still largely white world of status and power of the upper echelons of society. Bluntly, a white woman on your arm shows that you have made it. As such, this is separate from the aesthetic argument, since the idea would be that even a white woman plain by conventional white standards of attractiveness will still provide the aura of social prestige radiating from white-skin privilege. Indeed, one of the arguments that black women who object to such unions frequently use is that black men go out or end up with white women whom they would never consider if they were black and of the same comparative degree of attractiveness (assuming that some kind of interracial translation of such measurements is possible, i.e., a 6 on a white 10-point scale becoming an equivalent 6 on a black 10-point scale, somehow relativized to different phenotype). Under these circumstances in particular, the claim will be made that "it's only because she's white" that the black man is going out with her.

The more radical version of this accusation is that one is actually trying to achieve some kind of derivative personhood, personhood by proxy, in such marriages, insofar as black personhood is systematically denied in a racist society and the black man is likely to have internalized this judgment.[28] (Personhood and status are linked, but separate, since obviously whites can have the former while still wanting to increase their ranking by some metric of the latter, e.g., through climbing the corporate hierarchy.)

For both these sets of motivations, then, duties would arise *in addition* to the obvious ones of not using the white partner. (The latter set of duties is still pertinent since, while people don't usually object to having been chosen at least in part on the basis of their looks, they would presumably *not* want to be chosen merely on the basis of being an abstract representative of an instrumental whiteness.) And these could perhaps be construed as duties to *oneself,* or duties to the *race* (or perhaps this could be collapsed into duties to oneself *insofar as* one is a member of the race, a subset of the more general duties we have to ourselves as humans). In modern moral theory, the notion of duties to oneself is most famously, of course, in Kant. His idea was that in general we owe respect to all persons, a respect generating duties of differing degrees of stringency, and since we are persons ourselves, this means we have duties to *our*selves (so that certain actions are wrong because we are *using* that self). The idea has been judged problematic by most contemporary philosophers, but some, for example, Thomas Hill, Jr., think that it is in fact a defensible and fruitful way of explicating the internal moral logic of the notion of self-respect.[29] So respecting ourselves precludes acting out of certain kinds of motivation. Applying this to the case of interracial marriage for reasons of types (iii) and (iv), then, the implication is that *even if the white woman is fully aware of, and has no problem with, the black man's motivation,* such marriage would be wrong because it endorses a racist set of values and as such implies a lack of respect for oneself and one's own race.

I think that, though the other arguments I have discussed are also employed, and taken seriously, this really captures the essential objection that many black women have to interracial relationships. And it coheres nicely with the interpretation of racism as an ideology which, in anti-Kantian fashion, systematically *denies* full personhood to certain groups of humans—in effect, the whole race is thought of as sub-persons, *Untermenschen*. The Jamaican activist Marcus Garvey, one of the most famous black leaders of the twentieth century, is celebrated for his insight that white supremacy had left blacks as "a race without respect," and correspondingly the notion of "dissin' " someone, so central to black popular culture, is arguably a recognition, on the level of folk wisdom, of the danger of this diminished moral standing.[30]

Could this then be seen as a friendly amendment to Kant? (I really mean "Kantianism" rather than Kant; in general Kant's own views on sexuality can't be taken seriously.) The immediate obstacle is that race is part of the phenomenal self deemed morally irrelevant, so how could we have duties to ourself based on racial membership? Or how could we have duties to the race that are differentiated from duties to abstract noumenal (and hence raceless) persons? But I think this objection can be finessed in the following way. The claim is not that, *because* we're black (or white, or any other race) we're *differentially* deserving of respect; this would indeed be inconsistent with Kantian principles, presupposing hierarchy rather than equality of value for different persons. So the argument is not that race does enter at the noumenal level. The claim is rather that the historic legacy of white racism has been a social ontology in which race has *not* been abstracted from, but used as an indicator of, one's personhood, so that those with a certain "phenomenal" phenotype have been seen as less than human and so undeserving of full (or any) respect. *Resistance* to this legacy therefore requires that one affirm one can be *both* black and a person, that the phenomenal does not correlate with a sub-par noumenal self. Retreat into typical philosophical abstraction ("we're all human—race doesn't matter") evades confronting this, since the terms on which humanity will have been defined will be *white* ones. So the "person" is tacitly constructed as white in the first place, which is why this hidden moral architecture, this colorlessness which is really colored white, has to be exposed to the light. Because of black socialization into this system of values, the fact is that marriage to a white woman *will* often be based on the continuing, if not consciously acknowledged, submission to this racist social ontology, and when it is, *will* imply a lack of racial self-respect, respect for one's race (as all other races) as equally entitled to take the full status of personhood. It is, finally, I believe, something like this moral perception which, even if not always clearly articulated, underlies many black women's intuition that there is often something questionable about these relationships.

But what—the obvious reply will be—if one is quite sure, or as sure as one can be about anything, that one is *not* marrying for such motivations? Here, the opponent of interracial marriages has at least two interesting fallback positions (as distinct, that is, from any of the other arguments previously discussed). First, what the critic may do is introduce an auxiliary *epistemic* thesis (our knowledge of our motivation) as distinct from the *substantive* thesis itself (what our motivation is). The argument would then be that, though in some cases black men's motivation might be pure, the combined effects of standard human self-opacity and the cognitive interference produced in these particular circumstances by the strong motivations for self-deception (who will want to admit to himself he's really trying to whiten his being?), mean that they can never *know* that it is pure, so the safest thing to do is to eschew such unions. If this fails, then there is, secondly, the ultimate fallback position of re-introducing a consequentialist framework to argue that even if (a) one's motivation is pure, *and* (b) one knows one's motivation is pure, there is always (c) the fact that, whatever one's motivation, one will be *perceived* by other blacks as having married out of racial self-contempt, thus reinforcing white superiority. And this (as one of my black female students coldly informed me when I was trying to defend a liberal position on the issue) will be "a slap in the face of black women everywhere." So the bottom line for critics is that one's actions will be perceived as being motivated by these self-despising beliefs, and—especially if one is a prominent black figure of high status, with a correspondingly enhanced range of racial spousal selection—this action will be sending a message to the world that, once you *do* have this option to choose: *black women just ain't good enough.*

IV

I have no neat, wrap-up conclusion to offer, since I think the issue is a complicated one about which a lot more could be said. Rather, my basic aim has been to demonstrate this complexity, and, as a corollary, to show the mistakenness of the knee-jerk white liberal (or, for that matter, black liberal) response that no defensible case could possibly be made for the existence of such a duty. Some of the arguments *are* obviously weak (e.g., #1), but others are stronger, though they may be of conjunctural strength (e.g., #2), involve empirical and normative claims which may or may not hold true (#3, 4, 5), or rest on speculative claims about motivation which are hard to disprove, with a consequentialist fallback line which may seem illegitimately to hold us hostage to others' perceptions (#6). Whether singly or in combination (to the extent that this is possible, bearing in mind that *different* normative frameworks have sometimes been used) they do yield at least a presumptive duty I will leave, perhaps somewhat evasively, for the reader to decide, and if so what kind of a duty it is.[31] At the very least I think I have shown that—using conventional moral theories, and without making racist assumptions about whites, or even appealing to any controversial separatist ideology—an interesting case can in fact be built for a position quite widespread in the "commonsense morality" of the black community.

One common, misguided white liberal reaction to racism has been to move from the anthropological premise that "race" (in the biological sense) doesn't exist, to the conclusion that "race" (in the social sense) doesn't exist either, so that the solution is to proclaim an (ostensibly) colorless universalism in which we pay no attention to race. Sometimes this is expressed in the claim that race is "constructed" (true enough) and therefore unreal. But neither conclusion follows (try walking through the next constructed brick wall you encounter). As Aristotle pointed out long ago, treating people equally doesn't necessarily mean treating them the same, and one could argue analogously that genuine race-neutrality actually requires not *blindness* to race but close attention to the difference race makes. The subtleties of unraveling and re-weaving conventional morality in a white-supremacist society gradually transforming itself have only just begun to be worked on by philosophers. If discussions such as this one have rarely, if ever, graced the pages of philosophy journals, this is arguably a consequence not of the unimportance of such debates but of the demographics of the profession, and the absence of voices speaking from the day-to-day lives and concerns of a significant sector of the population. We can expect that, with the demographic "browning" of America that is under way, leading to a minority white population some time late in the next century, and perhaps even (dare one hope . . . ?) some more non-white faces around APA meetings, such issues will increasingly begin to appear in these formerly jimcrowed white pages.

I would like to acknowledge the support of the Institute for the Humanities, University of Illinois at Chicago.

Notes

1. For discussions of racism in general, and racism and sex in particular, see, for example: Frantz Fanon, *Black Skin, White Masks*, trans. Charles Lam Markmann (1952; rpt. New York: Grove Weidenfeld, 1967); Winthrop D. Jordan, *White Over Black: American Attitudes Toward the Negro, 1550-1812* (1968; rpt. New York and London: W.W. Norton, 1977); St. Clair Drake, *Black Folk Here and There*, vol. I (Los Angeles: Center for Afro-American Studies, UCLA, 1987); John D'Emilio and Estelle B. Freedman, *Intimate Matters: A History of Sexuality in America* (New York: Harper & Row, 1988), chapter five; Calvin C. Hernton, *Sex and Racism in America* (1966, rpt. New York: Grove Press, 1988).

2. For the grisly details, see, for example, Ralph Ginzburg, ed., *100 Years of Lynchings* (1962; rpt. Baltimore, MD: Black Classic Press, 1988).

3. As Judge A. Leon Higginbotham, Jr. sardonically pointed out to Clarence Thomas, admonishing him for his cavalier disparagement of the work of civil rights activists, had it not been for their efforts, "if you and your present wife decided that you wanted to reside in Virginia [their present home], you would . . . have been violating the Racial Integrity Act of 1924, which the Virginia Supreme Court as late as 1966 said was consistent with the federal Constitution because of the overriding state interest in the institution of marriage. . . . [Y]ou could have been in the penitentiary today rather than serving as an Associate Justice of the United States Supreme Court." "An Open Letter to Justice Clarence Thomas from a Federal Judicial Colleague," *University of Pennsylvania Law Review*, 140 (1992); reprinted in Toni Morrison, ed., *Race-ing Justice, En-gendering Power: Essays on Anita Hill, Clarence Thomas, and the Construction of Social Reality* (New York: Pantheon Books, 1992), pp. 24–25.

4. For changing (and unchanging) depictions of blacks in United States cinema, see Donald Bogle, *Toms, Coons, Mulattoes, Mammies & Bucks: An Interpretive History of Blacks in American Films*, rev. ed. (1973; rpt. New York: Continuum, 1989).

5. William Shatner, with Chris Kreski, *Star Trek Memories* (New York: Harper Collins Publishers, 1993). Nichols disgustedly describes the backstage drama: "[The network suits were] telling me that the kiss would make the show impossible to air. . . . I mean, they even went so far as to suggest changing the scene so that Kirk gets paired off with Nurse Chapel and Spock ends up with me. Somehow, I guess, they found it more acceptable for a Vulcan to kiss me, for this alien to kiss this black woman, than for two humans with different coloring to do the same thing." *Star Trek Memories,* pp. 284–285. The network arranged for the scene to be shot twice, the first take

showing actual lip contact, the second take positioning the camera behind Shatner's back at the crucial moment, so that an actual kiss did not have to be shown—and did not in fact occur. The second take was the one eventually aired.

6. For an interesting discussion, see also the *Newsweek* cover story (June 10, 1991) on the movie, "Tackling a Taboo."

7. Gloria T. Hull, Patricia Bell Scott, and Barbara Smith, eds., *All the Women Are White, All the Blacks Are Men, But Some of Us Are Brave: Black Women's Studies* (Old Westbury, New York: The Feminist Press, 1982).

8. I should record here the fact that I have greatly benefited from exposure to, even when I have not always agreed with, the arguments put forward by my students in classroom discussion and essays submitted in the "African-American Philosophy" course I taught in Spring 1993.

9. For a discussion, see, for example, Stephen Jay Gould, *The Mismeasure of Man* (New York and London: W.W. Norton, 1981).

10. See, for example, chapter 10, "Satan," of *The Autobiography of Malcolm X,* as told to Alex Haley, (1965; rpt. New York: Ballantine Books, 1973).

11. "There are no races, there are only clines." Frank B. Livingstone, "On the Nonexistence of Human Races" (1962); rpt. in Sandra Harding, ed., *The "Racial" Economy of Science: Toward a Democratic Future* (Bloomington and Indianapolis: Indiana University Press, 1993).

12. The more radical objection made by some theorists is that the whole idea of quantifying intellectual ability as a single reified number, and then ranking people on a unilinear scale, is inherently incoherent: again, see Gould, *The Mismeasure of Man.* This is sometimes summed up in the *bon mot* that the only thing IQ tests measure is the ability to do well on IQ tests.

13. I have benefited here from Joyce Trebilcot's argument opposing sex roles: "Sex Roles: The Argument from Nature," *Ethics,* 85 (April 1975); rpt. in Garry Brodsky, John Troyer, and David Vance, eds., *Contemporary Readings in Social and Political Ethics* (Buffalo, New York: Prometheus Books, 1984).

14. Kwame Anthony Appiah, *In My Father's House: Africa in the Philosophy of Culture* (New York and Oxford: Oxford University Press, 1992) pp. 13–15.

15. As late as 1978, a national survey showed that "70% of whites . . . rejected interracial marriage on principle": cited in Douglas S. Massey and Nancy A. Denton, *American Apartheid: Segregation and the Making of the Underclass* (Cambridge, Mass.: Harvard University Press, 1993), p. 95. Indeed, as late as 1991, 20% of whites thought that interracial marriages should be *illegal:* General Social Survey, *New York Times* (Dec. 2, 1992), cited in Thomas E. Wartenberg, " 'But Would You Want Your Daughter to Marry One?' The Representation of Race and Racism in *Guess Who's Coming to Dinner," Journal of Social Philosophy,* Vol. XXV, 25th Anniversary Special Issue (June 1994), p. 129.

16. Though contemporary "melanin theory" is indigenous to the black community, the notion of "ice people" actually comes from the white Canadian author Michael Bradley's *The Iceman Inheritance: Prehistoric Sources of Western Man's Racism, Sexism and Aggression* (New York: Kayode, 1978; rpt. New York: Kayode, 1991).

17. See, for example, Samuel Scheffler, *Human Morality* (New York: Oxford University Press, 1992).

18. Black unemployment rates in recent decades have been at least twice as high as white unemployment rates, and for the category of young black men in the inner cities the rate approaches catastrophic proportions. Another tragic figure frequently cited is the 1990 study that showed that, on any given day in 1989, nearly 1 in 4 black men from the ages of 20 to 29 were either in prison, on parole, or on probation. (Update: In the short period since I originally wrote this article, this figure has risen to 1 in 3.) The leading cause of death for black men 15–34 is homicide. For some of these frightening statistics, see William Julius Wilson, *The Truly Disadvantaged: The Inner City, the Underclass, and Public Policy* (Chicago and London: The University of Chicago Press, 1987) and Andrew Hacker, *Two Nations: Black and White, Separate, Hostile, Unequal* (New York: Charles Scribner's Sons, 1992).

19. Terry McMillan's recent bestseller, *Waiting to Exhale* (1992; rpt. New York: Pocket Star Books, 1993), made into a 1995 movie, revolves in large part around this theme.

20. Wilson, *The Truly Disadvantaged*.

21. I have worked throughout within a heterosexual, and, some gays might say, heterosexist, framework. Why, it may be asked, should black women wait for black, or any other, men? Why shouldn't they embrace their sisters? I certainly don't mean to impugn the legitimacy of lesbian relationships—I think that gay relationships and marriages should be recognized—but, on established assumptions about people's sexual orientation, there will still be a majority of *straight* women for whom this is not an attractive solution. If these assumptions are wrong, of course, so that the whole concept of a basic sexual orientation is misleading in the first place, and sexuality is radically plastic, then some of these arguments won't work. But the *general* issue of racism and sex obviously isn't just an issue for straights.

22. See Richard Brandt, *A Theory of the Good and the Right* (New York: Oxford University Press, 1979).

23. For a fascinating discussion of the psychological ramifications of this, see Kathy Russell, Midge Wilson, and Ronald Hall, *The Color Complex: The Politics of Skin Color Among African Americans* (New York: Harcourt Brace Jovanovich, 1992).

24. And many other countries too, of course. Though I have implicitly focused on the United States throughout, many of these arguments would be applicable elsewhere also.

25. A quick riddle for the reader: name a black female movie star other than Whoopie Goldberg and Whitney Houston. My guess is that the average white reader will come up empty. Now think how remarkable this is in a country where for most of the century movies have epitomized American popular culture, and blacks make up 12% of the population.

26. The following discussion draws on *The Color Complex*. The notion of a racial "somatic norm" was first put forward by the Dutch sociologist Harmannus Hoetink; see, for example, *Caribbean Race Relations: A Study of Two Variants* (London: Oxford University Press, 1962).

27. It should be noted, though, that some researchers have argued, on anthropological evidence, that there is a pro-light-skinned aesthetic bias in *all*

societies, which pre-existed, though of course it will be reinforced by, colonialism and white racism.

28. Cf. Fanon, *Black Skin, White Masks,* p. 63: "I wish to be acknowledged not as *black* but as *white.* Now . . . who but a white woman can do this for me? By loving me she proves that I am worthy of white love. I am loved like a white man. I am a white man."

29. Thomas E. Hill, Jr., *Autonomy and Self-Respect* (Cambridge: Cambridge University Press, 1991), especially chapters 1 and 2.

30. Likewise, it is no accident that the work of black philosophers has so often focused on the particular importance of *self-respect* for blacks; see, for example, Laurence Thomas, "Self-Respect: Theory and Practice," and Bernard Boxill, "Self-Respect and Protest," both in Leonard Harris, ed., *Philosophy Born of Struggle: Anthology of Afro-American Philosophy from 1917* (Dubuque, Iowa: Kendall/Hunt Publishing Co., 1983).

31. As it turned out, this calculated evasiveness was in vain. Most of the people who have talked to me about this article since its original publication, including my white feminist friends, *have* interpreted me to be arguing that the overall balance of considerations is against black male/white female relationships. So let me repeat what I said: I do *not* actually take an overall position in this article, being primarily concerned to lay out and elucidate arguments in the black community that do not usually get a hearing. Any final judgment would require looking at the many obvious arguments on the other side, which I do not explore. (My colleague Sandra Bartky suggests to me that in the realm of sexuality the well-known "perversity of desire" renders such prescription largely pointless anyway.) The basic aim, as I stated at the beginning, was to bring a traditionally taboo subject into the open, show how conventional moral platitudes can be challenged when the realities of white racism are taken into account, and in general demonstrate that even on earth, let alone in heaven, there are far more things than are standardly dreamt of in white philosophy journals.

PART FIVE

Paternity and Responsibility

9

Bioethics and Fatherhood

Daniel Callahan

I. Introduction

For most of the rest of our culture, the twin issues of the meaning of masculinity (or maleness, depending on your tastes), and the significance of fatherhood are well-developed topics of public discussion. Whether as a response to feminism, on the one hand, or to independent uncertainties about what it means to be a male, on the other, the question of masculinity attracts considerable attention. While fatherhood was not exactly a neglected topic in years past, there seems little doubt that the nasty phenomena of more and more single-parent families, mainly headed by females, and a growing number of absent and neglectful fathers, has given the issue a fresh urgency. What does it mean to be a father? What is the importance of the father for the nurturing of children? What can be done to encourage and assist more responsible fatherhood? What is the relationship between fatherhood and masculinity?

These are interesting and important questions, and timely as well. One would, however, never guess that from reading the literature of bioethics. For whatever reason, that literature, when it focuses on gender at all, is almost exclusively interested in women. And when it focuses on parenthood, it almost exclusively focuses on motherhood. While the general topics of reproductive choices and artificial means of reproduction have had a central place in bioethics, the literature and debate have usually centered on women's choices or women's role in such things as surrogate motherhood and *in vitro* fertilization. Fathers and fatherhood are just absent from the discussion altogether.

161

The absence of fatherhood in the debate is puzzling, especially since the topic of artificial means of reproduction is a central one in the field. My surmise is that, because those means of reproduction depend so heavily upon anonymous male sperm donations, and since such donations are rarely questioned for their moral propriety, there has been no need or place to talk about fathers. They just don't really count in that brave new world of reproduction. I will return later to that topic. Of more general importance is whether fatherhood can be given a fresh look and a reinvigorated role in bioethics.

At the heart of the problem and future of parenthood, and thus of the most basic and indispensable kind of human nurturing, is a *relationship,* of men, women, and children bound together. Professionals seem to have lost a sense of and feel for that relationship—of the way men, women, and children need and best flourish in the company of the other. Instead, professionals have done conceptually what society has been doing legally and socially—treating men, women, and children as separate and distinguishable, with their own needs and rights. Thus we now speak easily of women's rights, and children's rights, and (hardly surprising, even if amusing) we have seen the growth of a men's rights movement. Doubtless there are some good reasons for this fragmenting development, the most important being the way earlier generations were prone to stack the family relationship, and its ground rules, too heavily in favor of men; or, where children were concerned, to treat them too much as the property of their parents, not as persons in their own right.

But it is time for some reintegration. The fragmentation is, unless corrected in the long run, going to be harmful for men, women, and children, both individually and in their relationship. A revived and reinvigorated place for fathers and the institution of fatherhood is as good a place as any to begin. I want to develop three points: (1) biological fatherhood carries with it permanent and nondispensable duties; (2) the rapid and widespread acceptance of artificial insemination donors was much too thoughtless and casual, but for just that reason symbolic of the devaluation of fatherhood; and (3) feminism as a movement has hurt both men and children, but also women, by its tendency to substantively displace fathers from a central role in the making of procreation decisions.

II. The Duties of Fatherhood

I begin here with the most simple and primitive of moral axioms, rarely articulated as such but as undeniable as anything can possibly be in ethics. The axiom is this: Human beings bear a moral responsibility for those voluntary acts that have an impact on the lives of others;

they are morally accountable for such acts. I will not discuss the many nuances and problems that this axiom raises: what counts as "voluntary," how great must be the impact upon others, and which effects of actions on others are morally more or less important.

In the case of biological fatherhood those nuances will not ordinarily be of great importance. From this moral axiom I will argue that given the obvious importance of procreation in bringing human life into existence, fathers have a significant moral responsibility for the children they voluntarily procreate. What human action could be more important than that which creates new life, the burden of which the newly born person must live with for the rest of his or her life? What causal connection could be more direct than biological procreation, without which human existence would not be possible? A father can hardly be held wholly responsible for *what* a child becomes—much will depend upon circumstances—but a father can be held responsible with the mother for the fact the child comes to be at all.

One philosopher has advanced the notion that our only serious moral obligations area those we voluntarily impose upon ourselves, as in specific contracts.[1] There cannot be, she says, involuntary obligations. This is not the place to debate the full implications of such a theory—which must systematically close its eyes to what it means to live in a community with other people—but it is pertinent to make a single point. Unless a male is utterly naive about the facts of procreation, to engage in voluntary sexual intercourse is to be responsible for what happens as a result. To enter into a contract with another is, at the least, to undertake a voluntary activity with a known likely outcome. Sexual intercourse for an informed male is fairly close to that, so even on a contract theory of moral obligation, intercourse shares many critical features with a contract. Society, curiously, seems to have been faster in establishing the moral and causal links between drinking and driving than between sexual activity and pregnancy. But that may be because society prefers to think that accidental, unwanted pregnancies come more from contraceptive ignorance and failure than from the sexual activities that require them; the former is a more comforting thought to sustain the sexual revolution.

From my moral axiom, therefore, and from what we know about the biology of human procreation, I believe there is no serious way of denying the moral seriousness of biological fatherhood and the existence of moral duties that follow from it. The most important moral statement might be this: Once a father, always a father. Because the relationship is biological rather than contractual, the natural bond cannot be abrogated or put aside. I conclude, that just as society cannot put aside the biological bond, so neither ought it put aside the moral bond, the set of obligations that go with that biological bond. If there are to be moral duties at all, then the biological bond is as fundamental and unavoidable as any that can be imagined.[2] Does this mean that each and every father has a full set of moral obligations toward the children he procreates? My answer is yes—unless he is mentally or financially incompetent to discharge those duties. To treat the matter otherwise is to assume that fatherhood *is* some kind of contractual relationship, one that can be set aside by some choice on the part of the father, or the mother and father together, or on the part of the state. This position does not preclude allowing one person to adopt the child of another, to play the role of father with a legal sanction to do so. This arrangement, however, is legitimate only when there are serious obstacles standing in the way of the biological father playing that role himself. Even then, however, he remains the biological father, and should the alternative arrangements for the child fail, he is once again responsible, and responsible whether he likes it or not, accepts it or not. The obligation stems from his original, irreversible act of procreation; so too is his moral obligation irreversible.

Imagine the following scenario. A father has, through the assorted legal ways society allows fathers to turn over their parental authority to another, legally ceased to act as a father and someone else is caring for the child. But imagine that the other person fails to adequately act as a father; fails, that is, to properly care for and nurture the child. The child then returns to the father and says: "You are still my father biologically; because of you I exist in this world. I need your help and you are obliged to give it to me." I have never been able to imagine even *one* moral reason why a father in that circumstance could disclaim responsibility, and disclaim it if, even in principle, there was someone else available who could take care of the child. A father is a father is a father.

III. Fatherhood and Artificial Insemination

I find it remarkable that, with hardly any public debate at all, the practice—indeed, institution—of artificial insemination by an anonymous male donor so easily slipped in. What could society have been thinking about? In this section I will argue that it is fundamentally wrong and should have no place in a civilized, much less a supposedly liberal society. It is wrong for just the reasons I have sketched in Section II about the moral obligations that go with fatherhood. A sperm donor whose sperm is successfully used to fertilize an ovum, which ovum proceeds through the usual phases of gestation, is a *father*. Nothing more, nothing less. He is as much a father biologically as the known sperm inseminator in a standard heterosexual relationship and sexual intercourse.

If he is thereby a biological father, he has all the duties of any other biological father. It is morally irrelevant that (1) the donor does not want to act as a father, (2) those who collect his sperm as medical brokers do not want him to act as a father, (3) the woman whose ovum he is fertilizing does not want him to act as a father, and (4) society is prepared to excuse him from the obligations of acting as a father. Fatherhood, because it is a biological condition, cannot be abrogated by personal desires or legal decisions. Nor can the moral obligations be abrogated either, unless there are reasons why they *cannot* be discharged, not simply that no one wants them to be discharged. Just as a "surrogate mother" is not a "surrogate" at all but a perfectly real and conventional biological mother, so also is a sperm donor whose sperm results in a child a perfectly real and conventional biological father.

Why was it decided to set all that aside? Why was it deemed acceptable for males to become fathers by becoming sperm donors but then to relieve them *totally* of all responsibility of being fathers, leaving this new father ignorant of who his child is and the child ignorant of who the father is? I was not present at that great cultural moment, but two reasons seem to have been paramount.

First, it was introduced under medical auspices and given a medical legitimation. Artificial Insemination by a Donor ("AID"), one author wrote, is "medically indicated in instances of the man's sterility, possible hereditary disease, rhesus incompatibility, or in most cases of oligospermia."[3] "Medically indicated?" But it does not cure anyone's disease—not some other would-be father who is sterile, or the women who receives the sperm who is perfectly capable of motherhood without donated sperm. What is cured, so to speak, is a couple's desire to have a child; but medicine does not ordinarily treat relational problems (save in psychotherapy), so there is no reason to call the matter medical at all. Moreover, of course, since artificial insemination only requires a single syringe, inserted in a well-known place, there is nothing "medical" even about the procedure.

As Daniel Wikler has nicely pointed out, the professional dominance of doctors in the history of AID is a perfect case of the medicalization of a nonmedical act, and the estabishment of a medical monopoly and legitimization as a result.[4] Just how far this medicalization has gone can be seen by the very language used to describe the procedure: "[Artificial Insemination] is of two basic types: homologous, when the semen is obtained from the husband (AIH); and heterologous, when the sperm is acquired from a donor (AID)."[5] I wonder how many males, working pleasurably to produce some sperm, understood themselves to be engaged in a heterologous activity? There is very little that medical science cannot dress up with a technical term.

The second reason for ready acceptance was probably that, in the name of helping someone to have a child, society seems to be willing to set aside any existing moral restraints and conventions. Perhaps in an underpopulated world, whose very existence is threatened by low birth rates, a case for artificial procreation might be made.

But it is hard to see why, in our world, where the problem of feckless and irresponsible male procreators is far more of a social crisis, society lets that one pass. One can well understand the urge, often desperate, to have a child. But it is less easy to understand an acceptance of the systematic downgrading of fatherhood brought about by the introduction of anonymous sperm donors. Or perhaps it was the case that fatherhood had already sunken to such a low state, and male irresponsibility was already so accepted, that no one saw a problem. It is as if everyone argued: Look, males have always been fathering children anonymously and irresponsibly; why not put this otherwise noxious trait to good use?

As a symbol of male irresponsibility—and a socially sanctioned symbol at that—one could hardly ask for anything better than artificial insemination with the sperm of anonymous donors. It raises male irresponsibility to the high level of a praised social institution, and it succeeds in getting males off the hook of fatherhood and parenthood in a strikingly effective and decisive way. The anonymity is an especially nice touch; no one will know who did what, and thus there can never be any moral accountability. That is the kind of world all of us have wished we could live in from time to time, especially in its sexual subdivision. From the perspective of the sperm donor, if the child's life turns out poorly, the donor will neither know about that nor inconveniently be called upon to provide help, fatherly help. Home free!

IV. Feminism and Fatherhood

As a movement, feminism has long had a dilemma on its hands. If women are to be free of the undue coercion and domination of males, they must establish their own independent sphere of activities and the necessary social and legal rights to protect that sphere. Women cannot and should not leave their fate in the hands of males, much less their reproductive fates. Meanwhile, feminists have also deplored feckless, irresponsible males who leave women in the lurch. Yet if males are to be encouraged to act more responsibly, to take seriously their duties to women and children, then they must be allowed to share the right to make decisions in those domains that bear on their activities and responsibilities. Males, moreover, have rights corresponding to their duties; they should be empowered to do that which their moral duties require of them.

For the most part, this dilemma has been resolved by the feminist movement in favor of stressing the independence of females from male control. This is evident in two important respects. First, in the abortion debate there has been a firm rejection of the claim that males should be either informed that a woman is considering an abortion or that the male should have a right to override her decision. The male should, in short, have neither a right to information nor choice about what happens to the conception.

Second, in its acceptance of single-parent procreation and motherhood, for both heterosexual and lesbian women, some branches of feminism have in effect declared fathers biologically irrelevant and socially unnecessary. Since this kind of motherhood requires, as a necessary condition, some male sperm (provided *in vitro* or *in vivo*), it has not been possible to dispense altogether with males. No such luck. But it has been possible to hold those males who assist such reproduction free of all responsibility for their action in providing the sperm. The only difference between the male who impregnates a woman in the course of sexual liaison and then disappears, and the man who is asked to disappear voluntarily after providing sperm, is that the latter kind of irresponsibility is, so to speak, licensed and legitimated. Indeed, it is treated as a kindly, beneficent action. The effect on the child is of course absolutely identical—an unknown, absent father.

Both of these moves seem understandable in the short run, but profoundly unhelpful to women in the long run. It is understandable why women would not want their abortion decision to depend upon male permission. They are the ones who will have to carry the child to term and nurture, as mothers, the child thereafter. It is no less understandable why some women want children without fathers. Some cannot find a male to marry but do not want to give up motherhood altogether; they view this as a course of necessity, a kind of lesser evil. Other women, for reasons of profound skepticism about males, or hostility toward them, simply want children apart from males altogether.

Please note that I said these motives are "understandable." I did not say they are justifiable. What is short-sighted about either of these choices is that, by their nullification of the moral obligations that ought to go with biological fatherhood, they contribute to the further infantilization of males, a phenomenon already well advanced in our society, and itself a long-standing source of harm for women.

If the obligations of males to take responsibility for the children they have procreated is sharply limited due to women deciding whether to grant males any rights, then males quickly get the message. That message is that the ordinary moral obligations that go with procreation are contingent and dispensable, not nearly as weighty as those of women. For even the most advanced feminists do not lightly allow women who have knowingly chosen to become mothers to jettison that obligation. Mothers are understood to be mothers forever, unlike fathers, who are understood to be fathers as long as no one has declared them free of responsibility. If you are a sperm donor, of course, that declaration can readily be had.

What social conditions are necessary to have the responsibilities of fatherhood taken seriously? The most obvious, it would seem, is a clear, powerful, and consistent social message to fathers: You are responsible for the lives of the children you procreate; you are always the father regardless of legal dispensations; only the gravest emergencies can relieve you of that obligation; you will be held liable if you fail in your duties; and, you will be given the necessary rights and prerogatives required to properly discharge your duties. Only recently has there been a concerted effort, long overdue, to require fathers to make good on child-support agreements. And only recently, and interestingly, has the importance of biological parenthood been sufficiently recognized to lower some of the barriers erected to keep adopted children from discovering the identity of their biological parents, including fathers.

Those feminists who believe that fathers should have no role in abortion decisions should reconsider that position or at least add some nuance. There are probably good reasons to not legally require that fathers be informed that the mother is considering an abortion; the possibilities of coercion and continuing stress thereafter are real and serious. But that is no reason to dispense with a *moral* requirement that the fathers be informed and their opinion requested if there are no overpowering reasons not to. The fetus that would be aborted is as much their doing as that of the mother, and the loss to the father can obviously be considerable. Acting as if the only serious consequences are for the woman is still another way of minimizing the importance of fatherhood.

Far too much is made of the fact that the woman actually carries the fetus. That does not make the child more hers than his, and in the lifetime span of procreation, childbearing, and childrearing, the nine-month period of gestation is a minute portion of that span. Only very young parents who have not experienced the troubles of teenage children or an adult child's marital breakup could think of the woman's pregnancy as an especially significant or difficult time compared with other phases of parenthood.

Fathers, in short, have a moral right to know that they are fathers and to have a voice in decisions about the outcome of pregnancy. To deny males such a right is also to reject the very concept of paternal responsibility for one's procreative actions. The right to be a father cannot rest upon someone else's decision to grant such a right; that is no right at all. If the right to be a father is that poorly based, then there will be no better basis for upholding the moral obligations of fathers, or holding them accountable for their actions. I see no possibility of having it both ways. Society often asserts as a general principle that rights entail obligations. In this case, I am arguing the converse: If society wants obligations taken seriously, rights must be recognized.

The argument for a father's moral right to knowledge and choice does not entail a corresponding legal right to force a woman to bear a child against her will. There are a number of prudential and practical reasons not to require legal notification that a woman plans to have an abortion or to require the father's permission. Such a requirement, I suspect, would be both unworkable and probably destructive of many marital relationships. But as a moral norm, this requirement is perfectly appropriate. It puts moral pressure on women to see the need to inform fathers they are fathers, and to withhold such knowledge only when there are serious moral reasons to do so.

Women should, in general, want to do everything possible to encourage fathers to take their role and duties seriously. Women, and the children they bear, only lose if men are allowed to remain infantile and irresponsible. The attempt to encourage more responsible fatherhood and the sharing of childbearing duties while simultaneously promoting the total independence of women in their childbearing decisions only sends a mixed message: Fathers should consider themselves responsible, but not too much; and they should share the choices and burdens of parenthood, but more the latter than the former, and all parents are created equal, but some are more equal than others.

I have mainly laid the emphasis so far on abortion decisions. But the same considerations apply when women, heterosexual or lesbian, make use of donated sperm deliberately to have a single-parent child. Women have been hurt throughout history by males who abandon their parental duties, leaving to women the task of raising the children. A sperm donor is doing exactly the same thing. The fact that he does it with social sanction does not change the outcome; one more male has been allowed to be a father without taking up the duties of fatherhood. Indeed, there is something symbolically destructive about using anonymous sperm donors to help women have children apart from a permanent marital relationship with the father.

For what action could more decisively declare the irrelevance of fatherhood than a specific effort to keep everyone ignorant? A male who would be a party to such an arrangement might well consider himself some kind of altruistic figure, helping women to get what they want. He would in reality be part of that grand old male tradition of fatherhood without tears, that wonderful fatherhood that permits all of the pleasures of procreation but none of its obligations. Women who use males in this way, allowing them to play once again that ancient role in a new guise, cannot fail to do harm both to women and parenthood.

V. Parenthood, Families, and Relationship

A great deal of fun is made these days of those old-fashioned families of the 1950s, especially the television versions, where the emphasis was placed on the family as a unit. They are spoofed in part because they failed to account for all of the families in those days that were simply not like that. Fair enough. They are derided as well because they often treated the women as empty-headed creatures good for nothing other than cleaning up after the kids and keeping father happy. And sometimes they are attacked because they did not present those fathers as strong leaders and role models for children. Rather, they portrayed fathers as weak and childish, capable of manipulation by wives and children.

But what the old-fashioned families saw clearly enough is that parenthood is a set of relationships, a complex web of rights, privileges, and duties as well as the more subtle interplay of morality in intimate relationships. Feminists have been prone to pose the problem of procreative rights as principally a female problem. Traditionalists have been wont to view fatherhood as a role of patriarchical hegemony. Both are wrong, however, because they fail to see the complexity of the relationship or to place the emphasis in the right place. Both mothers and fathers, as individual moral beings, have important roles as well as the rights and duties that go with those roles.

Those roles, most importantly, are conditioned by, and set in a context of, their mutuality. Each needs and is enriched by the role of the other. The obligations of the one are of benefit to the other; indeed, the mutuality of their obligations amplifies all of them. A mother can better be a mother if she has the active help of a father who takes his duties seriously. Likewise, the father will be a better father with the help of an equally serious mother. The child will, in turn, gain something from both of them, both individually and as a pair. It is important, therefore, that society return fatherhood to center stage not only for the sake of fathers, who will be forced to grow up, but also for mothers, who will benefit from a more mature notion of what fatherhood and parenthood are.

Notes

1. Judith J. Thompson, "A Defense of Abortion," 1 *Philosophy & Public Affairs* 47, 65 (1971).

2. James L. Nelson, "Parental Obligations and the Ethics of Surrogacy: A Causal Perspective," *Public Affairs Quarterly* 5, 49 (1991).

3. Mark S. Frankel, "Reproductive Technologies: Artificial Insemination," 4 *Encyclopedia of Bioethics* 1439, 1444 (Warren T. Reich ed., 1978).

4. Daniel Wikler & Norma J. Wikler, "Turkey-baster Babies: The Demedicalization of Artificial Insemination," 69 *Milbank Quarterly*. 5, 8 (1991).

5. Frankel, 1444.

10

The Facts of Fatherhood

Thomas W. Laqueur

This essay puts forward a labor theory of parenthood in which emotional work counts. I want to say at the onset, however, that it is not intended as a nuanced, balanced academic account of fatherhood or its vicissitudes. I write it in a grumpy, polemical mood.

In the first place I am annoyed that we lack a history of fatherhood, a silence which I regard as a sign of a more systemic pathology in our understanding of what being a man and being a father entail. There has unfortunately been no movement comparable to modern feminism to spur the study of men. Or conversely, history has been written almost exclusively as the history of men and therefore man-as-father has been subsumed under the history of a pervasive patriarchy—the history of inheritance and legitimate descent, the history of public authority and its transmission over generations. Fatherhood, insofar as it has been thought about at all, has been regarded as a backwater of the dominant history of public power. The sources, of course, support this view. Fathers before the eighteenth century appear in prescriptive texts about the family largely in their public roles, as heads of families or clans, as governors of the "little commonwealth," of the state within the state.

The rule of the patriarchy waned, but historians have not studied the cultural consequences for fathers of its recession. Instead, they have largely adopted the perspective of nineteenth-century ideologues: men belong to the public sphere of the marketplace and women to the private sphere of the family. A vast prescriptive literature explains how to be a good mother: essentially how to exercise proper moral influence and display appropriate affections in the home, duties that in earlier centuries would have fallen to the father. But there is little in the era of "separate spheres" on how to be the new public man in private. A rich and poignant source material on the affective relationship between fathers and children in the nineteenth century—Gladstone's account of watching for days by the bedside of his dying daughter, for example—speaks to the power of emotional bonds, but historians have largely ignored it. They have instead taken some Victorians at their word and written the father out of the family except as a parody of the domestic autocrat or as the representative of all those forces which stood in the way of the equality of the sexes.

Second, I write in the wake of Baby M and am annoyed with the neoessentialism it has spawned. Baby M was the case of the decade in my circles, a "representative anecdote" for ancient but ageless questions in the late twentieth century. Like most people, I saw some right on both sides and had little sympathy for the marketplace in babies that brought them together. On the one hand Mary Beth Whitehead this . . . ; on the other William Stern that . . . The baby broker who arranged the deal was manifestly an unsavory character, the twentieth-century avatar of the sweatshop owners who in ages past profited unconscionably from the flesh of women. It was difficult not to subscribe to the doctrine that the baby's best interests must come first and it was by no means consistently clear where these lay. Each day brought new emotional tugs as the narrative unfolded on the front pages of every paper.

I was surprised that, for so many people, this transaction between a working-class woman and a professional man (a biochemist) became an epic prism through which the evils of capitalism and class society were refracted. It did not seem newsworthy to me that the poor sold their bodies or that the rich exploited their willingness to do so. What else would they sell? Malthus had pointed out almost two centuries ago that those who labored physically gave of their flesh and in the long run earned just enough to maintain and replenish it. So had Marx, who also identified women as the agents of social re-production.

Admittedly, the contract entered into by Whitehead and Stern was stripped of all shreds of decency and aesthetic mystification, flatfootedly revealing the deal for what it was—not a womb rental but a baby sale. This is why the New Jersey Supreme Court ruled it unenforceable. Every account that one reads of the surrogate baby broker's operations, with its well-dressed couples sitting in little cubicles interviewing long lines of less well-dressed but hopeful, spiffed-up women seeking work as surrogates, conjures up distasteful reminders of depression labor exchanges, starlet casting couches, or academic hiring fairs. But there surely are no new horrors in this case. Basically the Baby M narratives are modern versions of the industrial novel and allied genres in which factory labor is portrayed as wage slavery; in which children's tiny thin fingers are metamorphosed into the pin wire they hour after hour produce; in which paupers, whose labor is worthless on the open market, are depicted pounding bones into meal so that they might remain just this side of starvation.[1] In short, I remain cynical when some commentators discover Mary Beth Whitehead as the anti-capitalist Everywoman. If "surrogate" mothers were as well organized as the doctors who perform the much more expensive *in vitro* fertilization or as unionized baseball players they would earn a decent wage—say $100,000 instead of the ludicrously low $10,000— and opposition to surrogacy as emblematic of the evils of a free market in labor might be considered muted. (Though of course then the story might shift to emphasize the power of money to dissolve the very fabric of social decency, another nineteenth-century trope.)

I am, however, primarily interested in this case as the occasion for a return to naturalism. Feminism has been the most powerful de-naturalizing theoretical force in my intellectual firmament and, more generally, a major influence in the academic and cultural affairs that concern me. I regard it as both true and liberating that "the idea that men and women are two mutually exclusive categories must arise out of something other than a nonexistent 'natural' opposition," and that "gender is a socially imposed division of the sexes."[2] A major strand of commentary on Baby M, however, rejects this tradition and instead insists that the category "mother" is natural, a given of the world outside culture. Phyllis Chesler, for example, in the major article of a special "Mothers" issue of *Ms* (May, 1988) argues that motherhood is a "fact," an ontologically different category than "fatherhood," which is an "idea." Thus, "in order for the *idea* [my emphasis] of fatherhood to triumph over the *fact* of motherhood," she says, "we had to see Bill as the 'birth father' and Mary Beth as the surrogate uterus." (Actually Chesler misstates the claims. Mary Beth has been, rightly or wrongly, called the "surrogate mother," not the "surrogate uterus." But since the point of the article seems to be that mother and uterus are more or less the same thing this may be an intentional prevarication.)

I resist this view for obvious emotional reasons: it assumes that being the "factual" parent entails a stronger connection to the child than being the "ideational" parent. (This assumption is widespread. During my daughter Hannah's five-week stay in the preemie nursery her caretakers, in the "social comments" column of her chart, routinely recorded my wife's visits to her incubator as "mother in to bond," whereas my appearances were usually noted with the affectively neutral "father visited.") While I do not want to argue against the primacy of material connection directly I do want to point out that it is not irrational to hold the opposite view and that, "in fact," the incorporeal quality of fatherhood has been the foundation of patriarchy's ideological edifice since the Greeks. In other words, simply stating that mothers have a greater material connection with the child is not to make an argument but to state a premise which historically has worked against Chesler's would-be conclusion. The Western philosophical tradition has generally valued idea over matter; manual labor for millennia was the great horizontal social divide. In other words, precisely because the mother's claim was "only" corporeal, because it was a matter of "fact," it was valued less.

I will recount some of the history of this discourse, but I also want to argue against its basic operating assumption: the unproblematic nature of fact especially in relation to such deeply cultural designations as mother or father and to the rights, emotions, or duties that are associated with them. The "facts" of motherhood—and of fatherhood for that matter—are not "given" but come into being as science progresses and as the adversaries in political struggles select what they need from the vast, ever-growing storehouses of knowledge. The idea that a child is of one's flesh and blood is very old while its biological correlatives and their cultural importance depend on the available supplies of fact and on their interpretation.

But the reason that the facts of motherhood and fatherhood are not "given" has less to do with what is known or not known than with the fundamental gap, recognized by David Hume, between facts and their meaning. *Is* does not imply *ought,* and more generally no fact or set of facts taken together entails or excludes a moral right or commitment. Laws, customs, and precepts, sentiments, emotion, and the power of the imagination make biological facts assume cultural significance. An Algonquin chief, confronted by a Jesuit in the seventeenth century with the standard European argument against women's promiscuity (how else would you know that a child is yours?), replied that he found it puzzling that whites could apparently only love "their" children, i.e., that only individual ownership entailed caring and affection.

Before proceeding I want to again warn my readers that some of my evidence and most of my passion arise from personal circumstance. I write as the father of a daughter to whom I am bound by the "facts" of a visceral love, not the molecular biology of reproduction. The fact of the matter is that from the instant the five-minute-old Hannah—a premature baby of 1430 grams who was born by Caesarean section—grasped my finger (I know this was due to reflex and not affection) I felt immensely powerful, and before the event, inconceivably strong bonds with her. Perhaps if practitioners of the various sub-specialties of endocrinology had been present they might have measured surges of neuro-transmitters and other hormones as strong as those that accompany parturition. But then what difference would that make—with what is one to feel if not with the body?

I also write as the would-be father, some sixteen months before Hannah came along, of a boy weighing something less than 800 grams who was aborted late one night—an induced stillbirth really—after twenty-four weeks of gestation because of a burst amniotic sac and the ensuing infection. I can recapture my sadness at his demise vividly and still regard the whole episode as one of the gloomiest of my life. Gail, my wife, was ambivalent about having the child—she was, she says, unprepared at age 40 for becoming pregnant the very first month at risk—and regards the abortion as a painful but not especially fraught episode which cleared the emotional ground to allow her to welcome Hannah's birth unequivocally.

Finally I write as the male member of a family in which gender roles are topsy-turvy. Hannah early on announced that she would prefer being a daddy to being a mommy because mommies had to go to work—hers is a lawyer—while daddies only had to go to their study. (As she has grown older and observed my not silent suffering as I finished a book begun the year she was born her views have been somewhat revised.) I am far guiltier of the stereotypical vices of motherhood—neurotic worry about Hannah's physical and mental well being, unfounded premonitions of danger, excessive emotional demands, and general nudginess—than is Gail. In short, my experiences—ignoring for the moment a vast ethnographic and somewhat smaller historical literature—make me suspect of the naturalness of "mother" or "father" in any culturally meaningful sense.

The association of fatherhood with ideas and motherhood with facts is ancient; only its moral valences have been recently reversed by some feminists. The Marquis de Sade suggests that the "idea" of fatherhood—the notion that a child is "born of the father's blood" and only incidentally of a mother's body—means that it "owes filial tenderness to him alone, an assertion not without its appealing qualities. . . ."[3] Sade is the most rabid of anti-maternalists and his argument is made to induce a girl to sexually defile and humiliate her mother; but his relative valuation of fact and idea is standard. The "idea" of fatherhood gave, and displayed, the power of patriarchy for much of Western history since the Greeks.

Bolingbrooke in *Richard II* (1, 3, 69) addresses his father as

"Oh thou, the earthly author of my blood,
Whose youthful spirit, in me regenerate."

He is author and authority because, like the poet who has in his mind the design for the verses that subsequently appear, he has the conceit for the child in him. The physical act of writing, or of producing the child, matters little. Conceiving a child in this model is a man's sparking of an idea in the uterus which contains, like a block of marble, a form waiting to be liberated. It is like writing on a piece of paper awaiting inscription. The "generation of things in Nature and the generation of things in Art take place in the same way," argued the great seventeenth-century physician William Harvey, who discovered the circulation of the blood. "Now the brain is the instrument of conception of the one . . . and of the other the uterus or egg."[4] And being the instrument is less elevated than being the author: "He," speaking of God, "was the author, thou the instrument," says King Henry in offering pardon to Warwick (*3 Henry VI*, 4, 6, 18).

But the idea of "father" as bound to his child in the way a poet is to verse, i.e., its genitor, is much older than Shakespeare. It is, argues Freud, one of the cornerstones of culture; believing in fathers, like believing in the Hebrew God, reflects the power of abstract thought and hence of civilization itself.

The "Moses religion's" insistence that God cannot be seen—the graven image proscription—"means that a sensory perception was given second place to what may be called an abstract idea." This God represents "a triumph of intellectuality over sensuality *[Triumph der Geistigkeit uber de Sinnlichkeit]*, or strictly speaking, an instinctual renunciation. . . ." Freud briefs precisely the same case for fathers as for God in his analysis of Aeschylus' *Eumenides,* which follows immediately his discussion of the Second Commandment. Orestes denies that he has killed his mother by denying that being born of her entails special bonds or obligation. Apollo makes the defense's case: appearances notwithstanding, no man has a mother. "The mother is no parent of that which is called her child, but only nurse of the new-planted seed that grows." She is but "a stranger." The only true parent is "he who mounts."[5]

Here is the founding myth of the Father. "Paternity" *[Vaterschaft],* Freud concludes, "is a supposition" and like belief in the Jewish God it is "based on an inference, a premise," while "maternity" *[Mutterschaft],* like the old gods, is based on evidence of the senses alone. The invention of paternity, like that of a transcendent God, was thus also "a momentous step"; it likewise—Freud repeats the phrase but with a more decisive military emphasis—was "a conquest *[einen Sieg]* of intellectuality over sensuality." It too represented a victory of the more elevated, the more refined, the more spiritual over the less refined, the sensory, the material. It too is a world-historical *"Kulturfortschritt,"* a great cultural stride forward.

Similarly, the great medieval encyclopedist Isidore of Seville could, without embarrassment, make three different claims about the nature of seed—that only men had *sperma,* that only women had *sperma,* and that both had *sperma*—which would be mutually contradictory if they were about the body but perfectly compatible if they were instead corporeal illustrations of cultural truths purer and more fundamental than biological "fact." Isidore's entire work is predicated on the belief that the origin of words informs one about the pristine, uncorrupted, essential nature of their referents, of a reality beyond the corrupt senses, beyond facts.

In the first case Isidore is explaining consanguinity and, as one would expect in a society in which inheritance and legitimacy pass through the father, he is at pains to emphasize the exclusive origins of the seed in the father's blood, in the purest, frothiest, white part of that blood shaken from the body as the foam is beaten from the sea as it crashes on the rocks.[6] For a child to have a father *means* that it is "from one blood," the father's; and conversely to be a father *is* to produce the substance, semen, through which blood is passed on to one's successors. Generation seems to happen without woman at all and there is no hint that blood—"that by which man is animated, and is sustained, and lives," as Isidore tells us elsewhere—could in any fashion be transmitted other than through the male.[7] Now case two, illegitimate descent. This presents a quite different biology: the child under these circumstances is from the *body* of the mother alone; it is "spurious," he explains, because "the ancients called the female genitalia the *spurium*" (9, 5, 24). So, while the legitimate child is from the froth of the father, the illegitimate child seems to come solely from factual flesh, from the seed of the mother's genitals, as if the father did not exist. And finally, when Isidore is explaining why children resemble their progenitors and is not interested in motherhood or fatherhood he remarks pragmatically that "newborns resemble fathers, if the semen of the father is potent, and resemble mothers if the mothers' semen is potent." Both parents, in this account, have seeds which engage in repeated combat for domination every time, and in each generation, a child is conceived (Isidore, 11, 1, 145).

These three distinct and mutually exclusive arguments are a dramatic illustration that much of the debate about the nature of the seed and of the bodies that produce it was in fact not about bodies at all but rather about power, legitimacy, and the politics of fatherhood. They are in principle not resolvable by recourse to the senses. One might of course argue that "just so" stories like Isidore's or Aeschylus' are simply no longer tenable given what has been known since the nineteenth century about conception. Modern biology makes perfectly clear what "mother" and "father" are. But science is relevant only if these stories are understood as reductionistic, as claiming to be true because of biology, which is, rightly, not the sort of claim Isidore and Aeschylus are making. The facts they adduce to illustrate essentially cultural claims may no longer be acceptable and we may persist in reading their cultural claims as based in a false biology. But the "fact" of women bearing children has never been in dispute and has nonetheless counted for relatively little historically in establishing their claims to recognition or authority over children or property.

Facts, as I suggested earlier, are but shifting sands for the construction of motherhood or fatherhood. They come and go and are ludicrously open to interpretation. Regnier de Graaf's discovery of the ovum in 1672 seemed to relegate the male/father to an unaccustomed and distinctly secondary role in reproduction. (Actually de Graaf discovered the follicle that bears his name but which he and others mistakenly took to be the egg. Karl Ernst von Baer in 1827 was the first to observe a mammalian egg and an unfertilized human egg was not seen until 1930.[8]) The female after de Graaf could be imagined to provide the matter for the fetus in a pre-formed if not immediately recognized form while the male "only serv'd to Actuate it." This, one contemporary observed, "derogates much from the dignity of the Male-Sex," which he thought was restored when "Mons. Leeuwenhoek by the Help of his Exquisite Microscope . . . detected Innumerable small *Animals* in the Masculine sperm, and by his Noble Discovery, at once removed that Difficulty. . . ."[9]

I hope by this egregious example to suggest that the form of the argument, and not just its factual premises, are flawed; both conclusions are silly. And, the discovery, still accepted, that neither egg nor sperm contains a pre-formed human but that the fetus develops epigenetically according to plans acquired from both parents does not settle the question of the comparative claims of mother or father, just as the mistaken notions of the past did not entail judgments of their comparative dignities.

Interpretations, not facts, are at issue. The Archbishop of Hartford announced in the *New York Times* on August 26, 1988, that he had quit the Democratic party because it supported abortion: "it is officially in favor of executing unborn babies whose only crime is that they temporarily occupy their mother's womb." No one would dispute that the "thing" in the mother's womb is, under some construction, an unborn baby. "Baby" is a common term for fetus as well as for a very young child and the phrase "the baby is kicking again" to refer to an intra-uterine action is generally acceptable; baby-as-fetus is indisputably only a temporary occupant. The Archbishop's interpretation is objectionable because he elides the difference between "baby-in-the-womb" and "baby-in-the-world," between the womb and any other space an infant might occupy, and therefore between abortion and execution. At issue here is meaning, not nature.

David Hume makes manifest the chasm between the two. A beautiful fish, a wild animal, a spectacular landscape, or indeed "anything that neither belongs, nor is related to us," he says, inspires in us no pride or vanity or sense of obligation. We might with perfect reason fear a minor injury to ourselves and care almost nothing about the deaths of millions of distant strangers. The fault is not with the objects themselves but with their relationship to us. They are too detached and distant to arouse passion. Only, Hume argues, when these "external objects acquire any particular relation to ourselves, and are associated or connected with us," do they engage the emotions.[10] Owning the "external object" seems for Hume to be the most obvious way for this to happen, although ownership itself is, of course, an immensely elastic notion. A biological parent, uncle, clan, "family" can "own" a child in such a fashion as to love and cherish it. But more generally Hume is suggesting that moral concern and action are engendered not by the logic of the relationship between human beings but by the degree to which the emotional and imaginative connections which entail love or obligation have been forged.

The "fact" of motherhood is precisely the psychic labor that goes into making these connections, into appropriating the fetus and then child into a mother's moral and emotional economy. The "fact" of fatherhood is of a like order. If a labor theory of values gives parents rights to a child, that labor is of the heart, not the hand. (The heart, of course, does its work through the hand; we feel through the body. But I will let the point stand in its polemical nakedness.)

While I was working as a volunteer in an old people's home I was attracted to, and ultimately became rather good friends with, a gay woman who was its director of activities. At lunch one day—she had alerted me that she wanted to discuss "something" and not just, as we usually did, schmooz—she asked whether I would consider donating sperm should she and her long-time lover decide, as they were on the verge of doing, to have a child. I was for her a generally appropriate donor—Jewish, fit, with no history of genetic disorders in my family. She was asking me also, she said, because she liked me. It was the first, and remains the only, time I had been asked by anyone, much less someone I liked, and so I was flattered and pleased.

I was also hesitant. My wife the lawyer raised serious legal difficulties with donating "owned" sperm, i.e., sperm that is not given or sold for anonymous distribution. I would remain legally liable for child-support for at least twenty-one years, not to speak of being generally entangled with the lives of a couple I liked but did not know well. (Anonymous sperm is alienated from its producer and loses its connection with him as if it were the jetsam and flotsam of the sea or an artisan's product in the marketplace. Semen, in other words, counts as one of these products of the body that can be alienated, like plasma and blood cells, and not like kidneys or eyes, whose marketing is forbidden.)

Legal issues, however, did not weigh heavily with me. The attractive part of the proposition—that I was being asked because of who I was and therefore that I was to be a father and not just a donor—also weighed mightily against it. A thought experiment with unpleasant results presented itself. I immediately imagined this would-be child as a version of Hannah, imagined that I could see her only occasionally and for short periods of time, imagined that her parents would take her back to their native Israel and that I would never see her again. Potential conflicts with my friend about this baby were almost palpable on the beautiful sunny afternoon of our lunch. In short, I was much too cathexed with this imaginary child to ever give up the sperm to produce her.

I recognize now, and did at the time, that my response was excessive. My reveries of fatherhood sprang from a fetishistic attachment to one among millions of rapidly replenished microscopic organisms—men make on the order of 400 billion sperm in a lifetime—swimming in an abundant, nondescript saline fluid. All that I was really being asked to do was to "produce" some semen—a not unpleasant process—and to give it to my friend so that *a* very, very tiny sperm—actually only its 4-5 micrometers long and 2.5 to 3.5 micrometers wide (c. 1/10,000 to 1/20,000 of an inch) head—might contribute the strands of DNA wafting about in it to her egg. Since we humans apparently share 95% of our genetic material with chimpanzees, the sperm in question must share a still higher percentage of base pairs with those of my fellow humans. In short, my unique contribution to the proposed engagement, that which I did not share with billions of other men and monkeys, was infinitesimally small. I was making a mountain out of much, much, much less than a molehill and not very much more than a molecule.

But this is as it should be. For much of history the problem has been to make men take responsibility for their children. Prince and pauper as circumstances required could easily deny the paternity that nature did so little to make evident. The double standard of sexual morality served to insure that however widely they sowed their wild oats the fruits of their wives' wombs would be unambiguously theirs. In fact, until very recently paternity was impossible to prove and much effort went into developing histo-immunological assays that could establish the biological link between a specific man and child. The state, of course, has an interest in making some male, generally the "biological father," responsible for supporting "his" children. In short, a great deal of cultural work has gone into giving meaning to a small bit of matter. Ironically, now that tests make it possible to identify the father with about 100% accuracy, women—those who want children *without* a father—have considerable difficulty obtaining sperm free of filiation. History, social policy, imagination, and culture continue to encumber this cell with its haploid of chromosomes.

In 1978, Mary K., a gay woman living in Sonoma County, California, decided that she wanted to have a child which she would "co-parent" with a close gay woman friend living nearby.[11] Mary wanted to find a sperm donor herself rather than use anonymous sperm for several reasons which she later more or less clearly articulated. She did not want to make the repeated trips to Berkeley, the location of the nearest sperm bank; she did not want to use a physician in her community who might be able to acquire sperm anonymously because she felt that as a nurse she could not be assured of confidentiality; and—this would come to haunt her—she wanted some vestige of an individual human being to be associated with the sperm and with the hoped-for baby. She wanted a "father" of some ill-defined sort, and after a month or so of looking around and after interviewing three potential donors, she was introduced one January evening to a young gay man, Jhordan C., who seemed to fit her needs. He would become the "father" of her child, despite the fact that he did not have the red hair that she had originally sought in a donor.

Neither Jhordan or Mary thought very rigorously about what they expected from their relationship or just what his paternal rights and obligations would be. Neither sought legal counsel; they signed no contract or other written understanding and resolved only the most basic practical details of the matter: Jhordan, upon being notified that Mary was ovulating, would journey to her house, and "produce" sperm, which she would introduce into herself. It took six months before Mary conceived and each of his visits was apparently attended by commonplace social intercourse—some chit chat, tea, and other pleasantries.

After Mary conceived she and Jhordan saw each other occasionally. She accepted his invitation to a small New Year's party at the home of one of his close friends. She testifies that he "reiterated" to her that "he wanted to be known as the father—and I told him I would let the child know who the biological father was—and that he wanted to travel with the child when the child was older." In all other respects she believed that they had an implicit understanding that she would be the child's guardian and primary parent; that Victoria T., Mary's friend, would be co-parent; and that Jhordan would play effectively no role in the life of *her* child.

On the basis of Jhordan's own testimony, he did not know precisely what he meant by wanting "to be known as the father." The court-appointed psychologist described him as a young man of unsettled plans and interests. But Jhordan knew that he wanted somehow to be acknowledged. He was upset when Mary informed him, some months before the birth, that his name would not be on the birth certificate and he became increasingly uneasy as he came to realize that he was being increasingly written out of the family drama that he had helped launch.

Mary admits that she too had been vague about what Jhordan's being her child's father meant to her and that he did have some grounds for his expectation that he would play some sort of paternal role. Language failed her when she tried to describe it:

I had thought about and I was considering whether or not I would tell Sean [not his real name] who the father was, but I didn't know if I would tell him as a father. Like he would know that Jhordan helped donate the sperm, but I did not know if he would ever know Jhordan—How do I say this? I didn't plan on Sean relating as a father. No.

The confusion of names and collapse of grammar here suggests precisely the underlying ambiguities of this case.

When Sean was born Mary felt increasingly threatened by Jhordan's insistence on seeing him, on displaying him to his family, on taking pictures to show to friends and relatives, and in general on acting like a parent, a role that Mary had thought was reserved for herself and Victoria. Jhordan, on the other hand, told the psychologist who interviewed him to determine his fitness as a parent that when "he looked into Sean's eyes, he 'saw his whole family there.' " Whatever uncertainties he might have felt before vanished in the face of his imagined flesh and blood.

Mary finally refused to allow Jhordan to see the baby at all and he eventually gave up trying. There matters might have rested had not, a year later, Mary applied for welfare. The state sued Jhordan for child support (it was after all his sperm) and he, of course, eagerly agreed to pay. Two years and two lawyers later he won visiting rights with Sean at the home of Mary's friend and co-parent, Victoria. These privileges were subsequently expanded. From here on the story is like that of countless divorced couples: quarrels about visitation hours and pick-up times, about where Sean would spend holidays and birthdays, about whether Jhordan allowed him to eat too much sugar, and about other of the many controversial niceties of child-raising that divide parents in even the tightest of families. A court promulgated guidelines and issued orders; an uneasy peace settled over all the parties.

The trial judge in this case was a rather old-fashioned sort who did not seem terribly interested in the subtleties of the law regarding the rights of sperm donors but believed that "blood is thicker than water" and that Sean both needed, and had "a right to," a father. Jhordan was the father and therefore ought, in the judge's view, to be given commensurate visitation rights.

Mary appealed (*Jhordan C. v Mary K.* [1986] 179 CA3d 386, 224 CR 530). The central question before the high court was how to interpret sections 7005(a) and (b) of the California Civil Code. These provide that if, under the supervision of a doctor, a married woman is inseminated by semen from a man who is not her husband, that man under certain circumstances is treated as if he were *not* the natural father while the husband is treated as if he were. Mary's lawyers argued that while their client's case did not quite fit under this statute it was close enough and that the only possible distinction was one of sexual orientation, which ought not to matter. Other California statutes provide that the law must not discriminate against unconventional parenting arrangements in adoption and other reproductive rights issues. If Mary had been married to someone and had acquired Jhordan's sperm in precisely the same circumstances—admittedly not meeting all the conditions of the statute—it would be ludicrous to suppose that the State would give him rights that infringed upon those of the husband. (A German court has held that a man has no claims on a child of a married woman even if he is acknowledged to be the "biological father." Today, as has been generally true for centuries, children born in wedlock are presumed to belong to the husband of the woman who bore them.)

Moreover, Mary's lawyers argued, section 7005a's reference to semen given "to a licensed physician" was not intended to limit the law's application only to such cases but reflected simply a legislative directive to insure proper health standards by recourse to a physician. Mary, because of her training as a nurse, was able to comply with this standard on her own. Her lawyers also cited another court case which held—admittedly in different circumstances—that

A child conceived through heterologous artificial insemination [i.e. with semen from a man other than the woman's husband] does not have a "natural father." . . . The anonymous donor of sperm can not be considered the "natural father," as he is no more responsible for the use made of his sperm than is a donor of blood or a kidney.

Echoes of Isidore of Seville. Jhordan might not have been anonymous but he was certainly a stranger to Mary.

His lawyers naturally argued for a stricter construal of section 7005a-b and the appeals court sided with them. By not employing a physician, the court agreed, Mary had excluded herself from the law's protection. Moreover, the court viewed the case before it as being more like those in which artificial insemination occurred within the context of an established relationship and in which the sperm donor retained paternal rights than it was like cases of anonymous donation. Jhordan's lawyer cited a New Jersey Supreme court case, for example, in which a man and a woman were dating and intended to marry. She wanted to bear his child but did not want to have pre-marital intercourse so they resorted to artificial insemination. Three months into the pregnancy they broke up and she declared that she wanted nothing more to do with him and that she certainly would not allow him to visit their child. He sued for paternity and won.

Mary and Jhordan were obviously not as intimately involved as this couple but, the court felt, neither were they the anonymous strangers envisaged by statute. Enough humanity remained in Jhordan's transaction with Mary to allow him to believe that his sperm, however introduced into Mary's body, retained some of him.

As this case and others like it suggest, the legal status of a sperm donor remains deeply problematic and, advises a National Lawyers Guild Handbook, those "consulted by a lesbian considering artificial insemination must be extremely careful to explain the ramifications of the various choices available to their clients."[12] Using a medically supervised sperm bank where the identity of the donor is unknown to the recipient is the most certain way to guarantee that the donor will not at some time in the future be construed as the father. Other possibilities include having a friend secure semen but keeping the source secret; using semen from multiple donors (not recommended because of possible immune reactions); using a known donor but having a physician as intermediary. Some lawyers recommend having the recipient pay the donor for his sperm and describing the transaction in an ordinary commercial contract of the sort with which the courts are familiar. And even if agreements between sperm donors and recipients are not predictably enforceable, lawyers suggest that the parties set down their understanding of their relationship as clearly as possible.

Any or all of these strategies might have stripped Jhordan's sperm of paternity, not just in the eyes of the law but more importantly in his heart, and might thus have saved Mary and her co-parent their struggles with the parental claims of a near stranger. Mary was wrong to eschew a doctor's mediation or at least underestimated the hold that a very small bit of matter can, in the right circumstances, have on a man's imagination.

In designating a physician as middleman the legislature did not blindly medicalize an essentially social transaction but sought rather to appropriate one of modern medicine's least attractive features—its lack of humanity—for a socially useful end. Everyone knows, even politicians, that artificial insemination does not require a physician. De-paternalizing sperm might. A strange doctor in a lab coat working amidst white formica furniture, high tech instruments, officious nurses, and harried receptionists in a boxy office in a nondescript glass and steel building set in a parking lot may offer cold comfort to the sick and needy; he or she might, however, be perfect at taking the sparkle off sperm.

Had Jhordan donated sperm not at Mary's house, where he was offered tea and conversation, but at a clinic; had he never spoken to her after the inseminations began but only to the doctor's nurse, who would have whisked away the vial of fresh semen; had he never seen Mary pregnant or celebrated New Year's Eve with her, the fetish of the sperm might have been broken. The doctor as broker would have performed his or her priestly function, de-blessed the sperm, and gotten rid of its "paternity." (This I imagine as the inversion of normal priestly work, providing extra emotional glue between the participants in weddings, funerals, and the like.) Similarly, selling sperm at a price fixed by contract—the lawyer or sperm bank owner as de-blessing agent—would take off some of its paternal blush. Without such rites, a father's material claim in his child is small but his imaginative claims can be as endless as a mother's. Great care must be taken to protect and not to squash them.

Because fatherhood is an "idea," it is not limited to men. In a recent case litigated in Alameda County, California (Lofton v. Flouroy), a woman was, rightly in my view, declared to be a child's father, if not its male parent. Ms. Lofton and Ms. Flouroy lived together and decided to have a child. Lofton's brother Larry donated the required sperm but expressed no interest in having any further role in the matter. Ms. Lofton introduced her brother's semen into Flouroy with a turkey baster, Flouroy became pregnant, and in due course a baby was born. The "birth mother" was listed on its birth certificate as "mother," and L. Loften—Linda, not Larry, but who was to know?—was listed as "father."

Everything went well and the women treated the child as theirs until, two years later, they split up. The mother kept the child and there matters might have rested had not, as in the case of Mary and Jhordan, the State intervened. Flouroy applied for welfare benefits, i.e., aid to dependent children, and when asked by the Family Support Bureau to identify the father she produced, in a moment of unabashed concreteness, the turkey baster. The Bureau, not amused, did what it was meant to do and went after the "father" on the birth certificate— Linda, it was surprised to learn, not Larry. Like Jhordan she welcomed the opportunity to claim paternity, did not dispute the claim and eagerly paid the judgment entered against her: child support, current and retroactive. She also demanded paternal visitation rights, which Ms. Flouroy resisted. Lofton then asked the court to compel mediation. It held that she was indeed a "psychological parent" and thus had standing to have her rights mediated. The other L. Lofton, Larry, makes no appearance in this drama.

Linda's claim is manifestly not biological nor even material. That she borrowed her brother's sperm or owned the turkey baster is irrelevant. What matters is that, in the emotional economy of her relationship with her lover and their child, she was the father, whatever that means, and enjoyed the rights and bore the obligations of that status. She invested the required emotional and imaginative capital in the impregnation, gestation, and subsequent life to make the child in some measure hers.

I hasten to add that I do not regard biology in all circumstances as counting for nothing. Women have claims with respect to the baby within them simply by virtue of spatial relations and rights to bodily integrity. These are not the right to be or not to be a mother as against the right to be or not to be a father, nor the claims of a person as against those of a non-person—the terms in which the abortion debate is usually put—but the right shared by all mentally competent adults to control and monitor corporeal boundaries, to maintain a body as theirs. Thus I would regard a court compelling a woman to bear a child against her will as a form of involuntary servitude however much its would-be father might wish for the child. And I would regard an enforced abortion as an even more egregious assault on her body. But this is not to acknowledge the "fact" of motherhood as much as the "fact" of flesh. History bears witness to the evils that ensue when the state abrogates a person's rights in her body.

The flesh does not make a mother's body an ahistorical font of motherhood and maternity. A writer who wants, but cannot herself have, a child and who finds surrogate motherhood morally unaccept-able "can not imagine" that "there are plenty of women now, the huge majority of surrogates who have, to hear them tell it, not suffered such a loss [as Mary Beth Whitehead's]."[13] While her empathic instincts extend easily to Whitehead she cannot, despite testimony to the contrary, conceive of a mother *not* feeling an instant and appar-ently unmediated bond to her child. Ms. Fleming cannot accept that feelings do not follow from flesh so that "surrogate mothers" who feel otherwise than they supposedly should must suffer, like un-class-conscious workers, from false consciousness.

Ms's special "Mothers Issue," quite apart from Chesler's article, is striking by its very cover—an airbrushed, soft-toned picture of a 1950s young Ivory Soap woman, with straight blond hair of the sort that waves in shampoo commercials, holding a blue-eyed baby to her bare bosom and looking dreamily out of the frame of the picture—which would have been denounced by feminists as perpetuating an unaccept-able stereotype of women had it appeared in *Family Circle* a decade ago. In 1988 it unashamedly represents the Mother in America's largest selling feminist magazine.

What exactly are the facts of motherhood and what of significance ought to follow from them? For advocates of Mrs. Whitehead's, like Phyllis Chesler, her egg and its genetic contents are not especially relevant. She shares with Bill, a.k.a. Dr. Stern, the provision of chromosomes. The critical fact is therefore her nine months of incuba-tion, which would remain a fact even if the fertilized egg she was bringing to term were not hers. Her claim, it appears, rests on labor, on her physical intimacy with the child within her, and would be just as strong if a second woman sought a stake in the child on the basis of her contribution of half its chromosomes.

I am immensely sympathetic to this view but not because of a fact of nature. Capitalist societies, as I suggested earlier, are not usually friendly to the notion that putting labor into a product entitles one to ownership or even to much credit. It is the rare company that gives its workers shares of stock. We associate a new production of *The Magic Flute* with David Hockney and not with those who sawed, hammered, and painted the sets; everyone knows that Walt Disney produced *Bambi* but only the "cognoscenti" could name even one of the artists who actually made the pictures. Having the idea or the plan is what counts, which is why Judge Sokoloff told Dr. Stern that in getting Melissa he was only getting what was already his. (The Judge should, of course, have said, "half his.")

I became so exercised by Baby M because Dr. Stern's claims have been reduced in some circles to his ownership of his sperm which, as I said earlier, amounts to owning very little. This puts him—all fathers—at a distinct material disadvantage to Mrs. Whitehead—all women—who contribute so much more matter. But, this essay has suggested, his claims, like hers, arise from the intense and profound bonding with a child, unborn and born, that its biological kinship might spark in the moral and affective imagination but which it does not entail.

The problem, of course, is that emotional capital does not accumulate steadily, visibly, and predictably as in a psychic payroll deduction plan. That is why, for example, it is unreasonable to demand of a woman specific performance on a surrogate mothering contract as if the baby were a piece of land or a work of art whose attributes would be well known to their vendor. A "surrogate mother," like a mother who offers to give up her baby for adoption to a stranger, must be allowed a reasonable time to change her mind and if she does, in the case of a surrogacy arrangement, be prepared to argue for her rights against those of the father.

Each parent would bring to such a battle claims to have made another person emotionally part of themselves. "Facts" like bearing the child would obviously be significant evidence but would not be unimpeachable, would not be nature speaking unproblematically to culture. While we can continue to look forward to continuing conflict over the competing claims of parents I suggest that we abandon the notion that biology—facts—will somehow provide the resolution. Neither, of course, will ideas alone in a world in which persons exist corporeally. The way out of the fact/idea dichotomy is to recognize its irrelevance in these matters. The "facts" of such socially powerful and significant categories as mother and father come into being only as culture imbues things, actions, and flesh with meaning. This is the process that demands our continued attention.

Notes

1. For an account of these industrial narratives see Catherine Gallagher, *The Industrial Reformation of English Fiction, 1832–1867* (Chicago: University of Chicago Press, 1985).

2. Gayle Rubin, "The Traffic in Women: Notes on the 'Political Economy' of Sex," in Rayna Reiter, ed., *Toward an Anthropology of Women* (New York: Monthly Review Press, 1975) pp. 179–180.

3. *Philosophy in the Bedroom* (New York: Grove Press, 1965) p. 106.

4. William Harvey, *Disputation Touching the Generation of Animals,* trans. Gweneth Whitteridge (Oxford: Oxford University Press, 1981) pp. 182–183.

5. Sigmund Freud, *Moses and Monotheism* (1939), in *The Standard Edition of the Complete Psychoanalytical Works,* ed. James Strachey (London: Hogarth Press) vol. 23, pp. 113–114; I have altered the translation slightly based on the standard German edition. Aeschylus, *The Eumenides,* trans. Richmond Lattimore, in David Greene and Lattimore, eds., *Greek Tragedies,* vol. 3 (Chicago: University of Chicago Press, 1960) pp. 26–28.

6. Isidore, *Etimologias [Etymologiarum],* ed. and trans. with facing Latin text by J. O. Reta and M. A. Marcos (Madrid: Biblioteca de Autores Christianos, 1983) 6, 4.

7. *Ibid.* 5, 5, 4. On blood, see 4, 5, 4.

8. See Thomas W. Laqueur, *Making Sex: Body and Gender from the Greeks to Freud* (Cambridge: Harvard University Press, 1990), for more extensive discussion of these points.

9. William Cowper, *Anatomy,* introduction, n.p.

10. David Hume, *A Treatise of Human Nature,* ed. L. A. Selby-Bigge (Oxford: Oxford University Press, 1965) 2, 1, 9, p. 303.

11. Civil Case no. A-027810. I am grateful to Donna Hutchins, Esq., of San Francisco for making available the various depositions, briefs, and other court papers on which I base the following discussion.

12. Roberta Achtenberg, ed., *Sexual Orientation and the Law* (New York: Clark, Boardman, Co. Ltd, 1989) section 1-70.

13. Anne Taylor Fleming, "Our Fascination with Baby M," *New York Times Magazine,* March 29, 1987, p. 87. There were at the time of this article about one thousand known "surrogate mothers."

PART SIX

Fatherhood and Manhood

11

Fatherhood and Nurturance

Larry May and Robert A. Strikwerda

I myself am still in doubts about matters concerning fathers.
—Sigmund Freud (1897)[1]

Shortly after the birth of our first children in the late 1980's, we were asked by several close friends how we liked "fatherhood." We found this question to be a bit puzzling. Why hadn't these people asked how we liked *parenthood*? What sort of things did they have in mind that we were expected to have done, as fathers, that would form the basis of our answers? At the time there were few if any experiences or feelings that we could put a finger on that would count as distinctly "fatherly." (Note the different connotations evoked by "mothering" a child versus "fathering" a child.) Yet, our lives certainly had changed. We had made a commitment to share equally in the raising of our children with our partners. But what was involved in being a parent was unknown. We did have some idea of the amount of *time* that was to be required, but the emotional and attitudinal changes that were, and continue to be, required were very much *terra incognita*. This paper is an attempt to frame some of our reflections on trying to be fathers who share equally in the parenting role.

There have been philosophical discussions of what fatherhood or parenthood should *not* be, in particular, not abusive, as well as discussions of the *duties* and responsibilities of a parent. But these establish limits, without developing a more positive sense of what fatherhood can be. It seems clearer what a bad father is than what a good father should be.[2] In this paper, we wish to advance the notion that being a father today, given our contemporary conditions, is best understood in terms of nurturance.[3] We take this notion of "fatherhood

193

as nurturance" to be an *ideal*, not something which is necessarily obligatory. Our philosophic experience has made us skeptical of transhistorical, trans-cultural claims about such things as ideals, and we recognize the limits of our personal experiences: white, male, heterosexual, middle-class. Nonetheless, we do think that the issues we raise have a wider relevance.

In arguing that fatherhood should today be ideally conceived in terms of nurturance we will first provide a brief history of modern conceptions of fatherhood. Second, we will analyze the notion of nurturance and argue that more traditional conceptions of fatherhood that are not drawn in terms of nurturance are quite anemic. Third, we will respond to several arguments against our thesis from biology and psychology. And finally we will explore some of the significant advantages to fathers, their children, their partners, and to society that will accrue when fathers see themselves as, and become, nurturers.

We will draw on philosophical works as well as our own experiences and those reported in social science literature. Our focus is philosophical: to see how the conception of fatherhood will change when men view themselves as nurturers, and to see how the conceptualization of nurturance may change when it is recognized that fatherhood, and not just motherhood, can be defined primarily by reference to nurturance. In discussing the ideal of fatherhood as nurturance we will be guided by parallels with the way feminists have come to reconceive motherhood.[4]

I. Conceiving Fatherhood

There are at least two alternative ideals of fatherhood that have been historically important: the father as ruler and the father as educator. Sir Robert Filmer, author of the 17th-century tract in political theory entitled *Patriarcha,* uses a conception of fatherhood to dispute the growing movement of the time toward equality and natural liberty. He contends that it cannot be true that all are created equal, for God created one man, Adam, before all others, and made this man the father of us all. As Filmer states it, "not only Adam, but the succeeding Patriarches had, by right of fatherhood, royal authority over their children."[5] Filmer continues, "I see not then how the children of Adam, or of any man else, can be free from subjection to their parents."[6] And while he here uses parent rather than father, it is clear, as John Locke ably demonstrated, that Filmer was not thinking of female parents.

It was Filmer's intent to develop an analogy between a king and his subjects, on the one hand, and a father and his children, on the other hand. The father had absolute right over his children because of his legacy from Adam and also because he was, supposedly, the first cause of the conception of the child. These factors gave to a father a kind of property right in the child that the mother did not have. Similarly, a king had an absolute right to rule as a legacy from Adam, as first ruler, and as the literal father of all people, a right which could not be shared by others. Today, it is hard to see what kind of analogy could be drawn from family life. Perhaps, just as we have turned increasingly to democratic forms of rulership so there has been an increasing interest in role-sharing among parents.

Nine years after Filmer's book first appeared in print, John Locke began his *Two Treatises of Government* by soundly criticizing Filmer. He attacks Filmer's contention that "all power was originally in the father"[7] and that this gives fathers "absolute power over their children."[8] But, Locke argues, it is a mistake to focus so exclusively on only one of the two necessary parties in the procreative act. Rather, both mothers and fathers have an absolute claim on their children, since both performed necessary roles in begetting. It is parents rather than merely fathers that can lay claim to their children as property. And hence fathers and mothers are equals, Locke argued, in that they are equally absolute rulers over their children. Despite their differences, for Locke as well as for Filmer, parenthood is still conceived as rulership.

Rousseau develops a different ideal by extending Locke's point about equality and softening his conclusion about the consequences of this equality. In the *Discourse on the Origin and the Foundation of Inequality Among Men*, Rousseau talks of the "gentleness" of paternal authority:[9]

> by the Law of Nature the Father is the Child's master only as long as it needs his help, that beyond that point they become equal, and that then the son, perfectly independent of the Father, owes him only respect and not obedience. . . .

Freedom is characterized as a "gift of Nature" of which "Parents had no right to divest" their children.[10] In his *Emile*, Rousseau is quite strident in opposing the tradition which Filmer and Locke had embraced:[11]

> A father who engenders and feeds children, does with that only a third of his task. He owes to his species men; he owes to society sociable men; he owes to the state citizens. Every man who can pay this triple debt and does not do so is culpable, and more culpable perhaps when he pays it halfway. He who cannot fulfill the duties of a father has no right to become one.

Rousseau rails against fathers who find substitutes to fulfill their duties, whether these be hired caretakers or their wives. A major fear is that

multiplying caregivers will lead to conflicting interpretations of right
behavior, thus weakening the respect for the rule of law that Rousseau
stresses fathers should be inculcating. He expects good fathers to
show love and benevolence to their children, but his ideal is the father
as educator, an educator of "sociable men" and citizens,[12] not the
father as nurturer.

Historians have pointed out that there is a significant shift in the way
that the family is organized and conceptualized with the onset of the
19th century. Previously, the family was typically a unit that sought to
provide for the needs of its members by joint collaboration, epitomized
by the cottage industries of the early industrial revolution, and by
family-run farms. In the 19th century, it became possible and often
necessary for one member of the family to support the family by
working long hours outside the home. And it was almost always the
man who left the home to find a job, and the woman who stayed at
home with the children. Various theorists reflected this situation in
their conceptualization of the roles of mothers and fathers.[13]

The effects of these changes were evident as we grew up in the
1950's. Parenting was what women did, and it was characterized as
mainly involving the nurturance of children. Men worried about the
financial security of their families, but rarely did they think of themselves as parents, except when it came to disciplining a recalcitrant
child and introducing one's male children into various male activities.
Fatherhood meant earning money, fixing the sink, and cutting the
grass. Being a father had little to do with interacting with children.
Except for an apparent greater emphasis on "providing," fatherhood
was pretty much as it had been conceived in the 17th-century rulership
ideal, with little understanding of even the educative roles that Rousseau had assigned to fathers.

II. Contemporary Types of Fatherhood

Today, due in part to the feminist movement, many heterosexual
relationships aspire to be egalitarian (indeed many prefer the term
"partnership" over marriage to describe significant relationships).
Fathers don't breast-feed or give birth, but otherwise some fathers
perform most if not all of the childrearing tasks that were once the
exclusive domain of traditional mothers. Most fathers are involved to
a greater extent in child-raising than their fathers were. Given these
new realities for men, the door is now open for conceiving of fatherhood as nurturance.

We see our inability to think of our care-taking as "fatherly" as due
to a conceptual disorder, a gap between what we were doing and how
we thought of ourselves, and our activities. On reflection, though, it

seems clear that what we are doing as fathers is quite similar to what, when done by mothers, is called nurturance. We see nurturance as a complex, multi-level notion. To be a nurturer is 1) to display caring behavior for an extended period of time, 2) to have an intellectual commitment to that caring, and 3) to identify oneself as a nurturing person. Nurturance is not simple caring, since as we will argue, nurturance requires a sustained effort toward a goal, and at least in practice, we do not think these activities can be sustained without a conscious effort and emotional identification.

The Oxford English Dictionary gives a number of related senses of nurturance. One is that of providing life-sustaining food, especially for an infant, probably the most common usage today. A second sense of nurturance is the support and rearing which leads to maturity. The first of these etymological stems is clearly linked to the mother's role in breast-feeding. But the second also has this identification in some cultures since it is the mother who raises the child to maturity as well. In the latter sense, nurturance is more than simply caring since it must proceed over a lengthy time-frame, from infancy to maturity. In addition, the dictionary definitions also list "to discipline and chasten" as a now obsolete meaning of nurture, implying that there is a sense of responsibility to nurturance that goes beyond that of simple caring.[14] We think that it is important to reinstate the idea that some forms of nurturance will typically involve discipline, a traditional domain of fathers.

The concept of nurturance has been closely linked to that of caring, and both have been closely identified with the experiences of women as mothers. In an influential study, Nel Noddings talks of three main components to caring: "receptivity, relatedness, and responsiveness."[15] But while important, these characteristics do not quite capture what is distinctive in nurturing. For the nurturer is not just receptive, but receptive in a particular way. And likewise the responsiveness is necessarily of a particular sort, which is based on the fact that the nurturer is related to a child, or an elderly parent, or a sick person as someone who has assumed the role of, and now identifies oneself as, a primary provider of what the child, parent or sick person needs. Thus nurturing involves fulfilling a responsibility to care for the other. The responsibility is normally defined in terms of a social role, such as parent or teacher, involving socially ascribed expectations, although this need not be true as is seen in the case of a mentor. These responsibilities of nurturing, in distinction from simple caring, also involve a commitment over some appreciable period of time, the time necessary to bring the subject to some end state such as health or adulthood.

Since fathers have often been given the role of disciplinarian and, following Rousseau, have sometimes been seen as chief educators of young children, they have engaged in some nurturing behavior toward their children. But they have not conceived of themselves as nurturers because there has been an overemphasis on the "to feed" dimension of nurturance. If we lay stress on nourishment as metaphor rather than literal meaning, then we come away with an understanding of nurturance as: sustained care including education and discipline, toward mature development. Such a definition of nurturance leaves ample room for fathers today, and gives us the opening we need to reconceptualize fatherhood in terms of nurturance.

It may be helpful if we situate our ideal of the nurturant father over against three other contemporary "types" of fathers. Two of these we could call "ideal types" since they incorporate an identifiable ideal, just as we found in the ideals of father as nurturer or educator. But at least one of these types, "the augmented traditional father," will be criticized precisely because it is incoherent in its "ideal." We freely admit that these "ideal types" are idealizations. Many contemporary fathers do not represent anything like the idealizations we will characterize. Some are either abusive to, or neglectful of, their children. In other families, finances are constrained to the point that one or both parents have to work such long hours that it is impossible for them to be the sort of parents they may otherwise wish to be. Our concern, though, is with what is the proper goal to which contemporary fathers should aspire.

The first contemporary type is that of *the traditional father,* working outside the home, understood in terms of pursuing a job or profession away from the hearth as well as in terms of maintaining the exterior of the house, the yard and the car. Such a father promotes a conventional image of strength, the provider and arranger of all things in the public realm. The older ideal of father as ruler has mutated into that of bureaucratic manager. Here there is a neat division between mother and father, what might be called separate spheres. Mothers are supposedly sovereign in the home, fathers are sovereign, as far as their family is concerned, outside the home. In the home itself, the father's major responsibility is that of disciplinarian, and secondarily one of role model for male children.

The second "type" of father is *the augmented traditional father.* Here the central aspects of the traditional father are maintained but with an acknowledgment of the pressures of the dual career family. This father cooks dinner when his partner is working late, or at least takes the kids out to dinner. He also does the laundry occasionally, and a bit of light housekeeping when things get really bad. He consoles and cares for his children on occasion, but perhaps as much to help out his partner as for the sake of the children directly. She is the one who worries about the children's overall development, their clothes and the household. Even if the time commitment of such a father to non-traditional male parenting activities is considerable, it is not a commitment that is central to his self-conception.

Third, there is what Calvin Trillin has called a SNAG, a sensitive new age guy.[16] Diane Ehrensaft describes one typical pattern of men who are trying to be fully equal parents. One sign of this is that some men claim to want a female rather than a male first offspring. Here's a bit of dialogue:[17]

> I really wanted a girl. I absolutely abhor male culture and have since I was a young boy. I do not like that kind of teasing, aggressive boys' play.

These men typically recall "the pain of their own boyhood and their early alienation from boy culture." Ehrensaft points out that if a boy was born to these men, they "discovered great joy and fulfillment in their relationships with their sons."[18] However, their bias against most things male very likely influences how such fathers parent. Ehrensaft also finds an interesting difference between the way that these fathers differ from mothers in the families she studied. "The man describes his relationship with his child as 'intimate.' The woman instead chooses the term 'nurturant.' "[19] Women typically see and describe their role as one of "protective bonding toward a small, helpless human being." The new age men studied have what Ehrensaft calls a "hunger for intimacy."[20] One father describes his relationship as follows:

> Kids are so spontaneous. No layers of social conventions. You can laugh, make silly jokes. You can't do that with adults. . . . With children, you can be a child with them.

This third "type" of father often seeks the kind of fulfillment in his children that he hasn't found in any of his other relationships.

We find all three of these types to be inadequate. The "traditional father" presupposes an economic division of labor which is quickly becoming obsolete. In addition, as feminists have long maintained, it perpetuates a stifling split of responsibilities along gender lines. Such a split deprives mothers of rewarding lives outside the home just as it deprives fathers of the rewards of nurturance. The traditional father may have known his place, but he barely knew his children, and more often than not was isolated from them when they were children and when they became adults.

The "augmented traditional father" is a bit harder to critique, especially if one sharpens the picture of the type. Suppose such a father devotes an extensive amount of time to child-care, an amount at least equivalent to that of his partner, and he thereby plays a major role in satisfying the needs of his children. But if he still does not see himself as a nurturing person, if nurturance has not entered into his self-conception, he will not be able to appreciate his accomplishments as a good father, nor will he attain the kind of satisfaction *within* the home that will free him from the need constantly to seek accomplishment only *outside* the home.

In this context consider the case of Stuart, a history professor who spends a lot of time caring for his infant child. Asked what he does when the baby is awake he says:[21]

> I try to do something constructive still, maybe a little reading or some project around the house . . . sometimes I'll be in the same room with him, other times I'll just let him play by himself.

Stuart seems to think that the time he spends in caring for his child is not constructive time. It is not enough for him to be intellectually committed to parenting, for this is not adequate for sustaining oneself in this role over time, or so has been our experience. The augmented traditional fathers, like Stuart, will not identify themselves as nurturers and they will have difficulty being motivated to be other than mere helpers, even though they may actually do as much child-rearing work as their partners.

The third type which conceives of fatherhood in terms of intimacy is also seriously flawed. There certainly are wonderful moments of spontaneity and personal directness in our relationships with our children, but this intimacy needs to be securely placed in a larger context. For example, Bob and the kids were having great fun jumping in the waves at Lake Michigan, reliving one of Bob's favorite childhood memories. But he did not notice that his daughter was moving quite close to a log, and suddenly a big wave propelled her against the log. The moment encapsulates the need to protect one's children, to remember to move them further down the beach out of the range of debris so they can continue to grow toward maturity. Communing with them is hardly enough.

We see nurturant fathers as closer to the mothers than to the new age fathers in Ehrensaft's study, especially given the stress on reciprocity and intimacy rather than caregiving. Personally, we would choose "nurturance" over "intimacy" in describing our roles as fathers. Do sensitive, new age fathers give up on those children who don't reward their fathers with intimate relationships? Fatherhood would not be worth much if this were the case. Intimacy involves full reciprocity; intimates know each other and reveal themselves to each other as equals. Nurturance can involve reciprocity, although it is not a necessary condition for it. But most often the kind of reciprocity involved in nurturance is partial rather than full. While our children normally display love in return for the love we show toward them, we continue to love them even when they are immersed in the nihilism and rebelliousness of the terrible two's. Also, while our children clearly add considerably to the growth process of their adult parents, this is not, nor should it be expected to be, comparable to what parents add to the development of their children.

To pick just one domain where much attention has recently been focused, it is clear that parents should not view their children as intimates in the sense of satisfying sexual or other emotional needs for the parent. The child who is regarded as the parent's sexual intimate is obviously endangered. In less extreme cases, the child is often asked to bear the kind of reciprocal role which he or she is either incapable of or which will almost certainly lead to developmental difficulties down the road. Certainly there will be intimate moments between father and child, but these should best be seen within the broader responsibilities of nurturing relations.

These three ideals are not so problematic as to be morally impermissible. They have greater problems than is true of the nurturant ideal, but they don't necessarily violate any duties of parents or rights of children. Rather the nurturant father ideal is proposed as in many respects superior to these other ideals, given the contemporary situation of many men. But the other ideals may themselves also have merits, especially within the context of very different social circumstances than those with which we are familiar.

III. Why Shouldn't Fathers Nurture?

Various reasons have been given for thinking that fathers should not conceive of themselves as nurturers. We consider the following positions. First, there are those who point to the biological differences between men and women, arguing that since men don't have wombs or breasts they are not constituted to be nurturers, and it would be harmful to the physical development of their children for men to try to nurture young children the way that women do. Second, there are psychological arguments indicating that women bond more easily with young children, and that it would be harmful to the psychological development of small children for men to play a major role in early childrearing. Third, there are positions which combine physical and psychological arguments together. In all three cases, we will provide counterarguments and counterexamples to these positions.

It has seemed most obvious that the role of fathers should be different from that of mothers when a child is a newborn. Fathers cannot give birth and they cannot breast-feed their newborns. They have not experienced the tremendous change in hormones which occurs to a woman during the late stages of pregnancy, changes which increase the so-called maternal instinct.[22] Since men have neither the physical organs which are uniquely suited for childrearing, nor the hormonal/instinctual drives to care for children, it is thought that they would be ill-advised to conceive of themselves as nurturers.

Nonetheless, increasingly fathers are taking a more active role in the birthing process. A nationwide group supporting natural childbirth refers to fathers as "coaches." This terminology is quite revealing. Of course there is the vaguely sexist connotation that the men are "in charge" of the birthing process, mothers being the mere team players. But beyond this, the role assigned to fathers is one of helping and even directing, rather than merely passively sitting in the waiting room, with cigars at the ready.

There is no reason to think that men can't bottle-feed as well as women, and little reason to think that birthing and breast-feeding *must* place the woman at the center of the infant's life in ways which push men off center. Fathers who assist at birth and who bottle-feed their infants would seem to have just as strong a potential to care for these infants as would mothers. The old thesis that women are instinctually better caregivers has met with strong opposition from most scientific quarters. One book on motherhood puts the point this way:[23]

> there are now no operative biological constraints that confine motherhood to one sex and make women of necessity more capable caregivers . . . nothing but tradition sends men out to work and keeps women at home.

It is interesting, though, that even this author devotes only a few pages to fatherhood, employing the term motherhood to cover the roles that are assumed by both female and male caregivers.

Aside from the physical argument, some have made a psychological argument in support of giving mothers priority over fathers in terms of nurturance. Breast-feeding is often characterized as the ultimate bonding process between women and newborns. Freud held that:[24]

> The libido there follows the paths of narcissistic needs and attaches itself to the objects which ensure the satisfaction of those needs. In this way the mother, who satisfies the child's hunger, becomes its first love-object and certainly also its first protection against all the undefined dangers which threaten it in the external world—its first protection against anxiety, we may say.

Freudian theory has made great use of the claim that both male and female children initially form their first attachments with their mothers, and then experience separation at weaning. Nancy Chodorow, quoting Edith Jacobson, talks of a "primitive, first, visual mother-image" that occurs in the feeding process, and which becomes the focus of all "libidinal stimulation and gratification" as well as the center of all memories of both positive and negative feelings of infancy.[25]

While breast-feeding may be important for many children, it is by no means a necessity since many children are not breast-fed. Many American children raised in the 1950's were bottle-fed and virtually all adopted infants, then and now, do not form their first attachments to their female parents through breast-feeding. The Freudian theorists who put so much emphasis on breast-feeding are really only addressing a portion of the infants in Western culture. Similarly the Freudian emphasis on penis envy and the oedipal complex have been recently discredited for the unjustified way that Freud and his followers attempted to generalize from an impoverished sample of cases.[26]

In 1956, Bruno Bettelheim provided one of the stronger versions of the view which we oppose by combining elements from biology and psychology. He argued that a father[27]

> undergoes no physiological and emotional changes comparable to the mother's, [and] has no comparable feelings of contributing intimately and directly to the baby's welfare. . . . When he tries to find greater fulfillment of his fatherhood by doing more for the child along the lines only mothers used to follow, the result is that he finds less rather than more fulfillment, not only for his fatherhood, but also for his manhood. . . . the relationship between father and child never was and cannot now be built principally around child-caring experiences. It is built around a man's function in society: moral, economic, political.

And Allan Bloom quite recently made a similar point when he said that the contemporary problems in the American family are traceable to the fact that men are trying to be child caretakers and women are trying to find achievement outside the home.[28]

In response to Bettelheim it is perhaps enough to refer to our own experiences, since all that is necessary to refute so absolutist a statement is one counterexample. It is simply not true that we experienced only frustration and loss of manliness when we nurtured our children. And in any event we find it odd indeed to think that men could establish much of a relationship at all with their children based solely on their economic or political functions. Perhaps when one's children are adults, such a basis for relationship will work, but with young children, to say nothing of infants and newborns, economics and politics are simply not a part of their conscious lives.

It is striking that Bettelheim seems to accept as given that the contemporary western social roles of men are the primary roles with which all fathers must identify. This is an example of the tendency in much of the literature about fatherhood to generalize from the basis of one narrow cultural perspective. There is, though, a lesson that can be learned from Bettelheim, although not one he intended. If men do not alter their self-conceptions and patterns of behavior, and if they instead just increase the time they spend with their children, problems will likely develop. They will indeed feel frustrated. And there will be more time to encourage their sons to be aggressive junior warriors and their daughters to be demure or submissive. Perhaps it would be better for *these* fathers to stay out of the child-raising domain.

Bloom's contemporary version of Bettelheim's argument is equally suspicious, although perhaps more subtle. The American family so idealized by conservative commentators like Bloom was very short-lived, lasting for perhaps a decade and a half for the members of one class in one society. And many of the women who were locked into the role of mother in those years express much regret for their lost life opportunities. Working class women and men never had the luxury so completely to separate the public and private spheres. But surely Bloom has picked the wrong target even if he is correct about the breakup of the family structure. So-called problem children in contemporary society do not result from those families where men want to nurture but rather from families where neither partner wants to, or is able to, nurture. It is hard to imagine that anyone would seriously maintain that having two nurturing parents is worse than having only one. Bloom seems to be able to envision only two alternatives, either one real nurturer, "the mom," or two inadequate ones; he fails to allow that two could nurture equally well. We conclude that none of these arguments give us any reason to think that there are insurmountable obstacles to our ideal of fathers as nurturers. In the next section, we will conclude by further discussing some of these difficulties as well as the positive advantages of this ideal of nurturance.

IV. Burdens and Benefits for the Nurturing Father

For those fathers who have a serious commitment to nurturance, even in the most egalitarian family settings, they often find that they are not as good at the mundane, day-to-day matters as their female partners. Men are socialized to be task-oriented and yet child-rearing involves a continuous, ephemeral process which involves endless repetition of tasks which are so seemingly simple as to be boring. If a task is completed, it typically has to be done again the next day—laundry, for example. Frustration and impatience are common feelings of men, although this is also true of many women, who are intimately involved in raising small children. (Perhaps this has given rise to views such as those of Bettelheim.) Part of the difficulty may be that men are not raised to know "how" to take care of children or to place value in the virtue of constancy. Yet another part of the problem also may be that men lack sensitivity to the needs of others, especially children who cannot yet express their needs straightforwardly.[29] Men who find it easy to remember to schedule regular maintenance appointments for their cars find it difficult to remember to schedule regular check-ups for their kids.

Regardless of the difficulties, there are compensating benefits for fathers, although some of them are hard to see at the time. Consider an example. You awaken out of a deep sleep, just a little light coming through the windows. Your four-year-old son is crying in the bathroom. He has diarrhea and has soiled his pajamas. You try to comfort him. He's feeling guilty and very unhappy. You put one arm around him, telling him it's OK. "These things just happen." With more hugs he begins to quiet down. He says with surprise, "it just came out, Dad." You say, yes, that sometimes happens when you're sick, "It's called diarrhea." He tries the word out a few times. You finish cleaning him up. You put him back in bed, and pat him for a while, more than he needs for he's already asleep. You feel like a father, even as you realize that you will be dead on your feet at work the next day. But as tired as you felt at the time, these images will come back to you often, with a warm sense of accomplishment.

For both of us, we were struck by the simplicity of our own child-care successes. In the early months, we both found that we could indeed calm our seemingly inconsolable newborns. If we paid attention to the child, and did the obvious things like changing diapers, feeding, and cuddling, and did not let ourselves get impatient, our kids could be comforted by the hugs and attention of their fathers. We could be the nurturers, although it was very good to have our female partners there to act as coaches, to turn the birth class language on its head. And here the sense of accomplishment was palpable and surely more than compensated for the burdens of fatherhood which Bettelheim discussed.

Fathers of newborn infants need to be wary of the patterns that get established early. The lack of socialization to comfort and cuddle and nurse should not be allowed to push men away from newborns and young children, for it will later be hard to get back into the middle of the child-rearing enterprise. The model of the adoptive parent should give all fathers cause for hope—most women who adopt learn to parent newborn children as a form of on-the-job training, where hormones have very little to do with it. Most men can also learn to deal with the psychological needs of the newborn child quite effectively. Even though men bring different skills to the parenting role, it is important that in the first year of life men not abdicate in favor of their somewhat more at ease female partners. Virginia Held has written:[30]

Taking care of small children for a few years of one's life is an incredibly interesting and satisfying kind of work. . . . I hardly expect that fathers would be so foolish as to let mothers get more than their fair share of the best work of young adulthood and let grandmothers get more than their fair share of the best work of late middle age. If fathers *would* be that foolish, they would still be entitled to equality, and mothers would have an obligation to help them realize it.

Fathers should also be resistant to the separate spheres approach, even in the face of the frustrations of child caretaking, because of the many positive benefits they can provide to *others* by their involvement in early child-raising. First, there are obvious benefits to the family from having two caregivers, who can alternate tasks, and so on. But these accrue to lesbian parents as well. A second major benefit concerns the development of the children. They no longer have to deal with a parent who is both there and not there, a person obviously of great importance in the family, but yet without much identity for the kids. Larry's father was around so little when he was growing up that he was left with no image of what males in a household were supposed to do. Thirdly, mothers will benefit from having partners who are more than just "helpers," hopefully sharing equally in the burdens of parenthood.

As fathers begin to see themselves as nurturers, their disciplinary roles will take on a different, more positive aspect for themselves and their children. In the recent past, when men disciplined their children they were able to retreat to office or backyard after punishment had been inflicted, thereby effectively avoiding the aftermath of punishment. As fathers take on greater shares in all aspects of the parenting process, they will have to contend with the child both before and after discipline is called for. This will make the disciplining task both more challenging and more beneficial for both child and father. Fathers cannot any longer be like the hooded executioners of the Middle Ages who evaded community displeasure for their acts. Fathers will have to face their own feelings of regret or shame for having inappropriately punished as well as the need to rebuild trust and a positive sense of self-worth in the child. And the trusting relationship that develops will have strongly positive payoffs for the future relationship between father and older child. In addition, their work in the family will be something about which they can feel a sense of accomplishment.

Men are generally socialized in Western culture to be competent in the public world, but not in the private world. While these categories are definitely not as clear-cut and mutually exclusive as was previously thought, there is a sense in which boys are brought up to prefer to be, and to become, competent in the sandlot baseball diamonds, the newspaper routes and the great outdoors generally rather than the confines of the home. Girls are often brought up to prefer to be, and to become, competent in the skills and tasks associated with the home.

Yet, clearly child-raising should not typecast our children in this way, even though it has done so for those who are already adults. Many of the difficulties women experience today in the so-called "man's world of the (paid) workplace" are traceable to these differential, and disproportionately disabling, socializations. A recent study of Mary and Elizabeth Tudor, daughters of Henry VIII, reveals that some girls have been able to reverse the typical socialization, just as Elizabeth did, in the face of even greater social pressures than exist today. But most girls follow the path of Mary Tudor, feeling that they need to rely on a male to handle their public affairs. In Mary's case this clearly worked to her detriment.[31]

In this time of transition, nurturing fathers could use their socialized *public* skills to provide positive socialization especially for their girl children. Due to their socialization, men are better able to teach kids how to fend for themselves, especially how to assert themselves into a sometimes hostile world or sandbox. Given the differential socializations already experienced by adults today, fathers will be somewhat better at such roles than mothers. And by this we do not mean merely teaching girls to throw a ball "properly" (that is, not like a girl).[32] Rather, we have in mind taking children on regular outings to the playground or museum or just to the corner store and talking to one's children about strategies for coping with disparate problems, especially with male strangers, that can be encountered along the way.

But such limited roles for fathers are only the tip of the iceberg of what men can offer to the child-raising enterprise. Giving our children a broader, more expansive view of what men and women are capable of is perhaps the most important long-range developmental benefit of having a nurturing father. Daughters can hope to be mothers *and* firefighters, and sons can hope to be fathers *and* day-care teachers when they grow up. And if we are right about the benefits to future generations of children from having two nurturers rather than one, it can never be too early to start socializing boys, due to role modeling, to begin to identify themselves as nurturers. It is not easy to counteract the influences of television, as well as the influences of other children and their parents.

Now looking back, we have a greater confidence in the ability of men to overcome their role requirements. This is quite apparent in the nurturing care Bob's father (and grandfather) gave to his mentally retarded sister, the youngest in the family. Here in an unusual situation that fell outside normal circumstances they could display a care not expected from them in their "normal" roles. This greater display of nurturance by men as they grow older is apparently quite common.[33] But it was not a primary element as we grew up; for the most part our fathers were off working to provide for us, while our mothers actually delivered the goods.

We have tried to indicate that the burdens will be outweighed by the benefits that accrue to male nurturers and their families from adapting their socialization to cope with the needs of their children. But there is a further, social benefit. When men identify themselves as caregivers of their children, this will end, we hope, the noxious definition of certain issues as "women's issues," where humane parental leave policies, day care support, and the like remain defined as those of a "special interest," instead of the concern for the next generation of our society.

Fatherhood needs to be reconceptualized so that it takes account of the way that fathers have traditionally nurtured their children, and the ways that today's fathers can extend that nurturance so that it becomes the dominant characteristic of their role as fathers. We have argued for an ideal characterization of fatherhood in terms of nurturance which corresponds to the experiences many contemporary fathers are having or at least would aspire to. The ideal of fatherhood can be defined by reference to that dimension of nurturance which involves *caring* and *rearing toward maturity*, involving nourishment, but also humane discipline and creative education into the public domain. We hope this very preliminary analysis of nurturance in fatherhood will inspire as much work on the changing roles for men in our culture as has been spawned for the changing roles of women by recent feminist literature.[34]

Notes

1. *The Letters of Sigmund Freud, 1873–1939*, edited by Ernst Freud, translated by Tania Stern and James Stern, London: Hogarth, 1961, p. 237.

2. Mike W. Martin, in his chapter "Parents and Children" in *Everyday Morality*, Belmont, CA: Wadsworth, 1989, provides a good survey of such discussions. He concludes, without elaborating, by saying "Love is the aim and ideal of parent-child relationships. It is itself an ideal, not a duty" (p. 250). Our essay is an attempt to sketch the specific form of that love.

3. Some feminists have questioned the use of the term parenting to describe what fathers do, preferring instead to say that fathers *mother*. See Sara Ruddick, "Thinking about Fathers," in *Conflicts In Feminism*, edited by Marianne Hirsch and Evelyn Fox Keller, NY: Routledge, Chapman and Hall, 1990; and Sara Rae Peterson, "Against Parenting" in *Mothering*, edited by Joyce Trebilcot, Totowa, NJ: Rowman and Allanheld, 1983. Throughout this paper we give reasons for preferring to say that mothers and fathers *nurture*.

4. For some of the best in this literature see Angela Baron McBride, *The Growth and Development of Mothers*, NY: Harper and Row, 1973, especially chapter 8; and Joyce Trebilcot, editor, *Mothering*, op. cit.

5. Robert Filmer, *Patriarcha and Other Political Works*, edited by Peter Laslett, Oxford: Basil Blackwell Publishers, 1949, p. 57.

6. Ibid.

7. John Locke, *Two Treatises of Government*, edited by Peter Laslett, NY: Mentor Books, 1965, paragraph 62, p. 222.

8. Ibid., paragraph 52, p. 214.

9. Jean-Jacques Rousseau, *The First and Second Discourses*, edited and translated by Victor Gourevitch, NY: Harper and Row, 1986, Part II, paragraph 40, p. 188.

10. Ibid., paragraph 42, p. 190.

11. Jean-Jacques Rousseau, *Emile*, translated by Allan Bloom, NY: Basic Books, 1979, p. 48.

12. See Penny Weiss and Anne Harper, "Rousseau's Political Defense of the Sex-roled Family," *Hypatia*, vol. 5, no. 3 (Fall 1990) pp. 99–102.

13. See Arthur Schopenhauer, "On Women" in *Schopenhauer Selections*, NY: Charles Scribner's Sons, 1928, p. 435–446.

14. See *The Oxford English Dictionary*, p. 608.

15. Nel Noddings, *Caring*, Berkeley: University of California Press, 1984, p. 2.

16. Calvin Trillin, "Generation Rap," *Eleven Magazine* (the magazine of WTTW, Chicago), February 1990, p. 6.

17. Diane Ehrensaft, *Parenting Together: Men, Women, and Sharing the Care of their Children*, NY: Free Press, 1987, p. 138.

18. Ibid.

19. Ibid., p. 35.

20. Ibid., p. 126.

21. R. LaRossa and M.M. LaRossa, *Transition to Parenthood*, Beverly Hills, CA: Sage, 1981, cited in Alice S. Rossi, "Gender and Parenthood," *American Sociological Review*, volume 49, 1984, p. 7

22. For a critical discussion of this claim, see Caroline Whitbeck's essay "The Maternal Instinct," *The Philosophical Forum*, vol. 6, nos. 2–3, Winter-Spring 1974–1975.

23. Rudolph Schaffer, *Mothering*, Cambridge: Harvard University Press, 1977, p. 104.

24. Sigmund Freud, *The Future of an Illusion*, translated by W.D. Robson-Scott, NY: Anchor Books, [1927] 1964, p. 34.

25. Nancy Chodorow, *The Reproduction of Mothering: Psychoanalysis and the Sociology of Gender*, Berkeley: The University of California Press, 1978, p. 65.

26. See David Willbern's essay "Father and Daughter in Freudian Theory," in *Daughters and Fathers*, edited by Lynda E. Boose and Betty S. Flowers, Baltimore: The Johns Hopkins University Press, 1989.

27. Bruno Bettelheim, "Fathers Shouldn't Try to be Mothers," reprinted in *Feminist Frameworks*, edited by Allison Jagger and Paula Rothenberg, NY: McGraw-Hill, 1984, p. 308.

28. See Allan Bloom, *The Closing of the American Mind*, NY: Simon and Schuster, 1987, cited and discussed in Susan Moller Okin, *Justice, Gender and the Family*, New York: Basic Books, 1989, pp. 33–40, especially p. 35.

29. See our essay, "Male Friendship and Intimacy," reprinted from *Hypatia* in this volume.

30. Virginia Held, "The Equal Obligations of Mothers and Fathers," in *Having Children*, edited by Onora O'Neill and William Ruddick, New York: Oxford University Press, 1979, p. 238.

31. Leah S. Marcus, "Erasing the Stigma of Daughterhood: Mary I, Elizabeth I and Henry VIII," in *Daughters and Fathers*, op. cit.

32. See Iris Young's provocative essay, "Throwing Like a Girl: A Phenomenology of Feminine Body Comportment, Motility and Spatiality," in *Throwing Like a Girl and Other Essays in Feminist Philosophy and Social Theory*, Bloomington: Indiana University Press, 1990, pp. 141–169.

33. See Rossi, op. cit., p. 9: "It has been noted in a variety of studies that with age, men become less assertive, more tender and nurturant. . . ."

34. We are grateful for comments and suggestions supplied by Penny Weiss, Marilyn Friedman, Loretta Kensinger and the participants in the Women's Studies Symposium held at Purdue University in April of 1991.

12

About Losing It: The Fear
of Impotence

Lucy Candib and Richard Schmitt

In their lifetime at least half of all men will experience impotence for shorter or longer periods. Between 7–9 percent of all men are said to be permanently impotent. That percentage figure climbs significantly after age 50.[1] It is not certain how accurate these figures are, but it is certain that regardless of the incidence of impotence, the fear of it is pervasive among men. Men are deathly afraid of being impotent. In this paper, we want to examine this fear of impotence—the meaning impotence holds for men in our society and what that tells us about male conceptions of sexuality and of what it means to be a man. We will want to argue that male fear of impotence is an expression of the pervasive belief among men that their identity and worth depends on their ability to dominate women.

There are, of course, many different masculinities with different relationships to various kinds of power (class, race, sexual orientation, education, etc.) (Ramazanoglu 1992) but common, we would argue, to most of the very complex ways of being a man is the fear of impotence.[2] For heterosexual men, impotence means the erosion of the capacity to perform intromission (insertion of the penis in the vagina), whether or not the owner of the penis is interested in that act in any given situation or not. This fear may be more or less central to any given man, just as any given man's sexuality may be more or less active in his way of being in the world, varying also at different times in his life. Nevertheless, a functioning penis is central to the self-definition of manhood, and the possibility of its loss questions the very core of what it means to be a man.[3]

Among profeminist men, the dominant conceptions of male sexuality have been subjected to sharp criticisms. Such men abhor and actively and courageously oppose the male attitudes and beliefs that identify masculine identity with the domination of women, particularly the domination of women through the erect penis. But some profeminist men will nevertheless panic when confronted with their own impotence—whether due to disease or due to aging. This panic, we argue, springs from attitudes and beliefs that these men not only do not hold but have been actively criticizing and opposing through a range of political actions. They need to see that their fear is a hangover from a kind of masculinity that they rejected long ago. The implication of our discussion is that as long as men are not willing to surrender the fear of impotence, they have not yet completely surrendered the unexamined assumption that to be a man, one must dominate women sexually. It is not enough to speak out against the pervasive misogyny among men. Each profeminist man must recognize that his fear of impotence serves to perpetuate the beliefs and values that locate a man's identity in his ability to dominate women. On the bright side, each man's likelihood of impotence offers an opportunity to examine life without erectile dominance, an ordinary feature of the life of women.

Who's Afraid of Impotence?

Richard: About twenty years ago, when I was approaching fifty, I thought that it was getting time to begin thinking about getting older so I went out and bought Simone de Beauvoir's *The Coming of Age* (1972). Like other books of de Beauvoir's, this one begins with a wealth of factual material: historical facts about aging and a survey about its biology, including brief descriptions of the ways in which men's sexuality changes with age. De Beauvoir describes how male orgasms become less urgent and overpowering and how, after a while, erections become more difficult and are more difficult to maintain. Today these are familiar facts to me that neither startle nor frighten me. Then, I panicked at the very idea of losing my erectile powers. I was frightened and angry at the very suggestion that I might one day be impotent. I put down the book and never read beyond those early pages since.

Lucy: Our friend Peter, a gentle child psychologist, has high blood pressure. He is a bit overweight and his cholesterol is elevated. When I urged him to get his blood pressure treated, he balked—he had heard that impotence is a side effect of blood pressure medications.

"Anything but impotence," he said. High blood pressure tends to shorten one's life span. It increases the likelihood of having a heart attack or a stroke and thus of dying miserably, often being a burden to one's family. These are not pleasant prospects. One would think that a reasonable person, like Peter, would do everything possible to avoid this. But the fear of impotence outweighs all those considerations. If the choice is between avoiding a stroke and avoiding impotence, there is no doubt that most important of all to Peter is avoiding impotence.

We do not think that Richard's reaction to de Beauvoir's book or Peter's worries about his high blood pressure medicine are at all unusual. There are good reasons to believe that the very idea of impotence fills most men with dread. One striking indication of that pervasive fear is the fact that in the burgeoning men's literature, impotence is mentioned very rarely and only rather cursorily. What few discussions there are tend to be written by women (Ramazanoglu 1992).

Many men make choices like Peter's. When healthy men, provided with a hypothetical situation of prostate cancer, considered the treatment options, they chose the less effective therapy over the one that promises a greater life expectancy because impotence is much more likely to result from the more effective therapy. Patients have a choice between radiation therapy and excision of the diseased prostate. Radiation is believed to be less effective, but causes impotence in relatively few cases. Patients undergoing surgery have a better life expectancy but are more likely to be rendered impotent by the operation. More than two-thirds of the group of men studied chose the less effective therapy because it would leave their sexual functioning intact (Singer et al. 1991). This choice was "independent of age, interest in sex, frequency of sexual intercourse, and ability to achieve erections . . ." (Ofman 1995). In other words, even men who were already impotent would not choose a treatment that would make that impotence inevitable. The conclusion is inescapable that for many men life is not worth living if they are impotent. This belief has a long history. A passage in the Old Testament suggests that God punishes Abimelech with impotence for thinking about having sex with Sara, the wife of Abraham. God says to Abimelech "You are as good as dead . . ." (Genesis 20 2-6); (Rosen & Leiblum 1992). Even among the patriarchs of the Old Testament, impotence was a devastating punishment.

The same observation has been made by many other psychologists and therapists: for many men the erection—instantaneous, hard, enormous and indefatigable—is the center of their manhood. What men fear most is the loss of that, in most cases, mythical sexual power. The man with erectile difficulties feels like "an absolute nothing"—he does not feel like a man (Zilbergeld 1992). Many observers add that male potency is always precarious. Since, in the dominant view, masculinity rests on the size of one's erection, or how long it lasts, and on the frequency, masculinity is never a settled possession. It must constantly be reasserted, and is always impaired by any erectile failure, premature ejaculation, or failure (whether real or imagined matters little) to satisfy one's female partner (Tiefer 1986). Dominant masculinity is always under a cloud because of the permanent threat of temporary or permanent impotence.

This same fear of impotence is the central message in more than one famous novel. The hero of Hemingway's *The Sun Also Rises,* Jake Barnes, was wounded on the Italian front in World War I. His wound rendered him impotent. Impotence is so frightening that you could not possibly talk about it. In the entire novel the dread word "impotence" is mentioned only once when his friend Bill tells Jake that everyone thinks that he is impotent. Jake replies that he "just had an accident." Bill states, "That's the sort of thing that can never be spoken of." While Jake is still in the hospital, the Italian liaison colonel visits him and declares: "You have given more than your life." Sexual potency is worth more than one's life because without it, life is not worth living. The rest of the novel develops that theme by telling the story about Jake and Brett. Jake is in love with Lady Brett Ashley, and she loves him. But his impotence makes any permanent relation between them impossible, for a non-sexual relation is not acceptable to either of them. One can understand that. But Hemingway assumes that without a functioning penis, sexual relations are impossible.[4] That is the basic premise of the entire story. It is so basic that it is never even put into words (Hemingway 1926).

Clifford, the husband in D. H. Lawrence's *Lady Chatterly's Lover,* was also wounded in World War I and returns home a paraplegic to his wife Constance Chatterly. Sexual relations are out of the question, of course, because, like Hemingway, Lawrence assumes that sexual relations consist of coitus and little else. As a consequence, the two Chatterleys live in an emotional void, an abstract, arid, intellectual world that is not quite real. A man can be a real person only if he has a functioning penis; a woman attains reality only in vaginal intercourse with a real man (Lawrence 1957).

The medical profession does not help allay these fears. In part it simply responds to and in part it perpetuates the fears which are those of the majority of patients as well as of (male) medical practitioners who deal with sexual malfunctions. A number of remedies are available to the impotent man. Urologists have developed a panoply of penile implants—semi-rigid plastic rods that provide a permanent erection as well as plastic rods with a joint in them so that a part of the penis can be bent up or out of the way when an erection is not needed. Currently fashionable are inflatable cylinders implanted in the penis that can be pumped up to simulate an erection by squeezing a pump implanted in the scrotum. Alternative therapies include self-administered injections into the penis that provide an erection lasting for several hours and vacuum pumps that serve to pull the blood into the penis for an erection that is then maintained by means of a tight ring at the base of the penis to prevent the blood from flowing out again (Krane et al. 1989; Kim & Carson 1993).

The aim of these surgical and medical interventions is "to reconstruct or repair the penis so that coitus can be resumed." (Melman & Tiefer 1992) The road to this goal is a long and difficult one, requiring many visits to different doctors' offices, batteries of tests, operations, in the case of implants, and often more than one operation if the implants malfunction. The impotent patient begins with a visit to his physician who will refer him to the endocrinologist/urologist for more tests.[5] The urologist will subject the patient to various neurological and vascular tests, including a measurement of the blood pressure of the penis. That may involve injecting him with a drug that will give him an erection. The medical literature rarely refers to the acute embarrassment the patient may well feel under those conditions. After all that, the urologist may well send him home with one of several devices to test nocturnal erections. A sizable battery of additional tests is available and will no doubt be used by one or the other physician (Krane et al. 1989). Not all urologists, however, are persuaded of the usefulness of all these tests. Some point out that as long as the mechanisms of erections are poorly understood, test results are open to several interpretations and therefore not very useful (Jeffcoate 1991).

After the evaluation, the patient needs to decide whether to have an implant and what kind to have inserted. Despite routine preoperative information, post-operative interviews suggest that patients have a hazy understanding at best of what kind of procedure was done and why (Tiefer et al. 1991). The literature is vague with regard to patient satisfaction, but 36-40 percent of men who receive an implant experience some kind of device failure or require reoperation due to malfunction, erosion of tissue, or pain (Kabalin & Kessler 1989; Tiefer et al. 1991). Bendable implants may break; inflatable ones may begin to leak. In one study of patients who required reoperation after an initial implant, the average patient underwent 2.5 operations within a period of several years (Tiefer et al. 1991). All the patients in this study, with one exception, chose to replace their implant with a new one. Presumably they preferred having them. But once healed from the operation, there were still difficulties. Many men worry about the implant not functioning. Some men still worry about sexual inadequacy, and many are disappointed that with the implant there is "noticeably less size, less rigidity, and less sensation." Other men tend to conceal the fact that they have an implant at all and worry about being found out (Tiefer et al. 1991).

Why does anyone subject himself to this prolonged agony? The answer is unambiguous. Impotent men feel that they have lost their manhood; the prosthesis or other medical interventions restore that sense of manhood. The medical literature speaks repetitively about "restoring erectile function." According to the NIH Consensus Conference on Impotence, "Contrary to current public and professional opinion, many cases of erectile dysfunction can be successfully managed with appropriately selected therapy" (National Institutes of Health 1992). It is clear that "managing" sexual dysfunction refers to restoring an erect penis—or a reasonable facsimile. Many surgeons, urologists and other medical authors write in glowing terms about repairing the damage of impotence by means of various medical procedures.

> Ever increasing versatility, reliability and patient satisfaction continue to make the penile prosthesis the gold standard of impotence therapy (Kim & Carson 1993).

This statement may be more explicit than some but its confidence in medicine's curative powers for sexual disabilities is not at all unusual.

There is, interestingly enough, very little information about the extent to which all these medical interventions restore sexual functioning, in a more generous sense—restore men, or couples, to a happy, affectionate and joyful sex life. There is also no discussion of sexual orientation among the men undergoing therapy although at least one of the patients in the study of men undergoing reoperation had identified himself as gay. The vast bulk of articles about therapies of impotence are concerned with the very technical details. The main interest is in making the penis stand up again. Only very few authors—most, if not all of them women—have noticed that the ability to have erections sufficient for intra-vaginal orgasms, and perhaps for producing vaginal orgasms in a woman partner, has very little to do with a satisfactory sex-life. To begin with, it is obvious that the erect penis can be employed in loving, but it can also be used for rape. It can function in self-centered male sex that pays no attention to the needs and desires, or even the person of the partner. What is more, it very often does not function in just that way. In the study of recipients of penile implants who required reoperation, four of the six single men told few partners about their implant and two told none at all. Six of the twelve men with steady partners refused to allow their female partner to be interviewed. Of the six women partners who were interviewed, three stated that, had it been their decision (particularly the decision for reoperation), they would not have chosen another prosthesis, one because of pain she has never mentioned, one because she felt it was unnatural, and one because she would have been "happier with affectionate sex without penetration'' (Tiefer et al. 1991). In Shere Hite's survey, no more than 30 percent of the women had orgasms only by means of penile-vaginal intercourse. Erections were not sufficient for them to have satisfactory sex-lives (Hite 1976). Clearly the focus on erection as essential to sexual satisfaction derives from a primarily male standpoint and does not reflect the sexual needs of many women. (We do not deny that many other women do feel that their male partners' erections are central to their sexual lives.)

The conclusion is inescapable that the prevalent medical approach to impotence both is a response to the prevailing fear of impotence and a means to perpetuate it. The identification of the erect penis with sexual relations and with manhood pervades the majority of medical discussions of impotence. There are very, very few writers in the field who understand that.

Despite all the current rhetoric in the field about sex and intimacy involving more than penile vaginal intercourse, the quest for the rigid erection appears to dominate both popular and professional interest. Moreover it seems likely that our diligence in finding new ways for overcoming erectile difficulties serves unwittingly to reinforce the male myth that rock-hard, ever available penises are a necessary component of male identity (Rosen & Leiblum 1992).

Why the Panic about Impotence? What Is the question?

It is tempting—and we did not resist that temptation sufficiently in an earlier version of this paper—to look for a general answer to the question why impotence is so frightening. One then looks for an answer that says: ''men are so frightened of impotence because they have certain specific characteristics, hold certain beliefs, engage in certain practices.'' But against that, one must point out that in individual cases one must give different explanations of why particular men are frightened of impotence: This man is afraid of failure in whatever he does. Fear of impotence is for him just one more instance of a generalized fear of failure. That other man is secretly suspecting himself of homosexual tendencies and for reasons we can only understand in the light of his entire intimate history, and the history of his childhood, that suspicion fills him with great dread. If he finds himself unable to function sexually with a woman, that old fear of homosexuality comes back with full force. Other men are afraid of women: that fear of women takes many different forms. Men fear castration or emasculation, they fear that this woman will try to run their life, that they will lose their independence or find themselves being dominated. Impotence is for them the unmistakable sign of the castrating or emasculating power of a particular woman. The fear of impotence is a fear of being robbed of one's powers by a woman. Some men are insecure in their relations to other persons—they are never sure that they are really loved. In relations to women that fear sometimes makes them anxious about "satisfying" women with whom they have sexual relations. Impotence means to them that they cannot satisfy women any more and thus are bound not to be loved.

There are many more different histories of individual men that explain, at one level, why these men are afraid of being impotent. There is no single explanation of this fear. But at the same time, these different explanations of the fear of impotence all pertain to the feelings of men who live in the same culture. What is more, these different explanations are intelligible only against the background of, or in the framework of a very specific conception of male identity. This man is afraid of failure and hence is afraid of impotence. *But why is impotence considered a failure?* This other man fears that he is a homosexual. *But why is homosexuality such a terrible threat to men?* That man fears being overpowered by women. *But why are erectile difficulties signs that one has been deprived of one's power?* This man fears that he cannot earn love if he cannot satisfy a woman sexually. But women satisfy one another sexually. *Why is an erect penis needed to satisfy a woman sexually?* Regardless of the specific causes of a man's fear of impotence, there are some general background conditions that alone make those specific explanations intelligible.

Why the Panic about Impotence? Current Explanations

There are a number of different suggestions that are made over and over concerning the pervasive conceptions of masculinity that underlie any specific explanations of the fear of impotence. They are all interesting, but for the reasons to be developed, not completely satisfactory.

The first of these suggestions is the following: The fear of impotence is overpowering, it has all the earmarks of a basic instinct. It seems deeply embedded in our persons and irresistible as is the fear of death, or the startle reaction to sudden loud noises. At first, these similarities are striking, but soon questions arise. There is some evidence that the fear of impotence is not universal but differs from culture to culture (National Institutes of Health 1992). Hence it has become a common place to say that sexuality is "socially constructed."

But the issue is not really whether the fear of impotence is "natural" or is "socially constructed." The issue is whether we can overcome that fear or not. It is often thought that instinctive reactions are not under our control and that, hence, if the fear of impotence were such an instinctual reaction, we would have to resign ourselves to it. But clearly we do not resign ourselves to living with other "reflexes." Perhaps some reflexes, like blinking, are not controllable, but the fear of death, although very powerful and surely instinctual, can be overcome. It is, after all, the object of military training to enable men and women to invite death for the sake of carrying out commands, or for the sake of protecting their comrades (Gray 1992). There are other situations where the fear of death can be put aside: we know many stories of heroic rescues, of parents endangering or even sacrificing their lives for the sake of their children. There are many examples of people resisting oppression valiantly over long periods of time and running great risks in doing so. Gandhi, Martin Luther King, or Nelson Mandela are famous instances. Many of their followers whose names are not recorded in history books showed equal courage. Other examples of overcoming "instinctive" needs are mothers giving food to their children at their own expense—living with hunger in order that children might eat. Even inborn instincts can be tamed, and we can train ourselves to keep them in check or to overcome them. The same is true of sexual desire. Men and women have chosen to live celibate lives and, although it may have been a struggle, have succeeded in doing so. Men and women have fasted for long periods of time and have overcome the need to eat and drink. The needs of the body, its desires and fears are very powerful, but can be mastered, at least by those who have made it a priority. When it comes to the fear of impotence, it has always been treated as "natural." No one has deemed it worth considering that one try to overcome it. Where is the man who even recognizes that he should learn not to be afraid of impotence? No doubt that is possible, but men have rarely if ever considered the possibility or found reasons for doing so.[6] We must ask why being a man requires fearlessness in the face of danger and the threat of dying, but allows and even encourages in men a mindless panic at the very thought of impotence. Men are supposed to be powerful. But that requires that one be able to face bravely the possibility of losing power. Why have men not shown courage in the face of the threat of impotence? The irresistible force of the fear of impotence is not purely natural. It is supported actively by men who have never considered overcoming this fear as they have tried to overcome the fear of death. It is often said that the fear of impotence stems from the fact that men are, in general, oriented towards performance and that, in particular, they think of sexuality not as a form of a relationship to another person but as a performance (Zilbergeld 1992). But while this observation is, of course, correct it does not serve to explain the fear of impotence. In order to see this we need to think a moment about performances. Consider athletes, or musicians, poets or great thinkers. Their performances are, above all, public. They have an audience and that audience applauds their exceptional performance.

But sexual performances are not public; they do not "play to the house." They are performances in a different sense, namely insofar as the activity is challenging and requires concentration on the task at hand. It is an activity that can cause constant anxiety because failure is always possible. Sexuality as performance is taking on a challenge, one that we do not always manage to meet.

It seems true that for many men, sexuality is something like that kind of performance, that it is a challenge, that one can meet this challenge more or less adequately, or more or less successfully. It is also true that one can be very competitive about the ways in which one can meet that challenge. One can publicly brag about one's sexual performances—and men spend a good deal of time doing just that—and secretly fear that many other men are much better sexual performers.

But if we think about it, the fact that men regard sexuality as a performance, as a challenge, still does not explain why it should cause us such extreme anxiety and why, consequently, impotence should be so frightening. To be sure, once impotent, you are no longer able to perform. But there are many things which we could do at some time and can no longer do at others which do not cause us such great anxiety. Other things which we could never do adequately nevertheless do not impair our sense of ourselves or cause us great pain. Both of us, Lucy and Richard, at some time in our lives took violin lessons. Neither of us ever played even acceptably. Neither of us worry about that in the way Richard worried about the onset of impotence. Sexuality is not just a performance, it is a performance that plays a very special role in a man's life.

Irv Zola writes about how, after a bout with polio at age sixteen that affected the lower part of his body, he awoke with a morning erection. He was ecstatic. Within a week, he was able to masturbate to orgasm. He describes this not as a performance issue, though for certain it meant he could perform, but rather as an identity issue. Being able to have an erection and to ejaculate meant he still had an identity as a man. This, at least, he was able to rescue from an adolescent awareness of himself as someone whom others would regard as a cripple (Zola 1982). Here we get closer to the sources of the fear of impotence: sexual power is integral to male identity, to who one is as a man. The impotent man is not a man and a man who is not a man is . . . what?

Male sexuality is a challenge to one's identity as a man. It is not the performance as doing something skillfully that matters as much as the performance as something at which one could fail. If one fails, one fails the supreme test that allows one to assert one's identity as a man. Understanding that, however, does not explain adequately why impotence is so frightening, for we surely need to ask how sexuality came to be thought of as the supreme test of being who one is, a man. How did sexual functioning become this special test which not all men can pass—a test that a man must pass over and over again until he is no longer able to do so?

There is another question about male sexuality as performance. Even if one thinks of sexuality as a kind of performance—which we, Lucy and Richard, do not—one can think of it in very different ways. One can think of it as an act of reproduction. Here children are the signs of a good performance. One can think of it as giving oneself or others pleasures. One succeeds to the extent that oneself and/or the other experience pleasure. One can think of it as the union with another person and one succeeds to the extent that sexual relations make two persons into "one flesh." In all of these kinds of performances, an erect penis is nice and useful but it is not indispensable. But the sort of male performance that allows one to claim to be a man requires, as a necessary and perhaps even sufficient condition, that one have an ever-erect, big, hard penis.[7] But paradoxically whether our penis is that way, is mostly a matter of physiology. It is not a matter of performance at all because it is not under one's control.[8]

Other theorists try to explain the fear of impotence by pointing out that male sexuality is intended as a means for dominating women (Boyle 1993). This observation is, once again, correct but does not suffice to explain the panic in the face of impotence. In the political realm, the powerful will yield in one place if they must in order to preserve their power. They allow, for instance, the establishment of trade unions but then try to blunt the power of those organizations by more roundabout means. They enable some African Americans access to the professional middle class, only to bear down even harder on those who remain poor. They open certain opportunities to women, and do not balk at addressing them as "Ms" but at the same time, the powerful assure that the mass media reinforce traditional stereotypes of male and female roles, and of women as sexual objects. In any power struggle, the dominant group may well be forced to make some concessions. They will then try to regain lost ground by some alternative strategy. But in their power-struggle with women, men seem not to be able to concede sexual domination through the erect penis. The need for penile rigidity cannot be compromised. It remains to explain why male domination of women is specifically domination with the erect penis and why men cannot compromise on the method of domination. Male domination of women is unlike other examples of domination in that respect. Its inflexibility still remains to be explained.

This becomes only too clear if we consider the conception (and practice) of sexuality implicit in the myth of the ever-hard, ever-erect, huge penis. Male erection is a central element in domination over women in two ways: first, there is the familiar domination of the penis in ordinary (hetero)sexual relations. But secondly, there is the reality that for many men, the point of an erection is to use it. Men's sexual urges are said—by men—to be irresistible; they see women as provoking their arousal and hence regard women as responsible for the sexual act that results. Such men hold it to be their right to have sex when they have an erection, whether or not the partner is willing. While apparently a minority of men have engaged in rape (4.3 percent of college males) (Koss & Leonard 1985), over a third of college men would rape if they were assured they would not get caught (Briere & Malamuth 1983; Tieger 1981). Rape is clearly an extension of the male idea that erections are there to be used, and women are there to use erections on. Although rape is fundamentally an act based more on power over than on sex, nevertheless, an erection is a prerequisite for rape and is essential to the definition of rape—penetration by the erect penis against the will of the other. The occurrence of rape is simply an extreme form of the prevailing male attitudes towards their own sexuality and women's role in connection to it.[9]

Erection, however, is not only a personal phenomenon; among some male peer groups the social expectation of sequential or group sex with an anonymous female—a "gang bang"—reveals that being able to have sex on demand in the company of male peers regardless of the wishes or condition of the woman is a criterion of membership in the group (Sanday 1990; Martin & Hummer 1989). The relationship among men is what is important here; they are doing it in each other's company and showing support for group value of domination over women and ability to have sex at the group's behest. Davion points out that men engaging in forced sex are not interested in the woman but "are far more interested in impressing each other" (Davion 1995). (She reports her experience in foiling a group attack by connecting personally with one attacker who looked apprehensive. When the rest of the men turned on him, calling him a "pussy," and began beating him up and threatening to rape him, she was able to escape with an injured male companion.) Such attitudes are supported by social structures such as fraternities in which the members regard sexual coercion of women as normal. In fact, the ability to have sex in this setting may be used in some male peer groups to "prove" masculinity—e.g., the ability to have and use erection is socially mandated to be part of peer group.

Clearly there are subgroups of men who subscribe to the values described as "hypermasculinity" or "compulsive masculinity"— dimensions associated with the traditional male role: (1) toughness, fearlessness and fighting; (2) preoccupation with developing an athletic physique; (3) sexual athleticism and the concept of women as conquest objects; and (4) defiance of authority (Scully 1990). But rape and the culture of domination over women on which it depends is not just a part of the socialization of a subgroup of men. All women live in fear of rape and protectively modify their activities to minimize its likelihood (Ward et al. 1991; Furby et al. 1991).[10] The very frequency of rape (15.4 percent of college women) (Koss et al. 1987) and the invasion of the threat of rape into women's daily lives demonstrates how rape is a major dimension in men's domination of women. All men have some responsibility for the climate in which rape is prevalent because all men benefit from this climate (May & Strikwerda 1994). And all men are vulnerable to the threat that this climate means for them: if they can't get it up, they are not able to dominate women. In short, the erect penis is an instrument of terror in a rape climate. Even those who do not use their erection to dominate women still benefit from being the "good guys" or the "protectors." This climate creates and maintains the fear of impotence.

There is a pervasive conception of male identity in our society which requires erect penises, available whenever needed in sexual relations with women as the criterion of masculinity. Only against the background of that conception of what it means to be a man can we understand why the man who feels a failure fears impotence; why homosexuality is such a threat; why being dominated by women is so terrifying or why "satisfying" a woman sexually is assumed to involve coitus. The many different histories of the fear of impotence can only be understood against the background of this pervasive conception of male identity.

Why Domination with the Penis: A Hypothesis

But we need to ask more questions: why cannot men give up sexual domination and why must they dominate sexually through vaginal intercourse? It is obvious that men can control women's sexuality not only with firm erections but by many different means: By genital circumcision and infibulation, by keeping women sequestered in harems guarded by eunuchs, by imposing dress codes on them, by using religious threats or threats of physical violence and death if the sexual codes devised by men are not observed. The sexuality of women is controlled by means of legislation against "unnatural" intercourse, by economic or social sanctions against lesbianism. The men who devise and maintain these controls over women's sexuality may be impotent, or not. It makes no difference to the effectiveness of their control of women's sexuality.

But why, when men control the lives of women in so many ways, is sexual control by means of erections so important to men? Men dominate women but they do not do so exclusively or primarily sexually. The hard, ever-erect penis is not the only or even the most powerful weapon that men wield in the domination of women. Sexual domination is made possible and is sustained by a complex setting of other forms of domination: by physical violence, economic power, the power of the word. In the complex mechanism of social control the erect penis itself plays a minimal role except in the threat of rape, which, however important, applies to a minority of men. The control of women by men does not, by itself, explain why the erect penis is worth more than life itself and why impotence is so very frightening.[11] The explanations of the fear of male impotence offered so far were not sufficiently elaborate. Male domination of women is in many respects like racial or class or ethnic domination. But there is one important difference: men and women live very closely to one another in the ordinary family. Now, that was also true of the house slaves in the Slave South, but with this difference: whites always looked down on their slaves. Men, by contrast, love women. A great deal of outstanding poetry, music and art has been inspired by the love of men for women and a good deal of interesting, if not always great, philosophy has been written to illuminate men's love for women (Schmitt 1995, Chapter 5). The sexual domination of women by men remains opaque as long as one only pays attention to male domination, without, at the same time, reminding oneself that this domination is intimately entwined with love.

Most important is this fact: Unlike other relations between dominant and subordinate groups, men and women are singly intimate with one another—they have sexual relations, they share children, they work together in providing the necessities. They are literally naked in front of another. Even in cultural settings where that is not true, they see each other asleep, in pain, in moments of fear and weakness, in moments of anger. In many situations they spend many years in each others' company. Somehow, male domination of women is maintained in a setting where the strong are seen in their weak moments by those they dominate or are nursed through sickness and failure by their wives.

At the same time, men exploit women (Ferguson 1991). Women do more work and get fewer benefits. Men have more power in the distribution of domestic benefits—not to mention public benefits. But some of the benefits men derive from their relations to women are precisely nourishing, physical care, sexual satisfaction, bodily and emotional stroking, comforting in times of stress, etc. Women meet many physical and emotional needs of men—far more so than men meet women's needs. This means that men's relations to women are profoundly ambiguous (Ramazanoglu, 1992). Men love women[12] and dominate them. What is more, those two sides of male-female relations are not separable. The point of male domination is to get one's weakness needs met without reciprocating. If women are to get their physical and emotional needs met, they need, more often then not, to turn to other women. As a consequence, men cannot yield domination in the field of sexual relations. Sex is a center of their relations to women. But sexual desire gives power to the object of one's desire. Women can play hard to get, women can "tease," women can make themselves unavailable.[13] In some situations that only arouses greater ardor in men. But at the same time, these sexual pleasures of courtship, pursuit and final victory are a real threat to male power. It is very important to see that men react to that in a variety of ways—there is not just one way in which men respond to the ambiguity of their relations to women. Some men regard sexual relations to women primarily as temptations to weaken, to yield to the blandishments of women. But these men also know that yielding brings with it certain emasculation—remember Samson!—or death. Odysseus knew that if he listened to the songs of the Sirens and allowed himself to be enticed by them, it would mean certain death for him and his companions.[14]

In many cultures, men maintain their power by social segregation of women, assigning to them different tasks and imposing rules of conduct on them much more restrictive than those that apply to men. In the West, where the ideology of equal rights is more powerful, that cannot be done openly. The "double standard" must be surreptitious. In one of its forms, men transform sexuality so as to keep it under their control. Sexuality is transfigured from a wide range of activities between the bodies of two human beings—of whatever sex and gender—into a canonical form that only men can control. As long as men are potent, of all the aspects of heterosexual relations, they control their own penis most directly. Women can be as tender, or wild, acrobatic or lethargic as men. But the man alone has the penis. All of the forms of sexual love, of tenderness, of mutual pleasuring are, if admissible at all, admissible only as leading up to the main event, the intravaginal orgasm of the man. Once that is over it's time to go to sleep.

That is the reason why for so many men potency is essential to their position in the world. Surrendering potency means losing control over sexuality—as indeed it does. Losing control over sexuality means weakening at least one's genital supremacy in the relation to this woman. (Realistically, an impotent man is not usually at risk of losing emotional and material services from a long-term partner.) But this transformation of sexuality into exclusively genital sexuality imposes a heavy burden on men—the burden of having forever to prove their masculinity until the final, almost inevitable day when they are no longer able to do that. Nevertheless, in spite of the high price paid for the power to exploit women sexually, emotionally, and materially, the rewards are considerable.

Men's relations to women are profoundly ambiguous or, if one is willing to be more judgmental, duplicitous. Men expect love, tenderness, support for their thinking, their emotions and their physical needs and ailments. Such relationships of affection are difficult to combine with relationships of domination. Affectionate relations are not necessarily or not even very often egalitarian or reciprocal, but the opening towards equality and mutuality is usually there. Domination on the other hand does not permit movement towards equality, towards sharing. In this permanent dilemma men develop different sets of strategies to get their needs met without losing their power—power necessary to get their needs met. One of these strategies consists of masculinity defined as permanent sexual potency. The price men pay for adopting that strategy is the ever-present fear of impotence.

Here we need to meet another objection. Some readers may be willing to admit that the fear of impotence of many men is anchored in the prevailing conception of masculine identity as requiring central sexual domination of women, which requires the sort of perfect penis few men probably have. But the objection goes, what shall we say about the gentle men who are supportive of women, of feminism and do not dominate women sexually (or otherwise)? If these men—who are likely to be the majority of the readers of this paper—are afraid of impotence, that fear cannot be due to their desire to dominate women sexually. While that is, undoubtedly true, it is also beside the point. Male relations to women, like relations of whites to persons of color, are very complicated. They involve overt beliefs about women, they involve certain standard expectations of "normal" male and female behavior. But all of those are rooted in networks of barely and perhaps never articulated beliefs, barely conscious, which we have acquired over many years. Men who have given up a whole range of conscious beliefs about what women are like, what men should do to women and what women should do for men, do not thereby shed all the many beliefs that hover at the edge of everyday consciousness and rise to full awareness only on special occasions. No profeminist man can claim with a straight face that he has rid himself of all sexist beliefs. Some of them may surface to confront him to his great dismay on various unexpected occasions. One of these occasions is his erectile failure. He suddenly finds himself terrified. He can then say that he does not know why he is so frightened, and let it go at that. He can concoct some explanation of his fear. But many of those, we saw earlier, are not adequate unless we assume the prevailing conception of male identity in the background. Or he can use the crisis of impotence to recognize one set of sexists beliefs—most likely acquired as he was developing into a sexual being—and try to shed those by refusing to be frightened by impotence.

What We Must Do to Change

The fear of impotence is intelligible only against the background of traditional conceptions of masculinity, particularly of the need to and the ways to dominate women sexually. If men surrendered these beliefs, we would be rid of the fear of impotence. Conversely, freeing oneself of the fear of impotence will help in the effort to overcome the traditional values of men and the traditional image of a man as one who dominates women sexually. But surrendering these beliefs is not so easy for men socialized into the prevailing conceptions of masculinity. As we have seen, one needs to give up deeply entrenched conceptions of what it means to be a man, or of what it means to be someone, as a man. How does one do that?

Not being therapists with a wide range of experiences of peoples' sexual problems and how they solved them, we can only speak from our own experience. Richard, as he entered his sixties, gradually had more and more problems maintaining erections. At the same time, the sensations in his penis became less powerful and thus orgasms became more difficult to obtain and less pleasurable. The entire complexion of sexuality changed without a significant change in sexual interest.[15] At first I was enormously frightened and depressed. Lucy: For a long time it seemed that I wasn't tight enough or didn't move right etc., so that I took it as some measure of failure on my part. The increasing uncertainty of Richard's erection and ejaculation meant that Lucy could never be sure of what was going to happen in any sexual episode. At first that created a tension that postponed and sometimes obviated Lucy's trajectory to climax. It gradually became clear that the stimulation that Richard required for ejaculation was very different from what Lucy required. The situation dictated that we communicate about sex in a different way and have different expectations of any sexual event.

In fact, we had to begin to talk about sexuality in much more detail—something that Richard at least found difficult, if not repugnant. As sexuality changed, the changes had to be acknowledged and with it new needs. New pleasures had to be discovered and all of that needed to be said out loud. Richard needed to demystify impotence by talking about it to his men friends, but he also needed to talk to Lucy about it in order to exorcise the old ghosts of male performance, and the shame of sexual failure. With that sexuality changed also in that it became, in some ways, less burdened with the fear of male failure, or the woman's failure to enable the man to "function." At the same time it became more of a shared undertaking. Other projects we share, such as raising our children, or writing this paper, do get talked about a lot. Sexuality, once a topic for discussion, also becomes more clearly a joint project.

Gradually a new kind of sexual relations emerged between us—taking turns, more focus on the sensual, less focus on orgasm—all well-known recommendations for a satisfactory sex life, but in this situation, evolved in the context of Richard's physical changes, losses in some ways, gains in others. The increasingly open discussion of it between us meant that the shame associated with impotence was gradually diminished. Lucy urged Richard to talk about it with other men, and he slowly began to talk about it with men friends, one at a time. Richard also realized that impotence needed to be demystified for men: I needed to say that impotence was not such a terrible disaster. That required telling my male friends about it. That was a pretty scary thing to do. But, contrary to my expectations, none of them hooted with laughter and started putting me down. (Of course, Richard knew that none of his friends would do that and yet that was surely one of his fears.) They listened sympathetically. They shared sexual difficulties of their own. They appreciated the fact of Richard's talking about his impotence, as well as the political impulse behind it, namely to demystify impotence. Writing this paper and, as it were, "going public" as a man suffering from erectile differences is just one more step in the same process of asserting that male identity is not connected to the functioning of one's penis.

Of course, the erect penis, while a source of domination and rape, can also be a source of pleasure to a partner. A partner's pleasure from a man's erection may come from both an appreciation of the erection itself externally or from the sensation of the penis within the vagina (or hand, mouth or rectum). Some women also derive a sense of satisfaction from "giving" the man an erection.[16] Similarly, having an erection is a pleasure for a man—quite apart from the conventional meanings attached to hard erections, etc. The mere physical sensation is pleasurable. When erections become uncertain or altogether disappear, and ejaculatons become uncertain, both partners lose a number of sources of pleasure. We would be untruthful in saying that Richard's impotence has not been a loss for both of us. But we do not want to stop here—as most men and many couples do—for that leaves one with very few and very undesirable choices. Those are either grieving or sublimation, or alternatively, resorting to medical attempts at regaining erections in whatever way possible. (It is not clear to us whether the artificial penis restores the pleasurable sensations of male erections for men themselves, as distinct from the pleasure of being able to "get it up" at any time).

For us, though not necessarily for others (e.g., those men who have had radical prostate surgery), impotence has been inextricably linked with growing older. Susan Wendell points out the linkage between the oppression of the disabled and the old: "If all the disabled are to be fully integrated into society without symbolizing failure, then we have to change social values to recognize the value of depending on others and being depended upon. This would also reduce the fear and shame associated with dependency in old age—a condition most of us will reach." (Wendell 1989) While older men, to a point, hold great power socially, economically, and politically, this power is eroded in the popular mind by the association with "losing it" sexually. Popular wisdom holds that old men can't do it any more; they become the butt of jokes or the objects of more or less compassionate derision. The fear of impotence is an important ingredient in ageism directed against men (just as the pervasive preoccupation with women as sexual objects—closely connected to the fear of impotence—is an important ingredient in ageism directed against women) (Macdonald 1983). If men see their identity tied very closely to their ability to have erections any time, any place, then the loss of that ability—a loss that often accompanies aging—is indeed a loss of themselves. But that just shows, in a different perspective, the absurdity of resting one's identity, of who one is and what one derives respect and admiration for, on the youthful functioning of one's penis. Richard's contributions as a philosopher, an activist, and a person-in-relation have, if anything, accelerated in the last ten years, the same period that the functioning of his penis has become more tentative. Yet when potency comes to be what matters most, these gains in experience, insight and judgment that come with aging for some men count for nothing. But that failure to see the accomplishments that only aging makes possible is part and parcel of the outlook that regards the erect penis, as symbol of male domination, as more important than many of the valuable qualities of older men.

The vision of the less powerful can shed great light on the workings of the more powerful; those oppressed by racism can unravel the workings of the dominat group with greater specificity and greater accuracy than dominant group members (Collins 1990). Underlings have traditionally had to understand and predict the behavior of their masters to protect themselves. As well, the less powerful have the potential to imagine and practice less oppressive relations, based on their own understandings of how power works. The same parallels hold for those who become physically disabled in relation to the dominant able-bodied ideal. The writings of some of our friends in the disability rights movement led us to question not only what was and what was not "ablist" in the area of sexuality but also to see how the uncertainty of erectile function might open up other ways of being a man, other kinds of sexuality, and other possibilities for manhood. As Wendell points out (1989), in contrast to the able-bodied, disabled people know about other kinds of ways to be in their bodies and know about other kinds of sexuality. Disabilities whether sexual or other permit many possibilities of new strength and courage, of new pleasures that the able-bodied often miss because they are constrained by the preconceptions of what able-bodied life demands. We are not offering as a slogan the oxymoron, "Up with Impotence!" (which would gain no followers anyway) but rather want to share what we have gained by having come this far on the pathway in our own relationship.

What we have realized, from the vantage point of Richard's impotence, is how central the requirement of an erection is for male dominance. When the possibility of such domination is relinquished, new insights become possible. For us that means that impotence in its various forms permits a man to explore sexuality in ways not possible when driven by the demands and requirements of an erect penis. (Sexuality not centered on the penis is obvious within various kinds of women-centered sexuality, but is inaccessible to men with erections). In ordinary practice, the fear of impotence prevents men from ever recognizing that there are other ways that they could be sexual. Viewed from the other side, we argue that impotence allows a man to enter the world of not-male sexuality, and while it is not the same as female sexuality, it offers the option of choosing a new way of being sexual and an attendant practice not based on the centrality of erection. This may not be something that all men can strive toward, but it does open the possibility of letting go of the fear of impotence. The reality of waning erectile powers with aging offers men the opportunity to acknowledge and practice a sexual life not based on the physical embodiment of men's domination—the erect penis—and thus to make a step away from domination themselves.

Notes

1. The most commonly cited percentage of erectile difficulties for men of all ages is 7-9 percent (Frank et al., 1978), but that number is probably underestimated (Rosen and Leiblum, 1992). The percentage rises to 25 percent for men 65 and older (Krane et al., 1989).

2. We are writing this paper from the perspective of our own experience, particularly our heterosexual experience. We make no claims that the fear of impotence contains the same implications for gay men.

3. It is important to see, at the very outset, that masculinity is very complex and that masculinities are affected and vary with class, and race, sexual orientation, education, etc. Not only in order to understand that many of our generalizations may need modification, but also that because impotence and the fear of it has a somewhat different meaning and weight, depending on social status, power and level of education of different men. Hence facing up to the fear of impotence and trying to demystify it, may be easier for some men than for others.

4. Nor are these only the beliefs of literary men like Hemingway or Lawrence. The very same belief is cited by recipients of penile implants as a reason for their seeking surgical repair of their impotent penis (Tieffer et al., 1991).

5. This process is extensive and extremely unpleasant. But it has its lighter moments. Richard encountered an endocrinologist interested in Existentialism. He found himself lying stark naked on the examining table, discussing Kierkegaard while the endocrinologist was palpating his testicles.

6. Some men, especially older men, have been forced to resign themselves to their impotence. But as new prostheses and other medical procedures to replace their previous sexual powers become available they avail themselves of these replacements in large numbers. Resigning oneself to one's loss is not the same as overcoming the original fear of impotence.

7. In recent years, the medical establishment has insisted that impotence is largely a physical malfunction, or a combination of physical and psychological problems, rather than as had been thought earlier, primarily a psychological problem (Tiefer, 1986). This new medical orthodoxy has been attractive to men because it absolved them from responsibility for sexual failures or inadequacies. The pamphlet of Impotents Anonymous, a support organization for impotent men, advises us to "Understand chronic impotence for what it is—a treatable condition—like heart disease or a broken leg." But by the same token, potency is also a physical condition, that one has little or no control over and thus not something one can take credit for. But potency is a necessary if not sufficient condition for being a man. It turns out that the "performance" of being a man is not really a performance at all. Why do men brag about their potency, while they do not brag of not having a broken leg, or being free of heart-disease?

8. The matter is somewhat different in the case of premature ejaculation—a related but distinct sexual failure of men. There are techniques that enable men to postpone ejaculating for a certain amount of time (Kaplan, 1974).

9. Potential rapists are more likely to subscribe to callous attitudes toward women and to rape myths. Male arousal has a complex relationship to violent control over the other; laboratory studies with college men have shown that violent pornography increases antagonism toward women and intensifies male beliefs in rape myths: e.g., that victims are aroused by and are responsible for rape. Films that show positive consequences after aggressive sex increased male college students' acceptance of rape myths and violence toward women and diminished their negative reactions to rape (Scully, 1990). Thus erection is a very specific instrument of domination over women in the instance of rape, and men's attitudes toward that domination can be manipulated by media portrayals that link arousal to violence and diminish their sense of responsibility.

10. Furby et al. discovered a wide range of rape prevention strategies used by women. Women expressed many concerns about the negative consequences of these strategies. Men and women rated these strategies similarly except that "Men placed less importance on less dramatic and visible consequences, such as costs in freedom and mobility, recreational opportunities, inconvenience, and time, energy, or attention—suggesting an insensitivity to the daily toll paid by women in trying to reduce their risk of assault." Men find it really difficult to appreciate the price women pay daily for trying to remain safe in a society that is dangerous for them (Furby et al., p. 61).

11. There are other explanations of dominant conceptions of masculinity that are also very interesting but not completely adequate:

Thus Lisak (1203) suggests, following Chodorow and Dinnerstein, that men are more in need of reaffirming their masculinity to the extent that they do not learn how to be a man from a father who is present in the home and approachable. But that is a plausible explanation of the never ending insecurity many men feel about their masculinity if we take for granted the other underlying society-wide assumption that the worst thing that can happen to a man is to be "effeminate," to be like a woman—a belief that many women share. The absent father explains why some men have trouble learning how to be a man, but it does not make clear why learning to be a man and proving that one has learned one's lesson well are so terribly important.

12. We are writing this while in Ecuador. When you ride a bus, the radio plays. Most of the popular songs are songs sung by men to "Mi corazon, mi amor," and protest how the man cannot live without her. There is no reason to believe that all of this is mere propaganda. Men do not just dominate women; they also love them.

13. An experienced Ecuadorian family physician reports that sexual problems in marriage are common. Ecuadorian women are taught that a husband has a right to sex whenever he wants it; she must oblige. Marital rape cannot exist. But that does not mean that a woman enjoys such obligations. In fact, it is not an uncommon complaint among Ecuadorian men that their wives just lie there and spread their legs. In the social setting of this kind of marriage, not responding is the only possible form of resistance.

14. Warlike men are particularly subject to these fears. This has been documented by Theleweit for men in Germany (Theleweit, 1988), and by Gibson for men in the U.S. since the end of the Vietnam war (Gibson, 1994). Women and sexual love of women represent temptations that will destroy the man who succumbs to them. The most famous instance of that fear of women's sexuality is the mad bombardier in the film, *Dr. Strangelove* who speaks darkly and ominously about the danger of losing one's "vital fluids."

15. It seems clear that the changes that age brings to men's sexual experience differ for different men. Hence what follows describes our experience. Other men may well age sexually in different ways; their tasks may therefore also be different.

16. This point requires a lot more discussion. Many men when impotence first strikes blame their partner. In our relationship there certainly was a certain amount of that. Women who share the traditional outlook, often feel inadequate, not sufficiently attractive or sexual, if their male partner does not have adequate erections. In saying that the loss of man's erections is a loss also for his partner, we are not endorsing either of those reactions to impotence.

References

Boyle, Mary. "Sexual Dysfunction or Heterosexual Dysfunction?" *Feminism and Psychology* 3 (1993):73–88.
Briere, John, and Neil Malamuth. "Self-Reported Likelihood of Sexually Aggressive Behavior: Attitudinal versus Sexual Explanations." *Journal of Research in Personality* 17 (83):315–323.
Collins, Patricia. *Black Feminist Thought: Knowledge, Consciousness and the Politics of Empowerment* (New York: Routledge, 1990).
Davion, Victoria. "Rape, Group Responsibility and Trust." *Hypatia* 10 (1995):153–156.

De Beauvoir, Simone. *The Coming of Age* (New York: Putnam, 1972).

Ferguson, Ann. *Sexual Democracy: Women, Oppression and Revolution* (Boulder: Westview, 1991).

Frank, Ellen, Carol Anderson, and Debra Rubinstein. "Frequency in Sexual Dysfunction in 'Normal' Couples." *New England Journal of Medicine.* 299:111–115 (1978).

Furby, L., B. Fischoff, and M. Morgan. "Rape Prevention and Self-Defense: At What Price?" *Women's Studies International Forum* 14 (1991):49–62.

Gibson, James Walter. *Warrior Dreams: Manhood and Violence in Post-Vietnam America* (New York: Hill and Wang, 1994).

Gray, J. Glenn. "The Enduring Appeals of Battle" in May, Larry, and Robert A. Strikwerda, eds., *Rethinking Masculinity* (Lanham: Rowman & Littlefield, 1992):23–40.

Hemingway, Ernest. *The Sun Also Rises* (New York: Charles Scribner, 1926).

Hite, Shere. *The Hite Report* (New York: Dell, 1976).

Jeffcoate, W. J. "The Investigation of Impotence." *British Journal of Urology* 68 (1991):449–453.

Kabalin, John N., and Robert Kessler. "Penile Prosthesis Surgery: Review of Ten-Year Experience and Examination of Reoperations." *Urology* 33 (1989):17–19.

Kaplan, Helen. *The New Sex Therapy* (New York: Brunner-Maazel, 1974).

Kim, Jay H., and Culley C. Carson. "History of Urologic Prostheses for Impotence." *Problems in Urology* 7 (1993):283–287.

Koss, Mary P., and Kenneth E. Leonard. "Sexually Agressive Men: Empirical Findings and Theoretical Implications." in Malamuth, Neil, and Edward Donnerstein, eds., *Pornography and Sexual Agression* (New York: Academic Press, 1985).

Koss, Mary P., Christine A. Gidycz, and Nadine Wisniewski. "The Scope of Rape: Incidence and Prevalence of Sexual Agression and Victimization in a National Sample of Students in Higher Education." *Journal of Consulting and Clinical Psychology* 55 (1987):162–170.

Krane, Robert J., Irwin Goldstein, and Iñigo Saenz de Tejada. "Impotence." *New England Journal of Medicine* 24 (1989):1648–1659.

Lawrence, D. H. *Lady Chatterly's Lover* (New York: Grove Press, 1957).

Macdonald, Barbara, and Cynthia Rich. *Look Me In The Eye—Old Women Aging and Ageism* (San Francisco: Spinsters Aunt Lute, 1983).

Martin, Patricia Y., and Robert A. Hummer. "Fraternities and Rape on Campus." *Gender and Society* 3 (1989):457–473.

May, Larry, and Robert A. Strikwerda. "Men in Groups: Collective Responsibility for Rape." *Hypatia* 9 (1994):134–151.

Melman, Arnold, and Leonore Tiefer. "Surgery for Erectile Disorders: Operative Procedures and Psychological Issues." in Rosen, Raymond C., and Sandra R. Leiblum, eds. *Erectile Disorders: Assessment and Treatment* (New York: Guilford Press, 1992):255–282.

National Institutes of Health. *Consensus Development Conference Statement on Impotence.* (Bethesda: Office of Medical Applications Research, 1992).

Ofman, Ursula S. "Sexual Quality of Life of Men with Prostate Cancer." *Cancer Supplement* 75 (1995):1949–1956.

Ramazanoglu, Caroline. "What Can You Do with a Man?" *Women's Studies International Forum* 15 (1992):339–350.

Rosen, Raymond C., and Sandra R. Leiblum. "Erectile Disorders: An Overview of Historical Trends and Clinical Perspectives" in Rosen, Raymond C., and Sandra R. Leiblum, eds. *Erectile Disorders* (New York: Guilford, 1992):3–26.

Sanday, Peggy R. *Fraternity Gang Rape: Sex, Brotherhood and Privilege on Campus* (New York: New York University Press, 1990).

Schmitt, Richard. *Beyond Separateness: The Relational Nature of Human Beings, their Autonomy, Knowledge and Power* (Boulder: Westview, 1995).

Scully, Diana. *Understanding Sexual Violence: A Study of Convicted Rapists* (Boston: Unwin Hyman, 1990).

Singer, Peter, et al. "Sex or Survival: Trade-Offs between Quality and Quantity of Life." *Journal of Clinical Oncology* 9 (1991):328–334.

Theweleit, Klaus. *Male Fantasies* (Minneapolis: University of Minnesota Press, 1988).

Tiefer, Leonore. "In Pursuit of the Perfect Penis." *American Behavioral Scientist* 29 (1986):579–599.

Tiefer, Leonore, Steven Moss, and Arnold Melman. "Follow-Up of Patients and Partners Experiencing Penile Prosthesis Malfunction and Corrective Surgery." *Journal of Sex and Marital Therapy* 17 (1991):113–128.

Tieger, Todd. "Self-Rated Likelihood of Raping and Social Perception of Rape." *Journal of Research in Personality* 15 (1981):147–158.

Ward, S. K., et al. "Acquaintance Rape and College Social Scene." *Family Relations* 40 (1991):65–71.

Wendell, Susan. "Toward A Feminist Theory of Disability." *Hypatia* 4 (1989):104–124.

Zilbergeld, Bernie. "The Man behind the Broken Penis: Social and Psychological Determinants of Erectile Failure" in Rosen, Raymond C., and Sandra R. Leiblum, eds., *Erectile Disorders* (New York: Guilford, 1992):27–51.

Zola, Irving K. *Missing Pieces* (Philadelphia: Temple University Press, 1982).

PART SEVEN

Pornography and Sexuality

13

Pornography and the Alienation of Male Sexuality

Harry Brod

This paper is intended as a contribution to an ongoing discussion. It aims to augment, not refute or replace, what numerous commentators have said about pornography's role in the social construction of sexuality. I have several principal aims in this paper. My primary focus is to examine pornography's model of male sexuality. Furthermore, in the discussion of pornography's role in the social construction of sexuality, I wish to place more emphasis than is common on the social construction of pornography. As I hope to show, these are related questions. One reason I focus on the image of male sexuality in pornography is that I believe this aspect of the topic has been relatively neglected. In making this my topic here, I do not mean to suggest that this is the most essential part of the picture. Indeed, I am clear it is not. It seems clear enough to me that the main focus of discussion about the effects of pornography is and should be the harmful effects of pornography on women, its principal victims. Yet, there is much of significance which needs to be said about pornography's representation, or perhaps I should more accurately say misrepresentation, of male sexuality. My focus shall be on what is usually conceived of as

An earlier version of this chapter was presented at the Philosophers for Social Responsibility National Workshop on Pornography, Eastern Division Meetings of the American Philosophical Association, New York, December 1987. I am grateful to members of the audience, and to Roger Gottlieb, Lenore Langsdorf, Maria Papacostaki, and Ricky Sherover-Marcuse for helpful comments.

"normal" male sexuality, which for my purposes I take to be consensual, non-violent heterosexuality, as these terms are conventionally understood. I am aware of analyses which argue that this statement assumes distinctions which are at least highly problematic, if not outright false, which argue that this "normal" sexuality is itself coercive, both as compulsory heterosexuality and as containing implicit or explicit coercion and violence. My purpose is not to take issue with these analyses, but simply to present an analysis of neglected aspects of the links between mainstream male sexuality and pornography. I would argue that the aspect of the relation between male sexuality and pornography usually discussed, pornography's incitement to greater extremes of violence against women, presupposes such a connection with the more accepted mainstream. Without such a link, pornography's messages would be rejected by rather than assimilated into male culture. My intention is to supply this usually missing link.

My analysis proceeds from both feminist and Marxist theory. These are often taken to be theories which speak from the point of view of the oppressed, in advocacy for their interests. That they indeed are, but they are also more than that. For each claims not simply to speak for the oppressed in a partisan way, but also to speak a truth about the social whole, a truth perhaps spoken in the name of the oppressed, but a truth objectively valid for the whole. That is to say, Marxism is a theory which analyzes the ruling class as well as the proletariat, and feminism is a theory which analyzes men as well as women. It is not simply that Marxism is concerned with class, and feminism with gender, both being united by common concerns having to do with power. Just as Marxism understands class as power, rather than simply understanding class differences as differences of income, lifestyle, or opportunities, so the distinctive contribution of feminism is its understanding of gender as power, rather than simply as sex role differentiation. Neither class nor gender should be reified into being understood as fixed entities, which then differentially distribute power and its rewards. Rather, they are categories continually constituted in ongoing contestations over power. The violence endemic to both systems cannot be understood as externalized manifestations of some natural inner biological or psychological drives existing prior to the social order, but must be seen as emerging in and from the relations of power which constitute social structures. Just as capitalist exploitation is caused not by capitalists' excess greed but rather by the structural imperatives under which capitalism functions, so men's violence is not the manifestation of some inner male essence, but rather evidence of the bitterness and depth of the struggles through which genders are forged.[1]

For my purposes here, to identify this as a socialist feminist analysis is not, in the first instance, to proclaim allegiance to any particular set of doctrinal propositions, though I am confident that those I subscribe to would be included in any roundup of the usual suspects, but rather to articulate a methodological commitment to make questions of power central to questions of gender, and to understand gendered power in relation to economic power, and as historically, materially structured.[2] If one can understand the most intimate aspects of the lives of the dominant group in these terms, areas which would usually be taken to be the farthest afield from where one might expect these categories to be applicable, then I believe one has gone a long way toward validating claims of the power of socialist feminist theory to comprehend the totality of our social world. This is my intention here. I consider the analysis of male sexuality I shall be presenting part of a wider socialist feminist analysis of patriarchal capitalist masculinity, an analysis I have begun to develop elsewhere.[3]

As shall be abundantly clear, I do not take a "sexual liberationist" perspective on pornography. I am aware that many individuals, particularly various sexual minorities, make this claim on pornography's behalf. I do not minimize nor negate their personal experiences. In the context of our society's severe sexual repressiveness, pornography may indeed have a liberating function for certain individuals. But I do not believe an attitude of approval for pornography follows from this. Numerous drugs and devices which have greatly helped individual women have also been medical and social catastrophes—the one does not negate the other.

I shall be claiming that pornography has a negative impact on men's own sexuality. This is a claim that an aspect of an oppressive system, patriarchy, operates, at least in part, to the disadvantage of the group it privileges, men. This claim does not deny that the overall effect of the system is to operate in men's advantage, nor does it deny that the same aspect of the system under consideration, that is, male sexuality and pornography under patriarchy, might not also contribute to the expansion and maintenance of male power even as it also works to men's disadvantage. Indeed, I shall be arguing precisely for such complementarity. I am simply highlighting one of the "contradictions" in the system. My reasons for doing so are in the first instance simply analytic: to, as I said, bring to the fore relatively neglected aspects of the issue. Further, I also have political motivations for emphasizing this perspective. I view raising consciousness of the prices of male power as part of a strategy through which one could at least potentially mobilize men against pornography's destructive effects on both women and men.

It will aid the following discussion if I ask readers to call to mind a classic text in which it is argued that, among many other things, a system of domination also damages the dominant group, and prevents them from realizing their full humanity. The argument is that the dominant group is "alienated" in specific and identifiable ways. The text I have in mind is Marx's "Economic and Philosophic Manuscripts of 1844." Just as capitalists as well as workers are alienated under capitalism according to Marxist theory (in a certain restricted sense, even more so), so men, I shall argue, and in particular male modes of sexuality, are also alienated under patriarchy. In the interests of keeping this paper a manageable length, I shall here assume rather than articulate a working familiarity with Marx's concept of alienation, the process whereby one becomes a stranger to oneself and one's own powers come to be powers over and against one. Since later in the paper I make use of some of Marx's more economistic concepts, I should however simply note that I see more continuity than rupture between Marx's earlier, more philosophical writings and his later, more economic ones.[4] While much of this paper presents an analysis of men's consciousness, I should make clear that while alienation may register in one's consciousness (as I argue it does), I follow Marx in viewing alienation not primarily as a psychological state dependent on the individual's sensibilities or consciousness but as a condition inevitably caused by living within a system of alienation. I should also note that I consider what follows an appropriation, not a systematic interpretation, of some of Marx's concepts.

Alienated pornographic male sexuality can be understood as having two dimensions, what I call the objectification of the body and the loss of subjectivity. I shall consider each in greater detail, describing various aspects of pornographic male sexuality under each heading in a way which I hope brings out how they may be conceptualized in Marx's terms. Rather than then redoing the analysis in Marx's terms, I shall then simply cite Marx briefly to indicate the contours of such a translation.

1. Objectification of the Body

In terms of both its manifest image of and its effects on male sexuality, that is, in both intrinsic and consequentialist terms, pornography restricts male sensuality in favor of a genital, performance oriented male sexuality. Men become sexual acrobats endowed with oversized and overused organs which are, as the chapter title of a fine book on male sexuality describes, "The Fantasy Model of Sex: Two Feet Long, Hard as Steel, and Can Go All Night."[5] To speak non-euphemistically, using penile performance as an index of male strength and potency directly contradicts biological facts. There is no muscle tissue in the penis. Its erection when aroused results simply from increased blood flow to the area. All social mythology aside, the male erection is physiologically nothing more than localized high blood pressure. Yet this particular form of hypertension has attained mythic significance. Not only does this focusing of sexual attention on one organ increase male performance anxieties, but it also desensitizes other areas of the body from becoming what might otherwise be sources of pleasure. A colleague once told me that her favorite line in a lecture on male sexuality I used to give in a course I regularly taught was my declaration that the basic male sex organ is not the penis, but the skin.

The predominant image of women in pornography presents women as always sexually ready, willing, able, and eager. The necessary corollary to pornography's myth of female perpetual availability is its myth of male perpetual readiness. Just as the former fuels male misogyny when real-life women fail to perform to pornographic standards, so do men's failures to similarly perform fuel male insecurities. Furthermore, I would argue that this diminishes pleasure. Relating to one's body as a performance machine produces a split consciousness wherein part of one's attention is watching the machine, looking for flaws in its performance, even while one is supposedly immersed in the midst of sensual pleasure. This produces a self-distancing self-consciousness which mechanizes sex and reduces pleasure. (This is a problem perpetuated by numerous sexual self-help manuals, which treat sex as a matter of individual technique for fine-tuning the machine rather than as human interaction. I would add that men's sexual partners are also affected by this, as they can often intuit when they are being subjected to rote manipulation.)

2. Loss of Subjectivity

In the terms of discourse of what it understands to be "free" sex, pornographic sex comes "free" of the demands of emotional intimacy or commitment. It is commonly said as a generalization that women tend to connect sex with emotional intimacy more than men do. Without romantically blurring female sexuality into soft focus, if what is meant is how each gender consciously thinks or speaks of sex, I think this view is fair enough. But I find it takes what men say about sex, that it doesn't mean as much or the same thing to them, too much at face value. I would argue that men do feel similar needs for intimacy, but are trained to deny them, and are encouraged further to see physical affection and intimacy primarily if not exclusively in sexual terms. This leads to the familiar syndrome wherein, as one man put it:

> Although what most men want is physical affection, what they end up thinking they want is to be laid by a Playboy bunny.[6]

This puts a strain on male sexuality. Looking to sex to fulfill what are really non-sexual needs, men end up disappointed and frustrated. Sometimes they feel an unfilled void, and blame it on their or their partner's inadequate sexual performance. At other times they feel a discomfitting urgency or neediness to their sexuality, leading in some cases to what are increasingly recognized as sexual addiction disorders (therapists are here not talking about the traditional "perversions," but behaviors such as what is coming to be called a "Don Juan Syndrome," an obsessive pursuit of sexual "conquests"). A confession that sex is vastly overrated often lies beneath male sexual bravado. I would argue that sex seems overrated because men look to sex for the fulfillment of nonsexual emotional needs, a quest doomed to failure. Part of the reason for this failure is the priority of quantity over quality of sex which comes with sexuality's commodification. As human needs become subservient to market desires, the ground is laid for an increasing multiplication of desires to be exploited and filled by marketable commodities.[7]

For the most part the female in pornography is not one the man has yet to "conquer," but one already presented to him for the "taking." The female is primarily there as sex object, not sexual subject. Or, if she is not completely objectified, since men do want to be desired themselves, hers is at least a subjugated subjectivity. But one needs another independent subject, not an object or a captured subjectivity, if one either wants one's own prowess validated, or if one simply desires human interaction. Men functioning in the pornographic mode of male sexuality, in which men dominate women, are denied satisfaction of these human desires.[8] Denied recognition in the sexual interaction itself, they look to gain this recognition in wider social recognition of their "conquest."

To the pornographic mind, then, women become trophies awarded to the victor. For women to serve this purpose of achieving male social validation, a woman "conquered" by one must be a woman deemed desirable by others. Hence pornography both produces and reproduces uniform standards of female beauty. Male desires and tastes must be channeled into a single mode, with allowance for minor variations which obscure the fundamentally monolithic nature of the mold. Men's own subjectivity becomes masked to them, as historically and culturally specific and varying standards of beauty are made to appear natural and given. The ease with which men reach quick agreement on what makes a woman "attractive," evidenced in such things as the "1–10" rating scale of male banter and the reports of a computer program's success in predicting which of the contestants would be crowned "Miss America," demonstrates how deeply such standards have been internalized, and consequently the extent to which men are dominated by desires not authentically their own.

Lest anyone think that the analysis above is simply a philosopher's ruminations, too far removed from the actual experiences of most men, let me just offer one recent instantiation, from among many known to me, and even more, I am sure, I do not know. The following is from the *New York Times Magazine*'s "About Men" weekly column. In an article titled "Couch Dancing," the author describes his reactions to being taken to a place, a sort of cocktail bar, where women "clad only in the skimpiest of bikini underpants" would "dance" for a small group of men for a few minutes for about 25 or 30 dollars, men who "sat immobile, drinks in hand, glassy-eyed, tapping their feet to the disco music that throbbed through the room."

Men are supposed to like this kind of thing, and there is a quite natural part of each of us that does. But there is another part of us—of me, at least—that is not grateful for the traditional male sexual programming, not proud of the results. By a certain age, most modern men have been so surfeited with images of unattainably beautiful women in preposterous contexts that we risk losing the capacity to respond to the ordinarily beautiful women we love in our bedrooms. There have been too many times when I have guiltily resorted to impersonal fantasy because the genuine love I felt for a woman wasn't enough to convert feeling into performance. And in those sorry, secret moments, I have resented deeply my lifelong indoctrination into the esthetic of the centerfold.[9]

3. Alienation and Crisis

I believe that all of the above can be translated without great difficulty into a conceptual framework paralleling Marx's analysis of the alienation experienced by capitalists. The essential points are captured in two sentences from Marx's manuscripts:

1. *All* the physical and intellectual senses have been replaced by the simple alienation of *all* these senses; the sense of *having*.[10]
2. The wealthy man is at the same time one who *needs* a complex of human manifestations of life, and whose own self-realization exists as an inner necessity, a need.[11]

Both sentences speak to a loss of human interaction and self-realization. The first articulates how desires for conquest and control prevent input from the world. The second presents an alternative conception wherein wealth is measured by abilities for self-expression, rather than possession. Here Marx expresses his conceptualization of the state of alienation as a loss of sensuous fulfillment, poorly replaced by a pride of possession, and a lack of self-consciousness and hence actualization of one's own real desires and abilities. One could recast the preceding analysis of pornographic male sexuality through these categories. In Marx's own analysis, these are more properly conceived of as the results of alienation, rather than the process of alienation itself. This process is at its basis a process of inversion, a reversal of the subject-object relationship, in which one's active powers become estranged from one, and return to dominate one as an external force. It is this aspect which I believe is most useful in understanding the alienation of male sexuality of which pornography is part and parcel. How is it that men's power turns against them, so that pornography, in and by which men dominate women, comes to dominate men themselves?

To answer this question I shall find it useful to have recourse to two other concepts central to Marxism, the concept of "crisis" in the system and the concept of "imperialism."[12] Marx's conception of the economic crisis of capitalism is often misunderstood as a prophecy of a cataclysmic doomsday scenario for the death of capitalism. Under this interpretation, some look for a single event, perhaps like a stock market crash, to precipitate capitalism's demise. But such events are for Marx at most triggering events, particular crises, which can shake the system, if at all, only because of the far more important underlying structural general crisis of capitalism. This general crisis is increasingly capitalism's ordinary state, not an extraordinary occurrence. It is manifest in the ongoing fiscal crisis of the state as well as recurring crises of legitimacy, and results from basic contradictory tensions within capitalism. One way of expressing these tensions is to see them as a conflict between the classic laissez-faire capitalist market mode, wherein capitalists are free to run their own affairs as individuals, and the increasing inability of the capitalist class to run an increasingly complex system without centralized management. The result of this tension is that the state increasingly becomes a managerial committee for the capitalist class, and is increasingly called upon to perform functions previously left to individuals. As entrepreneurial and laissez-faire capitalism give way to corporate capitalism and the welfare state, the power of capitalism becomes increasingly depersonalized, increasingly reft from the hands of individual capitalists and collectivized, so that capitalists themselves come more and more under the domination of impersonal market forces no longer under their direct control.

To move now to the relevance of the above, there is currently a good deal of talk about a perceived crisis of masculinity, in which men are said to be confused by contradictory imperatives given them in the wake of the women's movement. Though the male ego feels uniquely beleaguered today, in fact such talk regularly surfaces in our culture— the 1890's in the United States, for example, was another period in which the air was full of a "crisis of masculinity" caused by the rise of the "New Woman" and other factors.[13] Now, I wish to put forward the hypothesis that these particular "crises" of masculinity are but surface manifestations of a much deeper and broader phenomenon which I call the "general crisis of patriarchy," paralleling Marx's general crisis of capitalism. Taking a very broad view, this crisis results from the increasing depersonalization of patriarchal power which occurs with the development of patriarchy from its pre-capitalist phase, where power really was often directly exercised by individual patriarchs, to its late capitalist phase where men collectively exercise power over women, but are themselves as individuals increasingly under the domination of those same patriarchal powers.[14] I would stress that the sense of there being a "crisis" of masculinity arises not from the decrease or increase in patriarchal power as such. Patriarchal imperatives for men to retain power over women remain in force throughout. But there is a shift in the mode of that power's exercise, and the sense of crisis results from the simultaneous promulgation throughout society of two conflicting modes of patriarchal power, the earlier more personal form and the later more institutional form. The crisis results from the incompatibility of the two conflicting ideals of masculinity embraced by the different forms of patriarchy, the increasing conflicts between behavioral and attitudinal norms in the political/ economic and the personal/familial spheres.

4. From Patriarchy to Fratriarchy

To engage for a moment in even broader speculation than that which I have so far permitted myself, I believe that much of the culture, law, and philosophy of the nineteenth century in particular can be re-interpreted as marking a decisive turn in this transition. I believe the passing of personal patriarchal power and its transformation into institutional patriarchal power in this period of the interrelated consolidation of corporate capitalism is evidenced in such phenomena as the rise of what one scholar has termed "judicial patriarchy," the new social regulation of masculinity through the courts and social welfare agencies, which through new support laws, poor laws, desertion laws and other changes transformed what were previously personal obligations into legal duties, as well as in the "Death of God" phenomenon and its aftermath.[15] That is to say, I believe the loss of the personal exercise of patriarchal power and its diffusion through the institutions of society is strongly implicated in the death of God the Father and the secularization of culture in the nineteenth century, as well as the modern and postmodern problem of grounding authority and values.

I would like to tentatively and preliminarily propose a new concept to reflect this shift in the nature of patriarchy caused by the deindividualization and collectivization of male power. Rather than speak simply of advanced capitalist patriarchy, the rule of the *fathers*, I suggest we speak of fratriarchy, the rule of the *brothers*. For the moment, I propose this concept more as a metaphor than as a sharply defined analytical tool, much as the concept of patriarchy was used when first popularized. I believe this concept better captures what I would argue is one of the key issues in conceptualizing contemporary masculinities, the disjunction between the facts of public male power and the feelings of individual male powerlessness. As opposed to the patriarch, who embodied many levels and kinds of authority in his single person, the brothers stand in uneasy relationships with each other, engaged in sibling rivalry while trying to keep the power of the family of man as a whole intact. I note that one of the consequences of the shift from patriarchy to fratriarchy is that some people become nostalgic for the authority of the benevolent patriarch, who if he was doing his job right at least prevented one of the great dangers of fratriarchy, fratricide, the brothers' killing each other. Furthermore, fratriarchy is an intra-generational concept, whereas patriarchy is intergenerational. Patriarchy, as a father-to-son transmission of authority, more directly inculcates traditional historically grounded authority, whereas the dimension of temporal continuity is rendered more problematic in fratriarchy's brother-to-brother relationships. I believe this helps capture the problematic nature of modern historical consciousness as it emerged from the nineteenth century, what I would argue is the most significant single philosophical theme of that century. If taken in Freudian directions, the concept of fratriarchy also speaks to the brothers' collusion to repress awareness of the violence which lies at the foundations of society.

To return to the present discussion, the debate over whether pornography reflects men's power or powerlessness, as taken up recently by Alan Soble in his book *Pornography: Marxism, Feminism, and the Future of Sexuality,* can be resolved if one makes a distinction such as I have proposed between personal and institutional male power. Soble cites men's use of pornographic fantasy as compensation for their powerlessness in the real world to argue that "pornography is therefore not so much an expression of male power as it is an expression of their lack of power."[16] In contrast, I would argue that by differentiating levels of power one should more accurately say that pornography is both an expression of men's public power and an expression of their lack of personal power. The argument of this paper is that pornography's image of male sexuality works to the detriment of men personally even as its image of female sexuality enhances the powers of patriarchy. It expresses the power of alienated sexuality, or, as one could equally well say, the alienated power of sexuality.

With this understanding, one can reconcile the two dominant but otherwise irreconcilable images of the straight male consumer of pornography: on the one hand the powerful rapist, using pornography to consummate his sexual violence, and on the other hand the shy recluse, using it to consummate his masturbatory fantasies. Both images have their degree of validity, and I believe it is a distinctive virtue of the analysis presented here that one can understand not only the merits of each depiction, but their interconnection.

5. Embodiment and Erotica

In the more reductionist and determinist strains of Marxism, pornography as ideology would be relegated to the superstructure of capitalism. I would like to suggest another conceptualization: that pornography is not part of patriarchal capitalism's superstructure, but part of its infrastructure. Its commodification of the body and interpersonal relationships paves the way for the ever more penetrating ingression of capitalist market relations into the deepest reaches of the individual's psychological makeup. The feminist slogan that "The Personal is Political" emerges at a particular historical moment, and should be understood not simply as an imperative declaration that what has previously been seen solely as personal should now be viewed politically, but also as a response to the real increasing politicization of personal life.

This aspect can be illuminated through the Marxist concept of imperialism. The classical Marxist analysis of imperialism argues that it is primarily motivated by two factors: exploitation of natural resources and extension of the market. In this vein, pornography should be understood as imperialism of the body. The greater public proliferation of pornography, from the "soft-core" pornography of much commercial advertising to the greater availability of "hard-core" pornography, proclaims the greater colonization of the body by the market.[17] The increasing use of the male body as a sex symbol in contemporary culture is evidence of advanced capitalism's increasing use of new styles of masculinity to promote images of men as consumers as well as producers.[18] Today's debates over the "real" meaning of masculinity can be understood in large part as a struggle between those espousing the "new man" style of masculinity more suited to advanced corporate, consumerist patriarchal capitalism and those who wish to return to an idealized version of "traditional" masculinity suited to a more production-oriented, entrepreneurial patriarchal capitalism.[19]

In a more theoretical context, one can see that part of the reason the pornography debate has been so divisive, placing on different sides of the question people who usually find themselves allies, is that discussions between civil libertarians and feminists have often been at cross purposes. Here one can begin to relate political theory not to political practice, but to metaphysical theory. The classical civil liberties perspective on the issue remains deeply embedded in a male theoretical discourse on the meaning of sexuality. The connection between the domination of nature and the domination of women has been argued from many Marxist and feminist points of view.[20] The pivot of this connection is the masculine overlay of the mind-body dualism onto the male-female dichotomy. Within this framework, morality par excellence consists in the masculinized mind restraining the feminized body, with sexual desires seen as the crucial test for these powers of restraint. From this point of view, the question of the morality of pornography is primarily the quantitative question of how much sexual display is allowed, with full civil libertarians opting to uphold the extreme end of this continuum, arguing that no sexual expression should be repressed. But the crucial question, for at least the very important strain of feminist theory which rejects these dualisms which frame the debate for the malestream mainstream, is not *how much* sexuality is displayed but rather *how* sexuality is displayed. These theories speak not of mind-body dualism, but of mind/body wholism, where the body is seen not as the limitation or barrier for the expression of the free moral self, but rather as the most immediate and intimate vehicle for the expression of that self. The question of sexual morality here is not that of restraining or releasing sexual desires as they are forced on the spiritual self by the temptations of the body, but that of constructing spirited and liberating sexual relationships with and through one's own and others' bodies. Here sexual freedom is not the classical liberal freedom *from* external restraint, but the more radical freedom *to* construct authentically expressive sexualities.

I have argued throughout this paper that pornography is a vehicle for the imposition of socially constructed sexuality, not a means for the expression of autonomously self-determined sexuality. (I would add that in contrasting imposed and authentic sexualities I am not endorsing a sexual essentialism, but simply carving out a space for more personal freedom.) Pornography is inherently about commercialized sex, about the eroticization of power and the power of eroticization. One can look to the term's etymology for confirmation of this point. It comes from the classical Greek "*pornographos*, meaning 'writing (sketching) of harlots,' " sometimes women captured in war.[21] Any distinction between pornography and erotica remains problematic, and cannot be drawn with absolute precision. Yet I believe some such distinction can and must be made. I would place the two terms not in absolute opposition, but at two ends of a continuum, with gray areas of necessity remaining between them. The gradations along the continuum are marked not by the explicitness of the portrayal of sexuality or the body, nor by the assertiveness vs. passivity of persons, nor by any categorization of sexual acts or activities, but by the extent to which autonomous personhood is attributed to the person or persons portrayed. Erotica portrays sexual subjects, manifesting their personhood in and through their bodies. Pornography depicts sex objects, persons reduced to their bodies. While the erotic nude presents the more pristine sexual body before the social persona is adopted through donning one's clothing, the pornographic nude portrays a body whose clothing has been more or less forcibly removed, where the absence of that clothing remains the most forceful presence in the image. Society's objectification remains present, indeed emphasized, in pornography, in a way in which it does not in erotica. Erotica, as sexual art, expresses a self, whereas pornography, as sexual commodity, markets one. The latter "works" because the operation it performs on women's bodies resonates with the "pornographizing" the male gaze does to women in other areas of society.[22] These distinctions remain problematic, to say the least, in their application, and disagreement in particular cases will no doubt remain. Much more work needs to be done before one would with any reasonable confidence distinguish authentic from imposed, personal from commercial, sexuality. Yet I believe this is the crucial question, and I believe these concepts correctly indicate the proper categories of analysis. Assuming a full definition of freedom as including autonomy and self-determination, pornography is therefore incompatible with real freedom.

6. Conclusions

It has often been noted that while socialist feminism is currently a major component of the array of feminisms one finds in academic feminism and women's studies, it is far less influential on the playing fields of practical politics.[23] While an analysis of male sexuality may seem an unlikely source to further socialist feminism's practical political agenda, I hope this paper's demonstration of the interconnections between intimate personal experiences and large-scale historical and social structures, especially in what may have initially seemed unlikely places, may serve as a useful methodological model for other investigations.

In one sense, this paper hopes to further the development of socialist feminist theory via a return to Hegel, especially the Hegel of the *Phenomenology*. Not only is Hegel's master-servant dialectic the *sine qua non* for the use of the concept of alienation in this paper, but the inspiration for a mode of analysis, which is true to the experimental consciousness of social actors while at the same time delimiting that consciousness by showing its partiality and placing it in a broader context, is rooted in Hegel's *Phenomenology*. It is not a coincidence that the major wave of socialist feminist theory and practice in the late 60's and early 70's coincided with a wave of Marxist interest in Hegel, and that current signs of a new feminist interest in Hegel coincide with signs of the resurgence of radical politics in the United States.[24] Analogous to the conception of socialist feminism I articulated in the Introduction to this paper, my conception of Hegelianism defines Hegelianism as method rather than doctrine.[25] In some sense, contemporary Marxism and feminism can already be said to be rooted in Hegel, in the case of Marxism through Marx himself, and in the case of feminism through Beauvoir's *The Second Sex*. A more explicitly Hegelian influenced socialist feminism would embody a theory and practice emphasizing the following themes: the dialectic between individual consciousness and social structure, a thoroughly historical epistemology, a non-dualistic metaphysics, an understanding of gender, class, and other differences as being constituted through interaction rather than consisting of isolated "roles," the priority of political over moralistic or economistic theory, a probing of the relations between state power and cultural hegemony, a program for reaching unity through difference rather than through sameness, a tolerance of if not preference for ambiguity and contradiction, and an orientation toward process over end product.[26]

I would like to conclude with some remarks on the practical import of this analysis. First of all, if the analysis of the relationship between pornography and consumerism and the argument about pornography leading to violence are correct, then a different conceptualization of the debate over the ethics of the feminist anti-pornography movement emerges. If one accepts, as I do, the idea that this movement is not against sex, but against sexual abuse, then the campaign against pornography is essentially not a call for censorship but a consumer campaign for product safety. The proper context for the debate over its practices is then not issues of free speech or civil liberties, but issues of business ethics. Or rather, this is the conclusion I reach remaining focused on pornography and male sexuality. But we should remember the broader context I alluded to at the beginning of this paper, the question of pornography's effects on women. In that context, women are not the consumers of pornography, but the consumed. Rather than invoking the consumer movement, perhaps we should then look to environmental protection as a model.[27] Following this line of reasoning, one could in principle then perhaps develop under the tort law of product liability an argument to accomplish much of the regulation of sexually explicit material some are now trying to achieve through legislative means, perhaps developing a new definition of "safe" sexual material.

Finally, for most of us most of our daily practice as academics consists of teaching rather than writing or reading in our fields. If one accepts the analysis I have presented, a central if not primary concern for us should therefore be how to integrate this analysis into our classrooms. I close by suggesting that we use this analysis and others like it from the emerging field of men's studies to demonstrate to the men in our classes the direct relevance of feminist analysis to their own lives, at the most intimate and personal levels, and that we look for ways to demonstrate to men that feminism can be personally empowering and liberating for them without glossing over, and in fact emphasizing, the corresponding truth that this will also require the surrender of male privilege.[28]

Notes

1. I am indebted for this formulation to Tim Carrigan, Bob Connell, and John Lee, "Toward a New Sociology of Masculinity," in Harry Brod, ed., *The Making of Masculinities: The New Men's Studies* (Boston: Allen & Unwin, 1987).

2. For the *locus classicus* of the redefinition of Marxism as method rather than doctrine, see Georg Lukács, *History and Class Consciousness: Studies in Marxist Dialectics*, trans. Rodney Livingstone (Cambridge, MA: MIT Press, 1972).

3. See my Introduction to Brod, *The Making of Masculinities*. For other recent books by men I consider to be engaged in essentially the same or a kindred project, see Jeff Hearn, *The Gender of Oppression: Men, Masculinity, and the Critique of Marxism* (New York: St. Martin's Press, 1987) and R. W. Connell, *Gender and Power* (Stanford, CA: Stanford University Press, 1987), particularly the concept of "hegemonic masculinity," also used in Carrigan, Connell, and Lee, "Toward A New Sociology of Masculinity." Needless to say, none of this work would be conceivable without the pioneering work of many women in women's studies.

4. For book-length treatments of Marx's concept of alienation, see István Mészáros, *Marx's Theory of Alienation* (New York: Harper & Row, 1972), and Bertell Ollman, *Alienation: Marx's Conception of Man in Capitalist Society* (Cambridge: Cambridge University Press, 1971).

5. Bernie Zilbergeld, *Male Sexuality: A Guide to Sexual Fulfillment* (Boston: Little, Brown and Company, 1978).

6. Michael Betzold, "How Pornography Shackles Men and Oppresses Women," in *For Men Against Sexism: A Book of Readings*, ed. Jon Snodgrass (Albion, CA: Times Change Press, 1977), p. 46.

7. I am grateful to Lenore Langsdorf and Paula Rothenberg for independently suggesting to me how this point would fit into my analysis.

8. See Jessica Benjamin, "The Bonds of Love: Rational Violence and Erotic Domination," *Feminist Studies* 6 (1980): 144–74.

9. Keith McWalter, "Couch Dancing," *New York Times Magazine*, December 6, 1987, p. 138.

10. Karl Marx, "Economic and Philosophic Manuscripts: Third Manu-

script," in *Early Writings*, ed. and trans. T. B. Bottomore (New York: McGraw-Hill, 1964), pp. 159–60.

11. Marx., pp. 164–65.

12. An earlier version of portions of the following argument appears in my article "Eros Thanatized: Pornography and Male Sexuality" with a "1988 Postscript," in Michael Kimmel, ed., *Men Confronting Pornography* (New York: Crown, 1989). The article originally appeared (without the postscript) in *Humanities in Society* 7 (1984) pp. 47–63.

13. See the essays by myself and Michael Kimmel in Brod, *The Making of Masculinities*.

14. Compare Carol Brown on the shift from private to public patriarchy: "Mothers, Fathers, and Children: From Private to Public Patriarchy" in Lydia Sargent, ed., *Women and Revolution* (Boston: South End Press, 1981).

15. According to Martha May in her paper " 'An Obligation on Every Man': Masculine Breadwinning and the Law in Nineteenth Century New York," presented at the American Historical Association, Chicago, Illinois, 1987, from which I learned of these changes, the term "judicial patriarchy" is taken from historian Michael Grossberg *Governing the Hearth: Law and the Family in Nineteenth Century America* (Chapel Hill: University of North Carolina Press, 1985) and "Crossing Boundaries: Nineteenth Century Domestic Relations Law and the Merger of Family and Legal History," *American Bar Foundation Research Journal* (1985): 799–847.

16. Alan Soble, *Pornography: Marxism, Feminism, and the Future of Sexuality* (New Haven: Yale University Press, 1986), p. 82. I agree with much of Soble's analysis of male sexuality in capitalism, and note the similarities between much of what he says about "dismemberment" and consumerism and my analysis here.

17. See John D'Emilio and Estelle B. Freedman, *Intimate Matters: A History of Sexuality in America* (New York: Harper & Row, 1988).

18. See Barbara Ehrenreich, *The Hearts of Men: American Dreams and the Flight from Commitment* (New York: Anchor-Doubleday, 1983); and Wolfgang Fritz Haug, *Critique of Commodity Aesthetics: Appearance, Sexuality, and Advertising in Capitalist Society*, trans. Robert Bock (Minneapolis: University of Minnesota Press, 1986).

19. See my "Work Clothes and Leisure Suits: The Class Basis and Bias of the Men's Movement," originally in *Changing Men* 11 (1983) 10–12 and 38–40, reprint in *Men's Lives: Readings in the Sociology of Men and Masculinity*, ed. Michael Kimmel and Michael Messner (New York: Macmillan, 1989).

20. This features prominently in the work of the Frankfurt school as well as contemporary ecofeminist theorists.

21. Rosemarie Tong, "Feminism, Pornography and Censorship," *Social Theory and Practice* 8 (1982): 1–17.

22. I learned to use "pornographize" as a verb in this way from Timothy Beneke's "Introduction" to his *Men on Rape* (New York: St. Martin's Press, 1982).

23. See the series of ten articles on "Socialist-Feminism Today" in *Socialist Review* 73–79 (1984–1985).

24. For recent feminist re-examinations of Hegel, see Heidi M. Raven, "Has Hegel Anything to Say to Feminists?", *The Owl of Minerva* 19 (1988)

149–68. Patricia Jagentowicz Mills, *Women, Nature, and Psyche* (New Haven: Yale University Press, 1987); and Susan M. Easton, "Hegel and Feminism," in David Lamb, ed., *Hegel and Modern Philosophy* (London: Croom Helm, 1987). Hegel enters contemporary radical legal thought primarily through the Critical Legal Studies movement. Especially relevant here is the work of Drucilla Cornell, for example, "Taking Hegel Seriously: Reflections on Beyond Objectivism and Relativism," *Cardozo Law Review* 7 (1985): 139; "Convention and Critique," *Cardozo Law Review* 7 (1986): 679; "Two Lectures on the Normative Dimensions of Community in the Law," *Tennessee Law Review* 54 (1987); 327; "Toward a Modern/Postmodern Reconstruction of Ethics," *University of Pennsylvania Law Review* 133 (1985): 291. See also papers from the Conference on "Hegel and Legal Theory," March 1988 at the Cardozo Law School of Yeshiva University, New York City, forthcoming in a special issue of the *Cardozo Law Review*. For signs of radical resurgence in the United States, I would cite such phenomena as the Jackson candidacy and the 1988 National Student Convention. In *The Nation* Jefferson Morley writes: "The most fundamental idea shared by popular movements East and West is the principle of 'civil society.' " Jefferson Morley, "On 'Civil Society,' " *The Nation*, May 7, 1988, p. 630.

25. I believe this is true to Hegel's own conception of Hegelianism, for Hegel put the Logic at the core of his system, and at the center of the Logic stands the transfiguration and transvaluation of form and content.

26. Much of the feminist critique of the philosophical mainstream echoes earlier critiques of the mainstream made in the name of "process thought." See *Feminism and Process Thought: The Harvard Divinity School/Claremont Center for Process Studies Symposium Papers*, ed. Sheila Greeve Davaney (Lewiston, NY: Edwin Mellen Press, 1981).

27. I am indebted to John Stoltenberg for this point.

28. I attempt to articulate this perspective principally in the following: *The Making of Masculinities*, Introduction and "The Case for Men's Studies"; *A Mensch Among Men: Explorations in Jewish Masculinity* (Freedom, CA: The Crossing Press, 1988), especially the Introduction; and "Why is This 'Men's Studies' Different From All Other Men's Studies?," *Journal of the National Association for Women Deans, Administrators, and Counselors* 49 (1986): pp. 44–49. See also generally the small men's movement magazines *Changing Men: Issues in Gender, Sex and Politics* (306 North Brooks St., Madison, WI 53715), *brother: The Newsletter of the National Organization for Changing Men* (1402 Greenfield Ave., #1, Los Angeles, CA 90025), and *Men's Studies Review* (Box 32, Harriman, TN 37748).

14

Erogenous Zones and Ambiguity: Sexuality and the Bodies of Women and Men

Laurence Thomas

Is that a pickle in your pocket, or are you happy to see me?
—Mae West

Introduction

If a man had sex with women only, but occasionally enjoyed watching homosexual films or merely admitted that from time to time he dreamt about having sex with men or men having sex, a great many would insist that he has (latent) homosexual desires. And no "real man" wants to have even latent homosexual desires. Indeed, openly

This is a slightly abbreviated version, with occasional alterations in the structure and content of the argument as well, of my chapter by the same title which originally appeared in Joseph Kuypers (ed.) *Men and Power* (Fernwood Publishing, 1996).

In writing this chapter, thanks are owed to many: My colleagues in France: Edward De Sapereira, Charlotte De Sapereira, Claire Zeppilli, and Carol Heidseick; to the students in my Philosophy 191 course (Spring of 1995), who were a most gracious and important sounding board for my initial attempt to put these ideas into essay form; and to Michael Patrick Evans and Joseph Kuypers for instructive comments upon the penultimate draft of this chapter. In thinking about matters of heterosexism over the years, Tom Foster Digby has been a godsend. Last, but certainly not least, I wish to thank Claudia Card and Larry May both of whom offered a most instructive set of comments not all of which I have been able to take into account.

admiring the physical appearances of another man is about as much as most "real men" can abide. Even then, if this admiration is not to occasion any suspicion of homosexuality, it had better be done with a certain bravado—"You look good/cool" versus "You look sexy." There are straight men and there are gay men: end of story, as in terms of social import bisexual men are but a version of gay men. Interestingly, the only context in which men are allowed to display (nearly) unrestrained physical affection for one another—usually for a dying partner—seems to be in the context of war. Or, so the cinema would have us believe. But then eroticism drops out of the picture.

Now, one naturally supposes that the category of straight and gay applies in a like manner to women. Well, yes and no. Contemporary popular and pornographic cinema presents very good evidence that things are significantly more complicated. Such thematically different movies as the *The Color Purple* and *Basic Instinct* portray considerable sexual energy between women without much bothering anyone, to say nothing of lesbian scenes in pornography. Were popular films to portray as much sexual energy between men that would surely be a problem. In straight pornography, any gay scene that occurs is apt to be very, very brief scene or a very small background part of a large sexual scene. We have a display of sexual energy between two people when they interact in ways that either or both parties would understandably find erotic to some extent or, in any case, it would be natural for the typical viewer to regard the interaction as being erotic to some extent. So actors performing a love scene have to do enough, given the conventions of the culture in which the film is being viewed, to at least be convincing to the viewing audience.

Interview with the Vampire is probably one of the most homoerotic movies ever produced for the general public. The movie just is about the intense need that one male vampire has for male vampire companionship. From the very first bite on the neck which is followed by the ascent into the air as the two men are locked in a blood-kiss (excuse me, I mean: bite) on the neck, sexual energy between males abounds. They are vampires, though; and that is absolutely crucial to the explanation for how all this explicit sexual energy between men remains relatively unproblematic for the audience. Because this energy occurs between vampires, the audience does not perceive the male-male sexual energy as either a recommendation or an endorsement. Vampires being perverse creatures, to begin with, can get away with (in the mind of the audience) doing perverse things. *Interview* is a far more homoerotic movie and thus displays far more sexual energy between men than the movie *Threesome*. This is so although *Threesome* is expressly about a ménage-à-trois between one woman and two men, with one man being sexually attracted to the other, and although the movie contains a sex scene at the end between the three where the two men are mildly animated by one another's sexual desire even as each is having sex with the woman who is between them. Not surprisingly, *Threesome* was not a commercial success in the United States. After all, this is not the sort of movie that together two straight guys might go out to see or that a straight guy would take a date to see; for no man would want anyone to think that he might have as a fantasy a ménage-à-trois involving himself, another man, and a woman. Had *Threesome* been about two women loving one man, it probably would have been a hit. In the hopes that their woman companion might take a liking to the idea, all sorts of men would want to see the film with her. Again! And again! Notice, too, that in order to portray intense sexual energy between women, we do not need the guise of vampires.

A question that certainly suggests itself, then, is: How can it be that society officially condemns homosexuality, and rather harshly at that, but yet accepts displays of intense sexual energy between women to a far greater degree than it accepts such displays between men? Now, this turns out to be a two-tiered question. For society consists of both women and men. Yet, it is not as if only men are accepting of displays of sexual energy between women, but women utterly abhor such displays. After all, it is between women that these displays occur and are portrayed for the eyes of both women and men to see. I assume that if women found displaying sexual attraction between themselves utterly abhorrent, we would certainly see far less of this sort of thing, except between lesbians. So, there is the very specific point that women are more accepting of displays of sexual energy between themselves than men are accepting of sexual energy between themselves. And one quite naturally asks: Why is that? In the hopes of gaining some insight into heterosexist attitudes on the part of men, it is this latter question that I want to answer in this essay.

Central to my answer is the difference between affirming and erotic sensuality. I take affirming sensuality to be a fundamental need among all human beings, and that in a sexist society men believe that they can turn only to women in order to obtain affirming sensuality, which is one reason why men have sought to control women. What is more, it is primarily in the context of sexual behavior that the desire for affirming sensuality often expresses itself among men.

Lest there be any misunderstanding, I hardly mean to deny that there are women who find lesbianism repulsive, and that many straight women generally do not want to be mistaken for being a lesbian or so accused. All the same, none of this detracts from the blatant reality that women are more accepting of displays of sexual energy between themselves than men are accepting of such displays between themselves. For such displays between women abound throughout Western culture, and is often instantiated by women who would never think of themselves as lesbians and who have little or no concern for their image as straight women being tarnished. Not so with men, who are generally concerned that they do not even invite the suspicion that they are gay. It is for these reasons that I said "yes and no" to the question whether the labels straight and gay apply in a like manner to women as they (the labels) apply to men. There seems to be an erogenous loop between being straight and gay that women can travel upon, but not so for men. This asymmetry between women and men is what I wish to explain.

Two caveats are in order. First, in talking about human beings, it is always important to remember that a pattern is not defeated by a single example to the contrary. For instance, the claim that the life expectancy of males in England is such-and-such is hardly defeated by the truth that there are males who die younger and males who die older. The account which I shall be developing of the asymmetery between women and men speaks to a difference in patterns in the lives of women and men, a pattern to which there are exceptions. Second, it is a most significant fact that men generally have a higher social status than women. Indeed, as Claudia Card (private communication) has observed, women (who were tomboys) look back with nostalgia at the days when they were tomboys, whereas men (who were sissies) never talk fondly of having been sissies. The arguments of this essay are very much consistent with these observations.

I. Bodies: Women and Men

In response to my question, it might seem that a natural line to take would draw upon both Carol Gilligan's *In a Different Voice* and Nancy Chodorow's *The Reproduction of Mothering*. Their view (speaking in broad terms) is that in a world where parenting is primarily the role of women, the boundaries of the self are less sharply drawn between females than is the case between males. Girls are to be like their mothers; but not boys, of course. There is something to this view. Yet, I suspect that these thinkers would not, for a moment, have thought that their views offered an explanation for why women are more accepting of displays of sexual energy between themselves than men are between themselves. This suggests that another approach might be more fruitful, without denying that sexism might be a factor.

I begin with an observation. Women have noted that breast-feeding an infant can be quite sensual. Yet, the sensuality of infant breast feeding does not usually result in anything close to full-scale sexual arousal on the mother's part. These reasons include everything from the infant being seen as an improper object of sexual attraction to the extremely strong social taboo against incest. In any case, what is of considerable interest given the concern of this essay is that women are able to view an extremely erogenous part of their anatomy in two radically different ways. Most significantly, it means that women quite successfully distinguish between the sensuality of breast-feeding and the sensuality of sexual intercourse. So, as a matter of logic: while good sexuality entails the sensual, the sensual does not entail the sexual. We might usefully distinguish between affirming sensuality and erotic sensuality, with breast feeding between a straightforward instance of affirming sensuality. (The adjective *good* is necessary, since it is certainly possible for there to be sex without sensuality. A person could be frigid, for example.)

Relatedly, there is the very important fact that the vaginal passage is also the birth passageway. Thus another extremely erogenous part of the woman's anatomy is inextricably tied to a most significant function—the giving of life—that is quite unconnected with sex. Let me hasten to add here that I have not claimed that giving birth is sensual in any way.

Taken together, these two considerations make it clear that as women conceive of their bodies, not only is sensuality a complicated phenomenon, not always connected to sex, but that the two central erogenous zones of the body serve a life-based purpose quite unrelated to sex. This complex bipartite conception of sensuality, ranging over affirming and erotic sensuality, is generally and routinely transmitted by mothers to their daughters, a point which I shall elaborate upon just before the conclusion of this section.

Needless to say, things are quite different with men's bodies. While men have nipples, their nipples do not supply nutrients. So for men this erogenous zone serves no significant life-based function unrelated to sex. In general, the penis is *the* central erogenous zone for men. And while sperm, of course, pass through the penis, it must be acknowledged that the penis serves no life-based function that comes even close to matching the saliency of bearing a child and giving birth to it. The penis is certainly not a passageway for human form. So, phenomenologically, the central erogenous zones of the male body serve no life-based function: male breasts serve no life-based purpose at all; and the emitting of sperm is more keenly associated with the pleasures of ejaculation than providing an ingredient that makes human life possible. As men conceive of their bodies, the sensual and the sexual are very nearly interchangeable. At any rate, the appreciation which men acquire of the difference between affirming and erotic sensuality is not informed by their body parts serving a life-based purpose.

Now, regarding the distinction between affirming and erotic sensuality, I do not claim that biology is destiny. Nothing I have said entails that, as a matter of biology, women and men are more suited to some social roles than others. I have said that owing to life-based functions women conceive of their bodies differently than men and that, in particular, biology requires women to conceive of sensuality in a more complicated way than it requires men to conceive of it. But perhaps even this is too strong. It would probably be better to say that biology favors women to see sensuality in a more complicated way. I have not claimed, nor have I meant to claim, that men cannot, owing to their biological make-up, conceive of sensuality between adults in such a way that it does not always involve sexuality. At the end of Section II below, I shall further explicate this point concerning being favored. For the moment observe that mothers and daughters routinely touch and embrace in a way that fathers and sons generally do not—at least not after the son is well into his pre-teen years. The force of "routinely" here is that whereas a sustained embrace between father and son is usually occasioned by some significant event, a like embrace between mother and daughter may simply be a part of a casual conversation that reaches a poignant or tender moment. Notice that in a like manner, it is often the case that women embrace one another, whereas this is rather rare among men. Moreover, women are depicted on television and in cinema as casually embracing and touching to a far greater extent than men are. Surely, the very pervasiveness of the difference between how women and men are depicted is not just a function of what men like, but it also reveals a level of comfort that women have with touch between one another that men do not have with touch between one another. In my view, it is the absence of continual experience that renders men so awkward at discerning the difference between affirming sensuality and erotic sensuality.

Of course, the line between affirming sensuality and erotic sensuality is a rather thin one that can be easily crossed either spatially (the touch was a little too close to . . .), temporally (the touch was a little too long), or physically (the touch was just a little too firm or intense). But non-verbal behavior in general is extremely subtle. A wink can be sexual or friendly, depending on the social setting and other facial features. Likewise for the difference between a look of sexual interest, a look that simply finds a feature of the face curious, and a look where one is merely in the line of vision. Yet, we manage remarkably well to make out the difference. Indeed, flirting at a distance would otherwise be impossible. All of this is so notwithstanding the obvious truth that what counts as flirting behavior is culturally-linked.

II. Sexual Ambiguity and Affirming Sensuality

Not having to reveal our true feelings can certainly be advantageous. In fact, given the right contexts, cultivated ambiguity can be quite enjoyable. Part of the joy of a certain kind of flirting, for instance, lies in its ambiguity, thereby allowing people to get a sense of their powers of sexual attractiveness or simply to engage in mild exploration without either party having to pay in the coin of commitment or rejection. Flirting can get out of hand in a number of ways, one of which is when it is taken too seriously. But that is just the point. If flirting gets out of hand precisely when it is taken too seriously, then flirting itself does not constitute a serious proposal, although that is what the flirting party may be warming up to. Flirting can also get out of hand by going on too long or by being directed at the wrong kind of person (say, a nun or a priest). In any event, flirting can be a way of masking keen sexual interest, or it may be just a way of having fun. And if the person flirting is good enough, then only if there has been self-disclosure need someone else ever know.

Along with the distinction between affirming and erotic sensuality drawn in the preceding section, I suggest that another factor in the explanation for why women are more accepting of displays of sexual energy between themselves than are men between themselves is that, in the context of physical interaction, women can generally be ambiguous about whether they are experiencing arousal in a way that men cannot. Let me explain.

In the context of physical interaction, there would be no ambiguity to speak of if sexual arousal in women were accompanied by a physical movement as blatantly revealing as the male erection. Mae West's quip (quoted at the beginning) gives voice to what I mean by blatantly revealing. The idea is that anyone familiar with the difference between a flaccid and an erect penis could, with even a most casual glance from across the room, say, easily recognize the latter on just about any nude adult male and would, in the case of any clothed adult male, readily associate a (heretofore absent) bulge in the groin area with an erect penis. A parallel claim cannot be made regarding women. This is neither to deny that there are bodily movements, such as erect nipples and an extended clitoris, that occur as a result of female arousal; nor to glorify the male erection. Rather, it is merely to point to a difference where there is one. Blushing is more apparent among people with very light skin than it is among people with very dark skin, although everyone blushes.

Nor, again, do I mean to deny that there are forms of behavior in which people can engage that are tell-tale signs of sexual interest. It should be noted, though, that many of these forms of behavior are culturally-tied and engaged in voluntarily, although they can appear driven by the very engine of desire itself. Indeed, part of what it means to be acculturated is to be able to display quite naturally learned behavior which, in that culture, is characteristically associated with having various feelings or beliefs. However, I am interested in autonomic displays of sexual arousals; and my thesis is that in the course of physical interaction, women can be more ambiguous about whether they are experiencing sexual arousal than men can be.

In this regard, we might usefully distinguish between shadow and substantive sexual arousal. I do not have a precise way of drawing this distinction, but I assume that sexual arousal admits of a continuum. I assume that, at one end, there are occasions when we are sexually aroused by some stimulus in the environment (something we see or hear), but that the arousal is not born of a longing for sexual satisfaction. Once the stimulus is no longer present, the arousal dissipates. This is what I am calling shadow arousal. At the other end, there are occasions when we are aroused and that arousal bespeaks or latches on to a longing for sexual satisfaction. This is what I am calling substantive arousal. To be sure, the line between the two can be crossed. In particular, a shadow arousal can become a substantive one. Consider the following story. At one institution where I taught, the majority of males rejected out right the idea of co-ed showers on their dormitory floor, much to the surprise of the women. (In the dormitory in question, shower stalls do not exist; rather, each floor has a large shower-room with a series of shower units.) These males were expressing their awareness that, although they might be preoccupied with going to class, and so not at that moment entertaining the idea of having sex, they were nonetheless susceptible to having a shadow erection given the mere presence of nude women in the same room.

Or, to take an example of a rather different sort, I imagine that just about every man has had the experience of having an erection and inferring from it that he was very much interested in obtaining sexual satisfaction, only to discover upon having sexual intercourse or masturbating that his sexual appetite was not nearly as pronounced as he had thought it was. On my account, this is to experience shadow sexual arousal. As this example reveals, it is possible to be mistaken about whether one is experiencing shadow or substantive sexual arousal. But is it not possible to be more or less hungry than one thought that one was? There is no reason to suppose that epistemic certainty is a feature of the sexual appetite. For the sake of completeness, I should mention, as Larry May has reminded me (personal communication), that there is a third category of erections which have nothing at all to do with sexual desire, namely the morning erection stemming from a full bladder.

In any case, the further point to be made here is that with men shadow sexual arousal has the very same bodily manifestation as sustained arousal, namely an erection; whereas with women the bodily responses associated with sustained arousal occur far less frequently with shadow arousal.

Now, for the sake of argument, let us make three assumptions:

(i) sustained arousals can be detected easily enough in whomever they might occur; whereas with shadow arousals only, it is generally men who leave a tell-tale sign, since shadow arousals in men take the very same form as sustained arousals, namely an erection; (ii) the line between affirming sensuality and erotic sensuality is thin enough that it can be unwittingly crossed; and (iii) it is very difficult for two people to display sufficient sexual energy between them to convince a viewer without running the risk of shadow arousal. Given human psychology, if (ii) is true, then (iii) is very likely to be true. (By the way, the argument does not presuppose that with men shadow arousal always results in an erection, but only that this happens with sufficient frequency. Nor does the argument presuppose that shadow arousal among women never results in bodily movements, but only that this is sufficiently infrequent or the movements are sufficiently less salient. Nor, finally, is it presupposed that deep feelings of arousal must always be accompanied by bodily movements on the part of either women or men. Recall my remarks about patterns at the end of the Introduction.)

In my view, then, it is no accident that many women are relatively comfortable with the ambiguity between affirming sensuality and erotic sensuality. The female-female scenes in such movies as the *The Color Purple* and *Basic Instinct* surely flaunt the ambiguity between affirming sensuality and erotic sensuality. And in my view what makes that flaunting possible is that, in the case of women, shadow arousals do not readily lend themselves to tell-tale bodily manifestations of arousal. For it must be remembered that those female-female scenes are generally convincing; and this requires the requisite frame of mind if only to produce shadow arousal. (Recall that typically a male can, absent extant feelings of sexual desire, bring himself to the point of ejaculation for entirely non-erotic purposes—to obtain a sperm count or to donate to a sperm-bank—by concentrating upon erotic images.) Yet because tell-tale bodily movements do not readily occur in women experiencing only shadow arousal, these scenes do not force the issue of whether or not the actors are in the least bit aroused sexually. In a female-female sexual scene, a woman could very well experience shadow arousal, but absent self-disclosure no one else need ever know. With men, on the other hand, the fact that shadow arousals are likely to yield an erection is precisely the problem. Hence it is no accident that there are virtually no male-male erotic scenes in movies for the general public. For an erection would force the issue that either or both male actors found the scene arousing. And the fact that the issue would be forced in this way is, indeed, the problem. It is this possibility of shadow arousal, and its concomitant erection, which in general men are absolutely unwilling to risk. For instance, in a gymnasium shower room with other men, every male knows that the one thing that he absolutely must not do, whatever else he might do, is have an erection.

No explanation, short of sheer uncontrollable spasms, would be a good one. Women do not seem to have a corresponding worry concerning erect breasts and clitoral extension. Among other things, surely this has to do with the comparative difference in saliency between these phenomena and an erect penis. By contrast, penis and breast size is, respectively, often a concern for both men and women.

As Claudia Card has reminded me (personal communication), the repulsion which heterosexual men have towards another man's erect penis or admiring another man's body is socially induced; for women have no trouble admiring one another's bodies; and I have certainly not denied this. Fortunately, this important truth is compatible with all that I have said about social ambiguity. Men are unwilling to risk shadow erection with their clothes on. For as Mae West's quip reveals, even with clothes on it is possible to be discerning enough. Two clothed men rubbing up against one another in a bar scene would know soon enough whether either or both were aroused. Not so with two women engaged in similar behavior. Even more so, men are unwilling to risk the possibility of shadow arousal in the nude.

The second part of the two-tiered question which I posed at the beginning of this essay reads: How can it be that society officially condemns homosexuality, and rather harshly at that, but yet accepts displays of intense sexual energy between women to a far greater degree than it accepts such displays between men? In sum, my answer is that, first of all, women generally have a richer view of their sensuality then men and, secondly, there is a range of ambiguity in the arena of sexual interaction that women have, but men lack. In both cases, this is due to the difference between the bodies of women and men. In practice, this difference has the effect of creating an erogenous loop, between being straight and gay, that women can travel upon. Not all women feel comfortable cruising this loop; and I have no made such a claim; but clearly, significantly many do. Not only that, those who do not feel comfortable seem to understand, if only from afar, that there is this erogenous loop for women.

I have carefully avoided saying that, as a matter of nature, women view sensuality in a more complex way than man; for I do not believe that is true. What I have said, in effect, is that women are favored by nature to view sensuality in a more complex way than men. This leaves unsettled what the actual outcomes will be like. Consider. A child both of whose parents have a Ph.D. is, from the standpoint of education, favored over the child both of whose parents have only a fifth-grade education. All the same, the former child may perform abysmally in school and the latter brilliantly. When it comes to attitudes and beliefs, how nature manifests itself is inextricably tied to the reality of the social circumstances in which we find ourselves. This is so even when some ways of seeing the world are favored by biology, as is presumably the case with women and the complexity of sensuality. But if what we see in the world of concrete objects can be very much a matter of our expectations, surely this is so with such a complex and amorphous phenomenon as sensuality. Social institutions can enable us to see more clearly that which we would see ever so dimly or not at all on our own.

Can there be a like erogenous loop for men? Surely, but we men would have to take a very different stance toward our bodies, attaching far less sexual significance to an erect penis than we presently do. Indeed, we would have to stop glorifying it. I shall say something about this possibility in the conclusion. However, I assume that a shift in male attitudes along this line must occur.

Now, to see how the account offered sheds a measure of light on sexism and the concern of men to control women: Let it be granted that affirming sensuality is in fact a deep psychological need on the part of women and men alike—that this need exists in the normal course of life, but is especially prevalent during times of crisis. Then, in view of the account of the differences in the bodies of women and men which I have developed, let it be also granted that only women in society are thought to be able to provide affirming sensuality. Together, these two considerations constitute an important reason, though not an utterly decisive reason, for men to want to control women. What is more, it would be a reason born of a sense of fragility on the part of men. Control is the issue here, because affirming sensuality is indispensable to our psychological well-being. Without control men cannot guarantee themselves access to the good of sensual affirmation.

In saying that men are fragile, the idea is that the self-identity of males as "real" men (that is, men who are not gay) can be so easily called into question. This is certainly so in comparison to the self-identity of females as "real" women (that is, women who are not lesbians). Whereas women can dance with one another although there are men available and share the same bed without automatically inviting the suspicion that they are lesbians, an analogous claim most certainly cannot be made for men. Men must studiously refrain from engaging in just about any form of behavior which would invite the suspicion that they are seeking nurturance from another male or that they are even comfortable with things appearing that way. And the socially acculturated man in Western culture is readily threatened in this way. This speaks to the very heart of the fragility of men. When they might turn to one another for the nurturance of affirming sensuality, they must either find a woman or do without that which they could provide for themselves, lest they should appear to be other than "real" men. What is going on here is, quite simply, the fact that "real" men invariably associate nurturance (between adults) with sex and so with their penis.

Suffice it to say that the lives of women would be different, for the worse, if they could only turn to men for the nurturance of affirming sensuality. American slavery, I am sure, would have taken a far greater toll than it did upon the lives of black women, but for the fact that they could turn to one another for the nurturance of affirming sensuality. Men must go through whatever psychological contortions that it takes to sustain this false view of themselves in the face of a reality that makes it clear, at least upon honest reflection, that things have to be otherwise. The case of children makes this abundantly clear. Girl and boy infants do not differ in their need for affection. Moreover, displays of affection among very young children themselves have no boundaries of gender. The explanation for the change here simply cannot be hormonal, since that would leave rather unexplained the blatant asymmetry between women and men.

III. Pornography and Lesbian Scenes

I believe that the account developed in the preceding sections, especially Section II, casts some light onto one of the most interesting questions that can be posed regarding the attraction of pornography: How is it that perfectly straight heterosexual men take such a liking to lesbian scenes—I mean scenes where the women are fully animated by one another's sexual passion, leaving no room for the interpretation that they are awaiting a man for complete sexual fulfillment? (Since pornographic films which cater to straight males almost invariably do not include a homosexual scene, certainly not one that is both explicit and enduring, the parallel question with respect to women does not arise.) Lesbian scenes are a common feature of most pornographic movies for straight men; and while in some instances lesbian sex is but a prelude to heterosexual sex, passionate lesbian scenes representing complete sexual ecstasy between two women are frequent enough. Yet, as a rule straight men do not generally regard these scenes as an affront to their masculinity; nor are they repulsed by passionate lesbian scenes. The very same men who are struck by the unnaturalness of male-male sexual passion, do not seem to find female-female sexual passion unnatural at all.

Whenever I put my initial question to men the most common answer essentially ignores what I asked. I am usually told that "Men like pleasing women; hence, the more the better." Perhaps. But as an answer to my question this response widely misses the explanatory mark. I did not ask why do men like watching pornographic scenes where the man has two or more female sexual partners. Nor did I ask why do men like watching pornographic scenes where women engage in (solitary) acts of self-eroticism. In this latter instance one can see how scenes of this sort are supposed to represent a prelude to the real act of sex, which is supposedly male vaginal penetration. A masturbating woman can be readily construed as wanting a man. Moreover, a straight man watching women masturbate can easily enough draw upon other straight sexual experiences to augment the moment of vicarious participation. Besides, I can only assume that some form of vicarious participation is going on. Otherwise, why are men just about always in pornographic scenes?

Passionate lesbian scenes, however, are a different story altogether. Indeed, precisely because the visual is so powerful, it is extremely difficult to see how these scenes could be inviting to men. On the contrary, scenes of this sort would seem to thwart vicarious participation. So to the typical response to my question, my counter-reply is: Watching passionate lesbian scenes would seem to be a most indirect route to the fantasy of pleasing women—so indirect as to appear off-course. At any rate, how is the pleasure that men take in watching these scenes to be squared with their supposedly inexorable heterosexual inclinations? For the ideological brush of heterosexuality entirely paints every aspect of one's sex life, including one's sexual fantasies. As I noted at the outset, even if in fact a man never had sex with men but only with women, in admitting that he fantasized about having sex with men or enjoyed watching scenes involving men having sex with one another such a man would, in the same breath, be admitting that his sexual orientation is decisively not 100% heterosexual. Why are men so indifferent to lesbian scenes of the sort that I have described?

The explanation that I shall offer for why men take such a liking to lesbian scenes is hardly complete. However, it does, I think, constitute an important beginning. There are, though, a couple of background assumptions to be mentioned. One is that male-male expressions of affirming sensuality generate far too much cognitive dissonance for most people and, in particular, for most men. The other is that, in their adult interactions, most men blur the distinction between affirming sensuality and erotic sensuality, with the latter overshadowing the former. As an aside, it is rather interesting that even for women male-male expressions of affirming sensuality generate a significant level of cognitive dissonance. This is because women frequently bemoan the fact that for men erotic sensuality often overshadows affirming sensuality which they (women) delight in for its own sake. Well, let me just say that women cannot have it both ways. If men are only "allowed" to express affirming sensuality towards women, it should hardly come as any surprise that this form of sensuality is often overshadowed by erotic sensuality. Need any one be reminded that women express affirming sensuality not only towards men but towards other women, and often with great intensity in either case. But this is another issue. Finally, and regarding a different matter, I take it for granted that people have an interest in sex. So what I mean to be explaining is not so much why men are attracted to lesbian scenes, but: *why they are not repulsed by them.*

Now, essentially, my explanation has to do with the account of ambiguity offered in Section II and, in particular, with the fact that shadow arousal among women is not as physically blatant as it is among women. For men, the mark of sexual arousal is the blatant physically revealing movement embodied in the erection. An erection is *the* salient sign that a man is ready for sex. To this, we need only add the consideration that, certainly in a sexist society, whether a woman is ready for sex is deemed irrelevant to a man's having sex with her, as defined in terms of vaginal penetration. Why, in the minds of some men, a woman need not even be conscious, so long as they can engage in vaginal penetration with her. Indeed, within a sexist framework, female readiness for sex is never the real issue, only male readiness is. In my view, then, the male fascination with lesbian pornographic scenes would not exist if female sexual readiness were accompanied by a physically blatant bodily movement. Suppose that whenever women were sufficiently aroused their chest expanded in such a way that their two breasts invariably seemed connected and took on the appearance of one breast with one nipple. Moreover, a fluid was produced upon orgasm. Then in the sex act whether or not a woman is aroused and whether or not she achieves orgasm would be settled matters in roughly the way that things now are with men. Then heterosexual men would have to take seriously that fact women are or are not ready for heterosexual sex in a way that they (men) do not now. If, whenever women were ready for sex, there would be the one-breast phenomenon, then men could not delude themselves into thinking that they had aroused a woman, as either a man succeeded in producing the appearance of the one breast or he did not; and women could not much deceive men about their success in arousing women. Most significantly, just how arousing lesbian scenes are would be clear to all—participants and viewers (if there are any). In particular, it would be rather clear whether a woman is aroused by women and not men, and conversely, or whether a woman is, in fact, aroused by both.

I maintain that this saliency with respect to sexual readiness would be too much for perfectly straight heterosexual men, if only because it would often force the issue of whether a man preferred having sex with a lesbian or a non-lesbian. As things stand, men often labor under the delusion that a woman—even a self-confessed lesbian—really wants sex in the form of vaginal penetration even if she is unwilling to admit it to herself. Well, in many cases that would change with the salience of one-breast appearance as a sign of sexual readiness. The "proof" would be in the manifest bodily display of women, as it presently is for men. Notice that absent an erection, no woman supposes that she has sufficiently aroused a man; nor does the man even try to pretend that he has been sufficiently aroused by the woman. Notice, too, what I have already said several times in various ways: Nothing in Western culture is taken as more decisive evidence of a man's homosexuality than his being moved to have an erection owing to the presence or thought of another man. By undercutting the possibility of certain illusions or forms of self-deception, the fiction of the one-breast appearance would make the enormous difference sketched above even as the idea of vaginal penetration remains unchanged.

(My aim in this fiction of the one-breast appearance has been to imagine a salient physical difference among women on the order of an erection, without losing the significant feature that an erogenous zone yet serves a life-based function. Even if in this scenario there would be some loss of ambiguity, because a one-breast appearance would be detectable enough, a bipartite conception of sensuality would still be very much informed by the breasts of the body; hence, in this regard, the breasts would still be fundamentally different from the penis.)

As I indicated when I began, I have offered only a partial explanation—a fundamental consideration, if you will—for why perfectly straight heterosexual men are so attracted to lesbian scenes. Indeed, if lesbian scenes are but women entertaining themselves in the absence of "real men," suffice it to say that I have sought to draw attention to an important consideration that makes it possible for men to maintain that illusion: Owing to the absence of perceived saliency with respect to female sexual arousal, men are able to avoid taking the sexual preferences of women seriously. Thus, à propos the lesbian scenes of pornography, the truth is that men are not forced to see lesbian scenes as women who are really lesbians who take no sexual interest in men. Hence, men can entertain the fantasy that a man could always make the difference in terms of the sexual fulfillment of these women. Needless to say, this illusory bubble would have difficulty forming, let alone being kept afloat, if the one-breast appearance were not a fiction. Interestingly, this consideration is supported if only obliquely by the truth that erect breasts can be achieved by putting ice or icy water upon them. By contrast, there is no corresponding way to achieve an erect penis. Nor would there be, so I would imagine, a corresponding way to achieve the one-breast appearance.

Let me note that arguments of this section do not entail that pornography must be morally wrong; for acts of erotic sensuality, alone, are not thereby sexist; hence, filming and viewing them need not be. In a world where male-identity was de-coupled from penis-identity, surely the character of pornography would be radically different, indeed, and pornography would no longer be vulnerable to many of the objections that people rightly have against it nowadays.

IV. Concluding Remarks: Sexual Malleability
and Moral Betterment

Biology is hardly decisive with respect to our conception of the erotic. So, it is not ludicrous to ask the question, as if for all practical purposes the answer could only be negative: "Could there be an erogenous loop for men between being straight and gay, as there is with women?" Nor is it ludicrous to suppose that men could view erections in a much more complicated way.

But what benefits might there be? Would it be enough if men were far less threatened by the depth of affection between one another? Would it be enough that *if* men were far less threatened by the depth of affection between one another, *then* female-male relationships would be less plagued by violence and assertions of power and control? Of course, as Andrea Dworkin implies in *Right-Wing Women,* if straightforward expressions of depth of affection were commonplace between men, then the relationships between women and men would be radically different. Specifically, women and, in particular, sex with women would not be the only routes available to men for meeting their emotional needs. Thus, as women and men endeavored to meet their emotional needs, there would be gender pairings of all sorts, and there would be people pairings of all sorts. If these pairings took place with honesty, integrity, and purity of heart: Would that be benefit enough? This would truly be a very different world, perhaps one that we really cannot imagine, because women would no longer be the sole purveyors of affirming sensuality which in a heterosexist world has been the essence of what leverage they have.

While I am not fixated on the male erection, I do often entertain the thought that this would be a better world indeed if penis-identity were not such a central part of male-identity. Things need not be this way. And every time I see a young son holding his father's hand, I know that male-identity could change for the better; for it is not given by biology that sons and fathers stop holding hands when sons reach their pre-teen years. And without at all supposing that everyone should be bisexual or some such thing, for I see no reason to suppose that homogeneity of sexual desire is itself a virtue, I am of the mind that this world would be a much better place if, as with affection between women generally, affection between men were a rich and on-going part of the lives of men generally.

Affirming sensuality is rightly regarded as a very prized moral and spiritual good. However, it is one which all human beings are capable of offering to one another, regardless of gender or sexual orientation. Not surprisingly, we have a world full of contortions when we attempt to limit affection to specific groups or to specific kinds of pairings; for affection in its purest form knows neither groups nor specific kinds of pairings but only affection and non-affection. In particular, if affirming sensuality is the prized good that I take it to be, it can be hardly surprising that men should take such an interest in controlling women, given the mistaken view that only women are capable of providing others with this good.

This chapter has a moral lesson to it. One thing more loathsome than controlling others in order to secure a basic need—affirming sensuality, in this case—is having a distorted self-concept which prevents us from seeing that we can provide for ourselves the very thing for which we are exercising power over others in order to obtain.

PART EIGHT

Oppression and Empowerment

15

Honor, Emasculation, and Empowerment

Leonard Harris

Honor is a form of reverence, esteem, exhausted regard, and deference an individual receives from others. Honor is accorded individuals that represent "certain archetypal patterns of behavior."[1] Honor is therefore a social good. That is, honor is a good that individuals can receive from others if they represent envious traits and behaviors.[2] Individuals of a generally despised or subjugated community are, however, normally considered incapable of representing envious traits or ascending to honorable social status. Such individuals are outside of the moral community, i.e., outside of a type of person, group, religion, class, or nation of primary value to those conferring honor. The African American community is the victim of racism, making it a subjugated community. Racism helps account for why honor has been an elusive good for African American males despite occasional examples of individually highly regarded African Americans. I argue that the honor accorded Dr. Martin L. King, Jr. does not defeat my claim that membership in the moral community is crucial for an individual to be honored.

A Conception of Honor

Parenting normally includes teaching children how to impose their wills—wiping their noses, deciding not to eat candy, exercising their preference for clothes, and discussing, arguing and using body language in ways that help convince. Parents are authorities whether they use tyrannical means of domination or discourse as a form of coercing and shaping behavior. Analogously, childrens' play includes means for children to impose their wills on one another. It may be that the play of boys evinces a greater concern for competition, rules and winning than girls; the play of girls may be more concerned with cooperation, sharing and keeping a game enjoyable rather than determining who wins. Nevertheless, both forms of play share the project of will imposition; the first through verifiable results and the second through a cohesion that allows deciding who is included and who excluded from the shared bonds. The use of threats, demands, pressure and aggressive behavior are features integral to the imposition of wills in both parenting and play.

There are tremendously varied ways and purposes through which individuals seek to have their wills imposed on others. However, the fact of imposing one's will is cross-culturally important as a way of securing regard from others and developing a sense of self-worth. The personalization of politics is telling in attitudes of children toward race, war, and social identity.[3] Caring, loving, and nurturing children to become soldiers or to be supportive of soldiers has occurred generation after generation in American history.[4]

Honor is a good often accorded because virtues and meritorious traits are assumed to be embodied by an agent. The willful obedience of children to their parents' most cherished expectations, for example, is a form of honoring one's parents. Honor reflects discrete and explicit social rankings and boundaries between agents. Failure to accord appropriate deferential behavior or appropriate regard for social rankings and boundaries, such as children cursing adults, bespeaks dishonor. Persons can be honored if they have no accomplishments, such as persons of noble birth, and honor can be bestowed on epic heroes as well as the dead. There are tremendously different forms of honor, different conceptions of what is required for a person to be honored, and different views about what counts as degradation. The above features of honor are certainly not exhaustive.

Peter Berger argues that honor in the modern world is no longer prevalent. He associates honor with socially imposed roles, chivalrous codes of behavior, and laws against insults to honor. However, for Berger, "A return to institutions will be *ipso facto* a return to honor." because institutions impose roles and establish hierarchies.[5] Contrary to Berger, normal social life has an array of hierarchies to support informal codes of honor. Moreover, the royal houses of Austria, England, Japan, and Saudi Arabia are faring well in modernity. A visit to nearly any multinational corporate headquarters, military barracks, or schoolyard might disabuse academicians of the illusion that conceptions of honor are not prevalent in modernity. Nonetheless, I intend to mean by honor a variety of forms of exalted accord. One way to see that honor is a social good and present a sample of its many forms is by considering what it is to be dishonored.

Honor and Emasculation

According to Orlando Patterson in *Slavery and Social Death,* slavery is the condition of being generally despised and natally alienated; incapable of defining descending generations or directing the course of ascending generations. "The dishonor the slave was compelled to experience sprang instead from that raw, human sense of debasement inherent in having no being except as an expression of another's being."[6] Contrary to Hegel and Marx, in Patterson's account, slaves were not necessarily workers, but they were never, however, accorded the status of moral persons. Moreover, male and female slaves, no matter how rich, were always under the threat of harm from any member of the slaveholding class—child, homeless free person, woman, man, or even pets of the free. "The absolute ruler . . . requires the ultimate slave; and the ultimate slave is best represented in the anomalous person of the eunuch."[7]

Eunuchs were absolutely incapable of redemption—they could father no future generations and they were usually despised. They were emasculated, not only because as a group they could not function as normal biological parents, nor hold the respect of their relatives if these were known, but because they lacked the possibility of empowerment over other men and dominance over women. As tax collectors, for example, they could shape the life chances of a tremendous range of wealthy as well as poor persons; they could never participate in shaping the next generation as their surrogates, vassals of their values, or as testaments to their love; nor could they dictate the flow of wealth from one generation to the next. As a group, eunuchs could not stop the children of their masters from becoming adults that would despise eunuchs any more than African American "nannies" could stop the children they raised on behalf of their masters from selling them or their children, beating their husbands, raping their daughters, or castrating their sons. Eunuchs existed completely for the other—bodies for sport, sex, status, guards, servants and administration—irredeemable physically, spiritually and socially. The dishonor of eunuchs was conditioned on the exclusion of the eunuch community from the moral community, i.e., the embodiment of virtues and meritorious traits by an individual eunuch was always tainted because individual eunuchs were members of, or perceived as members of, a generally despised community.

Thomas More's *Utopia* provides an excellent example of the importance performed by the boundary between membership in or exclusion from the moral community and the way that membership establishes what individual is potentially due deference. More considered slavery a substitute for death and an improvement in the life of the spiritually or virtue-dead person. In More's *Utopia* there are no positions of exalted honor. Rather, the society of Utopia itself is an honorable social entity. Utopia is reached only by accident or luck. Almost no one ever left Utopia. Slaves and colonized aliens are voluntary subjects or ones subjugated for their own benefit. In either case, they are always pleased to have been saved from their previous state of decadence. Everyone that lived outside of Utopia could be ranked as more or less degraded in comparison to everyone in Utopia. Persons were or became honored because they identified with, had the sentiments of, and conducted themselves in accordance with the norms of the social order in Utopia. That order is what More constructs as honorable. That is, social normality in *Utopia* is coterminous with nobility—everyone is in an exalted station and utopia itself is the highest earthly form of excellence.

The same is the case in *Ethiopia Unbound,* an idealized depiction of Africa by the noted Ghanian nationalist J. E. Casely Hayford (1866–1930).[8] Hayford's *Ethiopia Unbound* has a hierarchical character that functions to promote egalitarianism; polygamy, chiefs and provincial villages are grounded in Hayford's eyes on egalitarianism. The elite are exalted models of the best norms perceived as definitive of normality.

Utopias characteristically require the perfect ability of the Utopianites to impose their wills—wills that are coterminous with perfect virtue. Normal social life is thereby coterminous with exalted character virtues.[9] A utopia is thus the best, or best possible, social world. That is, honor and normality are coterminous; the abnormal, inferior and irredeemable exist outside of the honor of utopia's normality, i.e., outside the moral community.

The threat of being lynched is an example of the exclusion of African Americans from the moral community—a threat faced most often by African American males and a threat that existed independent of their virtues and merits.

Decapitation, torture, burning and starvation were some of the common practices used in the process of forming and controlling slave communities in the Americas. The vast majority of persons treated as cargo, chattel and fodder for plantations in the Americas were initially Black men. Moreover, it has been argued that "It was threat of honor lost, no less than slavery, that led them [southern American states] to secession and war."[10] Long after the formal end of American slavery in 1865, however, the project of exclusion of African Americans from the moral community continued. Trudier Harris, in *Exorcising*

Blackness describes an American mode of excluding Blacks from the moral community by its practice of lynching. Vicksburg, Mississippi, *Evening Post,* 1904:

> When the two Negroes were captured, they were tied to trees and while the funeral pyres were being prepared they were forced to suffer the most fiendish tortures. The blacks were forced to hold out their hands while one finger at a time was chopped off. The fingers were distributed as souvenirs. The ears of the murderers were cut off. Holbert was beaten severely, his skull was fractured, and one of his eyes, knocked out with a stick, hung by a shred from the socket. . . . The most excruciating form of punishment consisted in the use of a large corkscrew in the hands of some of the mob. This instrument was bored into the flesh of the man and woman, in the arms, legs and body, and then pulled out, the spirals tearing out big pieces of raw, quivering flesh every time it was withdrawn.[11]

Quivering flesh, taken by avid corkscrewers, was thrown to the crowd for souvenirs. The bodies were burned, and after cooling, pieces of charred flesh were taken from the ashes by white men, women and children for souvenirs. Shopkeepers and women of class occasionally used severed hands as ornamentation. This ritual of violence was not isolated to Mississippi: in almost every case of lynching Blacks in America, the same ritual was followed. With the increased accessibility of cameras, photographs of the crowd gloating over the body became a common feature of the ritual.

Approximately 25 percent of the lynchings studied by the NAACP in 1927 involved accusations of sexual harassment of white women as the justification for the lynching—the rest involved accusations of belligerence and property theft. When couples were lynched, the woman might be clubbed, hair cut and thrown to the crowd, fingers thrown to the crowd, corkscrewed through the breast and her flesh thrown to the crowd while the man was forced to watch what awaited him immediately upon completion of her torture. His genitals might be removed during his torturing and his "balls" later pickled as souvenirs.

Lynching bespeaks the importance of the body as an object for degradation to substantiate the submission of persons excluded from a moral community. Experiments on Black men are another example of the Black male body as a site for degradation.[12] In an excellent book, *Bad Blood: The Tuskegee Syphilis Experiment,* James Jones describes the "moral astigmatism" that allowed white government administrators, nurses, military personnel, entrepreneurs, doctors, news reporters and poor Black and white workers to participate in a study for over forty years on the "effects of untreated syphilis on [399] Black men in Macon County, Alabama."[13] An experiment without procedures, an experiment predicated on the intentional withholding of known effective treatments, an experiment about which generation after generation of well intentioned but astigmatic white physicians presented papers on at professional conferences, is an experiment that suggests why there should be a basic distrust of professionals and unreflective workers. Both may be ready practitioners of moral astigmatism if for no other reason than that they performed their duties, following precedents, or pursued professional self-promotion in approved utilitarian fashions. An unvirtuous character, authoritarian personality, nor evil intentions are necessary facets of persons deeply involved in perpetuating treatable pain and preventable misery. This is so because moral astigmatism often pervades relationships with persons excluded from the moral community.

The above forms of terror most often confronted by African American males are not intended to suggest a well designed conspiracy. They do suggest, however, a persistent pattern of immiseration and exclusion from the moral community. Honor is thereby an elusive good for African American males in a world dominated by male codes of honor.

Honor and Masculinity

Honor has been most often a masculine good in the sense that the ability to kill, destroy, compel others to subordinate themselves has been most often a power held by men. Men, for example, are most often the symbols of a nation's warriors, regardless of the roles played by women. Neither the women warriors of North Vietnam nor the women guerrillas of Algeria and Zimbabwe are memorialized in nearly as vast an array of statues, street names, or government sponsored ceremonies as are the men. Men have most often accorded the rewards and rituals of honor to other men within their communities.

Honor is not a masculine good when women accord women exalted regard independent of men or when the accord of exalted regard is not gender specific. Queens, women warriors, free women in slave holding societies and women of upper classes and statuses, for example, may be honored for similar reasons as men—they are empowered in ways in which persons lower on the scale of membership in the moral community, or persons exiled from that community, are excluded. Even if exalted regard is itself considered a masculine trait, it is nonetheless a trait that has been held by women as women, e.g., as goddesses and czarinas. The wife of any citizen of Athens held power over Aristotle because Aristotle, an outsider, a mete, could have become a slave but he could almost certainly never have ascended to citizen. Any Athenian that might have married Aristotle, regardless of how rich or wise he might have become, would have lowered her status. Citizenship, as a family-based good, excludes persons outside of its network. Whether considered immoral, demented, irredeemable inferior, a witch, or a tramp, every white woman held power over every Black, whether the Black was a model mother, husband, father, mistress, Christian, servant, or entrepreneur. Race, class, status, gender and citizenship can bifurcate who, and in what form, honor is accorded. Marriage, is an example of a social institution that bifurcates honor.

Marriage has historically provided men authority and status over women in almost every society, making patriarchy an oppressive norm. The status men gain by virtue of marriage, however, does not mean that all married men are held above all women: Married men of Turkish heritage are not held above German women in Germany, married or single; married French Muslim men of Arabic heritage face prejudice in France although under less suspicion than single Muslim men of Arabic heritage; white American married men are not held in greater regard than Japanese women in Japan; married Muslim Palestinian men are not held above Jewish women in Israel. The increase of honor in marriage for men is tied to their community. There may be a greater respect for married men over single men within as well as outside of their communities. However, neither marital status nor gender defeats status designation by nationality, ethnicity, or race. Community membership and relationships between communities, I believe, are extremely important in situating the type of regard available to a person.

It would seem to follow that an individual from a generally subjugated community could not be honored because, as I have argued, honor is a good tied to perceptions of who counts as a member of the moral community. Dr. Martin L. King, Jr. is honored, however, although the African American community has not ascended to exalted regard. The honor accorded Dr. King, I suggest in the following, does not defeat the idea that honor is a social good tied to moral communities.

Honor and Dr. King

Dr. King followed a principle of communal love; that principle was central to a protest movement that permanently transformed the world.[14] He imposed his will, a will that was simultaneously associated with the will of a large community of immiserated persons. The Aristotelian concept of honor requires that an individual embody virtues. This embodiment affords them the right to demand deference from others. The Aquinian concept of honor requires that an agent temper claims to deference with the recognition that ultimately good virtues and good acts are made possible by God. Both concepts required that an agent impose, or be capable of imposing, their will and both require that an agent to some degree embody virtues.[15] I suggest that a defensible depiction of the honor accorded Dr. King rests on an Aquinian conception of honor and an idea that was inconceivable in the middle ages: the idea that persons are nodally equal across lines of religion, nation, race, gender and age.

Ironically, the honor accorded Dr. King is associated with his promotion of communal love, an ideal that is also associated with femininity, passivity, and emotional abandon. It is certainly arguable that Dr. King's life contributed to a redefinition of masculinity— commitment to *agape,* strength through compassion, caring even at the expense of self-harm. Dr. King is not required to have lived some mystically perfect moral or normatively sanguine life—only that the life he did live was extraordinarily magnanimous. Dr. King is perceived as embodying virtues such as courage and tenacity, but these are subordinate to his image as a champion of non-violence and collective love. Arguments for a King memorial holiday, for example, do not rest on the family life of Dr. King as a model father or husband, a model minister, divinely annotated prophet, courageous savior of the polity or fearless defender of the nation.

Even if after a thorough research of white attitudes it's found that whites accord Dr. King honor because they perceive his will as one totally subservient and non-threatening to their will, it's still the case that the courage and magnanimous character required to love, care, be compassionate and sacrifice should have an important place in the social fabric of Americans. Regardless of this prescriptive claim about traits that should have a place in America's social fabric, is Dr. King a counter-example to my normative claim that honor is a social good?

Dr. King as Counter-example

If honor is a social good accorded to members of a moral community, and the African American community is often excluded from membership, it would seem to follow that Dr. King could not be generally honored. Dr. King therefore seems like a counter-example: If he is generally honored, then it is false that honor is a good accorded to members of a moral community when African Americans are understood as excluded by virtue of racism. If his ideas and methods are also perceived as "feminine" in the sense in which that which is feminine is considered somehow inferior, weak and submissive to that which is masculine, then the view of Dr. King's pacifism as consonant with the will of the dominant community gains warrant. Dr. King could thus be highly regarded (but not honored), like a good eunuch, because he was submissive to the will of the dominant community. If, however, Dr. King is highly regarded but not honored then we at least have an enigma: His non-violent direct action method and its results were the successful imposition of his will, yet, such impositions are normally reserved for members of the moral community.

A perception of Dr. King as submissive is, I believe, simply misguided. Dr. King prevailed, for example, despite attacks by the U.S. government's COINTELPRO (Counter-Intelligence Program) under J. Edgar Hoover's FBI, orchestrated to blackmail Dr. King into committing suicide and despite the attacks on his life by segregationists. Even if his ideas and methods are, or functioned, in ways subservient to the will of the dominant community they were instrumental in bringing substantive change. The laws and institutional rules of segregation, as well as avowed prejudicial beliefs, have all declined in direct response to the civil rights movement of which Dr. King was a major actor.

A perception of Dr. King as feminine, when feminine is construed as compliant, weak, and submissive expurgates Dr. King from being perceived as Black (already stereotyped inferior by race). The character of racial and gendered forms of oppression are not identical.[16] African American males, for example, do not face date rape or spouse abuse in anywhere near the proportion of women, Black or white. They are more likely to be the perpetrators of date rape and spouse abuse. They face, more than Black or white women, the likelihood of being unemployed. The minuscule group of middle class Black males fairs better than Black females, far worse than white males, and is far smaller in relation to their numbers than white females. Black males face the greatest likelihood of incarceration, regardless of guilt. For such reasons it's not intrinsically confusing to write about African American women and men facing multiple jeopardy (race, sex, gender and class)—the character of the jeopardies are interlaced yet distinct.

In another sense Dr. King is not a counter-example to the generality that honor is a social good accorded to members of a moral community: Non-violent direct action is not completely in the service and interest of the dominant community. The federal government and most states have instituted a Martin L. King, Jr. national holiday, for example, but they are under no pressure to disband their armies or militia thereby. The non-violent message of Dr. King's pacifism is selectively applied according to the will of the agents intoning his message. However, his pro-active method for imposing his will and his inclusion of African people as full members of the moral community are sources of ambivalence for the larger community. One feature of the ambivalence involves honoring Dr. King as an agent that promoted love *and* change, when change is often accompanied by unkindly threats, pressure and aggression.

Honor and Empowerment

The possibility of honor for individuals is integrally tied to the possibility of their community having, or potentially having, honorable status. Power, as Jennifer L. Hochschild uses it to depict a variety of goods (economic, political, internal motivation) imposing means and prospects regarding equal opportunity—is a function of community.[17] The moral community of America is most often conceived in ways that exclude the African American community. A perception of the African American community as capable of imposing its will, ranking above others, commanding deference—crucial features of normality—is contrary to America's perception of one of its least favored groups. Dr. King certainly imposed his will through tremendous labor, sacrificial love and non-violent resistance. However, the imposition of wills through threats, demands, pressure and aggressiveness are also features of normality.

One reason parents, soldiers, entrepreneurs, the poor, teachers and the elderly can be held in high regard is because they are perceived as persons who successfully manage exigencies against pressures to fail—exigencies that include, but are not restricted to, performances that have little or nothing to do with affective goods such as love, caring, compassion, or sacrificing. Parents, for example, clean, cook, wash, pay bills and are often blamed for the atrocities that their children commit but are rarely applauded if their children perform laudable acts. There are no national holidays, however, dedicated to good parenting. Even if parenting in the modern world can be said to be in some sense 'caused' by love, as distinct from the medieval view of parenting as a duty, the performances of generating income, paying bills, cleaning up after, and spending time that directly takes away from other enriching adult activities require tenacity, diligence, thrift, aggressiveness and discipline. There are, for example, more African American male single parents than white American male single parents in proportion to their numbers in society—but single fathering is hardly an image located in any social group's perception of African American males. Single parenting, for African American males, requires a willingness to do so despite the certainty that popular social media such as television, newspapers, novels, or church services will not offer much encouragement or recognition.

Parenting also requires tremendous aggressiveness and self-assurance for African Americans in general, and African American males in particular, to protect their children. Many grade school administrators, primarily male and white, and grade school teachers, primarily female and white, harbor and impose a daunting array of demeaning and destructive prejudices toward African Americans in general, and especially African American males. The history of research on administrator and teacher attitudes, detailing their prejudicial practices toward African American males is simply overwhelming: researchers may disagree on which array of prejudices and precisely how daunting, but they almost invariably portray a dismal picture of African American males receiving less attention, lower grades, harsher punishment and fewer awards than white children with identical or similar performance.[18] Successful parenting requires diligence, persistently arguing, demanding accountability and defending one's child against a barrage of prejudices against the very persons parents depend on for educating their children.

One of the most distressing features of aggressiveness and threatening behavior is that they are also implicated in the harms facing African American males. Black males receive harms in part because of the way they are socialized, not simply because of their sex.[19] Black on Black homicide, for example, is the cause of far more deaths than white on Black homicides. Black males physically inflict more harms on themselves than anyone else—it is impossible that this has nothing to do with their socialization and form of being nurtured. The imposition of wills through uncompromising or nearly uncompromising demands, mutually unpleasant encounters, aggressiveness, pressure and threats may function well or horribly. Honor is often accorded the powerful, for example, presidents, entrepreneurs, nobles and soldiers, through the conduits of their successful use of aggression and pressure for causes considered laudable. This, it seems to me, is true whether the honored are conceived as pure egalitarian pacifists ruled by affective emotions or absolute monarchical warlords ruled by meanness. Aggressiveness and threatening behaviors—traits that ruling groups tend to reserve as legitimate forms of behavior for themselves—may be tools that can help defend a person against an onslaught of social tyranny or help lift a person from the degradation of social death. Survival tools are invaluable in a chronically racist society that has obstacles from the improbability of prenatal care or fair treatment in grade school to the improbability of employment or income even nearly commensurate with others of similar endowment. Whether the traits of aggressiveness or threatening behavior are sources of harm or conduits for survival, they are features of social normality through which some forms of honor are obtained. Emasculation, however, is most assuredly not a basis for honor.

The attack on the African American male is arguably a sex-specific emasculating attack in the sense that African American men are the object, or at least African American men have received an undue array of harms, by virtue of their sexual socialization and race. It is a feminist issue in Ida B. Wells' sense—lynching for her was an issue for the nation and Africans as a people, yet it was particularly a feminist issue because Black men, sons and husbands, were its most frequent object. It is also fruitfully characterized as more than sex specific: it can be characterized as a part of an attack on the body of a people—a people long excluded from the moral community and continually under duress. This is so not because Black men are breadwinners (except for a small sector of middle-class Black men, Black men have less income than Black women), or because Black men are leaders (the percentage of Black elected officials has radically improved, but it hardly corresponds to the percentage of the Black U.S. population; civil rights leadership has been notoriously male dominated and almost completely chauvinist, there are no reasons why this should continue). It is an attack on the body of a people because in a certain sense "men" do not exist in social normality outside the context of associations, relations, networks, parents and ascending and descending generations of persons. Men do not exist in the sense of their sharing identical material assets, powers to command deference from persons outside their communities, or shape and execute life plans. Men of subjugated communities, for example, are characteristically emasculated. To be emasculated is to be disjoined from the possibility of empowerment across generations—a possibility that exists only in social connection.

The idea that in a certain way "men" do not exist as a social entity does not mean that "men" cannot be treated as an independent variable.[20] Without so doing it would be difficult to see chauvinist forms of gender oppression practiced by men across social entities of class, race, and ethnicity. It would also be difficult to see specifically gendered forms of male association. However, one of the limitations of treating "men" as an independent variable is the tremendous difference between what happens to men because of race, class, status and culture. Native American men, for example, are hardly in the same position as American men of any ethnicity or race—the former are not a part of the American nation nor do they have as a nation standing armies; it is not reasonable for Native American mothers and fathers to instill in their children an expectation of soldiering in an existing army as a possible future career. The disempowerment of African American men is, analogously, integrally tied to the status of the African American community.

The recognition accorded Dr. King bespeaks America's ambivalence about African American males as representative of envious traits and the African American community as members of America's moral community. It is certain that African American males are in multiple jeopardy—one of which is the elusive good of honor of the kind that we can easily identify with through normal social life—a social life the character of which is due substantive change.

Notes

1. J. K. Campbell, *Honour, Family and Patronage,* Oxford: Oxford University Press, 1964, p. 271. Also, according to Pitt-Rivers, "the claim to honor

depends always in the last resort, upon the ability of the claimant to impose himself. Might is the basis of right to precedence, which goes to the man who is bold enough to enforce his claim, regardless of what may be thought of his merits." Julian Pitt-Rivers "Honor" in *Encyclopedia of the Social Sciences,* 2d ed. New York: MacMillan Co., 1968, vol. 6, pp. 505.

2. The general idea that honor is a social good is not particularly unique, although the way I argue for this view and its application is hopefully of interest. Also see my "The Horror of Tradition or How to Burn Babylon and Build Benin While Reading *A Preface to a Twenty Volume Suicide Note,*" *Philosphical Forum,* XXIV: 1-3 (Fall-Spring 1992-93) 94–119.

An implication of my view of honor as a social good is that generally honoring an individual woman for virtues and merits associated with women as such is a function of whether "women" as a social group have status in the moral community and the sort of status that they have as a group. The analog for this is an African American male (Dr. King) and the African American community, social status in the moral community is the crucial factor shaping the possibility of honor for an individual.

3. See for example Robert Cole, *Political Life of Children,* Boston: Atlantic Monthly Press, 1986; Janice E. Hale-Benson, *Black Children,* Baltimore: The Johns Hopkins University Press, 1986.

4. See Bertram Wyatt-Brown, *Southern Honor: Ethics and Behavior in the Old South,* Oxford: London, 1982. Honor was an important variable shaping the cohesion of southerners; a cohesion sufficiently strong to compel tremendous sacrifice in defense of a segregated way of life. Also see Julian Pitt-Rivers, *Mediterranean Countrymen,* p. 80. Also see J. Pitt-Rivers, J. G. Peristiany, *Honor and Grace in Anthropology,* Cambridge: Cambridge University Press, 1992.

5. Peter Berger, "Peter Berger: On the Obsolescence of the Concept of Honour," in Michael Sandel, ed., *Liberalism and its Critics,* New York: New York University Press, 1984, p. 158.

6. Orlando Patterson, *Slavery and Social Death* Cambridge: Harvard University Press, 1982, p. 78. I am indebted to Patterson's work for comparing honor and degradation.

7. Patterson, *Slavery and Social Death,* p. 315.

8. J. E. Casely Hayford, *Ethiopia Unbound* (1911); *Gold Coast Native Institutions* (1903).

9. This is the case even if the utopia consists solely of women, imposing their wills on one another or imposing their wills on men, e.g., C. Gilman's *Herland,* New York: Pantheon Books, 1978, or S. S. Teppers's *The Gate to Women's Country,* New York: Foundation Books, 1988.

10. Wyatt-Brown, *Southern Honor,* p. 5. Also see Donald Yacovone, "Abolitionists and the 'Language of Fraternal Love,' " Mark C. Carnes, Clyde Griffen, eds., *Meanings for Manhood,* Chicago: University of Chicago Press, 1990, p. 85–94; Ladislav Holy, *Kingship, Honour and Solidarity,* Manchester: Manchester University Press, 1989, p. 125.

11. Trudier Harris, *Exorcising Blackness,* Bloomington: Indiana University Press, 1984, p. 2. This quote has been used in the literature on lynching as a fairly standard exmaple of the elements involved in the ritual.

12. See for examples of honor accorded various body parts and expressions,

Michel Feher, ed., *Fragments for a History of the Human Body*, Part One, Part Two, Part Three, New York: Urzone, Inc., 1989. Also see Philomena Essed, *Everyday Racism*, California: Hunter House, 1990.

13. James Jones, *Bad Blood: The Tuskegee Syphilis Experiment*, New York: Free Press, 1981.

14. See John Ansbro, *Making of a Mind*, New York: Orbis Books, 1982; Carson Clayborne, ed., *Eyes on the Prize*, New York: Penguin Books, 1991; James M. Washington, ed., *A Testament of Hope: The Essential Writings of Martin L. King., Jr.*, San Francisco: Harper & Row, Pub., 1986.

15. For comparison and contrast of Aristotelian and Aquinian concepts of honor see Maurice B. McNamee, S. J., *Honor and the Epic Hero*, New York: Holt, Rinehart and Winston, Inc., 1960.

16. See for example Bill Lawson, Howard McGary Jr., eds., *The Underclass*, Philadelphia: Temple University Press, 1992; A. Zegeye, J. Maxted, L. Harris, eds., *Exploitation and Exclusion*, London: Hans Zell Pub., 1991; Elizabeth Fox-Genovese, *Within the Plantation Household*, Chapel Hill: University of North Carolina Press, 1988; Bell Hooks, *Yearning*, Boston: South End Press, 1990; David Goldberg, *Anatomy of Racism*, Minneapolis: University of Minnesota Press, 1990;

17. Jennifer L. Hochschild, "Race, Class, Power, and Equal Opportunity," *Equal Opportunity*, ed., Norman Bowie, Colorado: Westview Press, 1988.

18. See for example Jonathan Kozol, *Death at an Early Age*, Boston: Houghton Mifflin, 1967; *Savage Inequalities*, New York: Crown Pub., 1991.

19. I am indebted to Trudier Palmer, University of Pittsburgh, for the importance of noting the influence of socialization here.

20. For examples of the fruitfulness of so doing, despite problems of how much to weigh the variable as a cause, see M. C. Carnes, C. Griffen, eds., *Meanings for Manhood*. See for my ideas of community and agency, "Historical Subjects and Interests: Race, Class, and Conflict," Michael Sprinkler et. al., eds., *The Year Left*, New York: Verso, 1986, pp. 91–106; "Columbus and the Identity of the Americas," *Annals of Scholarship*, 8:2 (Spring 1991) 287–299.

16

Are Men Oppressed?

Kenneth Clatterbaugh

The Question

In the words of feminist theorist Marilyn Frye: "It is a fundamental claim of feminism that women are oppressed"[1] At the same time, Frye and other feminists argue that men are *not* oppressed. Certain male writers, especially but not exclusively, from a men's rights perspective disagree; they make the counterclaim that men, too, are oppressed.[2] Indeed, some even argue that men are more oppressed than women.[3] In this paper, I am interested in the specific counterclaim that men are oppressed. But before we can assess the truth of any claim to oppression, we must first assess what it means to say that some group is oppressed? Only when we know what "oppression" means can we assess whether or not it is true that men are oppressed.

The structure of this paper is as follows. First, I articulate some generally agreed elements of most theories of oppression. Second, I discard three theories of oppression for obvious inadequacies. Third, I defend a theory of oppression, which I call "the dehumanization theory of oppression." Fourth, and finally, I argue that the claim that men are oppressed is *not* defensible on the dehumanization theory. At no time in my argument do I assume that women are oppressed, although I believe such a claim can be defended. I do not assume that women are oppressed because I do not need to argue that women are oppressed in order to show that men are not.

Common Ground

While there are several theories of oppression, most writers on oppression agree on a number of points, for example, most agree that oppression is social, systematic, and aimed at identifiable groups.[4] It is not a personal issue whether one is oppressed, because oppression is not directed toward individuals specifically. Individuals may be persecuted, but oppression typically falls on individuals in virtue of their membership in a group.[5] In fact, one of the aspects of oppression that makes it morally abhorrent is that it affect individuals regardless of their character, merit, or moral standing. Oppression issues blanket judgments, often grounded in stereotypes, through which individuals are treated as a type rather than as an individual. It matters not whether membership in the oppressed group is chosen or a consequence of birth.

Oppression of a group is systematic; that is, it exists throughout a society, usually over a substantial period of time, and the institutions of society interlock and reinforce each other in ways that create and maintain the oppression.[6] For example, oppressed groups may be denied access to valuable resources of the society and in turn their lack of such resources may be used as evidence that they should continue to be denied access. Thus, the practice feeds the justification and the justification supports the practice.

Oppression is only possible if there is a way of identifying the group to be oppressed.[7] There must be some set of common characteristics that are easily recognized and that mark out those and (almost) only those who are members of the target population. Where identification is difficult or impossible either the oppressive institutions fail or steps must be taken to ensure easier identification; ghettoization, wearing identification badges, or carrying passes may be ways of enhancing identification. Where it is possible to hide, members of oppressed groups may go "underground" or "closet" themselves. Such practices, besides extracting a personal toll on the individuals, do not usually end oppression unless they result in the extinction of the oppressed group.

Because oppression is social and systematic, social philosophers often treat oppression as a more serious injustice than being discriminated against, treated unfairly, or unequally, although oppression may well include each of these.[8] The remedy for oppression is correspondingly more threatening to the status quo; the solution to oppression is often a revolution or some great social upheaval, while inequality and discrimination typically seem to require only reform. Thus, the language of oppression is better suited to the needs of radicals who would restructure society rather than reformers who would fine tune it.

Discarded Theories of Oppression

In this section I reject three prevalent theories of oppression, which I identify as follows:

A. Psychological Theories

Some philosophers have argued that oppression is (largely) an internal state—feelings or beliefs. Thus, Judith Tormey states:

> [In oppression] one must be made . . . to have beliefs about oneself including beliefs about the proper social position one is to occupy that result in patterns of behavior which conform to an inferior or subsidiary social role, beliefs, which, in effect keep one down.[9]

B. Inequality Theories

Perhaps the best statement of the inequality theory is found in *Oppression: A Socio-History of Black-White Relations in America.* Here the authors define 'oppression':

> Oppression can be defined as a situation in which one or more identifiable segments of the population in a social system systematically and successfully act over a prolonged period of time to prevent another identifiable segment or segments . . . from attaining access to the scarce and valued resources [wealth, power, prestige] of that system.[10]

C. Limitation Theories

Limitation theories take a number of different forms, but the basic idea is that when options are denied to individuals in virtue of membership in a group, that limitation constitutes oppression. bell hooks, Alison Jaggar, and Marilyn Frye all seem to defend such a limitation theory of oppression:

> Being oppressed means the absence of choices.[11]
> Oppression is the imposition of unjust constraints on the freedom of individuals or groups.[12]
> The experience of oppressed people is that the living of one's life is confined and shaped by forces and barriers which are not accidental or occasional and hence avoidable, but are systematically related to each other in such a way as to catch one between and among them and restrict or penalize motion in any direction. It is the experience of being caged in: all avenues, in every direction, are blocked or booby trapped.[13]

Having briefly identified the three theories of oppression that we shall discard, it is now time to look at our reasons for rejecting them.

Psychological theories of oppression typically do not offer a definition of oppression because they focus on an effect of oppression rather than the state of being oppressed. It would be an ultimate form of blaming the victim to hold that people are oppressed simply because they feel oppressed or believe certain things about their social standing. If oppression were only a state of mind, the proper remedy for oppression would be therapy, not revolution. However, to deny that social oppression is *defined* by psychological states is not to deny that the psychology of oppression is important. Some understanding of the effect of oppression on human psychology is vital for those who are oppressed as well as those who work with the oppressed. But, because psychological theories leave unanswered the nature of social oppression, I shall not consider such theories further in this paper.

There is a generalized argument that undermines most efforts to explicate the concept of oppression in terms of inequality or limitation. It begins by asking: Are there social conditions in which the proposed oppressive conditions—inequality or limitation—obtain, but which fail to be oppressive? If there are, then we are justified in distinguishing oppressive inequality from simple inequality and oppressive limitation from simple limitation. The distinction in each case forces us back again to the question: "What is oppression?" Or, more simply, what is that extra condition that makes only *some* inequalities oppressive or only *some* limitations oppressive.

Consider a hypothetical case of inequality. Suppose that within a society there are two groups of people who for religious reasons have a tradition of ethnic animosity. They each control a certain amount of wealth, political power, and prestige. But they systematically discriminate against each other so that each can successfully deny to the other group any share of its wealth, political power, and prestige. Neither group is oppressed by this systematic discrimination, although hostility between the two groups might be extreme. That neither group is oppressed is easy to see where both groups are relatively powerful and wealthy, but even if the distribution of resources is unequal the relationship need not be one of oppression where each is able to hold onto its own resources. (The Walloons and Flemish of Belgium might be an actual case in point.) The point is that neither inequality nor successful denial is a sufficient condition for oppression.

One might object, at this point, that in the above case the inequality is not absolute; even the less advantaged group still controls some resources and power. Maybe we should count inequality as oppressive only when there is *absolute* denial of wealth, power, and prestige to a target group. But surely, this amendment is too strong. Groups can be oppressed even when they are not absolutely denied power and wealth. To make absolute denial a condition might well result in there being no oppressed groups or far fewer than we normally recognize. For example, we might have to eliminate Jews in tsarist Russia, even though they are probably a paradigm example of an oppressed group.

Consider one more example that shows that successful, systematic denial of scarce and valued resources will not do as an account of oppression. Consider two identifiable groups in society. One lives at subsistence level, and the other below subsistence level. The first group can survive only by denying to the subsistence group the resources and social power that they control. Surely, one could not accuse the subsistence group of oppressing the less fortunate group or even of doing anything wrong, if they successfully protect what they have. Here, I am assuming that the subsistence-level group can genuinely continue to exist only by protecting what they have and that they do not take unnecessary measures to protect their resources.

Limitation theories encounter a similar set of objections. There are obvious cases of limitation that are not oppressive; many limitations occur simply through circumstances such as weather, bad luck, ignorance, or well-intentioned human mistakes.[14] Therefore, trying to identify those patterns of limitation that are oppressive from those that are not shows the need for further conditions than simple limitation, unless we want to hold that *everyone* is oppressed. And, any theory that leads to the conclusion that everyone is oppressed is obviously less useful in sorting out oppressed peoples from nonoppressed peoples than a theory that clearly identifies some groups as oppressed and other as not oppressed. Thus, Jaggar tries to modify her limitation theory and argue that only certain kinds of constraints constitute oppression, namely, *unjust* constraints.

But even unjust constraints hardly constitute oppressive limitations. Are well-known Hollywood personalities oppressed because they cannot travel freely in the city or eat at a favorite restaurant without a crush of admirers? Surely, such constraint is unjust in that personalities are denied freedom from interference that is generally available to others. The basic point is that privilege in a society, even the kind of privilege antithetical to oppression, is compatible with unjust constraints. The prince who would be king or the Nazi who would be ideologically pure are subject to extreme unjust constraints, which may even be enforced by violence. Still it would be an unfortunate consequence of a theory of oppression that identifiable privileged groups that are systematically constrained are a paradigm of an oppressed group.

In part because she wants to rule out men as an oppressed group, Frye, too, struggles to discover further conditions on the limitations that make them oppressive. Thus, Frye argues for a benefit condition.

> The boundary that sets apart women's sphere is maintained and promoted by men generally for the benefit of men generally, and men do benefit from its existence, even the man who bumps into it and complains of the inconvenience. That barrier is protecting his classification and status as a male, as superior. . . .[15]

In the first place such a condition—women are oppressed by their limitations because men benefit from them—is unavailable to me since

I do not assume in this paper that women are oppressed. Second, Frye's condition does not seem to work. Although it is usually the case that oppressors benefit from oppression, it is not necessarily the case that the oppressors benefit. One need only consider an incompetent oppressor whose practices actually work to the short-term and/or long-term benefits of the oppressed. For example, imagine a people who due to natural catastrophe are dying and another group takes them in, saves their lives but enslaves them. In enslaving them, however, the second group out of laziness or lack of forethought turns over complete control of their technological society to the slaves, ultimately putting themselves completely at the mercy of the enslaved group. The enslaved group is oppressed, even if the short-term and long-term benefits accrue to them.

In view of this critique we are left with a need to discover more precisely what it is that makes a certain set of conditions oppressive. We, too readily, encounter inequalities and unjust constraints that are not oppressive. Our search for such a feature need not be an a priori project. We can discover such a feature when we examine the lives of those who are members of groups that serve as paradigms of oppressed populations. We can discover such a feature by comparing the lives of those groups to the lives of others who may also suffer from social harms such as discrimination, limitation, inequality, and exploitation, but who are not oppressed.

The Dehumanization Theory of Oppression

Rosa Parks once observed that she refused to give up her seat on the bus because she just wanted to be treated like a human being. Academic philosophers from Kant to Rawls have argued that everyone is entitled to equal respect as human beings. Similar themes have appealed to those who write about oppression. In *Pedagogy of the Oppressed,* Paulo Friere notes that "while both humanization and dehumanization are real alternatives, only the first is man's vocation. This vocation is constantly negated by . . . injustice, exploitation, oppression, and the violence of the oppressors."[16] Daniel McGuire in setting out the criteria for those who are entitled to preferential treatment notes that one criterion is that prejudice against those who are so entitled has reached the level of depersonalization.[17] Frye claims that women are not heard because they are excluded from the class of persons.[18] Finally, Sandra Lee Bartky notes that "psychological oppression is . . . separating of a person from some of the essential attributes of personhood."[19]

The common thread in each of these authors is the concept of *dehumanization* or *depersonalization.* The dehumanization theory that

I develop in this section holds that *oppression* is *the systematic dehumanization of an identifiable target human group*. To dehumanize a group is to deny that the members of that group possess the complete range of human abilities, needs, and wants that are valued at that time as important to being a human being. It also counts as dehumanizing to treat, overtly or covertly, a human group as if its members lack the abilities, needs, or wants of a more complete human being. It is not important whether the members of a group are conceived as *non*human or *defectively* human. Of course groups that are oppressed under one standard need not be oppressed under another. For example, if intelligence and moral sensitivity are two human making traits and one group of humans is denied intelligence (but not moral sensitivity) and another denied moral sensitivity (but not intelligence), then both may be oppressed. Similarly, a group may be oppressed at one time in history, but not at another because of changing standards.[20]

Of course what constitutes a complete human being is a social construct, which is historically and culturally relative. It may not even be an accurate and complete account of what humans really are at that point in history.[21] I am not claiming that a group is oppressed just because the historical concept of a complete human being leaves out some abilities, needs, or wants that humans in fact have. It is not a question of how well a group's perceived characteristics match their actual ones, but how well their perceived abilities, needs, and wants match what the broader society *values* as human-making.

Furthermore, a group is not oppressed if there are qualities included in being a human being that are denied them and that they in fact lack. Thus, it is not oppressive to treat people who cannot walk as if they cannot walk, although it would be oppressive to deny that they have other human needs, for example, needs for privacy and dignity. Again, a group is not oppressed if there are qualities included in being a human that are denied them and that society does not value as important to being human; most standards of beauty are such qualities. People need not conform to any particular standard of beauty to be fully human, although there are clearly privileges that are granted to those judged to be beautiful. Indeed, most of our abilities, needs, or wants are not deemed central enough to be human-making.

A social structure becomes oppressive under this definition, if it assumes, promotes, or treats the target population as if it were defective in any of the defining human abilities, needs, or wants. I use "social structure" in a very broad sense to include such items as social institutions, practices, policies, laws, humor, ideology, and work relations. Usually, when a group is oppressed in a society these social structures interlock and support each other. Thus, to take an example, if African-American children are denied access to education and therefore do not achieve in academic pursuits, the systems interlock when lack of achievement justifies continued denial of opportunity.

Let us illustrate the above rather abstract discussion of oppression with a concrete example drawn from a paradigm oppressed group, namely, slaves in the American colonies. Africans who found themselves enslaved were stripped of their nationality, their locality of origin, their name, religion, familial connections, and most human rights.[22] Myths were created concerning their inability to feel pain, cold, heat, and most especially their sexuality and lack of intelligence.[23] Laws forbade them to run away, to fight back, to defy in gesture or word the orders of a white person. "By the early 1700s, they were no longer defined as legal persons but as chattel property—little more than 'beasts of burden.' "[24]

The dehumanization, which began in slavery, continues well into the twentieth century. As late as 1933 there was a zero percent overlap between white and black traits as determined by whites, and there was no question as to which set of traits were valued as most truly human; by 1982 that overlap had increased to only 22 percent.[25]

Usually the valued trait that is denied an oppressed group will be a trait such as intelligence that is seen as underlying other traits such as the ability to behave morally or to have aesthetic appreciation.[26] Thus, it is sometimes argued that African-Americans, among others, lack intelligence and cannot benefit from having the rights of citizens or the responsibility of commerce.

> Moral judgement, like business judgement, social judgement, or any other kind of higher thought process, is a function of intelligence. Morality cannot flower and fruit if intelligence remains infantile.[27]

Coupled with the idea that intelligence of whole groups of individuals is impaired, this linking of traits can only lead to one conclusion, namely, that the social roles of individuals within these groups should be severely limited. Oppression always produces limitation.

> Among laboring men and servant girls there are thousands like them. . . . The tests have told truth. These boys are ineducable beyond the merest rudiments of training. No amount of school instruction will ever make them intelligent voters or capable citizens. . . . They represent the level of intelligence which is very, very common among . . . negroes.[28]

It is impossible to recapture the entire history of dehumanization of Africans who came in slavery and continued to live as American citizens. But this concrete example reveals the kind of evidence that one would pursue in order to determine if an identifiable group were being oppressed.

Furthermore, the dehumanization theory seems to fit well with the kind of preanalytic descriptions of oppression that are found among members of paradigm oppressed groups. Thus, Frederick Douglass, born a slave, recounts the appraisal of an estate on the death of a master:

> There was the intensified degredation of the spectacle. What an assemblage! Men and women, young and old, married and single; moral human beings, in open contempt of their humanity, leveled at a blow with horses, sheep, horned cattle, and swine . . . all holding the same rank in the scale of social existence. . . .[29]

Douglass' description contains the essentials of the dehumanization theory—human beings who can think and act morally are caught up in a society that systematically treats them as less than human, that is, lacking thought and moral capacity.

The dehumanization theory also makes it clear why some writers have confused limitation or inequality with oppression. If the oppressed are perceived as lacking some important human-making traits, then there will be justifications for denying those groups equal access to resources and restricting their choices. Thus, Andrew Carnegie argues in *Triumphant Democracy* that "the defective classes" cannot be expected to overcome "their inherent lack of abilities."[30] Limitation and inequality are the inevitable consequence of oppression, although, as our earlier discussion illustrates, limitation and inequality can have other causes as well.

Are Men Oppressed?

Now that we have a theory of oppression, let us turn to the issue of whether men can claim oppression. But, let us make it clear what we are asking. We are not concerned with the question of whether or not men fall into targeted (oppressed) groups. Men clearly have been and are oppressed as African-American, as Jews, as colonials. The question here is whether men, *as men,* have a claim to be oppressed in twentieth-century America? It is the arguments toward this conclusion that I shall now address.

There are three primary arguments to the conclusion the men are oppressed as men. The first is what I call the "socialization argument." According to this argument if socialization into restricted gender roles is oppressive for women, it is also oppressive for men. This argument depends upon the additional premise that socialization into gender roles is oppressive to women. The second argument, which I shall call the "cost argument," argues that the men are oppressed because there are great costs to being male, for example, men die younger than women and suffer more from stress-related diseases. Finally, there is the "expendability argument." Men's lives, it is argued, are seen as expendable and less valuable than women's lives. If men's lives are valued less, then men are oppressed, that is, seen as less than fully human.

A. The Socialization Argument

The first argument has its beginnings in the liberal profeminist men's movement.[31] According to liberal feminist analysis women are denied their full humanity by their restricted gender role.[32] Profeminist men argue, similarly, that men, too are subjected to restricted gender roles and are thereby denied their full humanity.[33] If such a restriction of gender roles is oppressive to women—and profeminist men assume that it is—then comparable restrictions for men are also oppressive. Women, for example, are discouraged or prevented from being assertive or independent, and women are also discouraged or prevented from becoming combat infantry or even parents who work outside the home. Men are discouraged or prevented from being emotionally expressive or noncompetitive, and men are also discouraged from becoming day-care workers or parents who do not work outside the home. Those who defend this argument speak of "oppressive, dehumanizing sex roles" or "the oppression we feel by being forced to conform to the narrow and lonely roles of men in this society."[34] The Berkeley Men's Center Manifesto declares that "we are oppressed by conditioning."[35] In short, men are socialized into a restricted set of roles and punished if they depart from these roles; women too are socialized into restricted gender roles and punished if they depart from these roles. If we assume women are oppressed by their restrictions then men, too, are oppressed by their restrictions.

There are many grounds on which this argument may be criticized. One might argue that the restrictions on women are not oppressive, so neither are the restrictions on men. However, such a line of argument is usually not available to profeminist men who are inclined to agree that the gender role restrictions on women are oppressive. A second line of criticism is to ask if there are not sufficient differences between the restrictions on women and the restrictions on men such that even if women are oppressed by restricted gender roles, men are not. This is the line of argument I wish to pursue in light of our discussion of oppression.

We have already noted that it does not seem to be plausible to view limitations or restrictions in themselves as oppressive. The reason is that members of privileged and dominant groups within society may be severely constrained in the social roles that they are allowed to play. Thus, if men are a privileged group within society and women are second-class citizens, they both may confront limitations or restrictions, but for quite different reasons. Let me illustrate. Imagine a young man who announces that he wants to be a nurse. While that occupation is less off-limits today than it was a decade ago, it is easy to imagine that he will be told that nursing is unworthy of him. Of course, he *could* be a nurse, if he tried, but doctors are more prestigious, better paid, and becoming a doctor is a more worthy challenge for the young man. A young woman who announces her intention to be a doctor may face a different set of objections. She is told that she *cannot* be a doctor; it requires abilities that she lacks, for example, a talent for science and mathematics, physical strength, or emotional toughness. In fact, as Mary Roth Walsh describes in her book *"Doctors Wanted: No Women Need Apply": Sexual Barriers in the Medical Profession, 1835–1975,* these are precisely the kinds of arguments that were used to restrict men and women to being doctors or nurses.

The point is simple, if there is a relevant parallel between men and women in their restricted gender roles, then both must be restricted for the same kinds of reasons. If men are restricted because they are being groomed for dominance and privilege and women are restricted because of perceived lack of abilities, then the latter but not the former restrictions are oppressive. And, since there is a strong *prima facie* case that men are perceived as reservoirs of valued human traits, especially relative to women, then it becomes incumbent on anyone using this argument to show that the reason for constraint is the same in each case, something that is very difficult to do and almost never attempted by those who favor this argument. We might speculate that the reason this argument has survived for the past twenty years is that those who offer it are satisfied to think of oppression only in terms of restrictions, rather than whether those restrictions arise from privilege or from dehumanization.

B. The Cost Argument

A second argument that presumably leads to the conclusion that men are oppressed is an argument that begins by pointing out that there are many harms that fall primarily on men. This argument, unlike the socialization argument, does not depend upon a parallel with the situation of women. Herb Goldberg, a psychologist who works with men, was one of the first to articulate this argument.

By what perverse logic can the male continue to imagine himself "top dog"? Emotionally repressed, out of touch with his body, alienated and isolated from other men, terrorized by the fear of failure, afraid to ask for help, thrown out at moments notice . . . when all he knows was how to work. . . . The male has become an artist in the creation of many hidden ways of killing himself.[36]

Since Goldberg's early writings, there have been several books and essays that take up the theme of costs or harms that fall disproportionally on men. Most recently Andrew Kimbrell echoes Goldberg's argument in *The Masculine Mystique*.[37] Both books argue that men are more likely to commit suicide, die younger, be homeless, die in battle, be alcoholic, go undiagnosed for certain mental diseases, take steroids, and suffer other harms that fall primarily on men. Kimbrell concludes that men are indeed oppressed because of these harms.[38]

For all the efforts to illustrate the costs of being a man, Goldberg and others make no effort to show that these costs are not the effects of privilege and dominance. It is not enough to say rhetorically: "how can the male continue to imagine himself 'top dog' " when he is subjected to a sufficiently long list of disorders. Profeminist male writers, whom Goldberg and others do not acknowledge, noted in the 1970s these same costs and attributed them to the dominant, competitive roles that men play.[39] It is a twist of logic to try to argue, as these authors do, that because there are costs in having power, one does not have power. The silliness of this position comes out in the following instantiation of the general argument, namely, that men are oppressed because only men are victims of political assassination.[40] What is left out is the fact that only men are deemed worthy of holding political office, so of course, only men are victims of political assassination. But this harm grows out of male privilege, the right to hold office, not men's oppression. Shorter life expectancy, access to drugs, fear of failure, and disorders due to competitive activities may well be the costs for men in a society that privileges them. By themselves these harms neither show nor fail to show oppression. Until a sustained argument is made that shows that the afflictions of masculinity are not the result of trying to maintain power and advantage, there is no reason to allow the cost argument to proceed. In its first premise this argument essentially begs the question; it assumes that the costs of masculinity constitute oppression. And, what may well drive this assumption is that costs or harms impose limits on men in what they do and such limitation is oppressive.[41]

C. The Expendability Argument

The first two arguments really get to the conclusion that men are oppressed by using a notion of oppression by which everyone is oppressed, namely, oppression as limitation. This third argument appears to be more compatible with the concept of oppression as dehumanization. The idea behind this argument is that violence against men is acceptable in a way that violence against women and children is not, and from this observation it is concluded that men's lives are valued less than other lives. Hence, men are dehumanized. Usually the claim that violence is more acceptable against men is supported by pointing out that only men are drafted, only men can serve in combat, men are "killed" more frequently on television, and domestic violence against men is not treated as a serious problem the way domestic violence against women is treated.

> Asked about women in combat at her confirmation hearings, then Supreme Court nominee Sandra Day O'Connor said she'd hate to see them come home in coffins. What are men, expendable in her eyes?[42]
>
> By *expecting* men to play life-threatening roles, we are less horrified when their lives are lost. By being less horrified, we can continue the assignment rather than look at our roles . . . *sponsoring* violence against men by turning to war films, murder mysteries, westerns, or TV movies in which men are killed routinely for our entertainment.[43]
>
> If . . . we turn to the only large nationally representative sample of spouse abuse . . . *we find that 12 percent of husbands are violent toward wives and 12 percent of wives were violent toward husbands.* A ratio of 1 to 1.[44]

Once again, however, there are a great many logical and factual questions that these arguments fail to address. The domestic violence studies that are used to support equal violence by each sex are purely behavioristic; that is, they study how many times a spouse slammed a door, threw an object, threatened with a knife, etc. There is no effort to study the context in which these behaviors occur.[45] When aggression is factored in, however, and defensive behavior excluded, men are overwhelmingly the violent aggressors.[46]

Those who offer the expendability argument never offer a criterion for determining when a social practice is acceptable. Sometimes they seem to slide from the fact that violence with men as victims is very widespread to the conclusion that it is acceptable or, what they take to be the same, men's lives are not valued.[47] Surely, some things that are widespread are acceptable, but not everything that is widespread is acceptable. And given the penalties for violent acts, social instructions against violent acts, and moral codes prohibiting violent acts prevalent in American society today, it is difficult to see how anyone could infer that violence against men is acceptable.

Finally, however, we again face the same serious oversight in this argument that occurs in the previous two arguments. Is the fact that only men are drafted and used in combat the result of valuing men's lives less or the result of a patriarchal society that through its institutions holds that only men are capable of being soldiers, that only men have the courage, strength, and military intelligence to defend their country. Women, on the other hand, are the property and spoils of war that victors take along with the roads, homes, farms, and factories of the vanquished.[48] Indeed, by the 1990s women and children have come to constitute 80 percent of the casualties of modern warfare.[49] The history of trying to bring women into the military suggests that it is not because men are valued less than women that only men are drafted, but that men are valued more. Add to this male privilege the fact that the military has provided a primary road of upward mobility for men through elaborate subsidizations in insurance, home loans, educational opportunities, preferential hiring, and tax benefits and the fact that very few men who serve see combat and that those who do are often poor or men of color and the military looks more like a structure for the advancement of male privilege than a source of male oppression.[50]

Conclusion

The arguments intended to show that men as men are oppressed fail. They either depend upon an inadequate notion of oppression as limitation or they simply beg the question by assuming that if only men are drafted, then men are valued less or by assuming that if there are harms that fall most heavily on men, then men are oppressed. But, assumptions, no matter how often repeated, do not merit belief until they are supported.

It is not hard to imagine a possible world in which men are systematically dehumanized—such a world would be very different from the actual world. Imagine that our world is suddenly controlled by humanoid aliens who establish a new hegemony over the traits that are valued as human-making. They reverse or revise the traits that have been held to belong specifically to males and for which males have been socialized. An elaborate science develops that teaches that men are overly controlled by their genitals and the emotion of anger; their so-called rational abilities are, in this new world, seen as rationalizations to support their biological and emotional demands. Male achievement in the arts, literature, philosophy, and sport are expunged from the pages of history and/or treated as trivial accomplishments. The new set of valued traits installed as human-making include many of the traits in which men have not traditionally excelled. A crisis ensues in which men lose confidence in themselves and strive to live up to the new concept, although hardly any are seen as doing so. In short, men do not fare as well as women in this new society; they are viewed as defective women and, therefore, by that norm as defective human beings. In such a world men would be oppressed.

The kind of case it would take to argue that women are oppressed has been made by feminist theorists on behalf of women. Women as an identifiable group have been treated as defective males whose talents and achievements constitute a norm. Women who do achieve have to be marginalized or eliminated from history. In Western science there is a long-standing debate as to whether women have the requisite abilities, needs, and wants, be it in medicine, sports, artistic expression, religion, or science itself, to live up to the male norm.[51] And many scientists concluded that women were wanting in genius, creativity, spirituality, and political ability. On the positive side, women have made crucial gains against their exclusion by simply demonstrating that they do have the requisite abilities and talents to do the very things from which they have been excluded. However, many feminists are not satisfied with proving that women are as good as men; they demand a new set of valued traits for all persons that are a fairer set for men and women, a conception that does not readily lend itself to the dehumanization of any group.

We have examined four theories of oppression and defended the dehumanization theory as the most viable. But when this theory is applied to the arguments that purport to show that men *as men* are oppressed, that conclusion is found wanting. At best such arguments rest on one of the inadequate theories of oppression; at worst they are disingenuous.

Notes

1. Marilyn Frye, *The Politics of Reality: Essays in Feminist Theory* (Trumansburg, NY: The Crossing Press, 1983), p. 1.

2. Herb Goldberg, *The Hazards of Being Male: Surviving the Myth of Masculine Privilege* (New York: Signet, 1976) or Andrew Kimbrell, *The Masculine Mystique, The Politics of Masculinity* (New York: Ballantine Books, 1995).

3. Roy Schenk, *The Other Side of the Coin: Causes and Consequences of Men's Oppression* (Madison, WI: Bioenergetics Press, 1982).

4. Frye, op. cit., p. 33. Jonathan H. Turner, Royce Singleton, Jr., and David Musick, *Oppression: A Socio-History of Black-White Relations in America* (Chicago: Nelson-Hall, 1984), p. 1. Iris M. Young, "Five Faces of Oppression," *The Philosophical Forum* 19:4 (Summer 1988), p. 275.

5. Frye, op. cit., p. 8.

6. Ibid, op. cit., p. 4; Turner, Singleton, and Musick, op. cit., p. 1; Young, op. cit., p. 275.

7. Frye, op. cit., p. 33; Turner, Singleton, and Musick, op. cit., p. 1; Young, op. cit., p. 275.

8. Young, op. cit., 271.

9. Judith Tormey, "Exploitation, Oppression, and Self-Sacrifice," *Women and Philosophy: Toward a Theory of Liberation,* eds. Carol C. Gould and Marx W. Wartofsky (New York: G. P. Putnam's Sons, 1980), pp. 206–21.

10. Turner, Singleton, and Musick, op. cit., pp. 1–2.

11. bell hooks, *Feminist Theory from Margin to Center* (Boston: South End Press, 1984), p. 5.

12. Alison M. Jaggar, *Feminist Politics and Human Nature* (Totowa, NJ: Rowman & Allanheld, 1983), p. 6

13. Frye. op. cit., p. 4.

14. Ibid., p. 10.

15. Ibid., p. 13.

16. Paulo Friere, *Pedagogy of the Oppressed* (New York: The Continuum Publishing Corporation, 1970), p. 28.

17. Daniel C. Maguire, *A New American Justice: Ending White Male Monopolies* (Garden City, NY: Doubleday, 1980), pp. 129–30.

18. Frye, op. cit., p. 50.

19. Sandra Lee Bartky, "On Psychological Oppression," *Philosophy for a New Generation,* eds. A. K. Bierman and James A. Gould (New York: Macmillan, 1981), pp. 418–29.

20. John Boswell, *Christianity, Social Tolerance, and Homosexuality: Gay People in Western Europe from the Beginning of the Christian Era to the Fourteenth Century* (Chicago: University of Chicago Press, 1980).

21. I am not claiming that there is a historical human essence. I am claiming that there is a difference between what humans are at one point in history and how humans are perceived at that point in history.

22. Cedric J. Robinson, *Black Marxism* (London: Zed Books, 1983), p. 105.

23. Stephen Jay Gould, *The Mismeasure of Man* (New York: W. W. Norton, 1981).

24. Turner, Singleton, and Musick, op. cit., pp. 15–17.

25. John F. Dovida and Samuel L. Gaetner, eds., *Prejudice, Discrimination, and Racism* (Orlando, FL: Academic Press, 1986), p. 6.

26. Gould, op. cit., pp. 158–74; Compare: Richard J. Herrnstein and Charles Murray, *The Bell Curve: Intelligence and Class Structure in American Life* (New York: Free Press, 1994).

27. L. M. Terman, *The Measure of Intelligence* (Boston: Houghton Mifflin, 1916), pp. 91–92.

28. Ibid.

29. Frederick Douglass, *Life and Time of Frederick Douglass* (New York: Macmillan, 1962), p. 96.

30. Andrew Carnegie, *Triumphant Democracy* (New York: Scribner's 1893), p. 176.

31. Kenneth Clatterbaugh, *Contemporary Perspectives on Masculinity: Men, Women, and Politics in Modern Society* (Boulder, CO: Westview, 1990), p. 52.

32. Betty Friedan, *The Feminine Mystique* (New York: Dell, 1963).

33. Jack Sawyer, "On Male Liberation," *Men and Masculinity,* eds. Joseph Pleck and Jack Sawyer (New York: Prentice-Hall, 1974), pp. 170–73.

34. Jeff Keith, "My Own Men's Liberation," *Men and Masculinity,* eds. Joseph H. Pleck and Jack Sawyer (New York: Prentice-Hall, 1974), pp. 81–88.

35. Berkeley Men's Center, "Berkeley Men's Center Manifesto," *Men and Masculinity,* eds. Joseph H. Pleck and Jack Sawyer (New York: Prentice-Hall, 1974), pp. 173–74.

36. Herb Goldberg, *The Hazards of Being Male: Surviving the Myth of Masculine Privilege* (New York: Signet, 1976), pp. 181–82.

37. Andrew Kimbrell, *The Masculine Mystique,* The Politics of Masculinity, New York: Ballantine Books, 1995). Compare: Warren Farrell, *The Myth of Male Power, Why Men are the Disposable Sex* (New York: Simon & Schuster, 1993), p. 1.

38. Kimbrell, op. cit., p. 3. Although Farrell draws up similar list, it should be noted that Farrell does not like the term 'oppression'; he prefers to speak of men as powerless, although the kind of powerlessness he describes is what most would call oppression—a kind of slavery to others. Farrell, op. cit., p. 40.

39. Marc Feigan Fasteau, *The Male Machine* (New York: McGraw-Hill, 1974), Jon Snodgrass, ed., *A Book of Readings for Men Against Sexism* (Albion, CA: Times Change Press, 1977), Deborah S. David and Robert Brannon, eds. *The Forty-nine Percent Majority* (New York: Random House, 1976).

40. Compare: Jack Kammer, " 'Male' is not a Four-Letter Word," *Wingspan, Inside the Men's Movement* (New York: St. Martin's Press, 1992), p. 63–71.

41. Kimbrell actually uses the metaphor of enclosure to describe the oppression of men, Kimbrell, op. cit., pp. 28–42. Compare: Farrell, op. cit., p. 38.

42. Dan Logan, "Woman in Combat," in *Men Freeing Men: Exploding the Myth of the Traditional Male* ed. Francis Baumli (Jersey City, NJ: New Atlantis, 1985), p. 239.

43. Warren Farrell, *Why Men Are the Way They Are* (New York: McGraw-Hill, 1986), p. 229.

44. Ibid., p. 228.

45. R. L. McNeely and Gloria Robinson-Simpson, "The Truth about Domestic Violence: A Falsely Framed Issue," *Social Work* (November-December 1987), pp. 485–90.

46. Lucy Berliner, "Domestic Violence: A Humanist or Feminist Issue," *Journal of Interpersonal Violence,* 5:1 (March, 1990), pp 128–29; and Michele Bograd, "Why We Need Gender to Understand Human Violence," *Journal of Interpersonal Violence,* 5:1 (March, 1990), pp. 132–35.

47. Fredric Hayward, "We Who are About to Die," in *Men Freeing Men: Exploding the Myth of the Traditional Male* ed. Francis Baumli (Jersey City, NJ: New Atlantis, 1985), p. 238–39.

48. Amnesty International, *Human Rights are Women's Right* (New York: Amnesty International Publications, 1995), pp. 17–56.

49. Ibid., p. 29.

50. *New York Times* byline, "Troop Cuts Make Army a Harder Place to Start," in *Seattle Post-Intelligencer* (May 7, 1990).

51. Carol Tavris, *The Mismeasure of Woman* (New York: Simon & Schuster, 1992).

Selected Recent Bibliography

Abbott, Franklin, editor. *New Men, New Minds: Breaking Male Tradition.* Freedom, CA: The Crossing Press, 1987.

Altman, Dennis. *AIDS in the Mind of America: The Social, Political and Psychological Impact of a New Epidemic.* New York: Anchor Press, 1986.

August, Eugene R. *Men's Studies: A Selected and Annotated Interdisciplinary Bibliography.* Littleton, CO: Libraries Unlimited, 1985.

Badinter, Elisabeth. *XY: On Masculine Identity.* New York: Columbia University Press, 1995.

Barrett, Robert L. *Gay Fathers.* Lexington, MA: Lexington Books, 1990.

Baumli, Francis, editor. *Men Freeing Men: Exploding the Myth of the Traditional Male.* Jersey City, NJ: New Atlantis, 1985.

Beneke, Timothy, editor. *Men on Rape.* New York: St. Martin's, 1982.

Benjamin, Jessica. "The Bonds of Love: Rational Violence and Erotic Domination." *Feminist Studies,* vol. 6, 1980.

Berger, M., Wallis, B., and Watson, S. *Constructing Masculinity.* New York: Routledge, 1995.

Berliner, Lucy. "Domestic Violence: A Humanist or Feminist Issue." *Journal of Interpersonal Violence,* vol. 5, March 1990.

Bettelheim, Bruno. "Fathers Shouldn't Try to Be Mothers." *Feminist Frameworks,* edited by Allison Jaggar and Paula Rothenberg. New York: McGraw-Hill, 1984.

Blount, Marcellus and George Cunningham. *Representing Black Men.* New York: Routledge, 1994.

Blum, Lawrence A. *Friendship, Altruism and Morality.* London: Routledge & Kegan Paul, 1981.

Bly, Robert. *Iron John.* Reading, MA: Addison-Wesley, 1990.

Boose, Linda, and Betty Flowers, editors. *Daughters and Fathers.* Baltimore: Johns Hopkins University Press, 1989.

Bordo, Susan. "The Cartesian Masculinization of Thought." *Signs,* vol. 11, Spring 1986.

Boswell, John. *Christianity, Social Tolerance, and Homosexuality: Gay People in Western Europe from the Beginning of the Christian Era to the Fourteenth Century.* Chicago: University of Chicago Press, 1980.

Brittan, Arthur. *Masculinity and Power.* Oxford: Basil Blackwell, 1989.

Brod, Harry, editor. *The Making of Masculinities: The New Men's Studies.* Boston: Allen & Unwin, 1987.

——, editor. *A Mensch Among Men: Explorations in Jewish Masculinity.* Freedom, CA: The Crossing Press, 1988.

——. "The New Men's Studies: From Feminist Theory to Gender Scholarship." *Hypatia,* vol. 2, Winter 1987.

——. "Work Clothes and Leisure Suits: The Class Basis and Bias in the Men's Movement." *Men's Lives: Readings in the Sociology of Masculinity,* edited by Michael Kimmel and Michael Messner. New York: Macmillan, 1989.

Brod, Harry and Michael Kaufman, editors. *Theorizing Masculinities.* Newbury Park: Sage, 1994.

Brown, Wendy. " 'Suppose Truth Were a Woman . . .': Plato's Subversion of Masculine Discourse." *Political Theory,* vol. 16, November 1988.

Cancian, Francesco. *Love in America: Gender and Self Development.* Cambridge: Cambridge University Press, 1987.

Carmeli, Yoram S. and Daphna Birenbaum-Carmeli. "The Predicament of Masculinity: Towards Understanding the Male's Experience of Infertility Treatments." *Sex Roles,* vol. 30, 1994.

Carnes, Mark C., and Clyde Griffen, editors. *Meanings for Manhood.* Chicago: University of Chicago Press, 1990.

Casas, J. M., B. R. Wagenheim and R. Banchero. "Hispanic Masculinity: Myth or Psychological Schema Meriting Clinical Consideration." *Hispanic Journal of Behavioral Sciences,* vol. 16, August 1994.

Christian, Harry. *The Making of Anti-Sexist Men.* New York: Routledge, 1994.

Clatterbaugh, Kenneth C. *Contemporary Perspectives on Masculinity: Men, Women and Politics in Modern Society.* Boulder, CO: Westview Press, 1990.

Collier, Richard. *Masculinity, Law and the Family.* New York: Routledge, 1994.

Connell, R. W. *Gender and Power.* Stanford, CA: Stanford University Press, 1987.

Cornwall, Andrea and Nancy Lindisfarne. *Dislocating Masculinity: Comparative Ethnographies.* New York: Routledge, 1994.

Craib, Ian. "Masculinity and Male Dominance." *Sociological Review,* vol. 35, November 1987.

Dellamore, Richard. *Masculine Desire: The Sexual Politics of Victorian Aestheticism.* Chapel Hill: University of North Carolina Press, 1990.

Doyle, James. *The Male Experience.* 2nd ed. Dubuque, IA: William C. Brown, 1989.

Dyer, Kate, editor. *Gays in Uniform: The Pentagon's Secret Reports.* Boston: Alyson Publications, 1991.

Edwards, Tim. *Erotics and Politics: Gay Male Sexuality, Masculinity and Feminism.* New York: Routledge, 1995.

Ehrenreich, Barbara. *The Hearts of Men: American Dreams and the Flight from Commitment.* Garden City, NY: Anchor Press, 1983.

Ehrensaft, Diane. *Parenting Together: Men, Women, and Sharing the Care of Their Children.* New York: Free Press, 1987.

Ellison, Marvin M. "Holding Up Our Half of the Sky: Male Gender Privilege as Problem and Resource for Liberation Ethics." *Journal of Feminist Studies in Religion*, vol. 9, 1993.

Farrell, Warren. *Why Men are the Way they Are*. New York: McGraw-Hill, 1986.

Finn, Geraldine. "Nobodies Speaking: Subjectivity, Sex and the Pornography Effect." *Philosophy Today*, vol. 33, Summer 1989.

Foucault, Michel. *The History of Sexuality, Vol. I: An Introduction*. Translated by R. Hurley. New York: Vintage Books, 1978.

Franklin, Clyde W. *The Changing Definition of Masculinity*. New York: Plenum Press, 1984.

———. *Men and Society*. Chicago: Nelson-Hall, 1988.

Gerzon, Mark. *A Choice of Heroes: The Changing Faces of American Manhood*. Boston: Houghton Mifflin, 1982.

Gilmore, David D. *Manhood in the Making: Cultural Concepts of Masculinity*. New Haven, CT: Yale University Press, 1990.

Glass, Leonard. "Man's Man/Ladies' Man: Motifs of Hypermasculinity." *Psychiatry*, vol. 47, August 1984.

Goodwin, Joseph P. *More Man Than You'll Ever Be: Gay Folklore and Acculturation in Middle America*. Bloomington: Indiana University Press, 1989.

Hacker, Andrew. *Two Nations: Black and White, Separate, Hostile, Unequal*. New York: Charles Scribner's Sons, 1991.

Halperin, David M. *One Hundred Years of Homosexuality and Other Essays on Greek Love*. New York: Routledge, 1990.

Hamilton, Mykol C. "Masculine Generic Terms and Misperception of AIDS Risk." *Journal of Applied Social Psychology*, vol. 18, November 1988.

Harris, I., J. B. Torres and D. Allender. "The Responses of African-American Men to Dominant Norms of Masculinity Within the United States." *Sex Roles*, vol. 31, December 1994.

Harris, Trudier. *Exorcising Blackness*. Bloomington: Indiana University Press, 1984.

Hartmann, Heidi. "The Family as the Locus of Gender, Class, and Political Struggle." *Signs*, vol. 6, 1981.

Hartsock, Nancy. *Money, Sex and Power: Toward a Feminist Historical Materialism*. New York: Longman, 1983.

Haug, Wolfgang Fritz. *Critique of Commodity Aesthetics: Appearance, Sexuality and Advertising in Capitalist Society*. Translated by Robert Bock. Minneapolis: University of Minnesota Press, 1986.

Hearn, Jeff. *The Gender of Oppression: Men, Masculinity, and the Critique of Marxism*. New York: St. Martin's, 1987.

Hearn, Jeff, and David H. J. Morgan, editors. *Men, Masculinities, and Social Theory*. London: Unwin Hyman, 1990.

Held, Virginia. "The Equal Obligations of Mothers and Fathers." *Having Children*, edited by Onora O'Neill and William Ruddick. New York: Oxford University Press, 1979.

Herdt, Gilbert H. *Guardians of the Flutes: Idioms of Masculinity*. New York: McGraw-Hill, 1981.

Herek, Gregory. "On Heterosexual Masculinity: Some Psychical Consequences of the Social Construction of Gender and Sexuality." *American Behavioral Scientist*, vol. 29, May/June 1986.

Hirsch, Marianne, and Evelyn Fox Keller, editors. *Conflicts in Feminism*. London: Routledge, 1990.

Hoberman, John. *Sport and Political Ideology*. Austin: University of Texas Press, 1984.

Hoch, Paul. *White Hero, Black Beast: Racism, Sexism, and the Mask of Masculinity*. London: Pluto Press, 1979.

Holden, Jonathon. "American Male Honor." *TriQuarterly*, no. 73, Fall 1988.

Hunter, Andrea G. and James Earl Davis. "Hidden Voices of Black Men: The Meaning, Structure, and Complexity of Manhood." *Journal of Black Studies*, vol. 25, September 1994.

Hutchins, Lorraine, and Lani Kaahumanu, editors. *Bi any other Name: Bisexual People Speak Out*. Boston: Alyson Publications, 1991.

Ingoldsby, Bron B. "The Latin American Family: Familism vs. Macho." *Journal of Comparative Family Studies*, vol. 22, Spring 1991.

Jardine, Alice, and Paul Smith, editors. *Men and Feminism*. New York: Methuen, 1987.

Johnson, Robert A. *Transformation: Understanding the Three Levels of Masculine Consciousness*. San Francisco: Harper, 1991.

Jones, Gerald, and Carol Nagy Jacklin. "Changes in Sexist Attitudes Toward Women during Introductory Women's and Men's Studies Courses." *Sex Roles*, vol. 18, May 1988.

Kaufman, Michael, editor. *Beyond Patriarchy: Essays by Men on Pleasure, Power and Change*. Toronto: Oxford University Press, 1987.

Keen, Sam. *Fire in the Belly: On Being a Man*. New York: Bantam Books, 1991.

Kimmel, Michael S., editor. *Changing Men: New Directions in Research on Men and Masculinity*. Newbury Park, CA: Sage Publications, 1987.

Kimmel, Michael S. "Toward Men's Studies: Introduction." *American Behavioral Scientist*, vol. 29, May/June 1986.

LaFollette, Hugh, and George Graham, editors. *Person to Person*. Philadelphia: Temple University Press, 1989.

Laqueur, Thomas. "The Facts of Fatherhood." *Conflicts in Feminism*, edited by Marianne Hirsch and Evelyn Fox Keller. London: Routledge, 1990.

Lauritzen, Paul. "A Feminist Ethic and the New Romanticism—Mothering as a Model of Moral Relations." *Hypatia*, vol. 4, Summer 1989.

Lisak, David. "Sexual Aggression, Masculinity and Fathers." *Signs*, vol. 16, Winter 1991.

Little, Roger. "Friendships in the Military Community." *Research in the Interweave of Social Roles*, vol. 2, edited by Helena Znaniecka and David Maines. Greenwich, CT: JAI Press, 1981.

Lloyd, Genevieve. "Selfhood, War, and Masculinity." *Feminist Challenges*, edited by Carole Pateman and Elizabeth Gross. Boston: Northeastern University Press, 1986.

McCreary, Donald R. "The Male Role and Avoiding Femininity." *Sex Roles*, vol. 31, November 1994.

McGill, Michael E. *The McGill Report on Male Intimacy*. New York: Holt, Rinehart and Winston, 1985.

MacKinnon, Catherine. "Pornography, Civil Rights and Speech." *Harvard Civil Liberties–Civil Rights Law Review*, 1985.

May, Larry. *Sharing Responsibility*. Chicago: University of Chicago Press, 1992.

Messner, Michael. "Boyhood, Organized Sports, and the Construction of Masculinities." *Journal of Contemporary Ethnography*, vol. 18, January 1990.

———. *Power at Play: Sports and the Problem of Masculinity*. Boston: Beacon Press, 1992.

Messner, Michael, and Donald Sabo, editors. *Sport, Men and the Gender Order*. Champaign, IL: Human Kinetics Books, 1990.

Metcalf, Andy, and Martin Humphries, editors. *The Sexuality of Men*. London: Pluto Press, 1985.

Miedzian, Miriam. *Boys Will Be Boys: Breaking the Link between Masculinity and Violence*. New York: Doubleday, 1991.

Miles, Rosalind. *Love, Sex, Death, and the Making of the Male*. New York: Summit Books, 1991.

Mirande, Alfredo. "Que Gaucho Es Ser Macho: It's a Drag to be Macho." *Astlan*, vol. 17/2, 1988.

Mitchell, Cary L. "Relationship of Femininity, Masculinity and Gender to Attribution of Responsibility." *Sex Roles*, vol. 16, February 1987.

Mohr, Richard. *Gays/Justice*. New York: Columbia University Press, 1988.

Money, John. *Gay, Straight, and In-Between: The Sexology of Erotic Orientation*. Oxford: Oxford University Press, 1988.

Murphy, Peter. "Toward a Feminist Masculinity." *Feminist Studies*, vol. 15, Summer 1989.

Murray, Mary. *The Law of the Father? Feminism and the Patriarchy*. New York: Routledge, 1994.

Myers, William R. "The Men's Movement and the Church: A Critical Review." *Religious Education*, vol. 87, Summer 1992.

Nelson, John O. "A Defense of Masculinism versus Feminism or, A Reply to Alison Jaggar and Feminists in General." *Public Affairs Quarterly*, vol. 7:3, July 1993.

Newburn, Tim and Elizabeth A. Stanko. *Just Boys Doing Business? Men, Masculinities and Crime*. New York: Routledge, 1995.

Pagels, Elaine. *Adam, Eve, and the Serpent*. New York: Vintage Books, 1988.

Parker, William. *Homosexuality: A Selected Bibliography*. Metuchen, NJ: Scarecrow Press, 1971; second supplement 1985.

Pedersen, Loren E. *Dark Hearts: The Unconscious Forces that Shape Men's Lives*. Boston: Shambhala Publications, 1991.

Plant, Richard. *The Pink Triangle: The Nazi War Against Homosexuals*. New York: Henry Holt and Company, 1986.

Pleck, Joseph H. *The Myth of Masculinity*. Cambridge, MA: MIT Press, 1981.

Poole, Ross. "Modernity, Rationality, and the 'Masculine.' " *Feminine/Masculine and Representation*, edited by Terry Threadgold and Anne Cranny-Francis. Sidney: George Allen & Unwin, 1990.

———. "Morality, Masculinity and the Market." *Radical Philosophy*, vol. 39, Spring 1985.

Pronger, Brian. *The Arena of Masculinity: Sports, Homosexuality and the Meaning of Sex*. New York: St. Martin's, 1990.

Puka, Bill. "The Liberation of Caring: A Different Voice for Gilligan's 'Different Voice'." *Hypatia*, vol. 5, Spring 1990.

Raphael, Ray. *The Men from the Boys: Rites of Passage in Male America*, Lincoln: University of Nebraska Press, 1988.

Redekop, Paul. "Sport and the Masculine Ethos: Some Implications for Family Interaction." *International Journal of Comparative Sociology*, vol. 25, September/December 1984.

Rhode, Deborah, editor. *Theoretical Perspectives on Sexual Difference*. New Haven, CT: Yale University Press, 1990.

Roberts, George W. "Brother to Brother: African-American Modes of Relating Among Men." *Journal of Black Studies*, vol. 24, June 1994.

Rowan, John. *The Horned God: Feminism and Men as Wounding and Healing*. London: Routledge & Kegan Paul, 1987.

Ruddick, Sara. "Thinking About Fathers." *Conflicts in Feminism*, edited by Marianne Hirsch and Evelyn Fox Keller. London: Routledge, 1990.

Schenk, Roy. *The Other Side of the Coin: Causes and Consequences of Men's Oppression*. Madison, WI: Bioenergetics Press, 1982.

Scott, Charles E. "The Pathology of the Father's Rule: Lacan and the Symbolic Order." *Thought*, vol. 61, March 1986.

Sedgwick, Eve Kosofsky. *Between Men: English Literature and Male Homosocial Desire*. New York: Columbia University Press, 1985.

Segal, Lynne. *Slow Motion: Changing Masculinities, Changing Men*. London: Virago, 1990.

Seidler, Victor J. *The Achilles Heel Reader: Men, Sexual Politics and Socialism*. London: Routledge, 1991.

———. *Recreating Sexual Politics: Men, Feminism, and Politics*. London: Routledge, 1991.

———. *Rediscovering Masculinity: Reason, Language and Sexuality*. London; New York: Routledge, 1989.

Snell, William, Rowland Miller, and Sharyn Belk. "Men's and Women's Emotional Disclosures: The Impact of Disclosure Recipient, Culture, and the Masculine Role." *Sex Roles*, vol. 21, October 1989.

Soble, Alan. *Pornography: Marxism, Feminism and the Future of Sexuality*. New Haven, CT: Yale University Press, 1986.

Stanko, Elizabeth A. and Kathy Hobdell. "Assault of Men: Masculinity and Male Victimization." *The British Journal of Criminology*, vol. 33, Summer 1993.

Staples, Robert. *Black Masculinity: The Black Male's Role in American Society*. San Francisco: Black Scholar Press, 1982.

Stoltenberg, John. *Refusing to be a Man*. Portland, OR: Breitenbush Books, 1989.

Strauss, Sylvia. *Traitors to the Masculine Cause: The Men's Campaigns for Women's Rights*. Westport, CT: Greenwood Press, 1982.

Thistlewaite, Susan B. "Great White Fathers." *Christianity and Crisis*, vol. 51, January 1992.

Thompson, Edward H. Jr. "The Maleness of Violence in Dating Relationships: An Appraisal of Stereotypes." *Sex Roles*, vol. 24, March 1991.

Tiefer, Leonore. "The Medicalization of Impotence: Normalizing Phallocentrism." *Gender & Society*, vol. 8, September 1994.

Tiger, Lionel. *Men in Groups.* New York: Marion Boyars, (1969) 1984.

Tjiattas, Mary, and Jean-Pierre Delaporte. "Foucault's Nominalism of the Sexual." *Philosophy Today*, vol. 32, Summer 1988.

Tong, Rosemarie. "Feminism, Pornography and Censorship." *Social Theory and Practice*, vol. 8, 1982.

Van Leeuwen, Mary S. "Why Christians Should Take the Men's Movement Seriously." *Perspectives*, vol. 7, May 1992.

Venter, Alexander. "A Theological Ethical Perspective on the Current Crisis in Masculinity and the Men's Movement." *Journal of Theology for Southern Africa*, no. 83, 1993.

Vetterling-Braggin, Mary, editor. *Femininity, Masculinity and Androgyny: A Modern Philosophical Discussion.* Totowa, NJ: Littlefield & Adams, 1982.

Voronina, Olga. "Soviet Patriarchy: Past and Present." *Hypatia*, vol. 8:4, Fall 1993.

Waters, Malcolm. "Patriarchy and Viriarchy: An Exploration and Reconstruction of Concepts of Masculine Domination." *Sociology*, vol. 23, May 1989.

Whitney, Catherine. *Uncommon Lives: Gay Men and Straight Women.* New York: Plume, 1990.

Wideman, John Edgar. *Brothers and Keepers.* New York: Holt, Rinehart and Winston, 1984.

Williams, Dorie Giles. "Gender, Masculinity-Femininity, and Emotional Intimacy in Same-Sex Friendship." *Sex Roles*, vol. 12, March 1985.

Williams, Walter L. *The Spirit and the Flesh: Sexual Diversity in American Indian Culture.* Boston: Beacon Press, 1986.

Wolf, James G. *Gay Priests.* New York: Harper and Row, 1989.

Woodhouse, Annie. *Fantastic Women: Sex, Gender and Transvestism.* New Brunswick, NJ: Rutgers University Press, 1989.

Young, Iris. *Throwing Like a Girl and Other Essays.* Bloomington: Indiana University Press, 1990.

Zaitchik, Matt C. and Donald L. Mosher. "Criminal Justice Implications of the Macho Personality Constellation." *Criminal Justice and Behavior*, vol. 20, September 1993.

Index

About the Contributors

Harry Brod teaches philosophy and gender studies at the University of Delaware. He is the author of *Hegel's Philosophy of Politics* (Westview, 1992). He has edited *The Making of Masculinities: The New Men's Studies* (Routledge, 1987), *A Mensch Among Men: Explorations in Jewish Masculinity* (Crossing Press, 1988) and *Theorizing Masculinities* (Sage, 1994).

Daniel Callahan is co-founder and president of the Hastings Center. He is the author of *Setting Limits* (Simon & Schuster, 1987) and *What Kind of Life* (Simon & Schuster, 1990).

Lucy Candib is a physician specializing in family medicine and obstetrics. She is the author of *Medicine and the Family* (Basic Books, 1995).

Kenneth Clatterbaugh teaches philosophy at the University of Washington, Seattle. He is the author of *Contemporary Perspectives on Masculinity* (Westview, 1990).

J. Glenn Gray taught philosophy for many years at Colorado College. He was the author of *The Warriors* (Harper & Row, 1959), *The Promise of Wisdom* (J. B. Lippincott, 1968), and *On Understanding Violence* (Harper & Row, 1970). He also edited and translated a number of Martin Heidegger's works.

Patrick Grim teaches philosophy at the State University of New York, Stony Brook. He is the author of *Incomplete Universe* (MIT, 1991). He has edited *Philosophy of Science and the Occult* (SUNY, 1982).

Leonard Harris teaches philosophy and African-American studies at Purdue University. He is the editor of *Philosophy Born of Struggle* (Kendall/Hunt, 1983), *The Philosophy of Alain Locke* (Temple, 1989), and *Exploitation and Exclusion: The Question of Race in Modern Capitalism* (Hans Zell, 1991).

Patrick D. Hopkins is a postdoctoral fellow in philosophy at Bowling Green State University in Ohio. He is just finishing an anthology on ethics, technology and gender. His research interests lie in the areas of social theory, gender studies, and the philosophy of technology.

Hugh LaFollette teaches philosophy at East Tennessee State University. He is the author of *Persons and Personal Relationships* (Blackwell, 1995), and *Brute Science* (Routledge, forthcoming). He has edited *World Hunger and Morality* (Prentice-Hall, 2nd edition 1996), and *Person to Person* (Temple, 1989).

Thomas W. Laqueur teaches history at the University of California, Berkeley. He is the author of *The Making of the Modern Body* (California, 1987), and *Making Sex: Body and Gender from Greeks to Freud* (Harvard, 1990).

Larry May teaches philosophy at Washington University in St. Louis. He is the author of *The Morality of Groups* (Notre Dame, 1987), *Sharing Responsibility* (Chicago, 1992), *The Socially Responsive Self* (Chicago, 1996), and is just finishing *Masculinity and Morality*. He has edited *Collective Responsibility* (Rowman & Littlefield, 1991), *Applied Ethics: A Multicultural Approach* (Prentice-Hall, 1994), *Mind and Morals: Ethics and Cognitive Science* (MIT/Bradford, 1996), *Hannah Arendt: Twenty Years Later* (MIT, 1996), and *Liberty, Equality, and Plurality* (Kansas, forthcoming).

Charles W. Mills teaches philosophy at the University of Illinois, Chicago.

Richard Schmitt teaches philosophy at Brown University. He is the author of *Martin Heidegger on Being Human* (Random House, 1969), *Alienation and Class* (Schenckman, 1983), *Introduction to Marx and Engels* (Westview, 1987), and *Beyond Separateness* (Westview, 1995).

Victor Seidler teaches philosophy at the University of London. He is the author of *Kant, Respect and Justice* (Routledge, 1986), *A Truer Liberty: Simone Weil and Marxism* (Routledge, 1989), *Recreating Sexual Politics* (Routledge, 1991), and *Unreasonable Men* (Routledge, 1994). He has edited *The Achilles Heel Reader* (Routledge, 1991).

Robert A. Strikwerda teaches philosophy at Indiana University, Kokomo. He has written on topics in the history of philosophy of social sciences and in applied ethics.

Robert Stufflebeam is a doctoral candidate in the Philosophy-Neuroscience-Psychology program at Washington University in St. Louis. He has edited *To Work at the Foundations: Essays in Memory* *of Aron Gurwitsch* (Kluwer, forthcoming). His research interests are in philosophy of mind, cognitive science, and philosophy of science.

Laurence Thomas teaches philosophy at Syracuse University. He is the author of *Living Morally* (Temple, 1989), and *Vessels of Evil: American Slavery and the Holocaust* (Temple, 1993).